I0814568

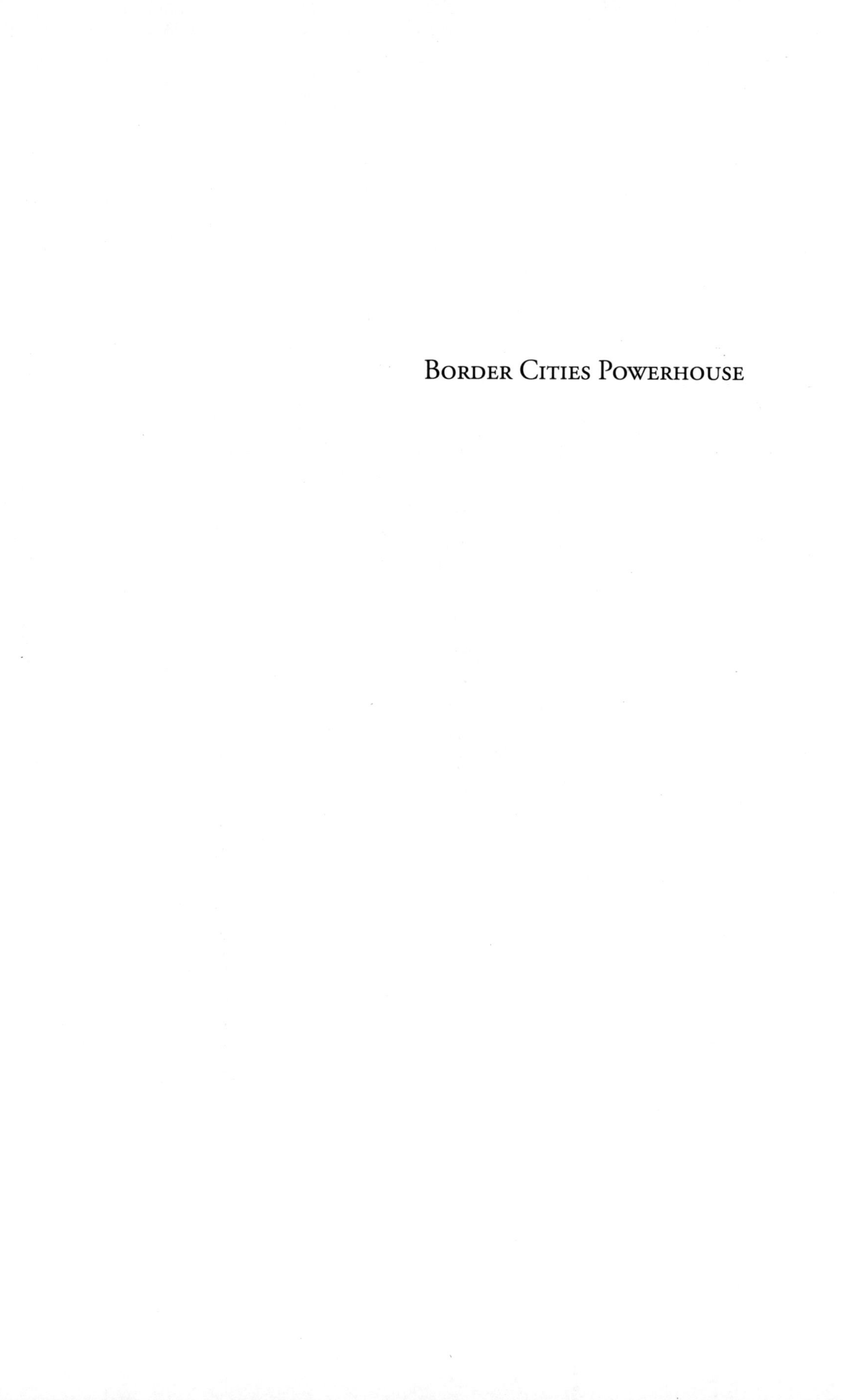

Border Cities Powerhouse

Border Cities Powerhouse:

The Rise of Windsor: 1900–1945

Patrick Brode

BIBLIOASIS
WINDSOR, ONTARIO

FIRST EDITION

Library and Archives Canada Cataloguing in Publication

Brode, Patrick, 1950-, author
Border cities powerhouse : the rise of Windsor 1901-1945 / Patrick Brode.

Issued in print and electronic formats.
ISBN 978-1-77196-157-8 (hardcover).--ISBN 978-1-77196-158-5 (ebook)

1. Windsor (Ont.)--History--20th century. 2. Windsor (Ont.)--Social conditions--20th century. 3. Windsor (Ont.)--Economic conditions--20th century. I. Title.

FC3099.W56B758 2017 971.3'32 C2016-907972-4
C2016-907973-2

Edited by Sharon Hanna
Copy-edited by Allana Amlin
Typeset and designed by Chris Andrechek

Published with the generous assistance of the Canada Council for the Arts and the Ontario Arts Council. Biblioasis also acknowledges the support of the Government of Canada through the Canada Book Fund and the Government of Ontario through the Ontario Book Publishing Tax Credit.

PRINTED AND BOUND IN USA

Photo credits:
Windsor Community Museum, Windsor, Ontario: 13, 49, 68, 72, 78, 92, 100, 126, 147.
McCord Museum of Canadian History, Montreal, Quebec: 29.
Charles Mady Collection: 89, 128.
Patrick Brode: 22, 30, 70, 110, 138.
Windsor Star: 44, 117, 123, 132, 136, 143.

Contents

Introduction / 7

Making the Devil's Wagons: 1901–1908 / 11
Power to the City: 1909–1913 / 27
Great War: 1914–1918 / 49
The Thirst: 1919–1921 / 79
Miracle Years: 1922–1926 / 99
Bridged And Tunnelled: 1927–1929 / 129
Surviving Hard Times: 1930–1934 / 147
City United: 1935 / 165
New Confidence: 1936–1941 / 175
Making A People's War: 1941–1944 / 197
Sacrifice And Victory: 1944–1945 / 217
Ford Strike: August–December 1945 / 231

Epilogue / 251
Appendices and Notes / 257
Index / 321

Introduction

On the evening of January 22, 1901, barely three weeks into the twentieth century, Windsor's Mayor John Davis and the aldermen of the City Council marched solemnly into a hushed Council Chamber that was hung with black bunting. News had just arrived that Queen Victoria, the only monarch the community had ever known, was dead. A resolution of condolence was passed and the meeting quietly adjourned. In the county town of Sandwich, just to Windsor's west, a similar scene was re-enacted in their council chamber. On Sandwich's streets, a French-Canadian store displayed the Union Jack and the French tricolour at half-staff. Storefronts in both communities featured large portraits of the late Queen draped in black ribbons.

The solemnity observed at the sovereign's passing was what would be expected in any proper town in Canada; and Windsor was a very proper town. At the beginning of the twentieth century, it was a small community of 12,000 mostly British residents living on the margins of Ontario. An unremarkable city, barely larger than a town, it was a place that many people passed through and few noticed. From its origin in 1836, Windsor was known simply as the ferry stop across the river from the American commercial hub of Detroit, Michigan. As a frontier town on the border with the tumultuous states, Windsor would bear witness to much of the political upheaval of the 19th Century. Throughout the Patriot War of the 1830s, the American Civil War and the Fenian Raids of 1866, Windsor was on the edge of conflict.

Yet by 1854, Windsor had become more than just a ferry stopover. The coming of the railway age had placed it on a much larger transcontinental network that linked it to North American trade. Connections were central to Windsor's very existence: the railways had literally put the town on the map. Shortly after the first trains of the Great Western Railway eased into the Goyeau Street station in 1854, Windsor was incorporated as a village. In 1858, it became incorporated as a town. It was as a rail hub that Windsor experienced its first growth spurt both in the employment of railway workers and the expansion of commerce. Its climb thereafter was gradual, and frequently subject to setbacks as one economic "panic" or another disrupted business.

A few enterprises, most notably Hiram Walker's distillery (founded 1858), achieved a degree of prominence. Significantly, this American citizen and Detroit resident had established one of the most dynamic business presences on the border. In his restless ambition to control all aspects of the distilling business, Hiram Walker expanded into farming to provide the natural products for his operations. As a result, his town of Walkerville became a bustling rival to Windsor and its main street of Walker Road a primordial industrial complex. To the west of Windsor lay the smaller, less vigorous town of Sandwich. While it had a proud tradition as the seat of local government, Sandwich had no access to railways and little prospect of development.

Within Windsor itself, a few leading industries began to emerge by the end of the century. The growth of these early industries was largely attributable to the protectionist measures in Sir John A. Macdonald's National Policy of 1879, which levied substantial tariffs on imported goods as a way to nurture local manufacturers. In order to avoid the cost of tariffs and sell to Canadian consumers, American manufacturers opened branch plants in the most accessible Canadian location. For many of them, the closest location, where they could best keep an eye on their investments, was the municipality just across the Detroit River: Windsor. As a result, the city fostered a branch plant economy with several American factories having taken advantage of its convenient location.

At the time of Victoria's death, the Canadian side of the Detroit River remained divided among the city of Windsor and the smaller towns of Walkerville and Sandwich. The explosive growth that was about to happen would have an impact on all of these riverfront communities in varying degrees. They would expand exponentially until they effectively became one urban conglomerate collectively known as the "Border Cities." While they were economically and socially interdependent, the Border Cities stubbornly resisted the political unification that would have enabled them to tackle the enormous issues raised by their growth in a deliberate and measured way. For Windsor, the forty-five years after the turn of the century would be one of the most incredible stories of urban expansion and industrial growth in Canadian history.

To the stolid aldermen who bowed their heads and solemnly marked the Queen's death, an unexpected world awaited them. Industrialism was about to alter the face of the Detroit River border and introduce vast new assembly plants, transforming the site of the ferry crossing into one of Canada's most dynamic cities. These factories would be operated by men and women who came from across the globe and made Windsor one of the first multicultural experiments in Canada. In their onion-domed churches or quiet basements, these newcomers followed different faiths and prayed in languages unfamiliar to those who had lived along the strait for generations. They also brought novel political concepts with them. Terms such as "fascism" and "communism" were unknown to the men who mourned Queen Victoria. But in a few short decades, Windsor's society would face open conflicts between labour and capital as well as between ethnic groups and religions. The story of how the community coped with these controversies is one of dramatic successes as well as of several spectacular failures. Ultimately, it was one of survival, in which the diverse individuals who made up the Border Cities merged into the larger community of the City of Windsor.

A postcard of the Windsor Armouries, circa 1905. To the right is Ouellette Square.

An early automotive plant showing skilled workers assembling engines in stationary cradles.

Chapter One
Making the Devil's Wagons
1901–1908

At least outwardly, Windsor was as British as any other place in southern Ontario. Less than a year after Queen Victoria's death, the city marked a joyous occasion when residents waving Union Jacks and singing patriotic songs welcomed back their soldiers from the first contingent sent to the South African War. Shortly thereafter in January 1902, the new drill shed, the armouries, was dedicated. A solid, imposing structure just off Ouellette Avenue, the armouries would become the focus of militia life and the scene of political and patriotic meetings. Its opening ceremonies were a grand affair and "With the blare of the band, the buzz of conversation, the clanking of officers' swords, the whole scene was a picture of animation." In a nod toward past glories, the officer's mess featured a portrait of Colonel John Prince, the controversial commander during the Patriot War of 1838.[1]

These celebrations were manifestations of Windsor's British heritage, for over half the city's residents claimed British descent. Yet, this outward appearance was balanced by the fact that the British-born segment of Windsor's population was about ten percent, roughly the same figure as for the American-born. While a city such as Toronto was indelibly British with almost 30 percent born in the United Kingdom, Windsor's population was more native-born and a far larger percent of its population had been raised in Essex County.[2] Whatever their allegiance, the majority of residents, almost 70 percent, were Protestant. Protestant clergymen were important public figures and the Rev. Bovington's sermons in the Baptist Church were widely attended. Together, the Anglican, Baptist, and Presbyterian churches were popular and authoritative institutions in the city's life.

In 1904, the Rev. F.A.P. Chadwick would deliver an "Imperial Sermon" in All Saints' Church to the men of the 21st Regiment Essex Fusiliers shortly before they left to represent the city at the St. Louis World's Fair. The church was draped in the national colours and an enormous Union Jack filled its centre aisle. Chadwick exhorted the men to remember that they carried with them not only Windsor's honour, but that of the British Army. The Methodists were no less fervent. After the original Methodist church on Windsor Avenue burned in 1904, plans were immediately made to build a fine new church on Ouellette near Wyandotte in the heart of the city's centre. Shortly after its completion, the church featured the famous evangelists Crossley and Hunter at a huge revival meeting in March 1907. Central Methodist could barely hold the throng who came to witness the eminent preachers "place Windsor in the grip of God."[3]

While not so flamboyant, St. Andrew's Presbyterian was one of the largest and most affluent congregations in the community. For over twenty years, from 1894 to 1915, the Rev. J.C. Tolmie was the minister of St. Andrew's and a powerful voice against social drinking and gambling. Interesting enough, the annual meeting of St. Andrew's also received a report on the progress of the "Chinese department."[4] The Presbyterians had been reaching out to one of the area's most exotic group of newcomers since 1890, when small numbers of Chinese had arrived in Windsor and taken over the laundry business. While regularly demeaned as the "washee-washee" men by the locals, the Chinese were courted by Presbyterians and many of them had become avid members of that church. A gathering in 1898 described how the Chinese attended Sabbath School and entertained their teacher with games from their native country. In 1902, the 188 members of Windsor's Chinese community were mostly men and boys (women were largely barred from immigrating to Canada) who were constantly in transit. While they were described as living "in splendid isolation," they invariably appeared on Sunday mornings, bibles tucked under their arms, marching in a group to St. Andrew's Sunday School.[5]

Another group of outsiders, who numbered almost as many members as the Chinese, were the local Jews. An *Evening Record* reporter attended the *Rosh Hashanah* services in 1900 and the trustees, Max Bernstein and Aaron Meretsky, explained the Jewish New Year ritual as the sound of the shofar echoed on Windsor's streets. While their numbers, perhaps forty families in all, did not enable them to support a rabbi, it was apparent that "the Jewish colony makes quite a respectable showing in commercial pursuits."[6] One of them, the grocer William Englander, was the first permanent Jewish resident in the town, and was elected an alderman in 1899. Englander also acted as treasurer of the tiny synagogue next to the fire station on Pitt Street. In 1905, the community resolved to build a fine concrete-block synagogue, Shaarey Zedek, on Mercer Street. One of the 1906 arrivals was a six-year-old boy, Dovid Avrum Croll, from Byelorussia (Belarus). As soon as he was old enough, David Croll (as he became known) was shining shoes, selling newspapers, and finding any way he could to get ahead. The community itself was slowly increasing and by 1910, Windsor's Jewish population would double to over 300 individuals.

While the Chinese and Jews were beginning to find a place in the city, the long-established black population was becoming increasingly marginalized. During the 1860s, the black community numbered almost a quarter of the town. But after the Civil War, many refugees returned to the states, and by 1901, black residents made up less than 5 percent of Windsor and the border towns. While schools had been integrated and black cultural activities such as the Frontier Club and the Emancipation Day Celebration had become entrenched as part of local life, blacks found themselves being increasing set apart from whites. By the beginning of the 20th century, local hotels refused to serve them and "The Southern aversion to the negro is evidently manifesting itself very strongly in this city." Customers at the British American and other hotels made it clear that "they do not care to stand behind a colored man in the café."[7] Lagoon Park in Sandwich was closed to black patrons in the summer of 1902. At the Labor Day parade of 1905, the longshoreman's union, one of the few trades open to blacks, was relegated to the back of the parade. The longshoremen refused to participate. Discrimination against blacks in public services would become an increasing fixture of the times.

Divided City

The main source of friction in the border, however, was between its two most dominant groups: Catholics and Protestants. While English-speaking Protestants formed the city's majority, Windsor's sizable Catholic minority made it unique among Ontario municipalities. Compared to cities such as Toronto or London where Catholics formed barely 15 percent of the population, in Windsor they totalled 30 percent. Unlike Toronto, where Catholics were reminded of their low status during the Orange Day parades and denied municipal jobs, in Windsor a few Catholics occupied prominent positions in law and government. Moreover, there was little of the overt animosity between the denominations that characterized most of the province. Prior to 1899, Catholics and Protestants had cooperated in operating one school board in which two of the public schools, St. Alphonsus and St. Francis, were effectively Catholic institutions. However, in 1899, Bishop Fergus McEvay ordered Windsor's Catholics to found a separate school board. This board was formed in November 1901 and it immediately petitioned the public board to transfer the two schools to its jurisdiction. Over the years, Catholics had paid the taxes which had financed them and they thought it just that this portion of the public board's property should be shared. The separate board's lawyer, Francis Cleary, drafted a petition outlining the history of the schools and requesting their transfer.[8] But the public board would not part with a single brick of their property. The battle-lines were drawn.

Not only would the public board refuse the separate board permission to collect taxes from its declared supporters, it even refused to appoint a committee to discuss dividing the assets. The school controversy created great bitterness not only in Windsor, but also in Sandwich where, despite the fact that Catholics formed a slight majority, the public board also refused to give up any of its assets. Sandwich's Mayor Girardot harangued the public board, reminding them that the town was almost evenly divided between Catholics and Protestants and that in the past "the most cordial entente and harmonious relations" had existed between the religions. The town's two schools, one Catholic and the other Protestant, had been built by the contributions of both communities. Now, Catholics were not only paying taxes to operate the public school, but were being billed to temporarily rent the other school which they had paid to build.[9] The public board enforced their ownership of all of the Sandwich schools with a court order, and the teaching nuns were confronted by the deputy-sheriff who told them to vacate the remaining school. When they attempted to re-occupy it, he threatened to make them leave by force.

In February 1902, Fr. Joseph Meunier told his congregation at St. Alphonsus to hold firm and that any member who wavered and sent a child to the public school faced excommunication. At the Baptist Church, Rev. Bovington gave a sermon whose topic was the "badge of servitude"—an obvious allusion to the strictures being placed on Catholics by their leaders.[10] In St. Andrew's, Rev. J.C. Tolmie proclaimed that no Protestant would ever tolerate such tyranny. In a balanced editorial, the *Evening Record* editor (Baptist elder Archibald McNee) reminded his Protestant readers that Catholics were acting within their legal rights and that the "resentful feelings" continually displayed by the public board were not productive. Catholics had contributed to the construction of the public schools and fairness demanded that they get at least some share of them. The editorial fell on deaf ears. Judge Michael McHugh, a leading Catholic and member of the public school board, pointed out that the two (former) Catholic public schools had barely any students attending them, and there was no reason why they should not be conveyed to the separate board. His colleagues refused to even consider a transfer and in May 1902, McHugh and the other Catholic members of the public board resigned in protest. The dispute had awakened deep feelings of animosity between denominations, and one of the Protestant members called out "Cowards!" as McHugh and his colleagues left the chamber. After a year and a half, nothing had been resolved and the provincial government was compelled to pass a statute appointing a High Court Justice to arbitrate the dispute. In February 1904, Justice William Street ordered that the St. Alphonsus and St. Francis sites be transferred to the separate board. Yet, even with a judicial order, the public board delayed complying, and a local priest wrote to Bishop McEvay that the Protestants "are not men they are worse than savages." It was not until September 1904 that Catholics in Windsor operated their own schools.[11]

A new source of discord added to the religious division: more than half of Windsor's Catholics (almost 18 percent of the city) were French-Canadians. While the rest of Ontario was Anglo-Protestant—in cities such as Toronto and London, fewer than one percent of the population was French-Canadian—Windsor and its environs was an ethnic mix very much at odds with the rest of the province. Irish and French eyed each other warily and jostled for control of schools and parishes. At the St. Patrick's Day dinner of 1903, Francis Cleary and Irish notables were out in force. Local French leader Gaspard Pacaud also attended and rose on behalf of "Frenchmen in general" and proclaimed that they were always "a friend to the Irish." It was an expedient comment, but one that was far from the truth. Since 1899, Pacaud had set his sights on Fr. Flannery, the pastor of St. Alphonsus. The following year, Pacaud was privately assured by the Catholic Bishop that as a result of "the recent agitation of the French members of the parish," a francophone priest would be appointed to that parish. Shortly thereafter, Joseph Meunier did replace Flannery. The controversy became public in December 1900, when Flannery defended himself and named Pacaud as the agitator who sought his removal. He pointed out that he could speak French, and conducted mass in that language. But he was not a French-Canadian, and concluded, "The only good reason I can see for this antipathy of Gaspard Pacaud is because I am Irish."[12]

Pacaud had indeed become the face of an aggressive French-language presence. His newspaper, *Le Progrès*, attacked a local customs officer for being an Orangeman. The implication was that only English-speaking Protestants got the most lucrative government posts. The *Evening Record* castigated *Le Progrès* for its "efforts to stir up race prejudices," but Pacaud maintained that French-Canadians were not getting their fair share of patronage.[13] Yet, it was on the question of who would control the parishes that French Catholics would come into direct conflict with their Irish co-religionists. Under the direction of Fr. Joseph-Napoléon Ferland, the chaplain at Hôtel-Dieu hospital, the French members of St. Alphonsus Church campaigned relentlessly after 1900 to make it a francophone parish. While Bishop McEvay nursed the hope that his parishes would be neither French nor Irish but Catholic, the reality was that one ethnic group or the other would seek to prevail. One solution was the founding of Immaculate Conception parish in the western part of the city in 1904 and the appointment of a bilingual pastor.[14] However, linguistic animosities within the Catholic family were far from resolved.

The River

Despite religious controversies, the one constant for those who lived at the strait was the Detroit River. At the beginning of the 20th century, it began to occur to the residents that the river might be more than just a mode of transportation. Some began to see it as a jewel—a bright, beautiful waterway that could be enjoyed by all. A riverfront park was first proposed in 1903, where "our citizens (can) enjoy the cooling breezes off the river and watch the passing boats." A small start was made the following year by converting a minute riverfront parcel between Church Street and Bruce Avenue into parkland. This proved to be a false start as the lands had to be leased from the Grand Trunk and the deal was not ratified by City Council. The railway insisted that the park benches and flower gardens be removed.[15] Most of the riverfront was still used by factories and the city itself was becoming increasingly grimy. On most days a black cloud of smoke from trains, ferries, and power plants hung in a pall over the city to the extent that one retailer complained that "the smoke obscures the light in the store." The waterfront itself was far from park-like, but rather formed a tenderloin district where, "colored dock employes and small boys continually engage in games of craps and cards."[16]

Yet the allure of the waterfront could not be denied. One poignant story illustrated just how much the river meant to those who lived there.[17] Jean Patterson, the daughter of Windsor's former Member of Parliament J.C. Patterson, had fallen in love with her father's secretary, Tom Watson. Patterson did not think Watson suitable, and had forbidden the match. Jean defied her father and married him anyway. For his part, Watson became a successful writer, but above all a sportsman who was devoted to the gun and rod, whose spare time was spent exploring the islands and byways along the Detroit River and Lake St. Clair. Watson died in 1904, only a few years after their marriage, and Jean honoured his wishes by having his cremated remains deposited in the same river "which had been the scene of his childhood joys and which he had loved so well."

Attracting "Live Industries"

The first decade of the new century was marked by a surge in Canada's economy propelled by the rapid peopling of the west. The prairies expanded at an unprecedented rate and millions of new acres were brought into production.

However, the flow of immigration largely bypassed southern Ontario, and industrial growth was increasingly centred in major cities such as Toronto and Hamilton. In Toronto, manufacturing employment was outstripping population growth, and by reducing tax assessment and water rates, the provincial capital was fostering a burgeoning industrial sector. By contrast, Windsor was burdened with high tax rates to pay for the sewers and macadam roads of previous administrations. John Davis, mayor by acclamation from 1897 to 1899, and elected two years thereafter, had made it one of his projects to pave Windsor's deplorable streets. After a business trip to England, Davis was impressed by the macadam paving using loose stones to form a semi-hard surface. He convinced Council in 1899 to embark on a program of spending $20,000 a year over ten years to end the era of muddy ruts.[18] Despite this improvement, few new industries were being attracted and the population remained far below that of its nearest rival, London.[19] When four new industries, including an electric light and tool factory, proposed setting up shop in Windsor in 1905 on condition that they be granted bonuses, the proposals failed to get the needed votes. "The citizens evidently do not wish live industries in the city," sighed former Mayor Oscar Fleming.

The *Monetary Times*, a financial magazine, surveyed the area in 1901 and found that Walkerville was doing well, as it had attracted a major U.S. subsidiary, the Canadian Bridge Company. These ironworks were a huge addition to the town, shoring up the industrial complex that was expanding down Walker Road and making it the "Manchester of Canada."[20] Quiet Sandwich was also undergoing something of a revival. In 1901 the Saginaw Lumber Company opened up a large sawmill in the town. The federal government came through with a new post office and customs building, which was completed in 1907. With paved roads and sidewalks, this was, as a newspaper called it, "the era of the New Sandwich."[21] While Sandwich was making some headway, the fact remained that Windsor had failed to attract any major new employer.

Yet the city still held enormous potential. In a 1905 editorial listing the municipality's advantages, the *Evening Record* noted that it was beautifully situated along the river, and that it attracted many Detroit families who liked to live along Windsor's quiet, tree-shrouded streets. The city was expanding its assets and in addition to the armouries, a new City Hall was about to be dedicated. One result of the public school board's decreased needs was the transfer of the old Central School to the City where it was refurbished, police cells installed in the basement, and the area around it transformed into a park. It became the City's new civic building in November 1904.[22] Windsor had also taken advantage of the largesse of Andrew Carnegie, becoming the first community in Ontario to obtain a "letter of promise" for a Carnegie library.

The city was so financially hard-pressed that a minority of aldermen objected to the cost of the building site. Nevertheless, in February 1902, after a bitter debate, Council finally agreed on the site at Victoria Avenue and Park Street. Carnegie's money was put to good use and Windsor opened a fine new library in 1903.[23]

Perhaps the most important public service, transportation, remained in private hands. The railway terminus at the foot of Goyeau Street was the nucleus for the factories, warehouses, and other goods-handling activities that extended along the railway line. In order to connect the railway yards and the industrial sites on Walker Road, the streetcars of the SW&A provided a "loop" to Walkerville along Wyandotte, which connected to the line along Sandwich Street. Far from being a novelty, streetcars had become a daily commuting necessity. It may be difficult to imagine the quiet streetscapes of this first decade where only a few horses and bicycles passed by and there was the occasional rumble of the streetcar. Entrepreneurs looked upon the streetcar as the transportation solution of the day and a new company, the Windsor, Essex, and Lakeshore Rapid Railway built a line from Windsor south to Kingsville. This extension was completed in 1907 and extended to Leamington the following year. In 1901, the Everett-Moore syndicate of Cleveland, which already owned the Detroit United Railway (DUR), bought the SW&A and one of its first acts was to extend the line to Amherstburg. This expanding web of connections also spread eastwards and on the afternoon of May 20, 1907, the first streetcar from Walkerville ran along the shores of Lake St. Clair to Tecumseh. *Habitant*

The corner of Wyandotte and Devonshire Road, Walkerville, circa 1905.

mothers came out and "waved an apron salute" as the cars of the Windsor & Tecumseh Railroad rolled by.[24] This line was also acquired by the SW&A and thereby became part of the network of the DUR. Significantly, the streetcar operations of Detroit and Windsor effectively formed one service.

Editorial cartoon protesting the ferry company's monopoly, November 16, 1906, *The Evening Record*.

Detroiters also monopolized the cross-border ferry service. Walter Campbell, the imperious president of the Detroit, Belle Isle and Windsor Ferry Company knew that the federal government alone controlled the cross-border ferry licenses. In 1895, Ottawa had mysteriously reduced the fee for the franchise to one dollar. While the ferries now provided a much more reliable service, it was a constant sore point that Ottawa had granted this valuable license to a Detroit company for a nominal sum. Moreover, Campbell knew that he was at liberty to control the fares. Even though Robert Sutherland, the Member of Parliament for North Essex, kept City Council informed, and backed their plea for more authority, Council was unable to seek a better deal with another operator. Archibald McNee, the influential publisher of the *Evening Record* and an alderman, campaigned vigorously throughout 1907 for a new deal with the ferry operator. However, Campbell treated McNee and the rest of Council with utter disdain and refused to meet with them.

This did not stand him in good stead when he appeared before the Minister of Inland Revenue in April 1907 seeking to get his license renewed. The Minister suggested that if he did not reach an understanding with the city that Ottawa might transfer the license to the municipality, or put it up for public competition.[25] Still, Campbell refused to bend and it was only when the Council appointed a ferry committee (which did not include McNee) that acceptable terms were agreed to. When a new lease was announced in March 1908, McNee, through the editorial columns of the *Evening Record*, growled that it was clear that the ferry company had made their own arrangement in Ottawa and that the city was "utterly impotent" in the outcome.[26] It was another measure of Windsor's uniqueness that its transportation facilities on both land and water were American monopolies operated from outside Canada and which often served to move workers from their Canadian homes to American factories.

One spinoff from the Saginaw Lumber plant in Sandwich was a proposal in December 1902 for a new "belt-line" railway, the Essex Terminal, to connect the lumber plant with other factories in the area south of the Detroit River. The plan was for a new line to transverse "the poorest part of Windsor—a section that was at present almost valueless" to the south of the existing developed lands and open up this vacant area for factories which could connect to the CPR or Grand Trunk freight routes.[27] The Essex Terminal proposal was backed by the Canadian Bridge Company, and was motivated in part by the prospect of connecting to a projected steel plant to be built in Ojibway. However, the torpor in Windsor's economy did not justify immediate action. The Essex Terminal Railway would eventually proceed, but the first section of the belt line would not be built until 1908.

Strangely enough, one business in Windsor was booming. The city had become a "Marriage Mill" for lovestruck couples in Michigan and Ohio who, for one reason or another, wanted to keep their union confidential. "American couples found marriage in Ontario so attractive, not because it was more binding, but because it was so secret."[28] Moreover, a license could be issued without any period of residence. Eager couples could cross the Detroit River on the morning ferry and return as spouses that afternoon. One Detroit policeman counselled an impatient couple that "over in Windsor they issue licenses at all hours, and by crossing over on the ferry you can get a license and be married and back here inside of an hour." As a result, huge numbers of Americans were crossing the border in the first decade of the century to get married in the border communities. Some Detroiters were annoyed by the situation, and they blamed hasty marriages in Windsor as the cause of "marital distemper" which resulted in a high American divorce rate. As clergymen charged for their services, a Windsor pulpit became a profitable and much desired location. However, City Clerk Stephen Lusted was not amused and he complained to the Registrar General about the impossibility of keeping an accurate record of this deluge of marriages. He also noted that divorced American women were seeking marriage licenses and passing themselves off as spinsters "as a ruse evidently intended to deceive." Lusted reported that "Windsor marriages are apparently as popular as ever," as in the first half of 1907, a remarkable 685 marriages were recorded in the municipality. A fluid border meant that vagaries in the law could be exploited and services unavailable on one side could be found on the other. In the coming years, there would be a constant ebb and flow of lovers, workers, and entrepreneurs between the border communities.

More than ever, Windsor was becoming a component in the growing industrial complex of greater Detroit, for Windsor held a reservoir of skilled workers who were able to staff industries on either side of the river at a moment's notice. In contrast to its previous role in the mid-19th century as a commercial hub, the Detroit of 1900 was more highly industrialized, with such a variety of metal fabricating and assembling crafts that "no single industry marked the city's manufacturing life."[29] Workers were flooding into the city at such a pace that Detroit's population of 285,000 was more than twenty-four times Windsor's size. Still, Windsor could fulfill a role for Detroit as a bedroom community where a portion of the workforce would be only a short ferry ride away. Thanks to the tariffs of the National Policy, Windsor boasted a few American subsidiaries. But it could not compete with centres such as Hamilton and London for "It is almost an impossibility to get the necessary vote in Windsor to carry a bonus by-law, as the non-resident and alien vote is so very large."[30] The city would clearly need fresh leadership to re-invigorate industry and match the dynamic growth of its American counterpart.

The Coming Men

On the cricket pitches of Essex County, Robert Sutherland had made a name for himself as one of the district's finest sportsmen. A tall, striking man, Sutherland was also an up-and-coming lawyer, a fixture in the law courts, St. Andrew's Church, City Council, and the Library Board. When he ran for Parliament as a Laurier Liberal in 1900, his opponents pointed out that he had once filed an application to join the anti-Catholic, Protestant Protective Association. Sutherland responded that once he had learned of the bigoted principles of that organization that he had gone no further. Moreover, in public life, he had been fair to all creeds and had been condemned as "a half Catholic and a poor Protestant" for his support of Hôtel-Dieu. The source of this slander, Sutherland revealed, was none other than the city's first mayor, Oscar Fleming. It was Fleming who had used the "sinister agency" of the PPA in the early 1890s and now sought to use it to undermine a fellow Protestant who was tolerant of his Catholic fellow citizens. Sutherland was heavily supported by French-Canadian Catholics and was easily elected.[31]

One of Sutherland's challenges was to deal with the early stirrings of labour unrest. In 1902, Windsor men who were taking strikers' jobs at Buhl Malleable Iron in Detroit were set upon and badly beaten. More violence occurred when the Canadian Bridge workers went on strike in April 1903 over increasing the workday from nine to ten hours. This time, Detroit men crossed the river to take Walkerville jobs. While the police kept order on the Canadian side, American unionists were sympathetic to their Canadian cohorts and on April 9, ambushed strikebreakers as they got off the ferry at the foot of Joseph Campau. In the ensuing riot, one man was shot and left for dead. Sutherland intervened in an attempt to resolve the dispute and met with the strikers at the Crown Inn in Walkerville to explain that management would drop its demands and the workday would remain nine hours. Thanks to his intervention, the strike was settled and he was given "a hearty vote of thanks" from the workers.[32] When he ran for re-election the following year, he would cite his services to labour as a reason for their support. In 1905, Sutherland would become the area's first MP to be selected as Speaker of the House of Commons. Part of his acceptance speech was delivered in French, the language of many of his constituents.[33]

Unlike Sutherland, Ernest S. Wigle was a pillar of the Anglo-Protestant commercial establishment. A descendant of Loyalists, Wigle was a Mason, a successful lawyer, and above all, a man's man. He was ruggedly handsome, and as well, an avid rugby player and soldier in the local militia. In 1905, his first of five consecutive terms as mayor, Wigle ran a tight ship and taxes went down. While he was careful about expenditures, he did back a plan to build a more efficient city-run electric light plant. But taxpayers were not ready for new projects and the plan was voted down in a referendum. His major success was in getting City Council to buy the lots at McDougall and Erie Streets in 1908 and set up playing fields.[34] Prior to this, the city had occupied "on sufferance" private lands and called them parks. This new recreation area (eventually named Wigle Park) replaced the impromptu setting of Ouellette Square as the site for baseball and football games. It was the beginning of the city's program to provide permanent space for recreation.

The other emerging figure, one who would have a far greater impact than either Wigle or Sutherland, was a prominent failure in business. In the 1890s, Gordon McGregor, the son of MP William McGregor, was considered a pleasant, but inconsequential, young man. "By early 1896 Gordon, at age twenty-two, was known more for his social comings and goings and bass-baritone voice than for his commercial aptitude or leadership."[35] He would be frequently noted in the society pages for singing at various functions and from 1887 to 1892, he worked as a salesman for a Detroit clothing store. Never a robust individual, McGregor travelled to Winnipeg in 1896 for a rest where the Winnipeg *Tribune* noted, "he is possessed of a fine sympathetic voice of good range." Shortly thereafter he was back in Windsor, but not well enough to assist his father in his 1896 re-election campaign. As did many men of the border cities, he courted a young lady, Harriet (Hattie) Dodds of Detroit. They were married in that city in 1898, and for a time lived in Detroit where Gordon worked as a bookkeeper. By 1902, William had become a principal in another venture and his son Gordon was hired on as manager.

The business was originally the Milner-Walker Wagon Works Company, a branch of the Hiram Walker empire. In his ceaseless quest to control all aspects of production, Hiram Walker entered into a wagon building scheme with an English manufacturer, William Milner, in 1897. The chosen site was a former sugar refinery, but was moved to a point just east of Walkerville next to the distillery. The enterprise began with a flurry of activity, for it was announced that several hundred men would be employed and that twenty-five wagons per day would be produced. However, after Hiram Walker's death in January 1899 and Milner's departure, the business flagged. Hiram Walker's successors saw no need to stay in the wagon business, and in December 1900, the works were purchased by William McGregor and Windsor banker John Curry. In 1902 they reorganized the enterprise as the Walkerville Wagon Works and installed Gordon McGregor as manager. While the factory had a substantial production capacity, it did not fare well. After March 1903, the workforce had dropped from 102 to 78. It was indebted up to $75,000 and it was said that the entire venture was at the point of collapse. By January 1904, it was announced that the business would be wound up and the remaining equipment moved to West Lorne.[36]

A young Gordon McGregor, circa 1890.

The Walkerville Wagon Works could easily have slipped away as had so many companies that came and went in those years. It would not have been missed, or long remembered. Instead, Gordon McGregor was about to take action, and his next steps would have a dramatic impact on Windsor and, for that matter, the industrial development of Canada.

The Modern Juggernaut

Henry Ford of Detroit first appeared in the Windsor *Evening Record* in the sports pages of January 1904. The newspaper recounted how Ford made "the wildest ride in the history of automobiling" across the ice of Anchor Bay in his "999" racer and set a new speed record for the mile. Ford appreciated that stunts such as this were sure to get press coverage and bring in new customers. A gaunt, intense perfectionist, Ford had been tinkering with the new technology since the mid-1890s. Together with James Couzens and Alexander Malcolmson, he started Ford Motor Company in 1903 and began the mass production of the Model A auto. The car sold well, and despite Ford's attempts to perfect every vehicle, the company met its production schedules. Detroit itself was a beehive of automotive innovation. The area had the critical mass of mechanics and metal machinists from bicycle and stove plants to staff this new industry. While the vast majority of new auto plants flashed across the scene and were quickly gone, Ford had shown that he could mass-produce a reliable car and make a good deal of money along the way.

Sometime after Ford set the new speed record, McGregor arranged a meeting, or possibly several meetings, with him. The exact dates and what was discussed were not recorded, but McGregor confided to his brother Don that, "There are men in Detroit, like Henry Ford, who say every farmer will soon be using an automobile. I don't see why we can't build autos right here."[37] However, the public remained skeptical (if not downright afraid) of the new machines. In a 1903 Grosse Pointe race, Barney Oldfield, travelling at the then unheard of speed of 60 miles per hour, lost control of his car and killed a spectator. Three years later, the *Evening Record* reported that the "modern juggernaut" of the automobile was regularly slaughtering those who went motoring on weekends. In 1904, Windsor's City Council considered a by-law to protect its citizens against "the benzene buggies (which) sail around corners without a limitation being placed on their speed, they carry no lights at night... run in the downtown at speeds exceeding six miles an hour."[38] Despite the dangers, nothing could halt the public's fascination with these new vehicles or the determination of inventors to profit from their production.

The National Cycle and Automobile Company occupied space in the Medbury Block from 1899 to 1902, and was perhaps the first Windsor company to consider (but not actually initiate) automobile manufacturing.[39] The first car to drive on Windsor's streets was possibly an early auto ferried over from Detroit by theatre magnate John Kunsky. Or perhaps the honour could go to a steam-powered buggy assembled by William Bulmer. Bulmer, a Great Lakes sailor who had passed a lifetime around steam engines, assembled his own boiler, attached it to a carriage, and with a ship's tiller to guide it, drove the vehicle out of his West London Street garage and navigated Windsor's streets in 1901. However versatile as an inventor, Bulmer was no businessman, and made no attempt to mass-produce his steamer.[40] What was available, to those few who could afford this novelty, was the Model A manufactured by Ford. By 1904, A.D. Bowlby, who had been a leading retailer of bicycles in the 1890s, was selling the Ford 2-cylinder cars in Windsor.[41] All of these imports were subject to a stiff 25 percent tariff that dampened sales.

It appears that between March and June 1904, McGregor courted Ford and presented him with a business plan whereby Ford components would be shipped across the river and assembled at McGregor's plant. The duty on components was far lower than that on assembled vehicles, so the finished cars could be sold in Canada at approximately the American production cost. Henry Ford visited southwestern Ontario in 1904, and noted that there were no serious competitors. Moreover, the Walker Road complex had the Canadian Bridge works which might supply frames as well as the Kerr Engine factory and other manufacturers, all of whom could supply parts to support automotive assembly. As McGregor would later succinctly recount, "After considerable trouble I got in contact with Mr. Henry Ford, Detroit, and succeeded in getting him interested."[42] Once Ford was on board, the task was left to McGregor to come up with the $125,000 in capital to start up the business. This was a formidable challenge, and with the help of banker John Curry, he solicited funds wherever he could. By July 1904, after imploring his friends, family, and professional associates, McGregor had completed his stock list. The arrangement to assemble Fords in Canada satisfied both parties. For Henry Ford, there was the attraction of selling not only to the Canadian market, but gaining entry into the British Empire's preferential tariff zone, all from a plant that he could easily visit from his Detroit office.

The first public hint of these business maneuvers was a small announcement in the *Evening Record* of July 2, 1904, that Gordon McGregor was trying to sell stock to set up an auto assembly factory. There was no mention of Henry Ford. It was generally understood that McGregor was trying to salvage his defunct wagon works and convert it to automobile production. If he succeeded in selling enough stock, then in the next winter he would use his building "for the manufacture of the 'devil wagons'."[43] By August 1904, everything was in place, and an agreement was reached with Ford for the transfer of patent rights and supervision to the Canadian company. At the first shareholders' meeting, Gordon McGregor became the secretary and effective head of the new company, while Henry Ford was appointed vice-president. Many of the parts would flow from either the Detroit plant or their suppliers. In anticipation of their new role for auto assembly, the vacant wagon works, which "smelled of painted wood, treated leather and must," was cleaned and readied. Production started in October 1904 with a few former wagon-workers and two mechanics on loan from the parent company. As historian David Roberts described it:

> McGregor's works was a slow, comparatively quiet operation, where hand tools were wielded by former carriage makers in greasy overalls. Aside from a steam-driven elevator, the only machinery was a drill press, reputedly powered by a belt that ran off the rear wheels of an automobile.[44]

At the end of October, McGregor drove the first Canadian assembled Model C down a Windsor street. By the end of the year he had turned out about 25 vehicles.

If McGregor lacked the volcanic vigour of Henry Ford, he made up for it with his exceptional organization and sales skills. In 1905, he strove to make

Ford of Canada the principal supplier of automobiles to Canadians from east to west. By the fall of that year, sales were being made in Winnipeg and Vancouver. Assembly processes were constantly improving and in the fall of 1906, one of Ford's Detroit mechanics, George Dickert, was dispatched to Walkerville to modernize production methods. He was struck by the smallness of the Canadian plant and that assembly was carried out on each vehicle on a pair of trestles. Once the engine, wheels, and frame had been attached to the chassis, the vehicle would be lifted by hand off the trestles and set onto the ground for completion. By the end of the year, under Dickert's direction, an electric generator and a drill press were installed. It was the harbinger of the end of the wagon days and the start of modern auto assembly.[45] The year after Dickert's arrival, production shot up to 327 vehicles. Ford of Canada was well on its way.

All the while, McGregor shored up his sales network. Going to trade shows and visiting dealerships, he ensured that the Ford brand was made available across Ontario and western Canada. When the Governor General visited the border communities on August 24, 1908, Gordon McGregor was there in a Ford to chauffeur the vice-regal party. By September 1908, it was reported that the company had made more than $18,000 in profits and had become the outright owner of their plant. Gordon McGregor was regularly praised by the *Evening Record* for his forward thinking and business acumen, for not only had Ford's been a stunning success in an entirely new industry, it had stimulated the relocation of additional industries to the border. Remarkably, this had all been accomplished with no incentives from the taxpayers. It almost passed without notice when Ford of Canada announced that in 1909, it would be coming out with an entirely new automobile: "a large touring car that will seat five passengers and will be driven by a 20-horsepower motor."[46]

It would be a product that would revolutionize how North Americans travelled.

Ford Motor Company of Canada in former Walkerville Wagon Works building, 1904.

Chapter Two
Power to the City
1909–1913

While the success of the new automobile assembly plants thrilled the public, established industries still remained the area's lifeblood. Walkerville had become the focus of a diversified complex that expanded well beyond Hiram Walker's distillery. Walker Road, its main street, had become the county's manufacturing dynamo. The area's largest employer, the Canadian Bridge Company (established in 1900), had over a thousand men on its payroll by 1913. Francis McMath, the company's founder, was an experienced American engineer who built a rapport with the Grand Trunk Railway and had obtained a blanket order from that railway to build all their bridges west of Winnipeg. In 1911, it became a point of area pride when Canadian Bridge was selected to help construct the new Quebec Bridge. Metal fabrication from companies such as Page Wire Fence and Kerr Engine Works dominated Walkerville's industrial core. Trussed Concrete Steel was established in 1907 and by 1913, it had about 200 men on staff providing Julius Kahn's latest designs in steel reinforced concrete buildings.[1] Throughout this expansion, the town's heavy industry was kept distinct from its budding residential area. The Walker family, through their real estate branch, the Walkerville Land and Building Company, was developing residential holdings south of Wyandotte Street and they had specific ideas on how this growth should proceed.

Garden City

The English writer Ebenezer Howard had already speculated that the city of the future should be laid out as a "Garden City." That is, it should be a "marriage of town and country, of rustic health and sanity and activity and urban knowledge..." The Garden City was to be neither a grimy urban slum nor a sprawl of houses across the rural landscape; rather, it was to provide a planned concentration of houses in a healthy environment with a green area surrounding the city proper. In October 1902, Walkerville's town council approved the extension of a road through part of farm lot 94 to become Garfield Street. The Board of Works had already committed itself to ensuring that this new road and all existing roads would be part of a model town, and that "Flowerbeds have been made and the planting of trees and shrubs will take but a short time."[2]

There were so many short streets in Walkerville that in 1904, it was proposed to rip up the still serviceable but unsightly block pavements and refashion the streets into flower-lined boulevards, thus enhancing what was "already the most beautiful town in western Ontario." Even federal officials of the Commission of Conservation took note and in 1917, Walkerville was complimented for its display of "very important features in common with the garden city type of development."[3] So concerned was the town with appearances that in 1903, at the apparent urging of Mrs. E.C. Walker, the existing street names were changed to reflect a more refined tone. Garfield Avenue became Windermere Road and Third Street became Argyle Road, to cite some examples. Elegance was further enhanced by the construction of spacious houses along these well-shaded streets for the use of the professional class. One of them, Stephen Griggs, purchased the Walkerville Brewery in 1907, and in that year moved into a large home designed by Albert Kahn on Kildare Road. Walkerville had become a place of comfortable charm and respectability. It was not by oversight that the developers had made no

Postcard of Kildare Road, Walkerville, circa 1910.

Bottling works, Hiram Walker & Sons, 1905.

provision for saloons or brothels, for these amenities had no place in the Garden City. But in any event, they were only a short streetcar ride away in Windsor.

Yet, all was not well with the business that founded the town. In June 1908, a U.S. Marshal seized 5,405 cases of Canadian Club at a Detroit warehouse. Walker's American competitors had convinced the authorities that Canadian Club was not really whisky at all, but a "compound of pure grain distillates," and should be relabelled under the *Pure Food and Drug Act* of 1906. The whisky wars raged over the next two years as the Walkers fought to keep their U.S. market open and restrain competitors who sold cheap liquor and marketed it as "Canadian whisky." Finally, President W.H. Taft ruled in December 1909 that whisky included "all potable liquor distilled from grain." Walker's good name was restored, and the company's lawyer exulted, "the label will not be changed."[4]

The time had come to enjoy some of the wealth that flowed from these potable liquors. From 1904–1905, Hiram Walker's son Edward constructed a private residence, "Willistead Manor" (named for his older brother Willis), not far from the rows of brick dwellings that housed his employees. Albert Kahn's design evoked the past, resulting in a massive, Tudor-Revival estate with stone and half-beam walls. The interior featured wide, exquisite staircases and ornately carved mantels over every hearth. Those fortunate enough to be invited within had never seen anything like it in southern Ontario. E. Chandler Walker and his wife Mary only lived in the mansion until his death in 1915. His widow returned to the US in 1921 and as the Walkers had no family, the mansion was donated to the people of Walkerville.

In 1904, the family also erected St. Mary's Anglican Church, just north of Willistead. The congregation had outgrown the early structure on Sandwich

Street, which in any event was regularly rattled by passing trains. St. Mary's was located in a park-like setting and its beautiful, ivy covered stone walls resembled nothing so much as an English country church. In an ecumenical gesture, Hiram Walker had once suggested that local Catholics could share the church. No such generosity was extended to the temperate Methodists and Walker had declined to contribute to or even sell land for a Methodist chapel. Nevertheless, they acquired land on a subdivision that was not under Walker control and built a small chapel in 1892. The community grew rapidly, and the cornerstone for the permanent structure, the Lincoln Road Methodist Church, was laid in September 1914.[5]

Not only was Methodism making advances, other Protestant denominations had expanded throughout the border area. St. Andrew's Presbyterian built a satellite church in Walkerville in 1908. In the same year, All Saints' assisted with the construction and dedication of another Anglican church, Ascension, on Windsor's west side. Evangelical rallies could pack Protestant churches, especially when a powerful speaker arrived to conduct a revival.[6] Moreover, with the introduction of the *Lord's Day Act* of 1906 there was not much else to do on Sundays. County Crown Attorney J.H. Rodd (an elder of the Methodist church) rigorously enforced the Act, and Sunday games of all sorts were barred; however, for the other six days, a few diversions were available.

St. Mary's Anglican Church under construction, 1904.

This Sporting Life—The Great "Rube"

Sportsmanship in the late 19th century was not refined and it was frequently downright crude. Dog fights were conducted just outside the city, and in 1902, the newspaper gleefully reported that "Ouellette Square is now being used as a prize ring. Yesterday afternoon several fights between small boys were pulled off in the midst of an admiring throng."[7] Far more civilized was organized sports, but even some of these were on the wane. By 1904, hockey had "dwindled to a mere recollection" in Windsor and the city did not field a team. Organized football had also disappeared and it was not until 1910 that Windsor entered a team in the Ontario Rugby league. They were thoroughly trounced by more experienced squads.[8] The one sport that was played, and that had developed an almost fanatical following, was baseball.

Very much the "working man's sport," baseball had become the game to play, and from 1900 to 1920, it was the country's most popular sport. Baseball teams sprouted everywhere from the "Windsor Colored Giants" to the team from Windsor Collegiate Institute. It was certainly huge in Windsor and between 1899 and 1905, the city regularly won the western Ontario amateur pennant. In 1903, Windsor's amateur squad won 19 of 23 games and the following year 32 out of 37. The undisputed leader of this dominant team, which brought so much pride to the area, was its pitcher, George "Rube" Deneau. An all-around athlete, Deneau was both a formidable pitcher and batter.[9] In 1904, he joined the Detroit Tigers as a "try-out," but did not make the roster. Still, his talent was undeniable, and a reporter urged him to expand his horizons beyond Windsor and "play baseball in a town where they pay men salaries. He's a pitcher and a good one." Deneau spent the next several seasons playing for semi-pro teams in Michigan and returned to Windsor in 1909 to captain "Deneau's Darlings" when it was thought that a border league might be formed. He won a number of memorable games through 1909, but in 1910 moved on to professional play. "Smiling" Rube became the player manager for the Berlin Green Sox and led them to the Canadian League pennant in 1911.

Very much in baseball's shadow was another sport which had also generated a local star whose career would be brief and tragic. Boxing was just coming into its own as a spectator sport and one of the finest boxers to emerge from the area was Willie Spracklin. Beginning in 1903, he fought a series of bouts in Michigan (some of them illegally staged) and developed a reputation as an up-and-comer. However, he was shot in a hunting accident and died in 1907.[10] Shortly after Spracklin's death, another Windsor boxer, Pierre Patrice "Patsy" Drouillard began his career in the ring at the age of 16. Fighting almost 20 bouts a year, he rose in the lightweight ranks and fought for the championship in Toronto in 1911. During the fight's second round, he broke bones in both hands yet still finished the bout, even though he lost on points. Drouillard came back the following year and won the championship and held the title for five years.[11] Significantly, two of the area's first sports stars, Rube Deneau and Patsy Drouillard, were both French-Canadians.

A Bedroom Community

In a less flamboyant fashion than Walkerville, Sandwich had done well in the first decade. By 1906, it was reported that "The sawmill and salt block of the Saginaw Salt & Lumber Co. is running full blast." The discovery of massive salt deposits had encouraged the Canadian Salt Company to build a chemical plant in the town in 1910. Located just below the mineral springs, the plant would not only process salt, but also caustic sodas and bleaching powders. Finally, in January 1912, the Essex Terminal completed the belt line to Sandwich and chemical products began to be shipped out to the major freight lines.[12] With the completion of these tracks, Sandwich ended the economic isolation it had endured since 1854.

For years, there was talk of a huge steel mill to be located south of Sandwich. While large blocks of land were assembled by Chicago investors, there was no hint of construction, only "a good deal of romance" in the notion of Sandwich becoming a second Gary, Indiana. For its part, Windsor had little success in attracting new industries. In 1908, Reo Motor Car, one of the wealthiest of the new car makers, leased the Medbury building in Windsor. But shortly thereafter they were lured away to St. Catharines by the prospect of the free use of a large factory.[13] Despite this setback, a strange thing was happening in Windsor. The city's population was still growing; in fact, it was experiencing a strong, sustained period of expansion. Even though the years 1907–1908 were gloomy economic times elsewhere, Windsor fairly blossomed. Banker John Curry was selling off housing lots at a furious pace and he boasted to a reporter that: "Real estate is on the boom."

The source of this demand lay in the recent industrial expansion, for houses were needed to accommodate the surge of workers coming in to man the factories. In the first decade of the 20th century, Walkerville doubled in population to 3,300. Windsor was also increasing at a remarkable pace and added 5,500 additional residents in the same period for a total of 17,829 in 1910. Walkerville was simply too small an area to accommodate the influx of workers while Windsor had the capacity to add more housing stock. But it was apparent that most of this increase in Windsor's population worked elsewhere.

Even the *Detroit News* observed in 1910 that while Windsor's industry was not growing, it remained "a charming residence suburb of Detroit."[14] However, in one remarkable year, a series of events would transform Windsor from a mere bedroom community to a vibrant industrial centre in its own right.

1910

Since 1854, the key to Windsor's existence and growth was rail traffic. Now that factor worked against it. Heavy industry relied on ready access to railways to haul freight, and Walkerville had a clear advantage. Both the Grand Trunk Railway along the riverfront and the Lake Erie, Essex and Detroit River Railway (sold in 1902 to the Pere Marquette) to the east of Walker Road provided freight service at the doorstep of industry. At the beginning of 1910, Windsor's new mayor, J.W. Hanna, was determined to improve the city's competitive position. He would be assisted by a special provincial statute that made it easier for it to provide bonuses to incoming industries. Giving bonuses to industries, either in the form of tax exemptions, interest-free loans, or outright grants, had been a common way for Ontario municipalities to stimulate investment and jobs. The system was easily abused and unscrupulous businessmen could siphon off money without actually making investments. To control bonusing, the *Municipal Act* of 1900 required the approval of two-thirds of all ratepayers. However, Windsor's special act did away with this requirement. The preamble to the statute explained that two to three thousand residents worked in Detroit, and since they did not return home until late in the evening, they were unable to vote. As a result of the "peculiar position of the city as to non-resident and absentee voters," the special act enabled the City Council by a three-fourths vote to approve free municipal power and water for ten years and to exempt newcomers from taxes for up to ten years without the public's consent. Windsor was back in the bonusing game. Mayor Hanna boasted to one investor; free municipal services were available without the troublesome need for a "vote of the people."[15]

This also made it possible for City Council to develop a plan to buy 40 acres of land from Giles to Tecumseh, between McDougall and Mercer, for $20,000 and then sell off parcels to prospective employers. The Essex Terminal Railway was selected to build the spur line to the new industrial site. It was Windsor's first attempt to create an industrial park.[16] The McDougall Street factory site would eventually emerge as a rival to Walker Road as a focus of industrial production. However popular this project, many residents feared that Windsor was becoming hemmed in by a growing network of railway tracks that blocked streets and divided neighbourhoods.

1910 would also see the completion of another railway marvel that secured Windsor's place in the transportation network. For decades, the Detroit River had been the great obstacle to the smooth transit of freight and passengers. In December 1909, the ice on the river was so bad that a Pere Marquette ferry was stuck solid for two days. The Grand Trunk Railway had already built an underwater tunnel between Port Huron, Michigan and Sarnia, Ontario. This left the Michigan Central Railway, the American main track from New York to Chicago through southern Ontario, at a severe competitive disadvantage. In 1904, the MCR was negotiating with the Grand Trunk about building a railway bridge at Windsor. But no agreement could be reached, and in any event the shipping interests required a bridge of such height that it was impractical. The MCR decided to go it alone and furthermore, to go under the river.[17]

William Wilgus, who had designed New York's Grand Central Terminal, came up with a novel engineering concept. Two parallel steel cylinders would be laid into a trench on the river bottom. The cylinders would be joined and covered with concrete to form an airtight "lung" and be big enough to accommodate two lines of railway tracks. Digging the approaches from either side of the river to connect to the lung proved especially difficult. While a huge boring machine dug the hole large enough to accommodate a locomotive, "muckers," working in a pressurized environment to keep the river from flooding the works, removed the debris. Falling clumps of clay, fires, and decompression sickness regularly killed and crippled men during the course of the excavation. But, thanks to the depression of 1907, there was a steady supply of men, most of them recent immigrants from Poland and Italy, who were desperate enough to go into "hell's kitchen" and take the place of the dead and injured. In 1909, when 200 muckers went on strike for better pay, they were summarily fired and replaced by outsiders brought

The Landsdowne car ferry crosses the Detroit River in winter, 1905. Passengers from the railway cars can be seen on the decks. (The Detroit Photographic Company)

in under police guard. By the time the MCR tunnel opened in 1910, twelve men had died building just the Canadian approach. Still, it was a major technological accomplishment for electric locomotives now crossed under the river (whether frozen or not) with passengers and freight in only 15 minutes. The river had ceased to be the barrier to commerce—but it had come at a heavy price.[18]

White Coal

At the beginning of the 20th century, Ontario had many economic advantages. Coal was not one of them. The absence of indigenous coal deposits placed the province at a distinct disadvantage to the United States in the race to industrialize. Most of Ontario had to rely on coal shipments from American fields where supplies were irregular and prices fluctuated. Windsor was unusual in that since 1893, it had access to the Gosfield Township natural gas fields. Gas power was so abundant in the area that natural gas was being illegally exported to Michigan.[19] As for electricity, the city had to rely on its antiquated 1895 plant which could not properly light its 175 street lamps and which frequently broke down, leaving neighbourhoods in darkness. The dynamos used direct current, which limited the distance the electricity could travel. In 1905, a by-law to go into a partnership with a private generating company was defeated. Finally, in order to operate its streetcars, the Detroit United Railway built a new 60-cycle power plant in 1910. This modern system could light the city (at a significant cost), run the streetcars, and as it was situated beside the salt company on Cameron Avenue, supply steam to separate the salt from rock.

Yet, even as this new plant was coming on line, other alternatives were presenting themselves. By the 1890s, the potential of water power from Niagara Falls was apparent and the discovery of alternating current made the transmission of electricity possible over great distances. The dream of cheap, hydroelectric power available across the province offered the possibility that Ontario could compete with, and perhaps even challenge, its American competitors.

In 1909, Windsor had its first encounter with the visionary of hydroelectricity. Adam Beck, the Mayor of London and a Member of the Provincial Parliament, was the province's most dynamic advocate of Niagara power. As a municipal leader and businessman, he knew that this cheap source of energy could transform the communities of southwestern Ontario. In the early 1900s, it appeared that the transmission of hydro would be under private control for the benefit of cities such as Toronto and Buffalo. Beck had successfully challenged this, and by 1907 he had created "a broad coalition of municipal activists behind his determination to build a publicly owned, provincial system."[20]

The first step was to unite the municipalities in support of the transmission lines. A plebiscite was called for January 4, 1909, to authorize Windsor to enter into a contract with the Hydro Electric Power Commission. Adam Beck twice came to the area to stump for the scheme. "You could make Windsor a big manufacturing centre by having ores shipped here and treated electrically," he exhorted his audience, "there are wonderful possibilities before you."[21] They applauded passionately, and the plebiscite was overwhelmingly approved.

The vote on the Niagara power by-law to enable Windsor to invest in the transmission line was to go to Windsor voters in June 1910 and the issue hardly seemed debatable. As part of the project, Beck proposed removing the existing street lights, installing 500 new ones and building a new $40,000 transmission plant. Electricity would be available at a cost that was barely a fifth of what the city was currently paying. The *Evening Record* exclaimed that, "The 'juice' will be cheap enough to cook with, and use in many other ways in the household."[22] But powerful interests (including the recently completed DUR plant) had lined up against hydroelectricity. Mayor Hanna was ambivalent about the project and in his inaugural address of 1910, he casually observed that "the power matter should not be lost sight of for although we now have natural gas in abundance it may happen that Niagara power will be desirable." To Alderman James Shepherd, Niagara power was essential and he led the campaign to bring the transmission lines to Windsor. Shepherd opposed exclusive grants to the Windsor Gas Company and wrote to Beck in April explaining to him that "conditions in our City are now taking shape to take up the question of Niagara power" and inviting him to come again to ensure that the by-law was passed. Shepherd worried that special interests were planning to block the coming of hydro, for it was apparent that both Windsor Gas and the DUR stood to lose a huge amount of their business. John Curry, Windsor's pre-eminent financier who had investments in both Windsor Gas and the DUR, led the opposition, warning that the cost of the transmission lines would increase taxes. As the by-law required approval by property owners (many of whom were female), the *Evening Record* felt that "timid, unthinking women" were being swayed by Curry's arguments.[23] Nevertheless, the "Power By-law" passed by a vote of 622–618. By this narrow margin, Windsor had voted for the cheap power that would be essential to its future.

Model T

As further proof that a new era had dawned, both the pro and con factions to the Power By-law had depended on automobiles to mobilize their forces: "Every automobile owner in the city was called on by one side or the other to lend his machine for the purpose of carrying voters to the polls, and the streets were full of flying speed wagons all day."[24] More than ever, Windsor was becoming a city of "speed wagons." Oshawa had McLaughlin and Toronto the Russell Motor and its "thoroughly Canadian car." But Windsor-Walkerville featured a variety of assemblers and parts makers, most of whom opened with great fanfare and then abruptly disappeared. It was a highly competitive environment and only those who could produce and sell survived. Regal Motors, the first to take a site in the new McDougall industrial park, opened in 1910 and lasted for only two years. Dominion Motor and Gramm Motor Truck also started up in 1910, and quietly departed in 1915 and 1914 respectively. Hupp Motor Car of Detroit had opened a solid five-acre factory in Windsor in 1911, and then closed in 1914. The American auto company E-M-F opened a branch plant in Walkerville in 1909. Shortly thereafter, the firm was acquired by Studebaker and began to produce the Studebaker '20' and '30.' Cutthroat competition marked the early years of the auto industry, and in the rush to innovate, there was much creative destruction before major producers would emerge to dominate the market.

Advertisement for Menard's Auto-Buggy, The Evening Record, February 8, 1908.

In those years, it seemed that anyone with a smattering of mechanical acumen and a willingness to take a chance could go into the auto business. Moise Menard, a blacksmith and wagon builder from Belle River, was attracted by all the tumult in Windsor and with the help of M.B. Covert of Detroit, designed a carriage powered by an engine. Menard eschewed the term "automobile" and called his high-wheel product an "auto-buggy." From his Windsor Wagon and Carriage Works at the corner of London and Caron streets, he began selling his auto-buggies in 1908. Unlike Gordon McGregor, Menard did not rely on imported parts, but manufactured and assembled his own components. This required painstaking piecework and made each auto an individual creation. Menard's auto-buggies did well for a short while, but the public soon lost interest in high-wheelers and wanted real automobiles. Still, Menard was a skilled mechanic and successfully shifted his production into heavy trucks and fire equipment. By 1917, he was operating as Menard Motor Truck.[25] W.E. Seagrave of Walkerville was also producing quality firefighting equipment and in 1910, he convinced Windsor to buy one of his aerial trucks. Perhaps the most impressive aspect of this sales performance was that at the time Windsor did not have enough water pressure to operate a hose on the ladder.[26]

Above all these hopefuls, Ford of Canada was building an enduring legacy and the foundation of it was an unlovely, but functional vehicle, the Model T Designed entirely by Detroit engineers, the "T" was light, durable, and affordably priced. By the summer of 1909, the Walkerville plant was operating at full capacity. Gordon McGregor decided that the time had come to expand his market and that August he began an around-the-world tour. While in Australia, McGregor, ever the consummate salesman, "drove a Model T into a town, asked the local bank manager to direct him to the wealthiest businessman in the area, and then entreated this businessman to take on the Ford dealership."[27] Even more outgoing than their American colleagues, Ford of Canada had established agencies in Australia, India, and South Africa. The *Evening Record* welcomed McGregor back in late January 1910 as a conquering hero. It was an amazing coup, for McGregor had effectively made Walkerville the capital city for Ford products to the British Empire outside of Great Britain. As a result of his salesmanship, "The world had already been neatly divided between Ford of Canada and the American company."[28]

1910 had also been a significant year in Detroit, for it marked the construction of the Highland Park assembly plant, which increased Ford's production by a factor of ten. In a limited reflection of this expansion, McGregor announced the Canadian branch's first major construction project in the summer of 1910: a three-storey structure behind the old carriage works on the riverfront. Albert Kahn, who had already designed much of the Hiram Walker offices and the Tudor splendour of Willistead Manor, proved that he could also design functional industrial facilities. Employing his brother Julius' trussed concrete reinforced walls and floors, he created a strong, well-lit assembly area that "embraced the stark new machine aesthetic of automobile production."[29] With 350,000 square feet of space, the three-storey "Plant 1" on the river would employ 2,500 men and be capable of producing 15,000 automobiles a year. Final assembly was on the third floor, and finished vehicles would be rolled down a ramp on the river side to ground level.

Plant 1 was one of the largest and most technologically advanced manufacturing spaces in Canada. A series of photographs taken in the plant in 1913 for the magazine *Canadian Machinery* displayed the most up to date equipment in the country. It was achieving such a level of sophistication that McGregor could shift from simply assembling the parts provided from Detroit to producing a few

Ford Plant 1, circa 1913.

of his own components as well as using parts from Canadian suppliers. Acting through his agents, the Bartlet law firm, McGregor steadily bought up land along the riverfront to expand the plant. The additional space enabled McGregor's chief mechanical engineer, George Dickert, to install Ford of Canada's first power conveyor in 1911. This would dramatically increase production from 1,280 cars in 1910 to 2,805 in 1911.[30] As for the Bartlet firm, while the family's patriarch, Alexander, died in December 1910, he and his sons had established a firm that would become not only McGregor's legal arm, but a city fixture.[31]

As for the men in Plant 1, work started at 7:30 a.m. and went on for ten hours, six days a week. Most of them walked or bicycled to the plant from nearby neighbourhoods. The half-hour lunches were spent swimming in the river or eating on the shipping dock. One man, who started on a drill press in 1909, recalled that at least initially the pace was tolerable for "most of the assembly operations were by hand." Over time, the pace quickened and tasks became repetitive and monotonous. However grinding the work, in some ways the Ford factory was family. In 1912, to celebrate a new production record, McGregor declared a half-holiday one Saturday and took the workers across the river to a Tigers game followed by a dinner.[32]

The 1911 Election and the Emerging Region

In many ways, Windsor had become very much a Detroit suburb. On Sundays, readers waited for bundles of the Detroit newspapers (the *Lord's Day Act* barred the Windsor press from publishing on Sunday) to arrive at the ferry landing for distribution. When Windsor finally got a professional baseball team in 1912, it was entered in the Border League with south-eastern Michigan teams. While Windsor did have a few amusements of its own, including the performers graduating from the Windsor Conservatory of Music (founded in 1901) and the silent movies available at the Windsor Theatre on Pitt Street, by and large the city looked toward Detroit for entertainment. When the "Detroit Theater" featured fresh-from-Broadway stars such as Florence Sylvester in "Babes in Toyland" in 1905, Windsorites flocked to get tickets. When the American League champion Tigers were playing at home, many of their fans came from across the river.

Conversely, one Canadian amusement park became a huge draw for Americans. Part of Isle aux Bois Blanc island had been purchased by the Detroit, Belle Isle & Windsor Ferry, and since 1898, it became a destination for Detroiters anxious to escape the grit of the city. Bob-Lo, as the park was known to its non-French speaking patrons, added attractions including bands, sports facilities and in 1906, an electric amusement ride. In order to get to the park, Detroiters boarded the excursion ship, the *S.S. Columbia.* With its mahogany panelling and gilded moldings, the *Columbia* was a floating monument to the *belle époque* and a brief reminder to its passengers of the finer things in life. In 1913, a dance pavilion (the largest in the world at that time) with an enormous glass wall and almost an acre of dance floor was opened on Bob-Lo.[33] The young Detroiters who flocked to the amusement rides, or hoped to meet a partner at the dance pavilion, were barely aware that they had left their own country.

Dance Pavilion at Bob-Lo Island, circa 1914.

Much like Detroit, Windsor was in the midst of a phenomenal growth spurt. McNulty Realty was building upscale houses on Victoria Avenue and its sales drive was oriented toward Detroiters. Americans who bought these stately homes "found that they could have the advantages of a quiet, suburban life and still be within three miles of downtown Detroit."[34] Moreover, Windsor was itself becoming an essential component of the industrial giant of Detroit. Starting in 1911, one new factory opened up every month in Windsor; and by far most of these factories were American branch plants.[35] Parts and machinery were being shipped across the river in an increasing flow to fuel the assembly lines of Windsor. Crossing the river to another country became a routine affair in the Detroit/Windsor conglomerate. No passport, or for that matter identification of any kind, was required to cross the border. "Over and back" was the phrase most locals gave to the border staff. Cross-border trade and traffic was the area's life-blood, and it would be the major issue arising in one of the most momentous elections in Canadian history.

By 1911, Sir Wilfrid Laurier's Liberals could take quiet pleasure in having governed Canada through a decade of solid growth. To cap his achievement, Laurier had negotiated a reciprocity agreement with the U.S. that enabled most natural products and a few manufactured goods to pass between the countries free of tariffs. Detroit businessmen were alive to the potential benefits of reciprocity and they had no doubt that it would be approved. However, it seemed to more fervent Canadian imperialists that reciprocity was an insidious attack on the British connection and the first step toward annexation. The subsequent election that September became a debate on the very nature of Canada and its relationship with the United States.[36] In Windsor, some of the harsher, anti-American tones of the campaign were muted. The city was far too closely tied to American industry to adopt the isolationist sentiments that marked other regions. In the Windsor area, the issue was not loyalty—it was jobs. In various departments of the Hiram Walker plant the following placard was prominently displayed:

THIS FIRM IS OPPOSED TO RECIPROCITY,
BELIEVING IT WOULD BE HIGHLY INJURIOUS
TO CANADA AS A WHOLE

The message could not have been clearer. Employees knew how they were to vote in the upcoming election if they wished to keep on working. It became an election about barley. Essex County farmers hoped that the new trade deal would eliminate the ruinous 30 cents a bushel tariff and open up the American Midwest to their product. At the same time, Hiram Walker's distillery wanted to keep the tariff in place to insure their supply of cheap, Canadian barley. They were not the only producers who warned of the perils of reciprocity. The manager of Canadian Salt advised his workers that the end of tariffs also meant the end of the company. When rival candidates met at the Sandwich courthouse, the Liberal, Dr. P.A. Dewar, pointed out that the grain farmers of Essex County were being "practically ruined" by the tariffs. His opponent, the sitting Conservative, Oliver Wilcox, thought the prevailing system was just what was needed, and a raucous crowd (well oiled by the free dispensation of Hiram Walker liquors) wildly applauded him.

One weapon the Liberals could count on was the presence of the grand old man himself: Sir Wilfrid Laurier. He arrived at the GTR Station on September 8, 1911, and was taken up in a Ford Model T driven by none other than Gordon McGregor and chauffeured through an enthusiastic crowd to Ouellette Square. There, the Liberal chieftain gave an impassioned defence of his policies. The presence on the dignitary's platform of McGregor, whose company had been founded by the existence of tariffs, seems highly contradictory. However, the family had identified with the Liberals since William McGregor's many years in Parliament. As well, Gordon may well have considered that his company was sufficiently entrenched to prosper without the need for protective tariffs. He would be one of the few industrialists to be seen with the Liberal leader. But it would not be enough. Despite carrying the rural, French-Canadian townships of North Essex, the Conservatives scored heavily in Windsor and Walkerville, and a triumphant mob carrying burning oil-soaked brooms marched through

Ford Model T assembly line, circa 1914.

the streets to celebrate the Conservative victory.[37] Detroit businessmen were taken aback by the result and the *Detroit News* reported that "Reciprocity is defeated and the returns are flabbergasting."

Deader than Kelsey's Nuts

One of the favourite phrases of American President Richard Nixon to describe something as permanently defunct was to say that it was "deader than Kelsey's nuts." The President likely did not appreciate that the phrase dated back to the wheel-maker John Kelsey who set up Kelsey Wheel in Detroit in 1910. His product was so reliable, the nuts so formidably fastened, that Henry Ford became one of his principal customers. In November 1913, Kelsey established a Windsor plant to provide the same product to Ford of Canada. It was the largest auto wheel plant in the country, and a tangible sign that Ford's parts could now be manufactured locally. The only disadvantage was that the plant required so many men that Detroit workers had to cross the river to Canada to maintain production.[38] The Detroit-Windsor area was now an eclectic hub of various auto manufacturing and parts suppliers. Obsessed with churning out ever lighter vehicles with new alloys and processes, Ford was diverting more of its parts production to stamping plants rather than casting. Dominion Stamping of Walkerville helped fill this demand on the Canadian side.[39] As for the most popular car in the country, the Model Ts were being produced by the Ford plant in ever greater quantities. From 2,805 in 1911, a heady 6,388 were built in 1912. Showrooms in Winnipeg and Vancouver, and as far as Melbourne to Johannesburg, prominently displayed and sold the automobiles of the border area.

This rapidly expanding industry needed workers, and it needed them immediately. Prior to 1905, Windsor had been a typical southern Ontario town with an average annual growth rate of 2.1 percent over the preceding ten years. However, between 1905 and 1914, its growth averaged 6.4 percent a year, and it had reached a population of 23,013 in 1914 (see Appendix A).[40] These statistics did not include the growing numbers of people moving into neighbouring municipalities. Walkerville and the township lands adjacent to the Ford complex were expanding even faster than Windsor. The question became where to put these new arrivals. In 1912, the Davis Farm Subdivision opened up an extended project for worker homes along Moy and Hall Avenues. A conglomerate formed by A.F. Healy, Leo Page, A. Chappus, and E. Morton, had acquired farm lots 92 and 93 from Mayor John Davis, and sold them off in 1912 for an enormous profit.[41] Sadly, the developers also levelled Moy

Hall, the grand mansion of Angus Macintosh and a sparkling jewel of the days of the fur trade. Only the gates were left facing the river. According to the *Evening Record* of 1910, this spread of development meant that "in five years' time Wyandotte Street from Windsor to Walkerville will be one solid business block."[42] It would have seemed logical that this growth would compel the three communities along the Detroit River to merge into one city. To the contrary, they were about to spawn two additional municipalities.

Market Gardens to Big Steel City

Overshadowing the enthusiasm for Ford was the announcement that U.S. Steel planned to buy great swathes of land south of Sandwich and build steel mills to rival those of Pittsburgh. This northern part of the lands at the "Petite Côte," the first permanent European settlement in Ontario, had changed little since 1749. French farmers still grew market vegetables, and the only development had been the Dominion Fish Hatchery. Rumours of an industrial project had been circulating for years, but seemed to become a reality at the beginning of 1913 with news that E.H. Gary, the President of U.S. Steel, had selected Ojibway for a $20 million steel plant. The announcement "spread over the city like wildfire" and the *Evening Record* was confidently predicted that:

> The quiet old county town (Sandwich) with its surrounding peaceful farms, will in a few years be transformed into a manufacturing metropolis, blazing with blast furnaces, roaring with mills, noisy with the traffic of a large city… and residential streets where thousands of employes will have their homes.[43]

The press forecast that steel mills would be going up by the spring and that another model city in the same style as Gary, Indiana, would soon arise. O.E. Fleming acted as the real estate agent for the steel company and bought the property of Detroit tobacco tycoon Daniel Scotten that was to be the nucleus for the development. Rail connections were guaranteed by Francis McMath, the head of Canadian Bridge (already associated with U.S. Steel), who with William Woolatt (Ojibway's first mayor) controlled the Essex Terminal Railway and assured that the connecting spurs would be extended. Democracy was cast aside and in its first years, the town would be run by an appointed commission composed of the founding industrialists.

Almost as soon as the announcement was made, speculators began to crowd in. Farmers subdivided their lands and purchasers waited in line for four days to be the first to buy these lots that they were certain would yield fistfuls of money. Lots were sold on the first day for $1,000 and a few days later were re-sold for $6,000.[44] Even Toronto was taking note and the *Globe* ran an article that this humble site of a few French truck farmers was about to become an industrial giant. The *Globe* writer thought that "the five municipalities of Ford City, Walkerville, Windsor, Sandwich and Ojibway (would become) the inevitable steel and auto centre of Canada."[45] Four years after its incorporation, and with the intervening uncertainties created by the First World War, there were no steel mills in Ojibway and only 75 people lived in the town.

Political cartoon from the Border Cities Star about the proposed U.S. Steel plant in Ojibway, June 14, 1913.

At the other end of the border area, the only thing Ford City had in common with Ojibway was that it was also originally a small, French-Canadian farming community. But Ford City was not built on dreams, but on the sweat, steel, and reality of Ford of Canada. Separated from the genteel neighbourhoods of Walkerville by the row of factories along Walker Road, Ford City would develop its own distinct identity based on its French foundations. François X. Drouillard was born on the family farm just to the east of Walker Road and his life mirrored the times. As a boy of fifteen, he had served in the militia during the Patriot War of 1838, and as a man, he had helped build Walker's first distillery. In his later years, he watched the wagon works turn into an automobile factory, and the private lane on his family's farm become Drouillard Road. The church of *Notre Dame du Lac,* situated on land donated by the Drouillard family and facing where the Detroit River branched out to Lake St. Clair, was the focus of their community. Without question, it was a French parish (the pastor was always a French-Canadian) and it followed the traditional way of life. On Christmas mornings, rows of altar boys singing *Il est* né le *Divin Enfant* would parade to the church for Mass and sermon in French. Following the destruction of the first wooden church in 1907, a fine Romanesque-style church was built and dedicated as Our Lady of the Rosary the following year.

By late 1912, it was apparent that the Ford industrial area should be separated from Sandwich East Township and become a separate municipality. By virtue of an Essex County by-law, "Ford City" was created in December 1912. While other names had been contemplated, including "Autoville," the community was so entirely a creation of the Ford company that bearing its name seemed inevitable.[46] In its first years, Ford City maintained its character as a small French enclave and its first four mayors were French, as was most of the village council. But this way of life could hardly withstand the blast of industry that was reshaping the area. Only eight months after its creation, Ford City was described in the press as a "lusty industrial infant." In addition to Ford, it contained Fisher Body, Dominion Stamping, and other plants that made this village one of the rising industrial stars of Canada. In discussions with hydro-electric officials, Ford City's Reeve Charles Montreuil announced in March 1913 that the village would take 3,000 horsepower from the service (Windsor planned on 5,000) as "the Ford Motor Co (is) becoming the largest consumer in his municipality."[47] Less than a year after its creation, Ford City was contemplating separating from Essex County altogether.

The riverfront was fast becoming the scene of technologies and industries piling up one over the other. From the railway of the 1850s in downtown Windsor to the latest automobile technology of the early 20th century in Ford City, and French farms and windmills of the 1700s on either side of them, the riverfront was an eclectic array of activity. The one thing the riverfront lacked was space for its own people. However, thanks to Alderman W.W. Lanspeary, the city had acquired lands in the east and west to expand its parks system and to landscape Giles Boulevard in 1912. The real breakthrough occurred later that year when the city finally closed a deal with the Grand Trunk Railway to lease the Riverside Park and build a dock at the foot of Church Street. It was a long awaited improvement that dedicated this small parcel of the riverfront for public enjoyment.[48] However, for the most part, the riverfront had been given over to factories and smokestacks. The resulting palls of smoke were quietly accepted by most people as a tangible sign of prosperity.

The summer of 1914, the last summer of peace for years to come, was marked by a bitter provincial election that raised the two passions that were to divide the community in the following decade. Since 1902, North Essex had been represented by a leading member of the Conservative party, Dr. J.O. Reaume. Raised to be a farmer like his forefathers, Reaume had been crippled in an accident and instead turned to the professions. He studied medicine at the Detroit College of Medicine, graduated in 1885, and attracted a wide clientele from among the French farmers of the northern part of Essex County. Conservative leader James P. Whitney had urged Reaume to run for office, and once Whitney became premier in 1905, Reaume was appointed to the cabinet. For his part, Reaume tried to stand up for bilingual education and challenged the influence of the Orange Lodge in Whitney's government.[49] In 1914, Windsor, Sandwich, and Walkerville were split off from North Essex and formed a separate riding. Thinking that the area had been represented for too long by a French-Catholic, Oscar Fleming challenged Reaume at a hastily called meeting and captured the nomination. Fleming, Windsor's first mayor in 1892, remained one of the city's most powerful lawyers and businessmen. However, Reaume had Whitney's backing and stayed in the race as an independent. The Liberals selected a popular but unlikely choice, Rev. J.C. Tolmie of St. Andrew's Presbyterian. While Reaume and Fleming battled each other, Tolmie campaigned on a platform to "abolish the bar" and forever end the curse of drink.

The contest in the remainder of northern Essex County could not have been more different. In June 1912, the Whitney government introduced "Regulation 17" which restricted the use of French to the first two years of school and required that all francophone children receive instruction in English. French-Canadians were inflamed, and their champion was the Liberal candidate, Sévérin Ducharme. At a passionate rally at *Notre Dame du Lac* (as Holy Rosary was still frequently called), Ducharme demanded that their language be respected. He was easily elected. In the city, Tolmie benefited from the Tory divide and a devout temperance man was chosen in what was likely the wettest constituency in Ontario. This campaign had raised two issues: bilingual schools and prohibition, which would come into sharper focus and divide the community in the coming years.[50]

Illuminating the Waterfront

Dusk was settling over the Detroit River on Saturday evening, September 12, 1914, as a tall, distinguished man strode into the Windsor armouries. Adam, now "Sir" Adam Beck had arrived to turn the switch and complete one of the greatest triumphs of his career. At exactly eight o'clock he would trigger the flow of power from Niagara Falls to the streets of Windsor.

Many doubted that this was possible, or even desirable. When Windsor balked at signing a contract with the Hydro Electric Power Commission, Mayor James Shepherd again called for Beck to come and address the Council in December 1912. There was no question as to where the "Power Minister" stood: "Hydro power was a natural monopoly, said Mr. Beck, because the people owned it themselves and shared in the profits. We will say to the Edison people that you can't come over here and compete with hydro power... We will tell them to stay where they are."[51] Council unanimously passed the contract that night and it was signed and sealed by Shepherd and Beck minutes thereafter. Shepherd, who as alderman and mayor had led the drive to bring hydroelectricity to Windsor, and who had also been a major backer of the industrial park and the first riverside park, was defeated for the mayoralty a few days after this event by Henry Clay, a lawyer who had taken no part in Windsor's improvement and who had been a persistent critic of development.

By November 1913, transmission cables reached southern Ontario and a "Hydro/Electric Commission of the City of Windsor" was created in December. An office was set up in a 12-foot by 12-foot room at the corner of Pitt and Ouellette. Oliver Perry, a young electrical engineer, arrived to serve as manager of the new system. "Thus, with the beginning of 1914 Windsor Hydro had everything but electricity and customers." It soon acquired an abundance of both. A substation was built and canvassers signed up scores of new customers. Many came to the office unsolicited after hearing about the wonders of hydroelectricity.[52]

As Beck stepped forward that evening of September 12, he was about to open the circuit for the longest electric transmission line in the world. Fully aware of the significance of the moment, he spared no expense to highlight its drama. His men were instructed to "have lots of light for the whole of Sandwich Street so that it would show up well from the river." To Beck, the extension of the line to Windsor would be a sweet victory for he "wanted Windsor to advertise the hydroelectric system to the Americans." When he turned the switch at exactly eight o'clock, the first surge of power lit up an enormous light display in the armouries. A reporter from the *Detroit News* described how searchlights mounted on the roof pierced the night sky and illuminated a large kite in the shape of an airship that hovered over the city. Instantly, the newly installed lights on Ouellette Avenue came on as did the lights along Sandwich Street. From power supplied by water falling at Niagara, lights sparkled and shone on the Detroit River as crowds of Detroiters looked on and marvelled.

The only disadvantage to this fabulous display was that it had come on the heels of momentous events in Europe. Instead of having all attention focused on this great triumph of human ingenuity, much of the public's interest was fixated on a distant and terrible war.

Chapter Three

Great War

1914–1918

The Civic Holiday of Monday, August 3, 1914, seemed especially ideal. It was a torrid weekend, and Windsor was all but evacuated as excursions headed off to Bob-Lo Island, cruises sailed downriver, and the Emancipation Day celebration gathered in Sandwich. Windsor's baseball team faced their archrivals, the "Independents," at Wigle Park. No one could suspect that it marked the end of an era, and that after that weekend the world would never be the same.

On August 4, Germany invaded neutral Belgium. Britain declared war against Germany and Austria-Hungary, and for the first time, Canada was a participant in a major conflict. Canada's impetuous Minister of Militia and Defence, Sam Hughes, discarded the existing plans for mobilization based on the county militia regiments, and instead implemented an *ad hoc* plan to assemble a mass of trained and untrained men and ship them to England for service. As a result, enthusiastic volunteers jammed into the Windsor armouries in the hope that they might be among the chosen. Recruits, some from the existing militia, and others with no military background, waited anxiously as a medical examiner measured their fitness for service. Those lucky enough to be selected were immediately sworn in and handed over to drill sergeants.[1]

The 21st Regiment Essex Fusiliers' commanding officer, Lt. Col. Ernest Wigle, had been returning from a business trip to England when war was declared and it was not until the afternoon of August 22 that he arrived on the afternoon train. For years, Wigle had been one of the city's most dominant political and commercial personalities. During five consecutive terms as mayor from 1905 to 1909, he balanced the city's finances and started work on the parks system. After that, he concentrated on his law firm, but still found time

Crowds wave farewell as the first group of volunteers leave the CPR station, August 1914.

to tussle in the mud with the men's rugby squad. Wigle seemed most comfortable in a rugged, male milieu and he had served in all ranks in the local militia since 1874. In 1912, he had become the Fusiliers' commanding officer. Now he had to tell his men that their regiment meant nothing to the authorities in Ottawa. Militiamen could volunteer to serve in the new battalions being formed and be selected along with civilians. Many did, and the first 210 recruits marched out of the armouries to the CPR train station on August 22 on their way to Valcartier camp in Quebec. "Cheers and music, sobs and tears were strangely mingled as close to a thousand civilians" crowded in to watch the train pull out.

Within days, three of the men were back in Windsor. One was underage and two were married men who did not have their wives' permission to enlist. Over the next several months, two further drafts of 250 men were recruited and sent out for training. In October, orders were issued for the formation of the 18th Battalion of the Canadian Expeditionary Force to be drawn from western Ontario volunteers. Wigle would be its commanding officer, and Captain Alan Prince, the great-grandson of John Prince of Battle of Windsor fame, would command "A" Company. An early premonition of the tragedies to come was delivered just before Christmas, 1914. George Wade, an Englishman who worked at the Walkerville plant of Page Wire, had received notice in August to rejoin his regiment. In December 1914, shortly after reaching the front, he was wounded and died before reaching hospital. He was the first Windsor resident to die in the war.

The Lady Searcher

After the initial burst of enthusiasm, life along the Detroit River returned to its normal rhythms. Patriotic teas and fundraisers for the Belgian refugees filled the social calendar. As Easter 1915 approached, unpleasant war news was put aside as Windsor women scoured Detroit department stores for the latest finery. It was well known that Detroit stores offered the best fashions at prices Windsor retailers rarely matched and it was routine for ladies to change into the purchases when returning to Canada to avoid paying duty. By March

1915, the federal government decided that the border region should start paying its proper share of excise taxes. On March 27, a female agent, Martha White, arrived in Windsor and began to search every woman returning on the ferry from Detroit and apprehended scores of them. Confronted by her, many women "weepingly brought the articles from many and strange hiding places." Several women were emotionally distraught by the ordeal and tried to telephone friends to secure their release. Confiscated clothing began to pile up and the floor of the customs shed began to resemble the "woman's section of a large department store."

Outrage at these inspections was not directed toward the smugglers who were breaking the law. Rather, Windsor residents were indignant that an outsider (the "Lady Searcher" as she became known) had descended from Ottawa to interfere with what was considered a local way of life. Former alderman Robert Timms best captured the prevailing feeling:

> Windsor is, except politically, part and parcel of the City of Detroit, and hundreds of valiant yeomen and yeowomen fare forth in the morning from our shores to the big parent sister on the other shore.... And shall those many hundreds of honest people be debarred from patronizing the ten cent or other stores without being fined when they step off the boat?[2]

Mrs. White was gone in a few days, and cross-border smuggling resumed its normal course. But this outside interference with local ways continued to rankle as an insult not to be borne.

In its initial phase, the war seemed to have hardly any effect on business. As far as heavy industry was concerned, it had no impact at all. Wars were fought by men, and it was thought that there was not much need to link manufacturing to the war effort. Ford Motor's production of civilian autos rose steadily and in lockstep with the American parent company, the price of a Model T was lowered to $540 in 1914. By the end of 1914, Gordon McGregor determined that the old wagon works had to go. A six-storey Albert Kahn-designed plant was built to provide a massive crane to speed up production and link assembly to parts areas. This enabled a spectacular rise from 15,657 finished vehicles in 1914 to 46,914 in 1918.[3] Already in 1914, Ford dominated the market, and 38 percent of the cars registered in Canada were Fords. In line with the "big parent" across the river, McGregor gathered the workers on the plant floor on April 21, 1915, to announce that Ford Canada would emulate the American company and institute a minimum wage of $4 a day for an eight-hour day. The assembly area rocked with cheers and photographers captured McGregor being all but embraced by his workforce.[4] It almost seemed as if the district was at peace, and not part of an Empire that was locked in a desperate struggle for survival.

As for those directly involved in the war, most were in training and there was little to report. One Windsor soldier, John Teahan, wrote from the training camp at Salisbury Plain, England, that "life in the trenches cannot possibly be worse," and that in the mud and rain of Salisbury, men were dying of disease at a furious rate. Late in January 1915, word arrived of Windsor's second death in the war. The casualty was Svend Raasted, a local real estate agent who had been drafted into the German army during a European trip, and who had died fighting for Germany. With little warning, this far-away war was about to come directly to Windsor.

Under Attack

As soon as the war began, armed guards were posted at the armouries and at federal buildings. Lt. Col. Wigle warned that there were thousands of Germans in Detroit who were plotting to attack Canadian installations and that every precaution should be taken. Locals found his concerns exaggerated, and there was more anxiety caused by trigger-happy guards at the armouries than with the possibility of saboteurs. But Wigle made a valid point, for in the decades after the Civil War, Germans were by far the largest single ethnic group coming to Detroit.[5] They were concentrated in the near east side around Gratiot. In this neighbourhood, German was the language on the street and German shops were commonplace. Many of these newcomers retained sympathies for their homeland and were willing to do what they could to advance Germany's cause. Moreover, the border was weakly defended and the remaining militia of the 21st Fusiliers were hard-pressed to find recruits who were willing to volunteer for home defence.

By the spring of 1915, a few firms started getting war contracts. Canadian Bridge was manufacturing shells and the Peabody Overall Company in Walkerville secured a huge contract for the production of trousers for the British army. At three o'clock in the morning of Monday, June 21, 1915, a huge explosion rocked the outer wall of the Peabody Building. The blast shattered the plant's windows and was so loud that Detroiters thought that the explosion had occurred in their city. Locals, most of them still in their nightclothes, rushed to the scene. Superficially, the damage appeared extensive for in addition to the shattered glass, portions of a sidewalk had been tossed several yards away. But the building itself was largely undamaged and its support pillars were intact. While the curious milled about the Peabody Building, troops at the armouries had heard a sharp bang at almost the same time as the initial explosion. Private Walter Banton inspected the grounds, discovered a bomb, and rather imprudently, carried it into the building. Fortunately, it appeared that the detonator had already gone off and failed to activate the dynamite. The device was disarmed.

"All Canada was aroused by the daring attempt" the *Evening Record* proclaimed, to stop the flow of trousers to the British army. Guards on public buildings were redoubled, and they were given orders to shoot to kill. Agents of both the Ontario Provincial Police and the Dominion Police were dispatched to Windsor to expedite the "apprehension of the dynamiters."[6] Authorities immediately suspected that a "Bomb-Bund" of German-Americans were behind the attacks. It was an accusation that Detroiters heatedly resented and a Detroit *Free Press* editorial held that, in the absence of proof, these accusations were most unfair.[7] Four days after the bombing, police arrested a Walkerville watchman, William Lefler, who gave a detailed confession of how the bombing attacks had been planned in Detroit by a German organization.

It soon became apparent that the German Foreign Office in New York was engaged in a widespread campaign to disrupt the war effort by attacking any targets of opportunity in Canada. As Lefler described it, their Detroit agent was Albert Kaltschmidt, the former manager of Tate Electric in Walkerville, who had been fired when the plant got a contract in 1915 to manufacture shrapnel shells. Kaltschmidt had never hidden his pro-German views and it was inevitable that he would be sacked. In May 1915, Kaltschmidt assembled a group of men including Lefler and one "Schmidt" (later identified as Karl Respa) to work out a plan of attack. Lefler and Respa conveyed the dynamite across the river concealed in automobiles and Respa planted the bombs.[8] Kaltschmidt denied any complicity. Respa, on the other hand, made an ill-advised trip to Bob-Lo Island with his family at the end of August. The amusement park had become so popular with Detroiters that few appreciated that it was in a foreign country. Police were alerted that one of their main suspects had strayed across the border, and Respa was arrested.

At Respa's trial in March 1916, the entire plot to bomb Windsor factories was revealed. The papers of captured German attaché Franz von Papen disclosed an extensive conspiracy to disrupt British military supplies flowing from North America. The Windsor and Walkerville bombings were part of this plan, and had been entrusted to von Papen's Detroit agent, Kaltschmidt. In his confession, Respa freely admitted to his part in the conspiracy. It did him little good, for at his trial the judge condemned Respa for being "a hired incendiary and assassin" and sentenced him to life in prison. Kaltschmidt would later be tried in Detroit for breaking American neutrality laws, as well

This political cartoon comments on the Peabody bomber Kaltschmidt being financed by German attache, Franz von Papen, *The Evening Record*, January 22, 1916.

as conspiracy to destroy military installations, and would serve five years in an American prison. In the end, there were few successful acts of sabotage carried out by German agents with practically no impact on Canada's war efforts.

One result of the bombing was the formation of a "Home Guard" unit to protect the border and designated facilities. Under the command of Major S.C. Robinson, the Guard was a poor-cousin of the real army and the municipality was expected to come up with the funds for uniforms and rifles. One measure of the low priority of home defence was Robinson's request to the women's auxiliary to hold a fundraiser so the Guard could buy a machine gun.[9]

Closer to Home

By the fall of 1915, the initial war enthusiasm had passed and the realization that it would be an extended, gruelling struggle had set in. In a thoughtful editorial, "A City That Found Itself," the *Evening Record* commented on Windsor's unusual role in the war effort:

> "Windsor is different." You have heard that many times. Somehow or other we were not exactly a typical Canadian city. New arrivals were wont to remark that we seemed to be "more Americanized" than most Canadian cities.
>
> Then the war came. For a time we continued in the way we were going. We were engrossed in material things… The war made little difference.
>
> Strangers told us Windsor was less affected by the war than any other place in Canada.
>
> We are coming to realize that we haven't done enough. Our vision broadens. No longer are we blinded by greed and selfishness. The war is coming closer to home.[10]

One way of doing more was to send additional men overseas, and Essex County was tasked with raising a new battalion, the 99th. Enlistment was now a public event. On one occasion when a group of ten men volunteered, they were marched to Wigle Park to take in a football game and be applauded by the crowd. But these volunteers were all were British-born or Americans. Few natives of Essex County were coming forward. As the winter of 1916 set in, recruits for the 99th were housed in the stables of the Windsor Driving Park, and satellite platoons were set up in Amherstburg, Essex, Kingsville and Leamington. Shaming methods were now being employed, and letters were directed to young men inquiring why they were not in uniform. Sergeants addressed factory workers at lunchtime and appealed to them to sign up.

Even with these methods, it was difficult to get the 99th up to strength. By the end of March 1916, the battalion was supposed to move out to London for training. This was disrupted when the men were paid at the end of the month and a riot ensued. Free-for-all fights became hourly occurrences that weekend as recruits went on a drunken rampage in downtown Windsor. There were too few military police to control them and Windsor police were hard-pressed to restore order. The following Monday, there were even more gaps in the ranks of the 99th, for as one officer observed, "some of the men who enlisted did so merely to get a place to stay and warm clothing and something to eat for the winter." He consoled himself with the notion that "Now that they are gone, the battalion will be much better off."[11]

Perhaps the reluctance to come forward was the result of news from the trenches. In June 1916, word arrived that "Curly" Allen, a legendary figure among the city's young men, a good-looking, headstrong youth who had fought in the South African War, the Mexican Revolution, and had paid his own way to England to enlist as a private, had been killed at the front. If Curly Allen could be mown down among thousands of others, then it seemed that courage and gallantry were of little value. Lt. Col. Wigle had returned to Windsor at the end of May 1916 to tend to his ill wife, and he recounted his war experiences to the press. He showed reporters some of his trench art, including a painting of his dugout with a bottle of Canadian Club perched on a table. While Wigle expressed optimism about the war and the eventual defeat of Germany, he also recounted how many of the officers in the 18th battalion had been hospitalized with shell shock. Even at this stage, there seemed to be little glamour or heroism in the struggle.

Non-Combatants

War or no war, industries were growing at a remarkable pace. Kelsey Wheel was supplying more products than ever to a flourishing automobile industry.

The Maxwell Motor Company appreciated Windsor's potential as a manufacturing centre and in February 1916, announced that a new plant was coming to the city. In a curious boast, Ford Motor published a huge advertisement that declared "The executives of the Canadian Ford Company make no consideration of the war."[12] It was true. Ford made no attempt to enter the munitions trade or supply any sizable number of vehicles for the military. In fact, its steady use of the railway system to transport raw materials and finished autos detracted from the space available to move war matériel. The purpose of the ad was apparently to reassure the public that the Canadian economy was so solid that it could afford to disregard the inconveniences caused by the war. Nevertheless, it was a public declaration that, as far as Ford and Gordon McGregor were concerned, making a profit remained the prime objective.

This profitability had a further impact on Windsor by diverting manpower into the factories. In lieu of the dangers and discomfort of army life, there was good-paying factory work to be had. Building statistics from 1914 onwards showed that Windsor, which only a decade previously had been little more than a town, now had a rate of growth that was only exceeded by Toronto and Montreal.[13] Construction could not meet the pace of demand and houses were sold as soon as a foundation was laid. Many of these new workers were East Europeans, and while the wages were attractive, they would be hard-pressed to find accommodations.

Many of the Poles and Russians who were coming to the border were concentrated in the boarding houses along Marion Avenue in Windsor's east end.

Holy Trinity Church under construction, 1917.

This was largely the result of a Ford City by-law that ordered that they not be allowed to crowd into boarding houses. In May 1913, a reporter watched as a group "on a pilgrimage to Windsor" from Ford City, and carrying their few possessions, were greeted by their countrymen at the "Polish city" on Marion Avenue. The reporter observed that thirty men were jammed into each boarding house along Marion, and that the mattresses were in steady use. When one man went to work, a man just returning took his place for "They sleep eight and ten in a bed, 24 hours a day." He estimated that the 300 members of "the colony" lived in eighteen houses. Similar concerns were expressed about the "Hungarian Colony" of 52 men jammed into one boarding house (locally referred to as "The Nest") on Parent Avenue. Neither Hungarians nor Poles were welcomed in Walkerville. A councillor moved that they needed a by-law to prevent "foreigners [from] buying property in the exclusive and aristocratic" town and he went on to note that "We have restricted the colored people, and I would far rather have a colored man living beside me than a Pole."

At the beginning of 1914, there had been a public outcry against the squalid conditions existing on Marion Avenue and that "the houses are reeking in filth." Sewers had not yet reached this area and drainage was a nightmare. "Bare feet is the order among the women. They walk about, or rather they wade about in the filth and stagnant water."[14] In January, Frank Wolsek, the "King" of the Marion Avenue Poles, appeared before City Council and explained that the problem lay in the sudden downturn in employment. Poles had been coming to Windsor for the past three years and when men were let go, invariably the foreigners were the first. City Council responded by addressing both problems. They authorized a sewer to be built to drain Marion Avenue and the unemployed from the neighbourhood were hired to build it. With the demands of industry after August 1914, employment was steady and a Board of Health survey in September 1916 observed that Marion Avenue was a clean and healthy place to live. As had previous excluded groups, the Poles rallied around their church. A sympathetic Protestant, Walter Bourg, donated land on the outskirts of the city to the community. The Poles devoted their own labour and money, and completed Holy Trinity Church in 1919.

East Europeans, with their strange languages and customs, were not seen as likely recruits for the King's army. Neither was that other group, women, which despite making up half of the city's population were effectively excluded from what was considered exclusively a man's conflict. The separate spheres continued much as before and women remained limited to their traditional roles as mothers and housekeepers. For upper class women, their participation in the war effort was a campaign initiated by the Women's Patriotic League to knit socks for the boys at the front. Hundreds of socks of wildly varying quality were being churned out, many by first-time knitters. Nevertheless, the League urged them to persevere for "as long as the war lasts the women must knit." Somewhat more practical were suggestions that Windsor's women fill in for the men who had left office jobs. One employer noted that there was an acute shortage in some clerical fields. He suggested that if things got worse, that women might have to help in the manufacture of munitions. But even in that event, he assured his readers that he did not expect "women of the upper classes should go in for munition making."[15] At the other end of the social scale, what was available to working women was manual labour. Scores of women were operating the sewing machines making uniforms at the Peabody plant textile works. Ford of Canada was primarily a male preserve, except for the magneto department where the intricate task of weaving copper wiring around magneto starters was entrusted to a female workforce.

Yet, in isolated instances, the roles available to women seemed to be changing. The *Evening Record* now featured a female reporter, Minnie Cage, who fed material to the women's page and the social column. In 1914, three women ran for school board trustee in Windsor. One woman even attained a degree of local prominence. Martha Dickinson had helped her father run the *Windsor World* newspaper in the late 1890s. A capable office worker, she became a clerk at City Hall in 1902. In 1914, when Stephen Lusted, her friend and colleague, was unable to carry on due to poor health, Martha Dickinson was appointed acting city clerk.[16] Lusted retired in 1920, Dickinson became city clerk in her own right and headed the Clerk's Department for the next 21 years. In her first years in office, the efficient Miss Dickinson was in charge of preparing the municipal voter lists—lists on which her name did not appear on account of her sex.

During the initial burst of enthusiasm in 1914, young black men were also eager to join the great adventure. None belonged to the Essex militia, which enforced a strict "whites-only" policy. Enlisting black volunteers was left up to the discretion of local commanders and most (as in Essex County) refused to accept blacks. The military was not unique, for racism pervaded Windsor's society. Black citizens had to fund their own ward in the tuberculosis hospital as they would not be accepted in the hospital itself. When a black man, Doran Dixon, was hired to deliver the mail in 1913, the rest of the deliverers threatened to resign. Only the intervention of MP Oliver Wilcox enabled him to keep his job. It was apparent that denying blacks the right to serve in the military was yet another method of denying them citizenship. Yet, some were so determined to serve that they travelled to other parts of Ontario in order to enlist, and several achieved distinction on the battlefield. One black Windsor volunteer, Walter Hewlitt, was frustrated by the refusal of Essex County recruiters to accept him, and he enlisted in London. Hewlitt would eventually serve with distinction in an overseas battalion.[17]

By the summer of 1916, the manpower drain was becoming critical and in July, Ottawa authorized the formation of a black labour battalion. Initially based in Nova Scotia and officered by white men, the No. 2 Construction Battalion would be one of the few ways that black Canadians could express their patriotism. In September 1916, twenty black men from Windsor enlisted in the battalion and were given an emotional farewell ceremony from the armouries. The ministers of the black churches exhorted them to uphold "the traditions of the race in their fight on the side of freedom and democracy."[18] They would serve in the forestry corps in France until the unit was disbanded in 1920.

Border Region at War

In some ways the war seemed to be an unfortunate, far-off event, disconnected from Windsor. There was no conscription until 1917, and those who wished to ignore events in Europe were safe to do so. Times were good, the factories were hiring, and Windsor's population grew steadily during the war years. The war only had an impact on those directly involved. In August 1916, news arrived that Walter Hoare, an officer from the 99th and the only son of Dr. Charles Hoare, had been killed shortly after his arrival in France. He was nineteen. At the same time his death was announced, the racing season began at the Windsor Driving Park, and aficionados poured across the border and packed the grandstand to catch the premier race. While a few families were in mourning, most of Windsor went about its normal business and pleasures.

One of those pleasures, horse racing, was becoming so popular in 1916 that two additional tracks, the Kenilworth and Devonshire Parks, were opened south of the city. In 1910, there had only been six racecourses in all of Ontario. Now there were three in Windsor alone. Unlike the Windsor Jockey Club, these parks were owned by outsiders (in Devonshire's case a Montreal syndicate) and served a Michigan clientele where horse racing had been prohibited. As a result, Detroit race enthusiasts likely outnumbered Canadians during the meets. In 1920, the Royal Commission in Racing Inquiry noted the explosive growth of racetracks around Windsor and that "they were largely dependent for their crowds on the city of Detroit." Some Windsor residents were aghast that their community hosted a pastime that was banned in the adjacent states. However, a motion in City Council requesting the Province to "protect the city from racetrack evils" was ignored.[19]

The sudden increase in interest in horse racing was another indication of the growing interdependence of Windsor and Detroit. American suppliers were forwarding essential war *matériel* through the MCR tunnel at Windsor to east coast ports for transit to Britain. In addition to the flow of *matériel*, the Detroit-Windsor region was a source of able-bodied men. Since the beginning of the war, young Detroiters were eager to volunteer for service in the Canadian army and Windsor was a prime recruiting station. R.H. Clarke, one of the first Detroiters to volunteer, went out with the first contingent. In late October 1916, he was reported wounded, and was praised as "probably [having] as much service at the front as any soldier." Also from the first contingent were three Detroit volunteers who were killed at Canada's first battle at Ypres. It was even reported that half the recruits in the 99th came across the border from the U.S.

Not only were men from Detroit and southern Michigan crossing the river to join the army, scores of ordinary workmen were also flowing across the border in search of places to live. Detroit was growing so fast there was simply no housing available. A reporter discovered an American family living in an unkempt boarding house on Goyeau Street where the wife explained that "We came to Detroit from Indiana and when we arrived we had to live in a tent."[20] While the Windsor boarding house was filthy, it was better than anything they could find on the American side of the river.

Another feature that defined the border region was its fondness for drink. Nevertheless, Windsor could not long resist the measures being applied in the rest of the province to advance the war effort. Perhaps the most disliked one for border residents was the growing sentiment in favour of the total prohibition on alcohol. In the past, whenever a plebiscite had been held on prohibition, Windsor and northern Essex County were one of the few holdouts opposing these restrictions. In the 1894 plebiscite, Ontario voted three to one in favour of banning alcohol. Windsor was the only city in the province to vote against it. In the early 1900s, rural communities became effectively dry by forbidding the issuance of any liquor licenses. Windsor was heading in the opposite direction. In 1912, based on its population, Windsor had twice as many licenses as London and five times as many as Toronto.[21]

Yet even in the border area there was a movement among the upper classes to limit access to drink. In 1913, Arsas Drouillard applied for a permit to sell liquor in a shop on the road named for his family, only a few paces from the Ford factory. Gordon McGregor personally appeared before the license commissioners and heatedly argued that placing a saloon at his plant gate was an invitation to disaster. McGregor explained that "We have probably 300 or 400 foreigners at work" (out of a total workforce of 1,400) who were "unaccustomed to the

Over 1,000 American troops are transported across the Detroit River on car ferry, Detroit, 1917.

strong drink of North America" and if they got their hands on liquor, productivity would decline and accidents would rise. Fellow industrialists along Walker Road also wanted no dives near their plants. Walter McGregor, Gordon's brother and manager of McGregor-Banwell Fence Company, reminded the commissioners that the "Dew Drop Inn" had supplied alcohol to the residents of "Hungry Hollow," the shanties that had been thrown up just to the south of the Ford factory. This area was "a positive disgrace and there is no worse slum district west of Toronto." In the midst of these capitalists, Fr. Lucien Beaudoin, the pastor of Our Lady of the Lake Church, adopted a slightly different argument. His concern lay with the rural French-Canadians who were also flooding into Ford City in search of industrial wages. "They are all poor people coming from the country" he noted, and to retain a decent family life they had to practise temperance. In contrast to his Protestant contemporaries, Fr. Beaudoin was no prohibitionist for "It is my duty as a priest to promote temperance—not prohibition." It was a measure of the easy availability of licenses that even in the face of this opposition, permission was granted to Drouillard. However, McGregor and his associates brought their influence to bear and the license was quickly revoked by provincial authorities.[22]

The pressure to impose prohibition as a necessary war measure was growing in Ontario. It was argued the workforce at munitions plants needed to stay sober and dedicated to their jobs. Besides, the soldiers at the front were making huge sacrifices and it was little enough for the civilian population to give up alcohol for the duration. The war accomplished what a battalion of temperance preachers had failed to do as numerous roadhouses across Essex County were ordered to close. Wolfgang Fellers, whose shanty "Wolf's" at Lesperance Road and Lake St. Clair had been a popular haunt for hunters and fishermen for decades, was ordered to shut down in July 1915. Stephen's Inn of Windsor and Louis Hébert's "Abars" in Sandwich East were also ordered to close. This was just the beginning. Ontario premier, Sir William Hearst, proposed a bill to halt the sale of liquor (the manufacture, ownership, and consumption of it were not affected) as of September 16, 1916. "The war has changed everything," he explained to the provincial assembly, and the people demanded prohibition. The *Ontario Temperance Act* passed unanimously. "A dry Ontario will be a prosperous Ontario"[23] proclaimed a jubilant Toronto *Globe.*

Windsor was not so sure. When September 16 arrived, there was nervous tension on the city's streets. "Up to 7 o'clock Saturday night all the bars of Windsor were crowded to their fullest capacity." As the dreaded hour approached, bartenders simply took out their remaining stock and placed it on the bar to be consumed by whoever could grab it first. These bottles, "slid along the polished surface until the contents disappeared, and then another one would be put up, only to meet the same fate."[24] When seven o'clock arrived and the bars had to close, the well-fuelled crowd headed out onto the streets and down to the ferry dock where a short trip deposited them at the Detroit bars. Righteousness could not be enforced in a border community where access to what was forbidden in Canada was only a short boat ride away on the U.S. side. If Ontario had gone dry, Windsor remained effectively wet.

Further wartime restrictions only accentuated the difference between the border region and the rest of the province. Reading the voluminous Detroit newspapers on Sunday mornings was a treasured custom in Windsor. While the publication and distribution of any newspapers was technically a breach of the *Lord's Day Act*, Windsor residents were used to getting their Sunday papers from across the river. In a move that was as popular as sending the Lady Searcher to the border, Toronto authorities decided in November 1916 to start enforcing the statute in Windsor. The move was condemned as unpatriotic, depriving interested citizens of vital war news, and insulting to Americans. This unwelcome enforcement compelled designated residents to cross the border to get newspapers for their neighbourhood all the while grumbling: "This country [is] getting to be as bad as Germany: booze *verboten*; Sunday papers *verboten*."[25]

Like it or not, a region had arisen that was neither entirely American nor Canadian, and residents along the border resented the dictates of a far-off government. An editorial in the *Evening Record* best captured local sentiments:

> Established residents of Windsor and Detroit understand each other thoroughly and mingle together in harmony... Hundreds of persons

> on this side cross to Detroit daily and find employment in the great city across the river.
>
> We get along in fine style. It is only when outside influences are exerted that friction arises.[26]

It was becoming increasingly apparent that "residents of Windsor saw their relationship with Detroit as a factor that distinguished them from their countrymen" and that even the opposition to such a supposedly innocuous issue as Sunday newspapers was something that "few outside their region could understand."[27]

Not only were the border cities developing a distinctiveness that set them apart from the rest of Ontario, they were also a collection of ethnicities that were unique in the province. These ethnic divisions mirrored the tensions that were dividing the country and were about to lead to one of the most violent episodes in the area's history.

The Battle of Ford City

Father Lucien Beaudoin, the beloved pastor of Our Lady of the Lake, had seen incredible changes since he first arrived from Quebec in 1891. In that year, when he assumed charge of the church, it was still *Notre Dame du Lac*, the spiritual home to a small French-Canadian farming village. It was a comfortable existence where the people worshipped, went to school, and lived their lives as their ancestors had for generations before them. Then came industrialization. With the rapid development of Ford of Canada after 1908, the parish saw rural French-Canadians moving in from the surrounding villages to take advantage of higher wages, even if it meant working in factories where English was the predominant language.

Worse still, a hostile provincial government enacted Regulation 17 in 1912 to curb the use of the French language in schools and ultimately obliterate the French language in Ontario. The impetus for this regulation came from the influx of Quebecers into eastern Ontario. Regions that had been English-Protestant now found themselves becoming overwhelmed by French-speaking Catholics. Many Orangemen asked: "Was even Ontario to be dominated by those twin evils, the Catholic hierarchy and the French language?"[28] At the Orange Lodge convention in Windsor in July 1916, members hoisted a huge streamer across Ouellette Avenue calling for "One Flag, One Language, One School." Mayor Jackson immediately ordered that it be taken down, but the point had been made. This sign was especially provocative in a city that was, if anything, becoming more francophone. Newcomers from the countryside and eastern Ontario increased the city's French-speaking population from 12.3 percent in 1901 to 17.8 percent in 1911. Despite the influx of French-Canadians, the school system had become a prime instrument of assimilation for "Children were even expected to learn their catechism and prayers in English in a school where half the student body was French-Canadian."[29]

Father Beaudoin shared his parishioners' unease that the times were rapidly changing and not to their advantage. In 1911, he visited the parish schools and discovered that the St. Joseph's Sisters in Walkerville were teaching French-speaking children how to say their prayers in English. Regulation 17 effectively disqualified Windsor's three bilingual schools from any further teaching of French after 1912. An outraged Beaudoin immediately ordered the sisters to stop. However, his order was countermanded by that other figure who was to instigate so much controversy, Bishop Michael Francis Fallon.

The "Mitred Warrior," as Fallon was so often called, was a cleric who was at war, and his enemies were the French-Canadians. Born in Kingston in 1867, he came from a close-knit Irish family and his life would embody numerous paradoxes. Stoutly opposed to bilingualism, he was fluently French. An avid Imperialist, he was descended from Irish Catholics who had barely survived the anti-Catholic penal laws. It was clear from his early years that he was a talented

Bishop Michael Francis Fallon at Assumption College's Golden Jubilee, 1920.

young man, destined for the priesthood. He took a doctorate in Rome in 1894 and was ordained that year. However, in his first assignment as vice-rector at the University of Ottawa, he resisted the institution of a bilingual curriculum and held out for studies exclusively in English. For this, Fallon was banished to Buffalo, New York. He would forever blame a French-Canadian cabal for the loss of his academic position and exile to an obscure parish. Yet in 1910, despite his lack of prominence (but ironically due to his fluency in French) he was consecrated Bishop of London. Already an imposing man, "The addition of the mitre at liturgical functions made him look almost gigantic. There are many stories still circulating that the mere sight of him in his episcopal vestments terrorized confirmation classes throughout the diocese."[30] French-Canadians, who were aware of his opposition to bilingual instruction, were appalled. Barely five weeks into his episcopacy, a memorandum of a meeting between Fallon and a provincial cabinet member was leaked to the press. At this meeting, Fallon maintained that "We are an English-speaking province" which had no place for bilingual schools. He quickly put this into effect in Essex County by forbidding teaching sisters in French communities to use French in their classrooms.

Father Beaudoin refused to sit back and let an Irish bishop crush a French-Canadian community that had existed for almost two centuries. He organized petitions from his parishes and others to Rome protesting Fallon's actions. The bishop responded with more provocations. In 1912, he severed the Walkerville section from Beaudoin's parish to create the English-speaking parish of St. Anne. Fallon did not consult Beaudoin and in the process, he removed one of the separate schools that had been paid for by Beaudoin's parishioners. Fallon informed the papal nuncio that Beaudoin was a "troublemaking priest" who was incompetent in English. Ten diocesan priests (three of them Irish) petitioned Rome in March 1914 defending Beaudoin. In response, Fallon organized a diocesan tribunal chaired by Fr. François Laurendeau, but under the bishop's direction, which compelled four of the priests to recant and submit. Three others were exiled from the diocese. Beaudoin would not give in, nor would he retract his statements.

The ongoing controversy left its mark on Beaudoin as he became increasingly debilitated and had to use crutches to go about his parish rounds. In June 1917, he went to Montreal for medical treatment and died there in August. At his funeral mass on August 22, Fallon administered the final insult when he named Laurendeau to succeed Beaudoin as pastor. The congregation was aghast. Here was the bishop's lackey, the one who assisted him in attacking French priests and crushing French education; a man who had played a role in the persecution of their beloved pastor; and who was now supposed to succeed

Guards on watch outside the church presbytery of Our Lady of the Lake, *Evening Record*, August 24, 1917.

him. Barely was the funeral mass over than parishioners entered the rectory, seized the new pastor's luggage, and threw it onto the street. He was told in no uncertain terms to leave and not come back. An around-the-clock blockade of the church was organized by a coordinating committee led by Stanislas Janisse, Dr. Damien Saint-Pierre, and Joseph de Grandpré. This revolt was not without allies. The archbishop of Quebec, Joseph Hallé, as well as most of Canada's French-speaking clergy supported the blockade. Such a display of open defiance was unheard of in the Catholic Church, and Fallon was initially at a loss as to how to react.

By early September 1917, Fallon decided to regain his property and he called on the provincial government. The bishop was widely admired by those in authority for his enthusiastic support for the war effort. Whatever police assistance he needed would be provided. On Saturday afternoon, September 8, there was apprehension that Fallon was about to make his move and at 1:30 p.m. Dr. Saint-Pierre learned that police were on their way. The doctor put the blockade pickets on alert, and the great bells pealed a warning for the people of Ford City to come and defend their church. Shortly after 2:00 p.m. when the police arrived, they confronted a scene out of a Victor Hugo novel with hundreds of men and women surrounding their church and screaming defiance. A reporter for the *Evening Record* left a memorable account of what happened next:

> Wars abroad were temporarily eclipsed Saturday by a miniature war in Ford City parish of Our Lady of the Lake when, acting under orders from the attorney-general, the Essex County, Walkerville, Ford City, and

> several provincial officers, hacked their way through a crowd of 3,000 people and forced an entrance to the church... The war had all the thrills and frills on a modest scale of a real war; its flags, cheers, tears, bloodshed, heroism, devotion, sacrifice, Amazonian legions...

About a dozen police used their billy clubs to force a path through the crowd and enable Laurendeau and the vicar-general, Fr. O'Connor, to enter the church. A phalanx of older women engaged the police with cudgels made of two-by-fours. The women seemed the most fearsome fighters of all and held off the police from getting into the rectory until at last:

> After the side door was smashed in and the women driven out they collected on the verandah and taunted the officers. There were jeers and mocking groans when Fr. O'Connor would appear outside the presbytery to confer with the police.
>
> When Mayor Montreuil appeared with a copy of the statutes and began reading the riot act some of the women shouted out, "*En Francais.*"

Nine men were arrested, and singing *La Marseillaise,* were dragged off to the Sandwich jail. Many were injured, including a seventy-two-year-old woman, but amazingly there were no fatalities. Amid the dying tumult, Fr. Laurendeau tried to address the combatants. He expressed his regrets, that he was only obeying the bishop's command, that he was partial to their language concerns and, above all, he hastened to assure them that he was not Irish.[31]

Many of the parishioners vowed to keep up a church boycott, and every morning Laurendeau would say Mass to a nearly empty church. But after a year, most of his parishioners drifted back, and this kindly man resumed the care of his flock. The Ford City Riot of 1917 was one of the most visible manifestations of impassioned resistance to the forces of anglicization and urbanization. Yet, ultimately it would be futile. The French-Canadian community that had been the foundation of the border area would find itself being slowly merged into a wider English-speaking and multi-ethnic city.

Kilties

By September 1916, sporadic reports of casualties gave way to almost daily accounts of men being killed and wounded in France. "Evidence is accumulating every day," the *Amherstburg Echo* reported, that "the boys of the Essex County 99th Battalion were in the thick of the recent fighting on the Somme

River." Many of these men had been taken out of the 99th soon after they arrived, and were sent as replacements to other front-line battalions. Captain Colley Ambery, of Walkerville, had just landed when he was "sent to fill up the wastage of the earlier battalions" and was killed. It was bad enough that so many young men were being lost, but even worse to think that they were being taken away from comrades and sent to die with men they barely knew. No more eager volunteers were coming forward and "recruiting across Canada was at a virtual standstill by the end of 1916."[32]

It was certainly at a standstill in Windsor. One of the men in charge of finding replacements for the hosts of men being killed in France was Gordon McGregor's younger brother Walter. In June 1916, he was made lieutenant colonel of another local battalion, the 241st, the "Canadian Scottish Borderers." In order to attract recruits, the battalion adopted an unusual flair, and instead of the standard-issue khaki trousers, its men sported the Highland kilt. Gordon McGregor even offered $25,000 to outfit the battalion in kilts of the McGregor tartan. The battalion became Windsor's own, and there was public resistance to a proposal that the unit be transferred to London. City Council passed a resolution that "the people of Windsor have regarded and still regard with justifiable pride the 241st as a local organization…" The battalion remained in Windsor. Picnics and lawn parties were held to celebrate those who came forward to serve, and church committees put forward the names of likely recruits. Despite this, few area men were tempted and in January 1917, Walter McGregor wrote to his mother that he was about to speak to an IODE meeting where he would "make a heart rending appeal to mothers and sisters to send their sons or brothers & who have already resisted any appeals made to them heretofore… I do not expect one recruit as a

Members of the 241st Battalion, November 1916.

Departure of 241st Battalion from GTR station, April 1917.

direct result. Not a man from Windsor has joined in January. What we get are from Detroit. Some are British or Canuck born but mostly U.S."[33]

The battalion's sergeants had even resorted to conducting "slacker hunts" by invading pool rooms and restaurants and cornering men out of uniform. During one of these hunts at a pool room, the proprietor flicked off the lights. Undeterred, the sergeants lighted matches and demanded of the men cowering under the tables why they were not fighting in France. These hunts bore few, if any, results. By the time the 241st paraded out of Windsor on its way to war on April 24, 1917, it still had only 500 men—200 fewer than the number specified for an overseas battalion. It received perhaps the most emotional send-off yet. The casualty lists had become a daily feature in the newspapers and everyone knew that many of the men who boarded the railcars at the Grand Trunk Station would never return. A massive crowd, 12,000 strong, jammed into the station to say goodbye. The bands played "Auld Lang Syne," "Oh Canada," and in a tribute to the many Americans in the 241st, "Dixie." With the recent entry of the U.S. into the conflict, the departure of the 241st was carried on the front page of the *Detroit News* as if it was an American regiment going off to war. After the last rail car left, a reporter noticed that most of the people left in the station were women who were crying inconsolably.[34]

Mobilizing the Home-Front

The war was transforming the world at the Detroit River in a bewildering variety of ways. In March 1917, war came to the very streets of Windsor when the Favorite Theatre showed films of the recent Battle of the Somme. Civilians were shocked to see newsreels of actual tank battles, where mechanical leviathans rolled over German defences. War even affected racial perceptions. When black troops were denied access to the main floor of a Windsor theatre in 1917, the proprietor was taken aback when white soldiers sided with their black comrades and demanded that they be treated with respect. The uniform transcended race.

By 1917, women were also starting to occupy roles that had previously been closed to them. One small unit of women had already achieved distinction during the war. Led by Windsor's Lt. Col. H.R. Casgrain, and staffed by several Essex County nurses, the No. 3 Stationary Hospital served in Greece and later on the Western front. Casgrain was most upset when the hospital was relocated to England and a local stationery dealer issued postcards featuring a soldier embracing a nursing sister and a caption: "No. 3 Stationary Hospital are holding their own." He demanded that the postcards be withdrawn as an insult to his staff. As the war dragged on the hospital incurred casualties and in one bombing raid, several nurses and orderlies were killed. One of the nursing sisters, May Whittaker of Sandwich, would be awarded the Order of the British Empire for her courage and endurance. Other women who stayed nearer to home were also being allowed to contribute to the war effort. "Farmerettes" was the name given to the middle-class girls who donned bloomers or overalls to work as Essex County farm labour.

Women serving near the Front, and urban females doing rough country work was turning the world on its head. Perhaps not as extreme, but also a sign of women taking over untraditional roles, was the appearance of female staff in Windsor's banks. Taking over from men who had enlisted, women were now regular features at financial institutions where, it was grudgingly admitted, "service has improved." In return for their war work, women were being given the vote by most provinces. Reversing years of opposition, Ontario's premier William Hearst declared in early 1917 that the war service of women had earned them the right to be taken "into partnership with men in the councils of the nation." The campaign for women's suffrage, which had been inconclusive for years, was finally put into effect. Windsor's roving female reporter, Minnie Cage, was disappointed to discover that most women in the city were indifferent, or even hostile, to this change. "All the suffragettes I've ever seen were so overbearing and mannish" a woman in charge of a department at C.H. Smith department store observed.[35]

Sacrifices were made by those who stayed behind, as well as by those who fought. In the absence of a social assistance network, the Patriotic Fund had been established in 1914 as a private fundraising organization to provide support for soldiers' families. Assistance varied according to what the community offered, and Windsor-area families were relatively better off than most as contributions were generous and donations were matched by municipal councils. This disparity was raised in Parliament when one M.P. pointed out that Walkerville citizens gave $11.18 per capita to the fund, the highest in the country, whereas Barrie residents gave only .28 cents.[36]

Coming to Grips with the River

Even in the midst of war, domestic problems could not be ignored. By 1914, it was apparent that the uncertain broth of the Detroit River was a major health problem. In that year, the civic beach at the foot of Bridge Avenue was closed as it was "exposing hosts of children to disease-laden waters." The rapidly swelling urban population discharged its waste directly into the Great Lakes, and the waterway was becoming little more than an open sewer. In 1912, Windsor's water engineers had quietly begun to chlorinate the city's water supply; no one noticed any difference, so the inevitable outcry against "doped" water was thereby avoided. Even so, whenever chlorine was not available—which occurred from time to time—it resulted in thousands of gallons of contaminated water being pumped into the City's mains. The Medical Officer of Health reported that in 1916, there were 153 cases of diphtheria and 14 related deaths. In 1917, there were 32 reported typhoid cases and four deaths. It was apparent that the water flowing outside the city was almost toxic and the *Evening Record* warned that "The only protection we have is the system of chlorination."[37] The problem became all the more urgent when the International Joint Commission, which had been established between Canada and the U.S. to protect the boundary waterways, reported in 1912 that pollution in the Detroit River was a major health hazard. However, with the area divided into five urban municipalities and two townships, a united effort to fight pollution was very unlikely.

In early 1915, elected representatives of the border municipalities formed a committee to discuss this lack of coordinated effort. In addition to public health concerns, they were frustrated by the area's inadequate transit system. The SW&A adamantly refused to extend any tracks into the new residential areas opening up in Windsor and Walkerville, and insisted that its franchise be extended to 1932 before it would consider new routes. Tired of being held for ransom by streetcar moguls, area politicians were ready for a bold new step in how the border was governed. In September 1915, they agreed that all services should come under public control and in a resolution that prefigured the eventual unification of the Border Cities, the mayors of Windsor and Walkerville urged the province to implement a joint commission that would control street railways, sewage, hydroelectricity, and water supply. In due course, they added the park system, streets, and fire protection. Such a step in metropolitan government was certainly radical, but it reflected the times. Samuel Morley Wickett, a Toronto politician and urban theorist, had urged in 1913 that Toronto's public transit be operated by the municipality instead of a profit-motivated concern.[38] Wickett had promoted the benefits of regional decision making to deal with larger concerns such as water and sewage. It was "through cooperation rather than annexation" that he thought a 30-mile wide area around Toronto could act in concert to deal with regional issues.

The provincial government thought Wickett's ideas too audacious and they had the same cautious response to the request from the Windsor border area. In February 1916, the border municipalities petitioned for a bill to unite street railways, water supply, sewage treatment and hydroelectricity under one utilities commission. When the proposal was considered in Toronto, the private bills committee pared it down to only water and sewage. Still, *The Essex Border Utilities Act* of April 1916 was a remarkable statute. It embodied the intention of Windsor, Walkerville, Sandwich, Ford City, Ojibway, and even that part of Sandwich West Township contiguous to the urban centre, to work together to provide a joint water supply and sewage disposal system. Morris Knowles, a civil engineer from Pittsburgh, was hired as consultant. His 1917 survey showing the area under the commission's jurisdiction, and his plans for a trunk sewer, reflected almost exactly the area that would become the modern City of Windsor half a century later.

Gordon McGregor, the dynamic head of Ford of Canada, chaired the Essex Border Utilities Commission (EBUC) in 1917. The *Evening Record* thought that at last something good had come from this terrible war:

> The war is teaching us the value of co-operation in the divisions of a nation under an efficient government. We are about to apply co-operation in our five towns by means of an efficient Essex border utilities commission, which is really a commission for the development of a great metropolitan area.

There were even proposals for a new municipal name: "South Detroit" was suggested by some, "Vimy Ridge" by others. However the term "Border Cities" had entered popular usage and was now commonly applied to the larger area. Knowles noted that the 1917 population of the Border Cities had skyrocketed to 36,000. By 1950, he estimated that it would rise to 173,000 (a remarkably accurate projection) and he pleaded with the Commission to provide for the "development of works ahead of the immediate needs" and laid out a "big utilities scheme" for shared services.[39] These initial hopes would not be realized as the individual municipalities advanced their separate interests. Ford City needed sewers now, not according to some future timetable. Windsor was shocked at the burden it was being asked to bear for services that might only serve future suburbs. Despite the creation of the EBUC, a centralized approach to public services remained unfulfilled, and Knowles' plans and drawings became mere curiosities. Still, the germ of the idea of a greater "metropolitan area" had been planted.

The Final Push

By 1917, there were no further volunteers to be had, and the Canadian divisions in Europe faced the prospect of being withdrawn from action due to the lack of reinforcements. Conservative Prime Minister Robert Borden announced in May 1917, that men would be forced into military service. By that fall, local tribunals in Windsor were hearing requests for exemptions from men who had reason to be excused from service. Men not excused were bound over for the army. Wartime demands resulted in the government becoming increasingly involved with the lives of its citizens. An Order-in-Council in May 1917 required Canadian men of military age (18–45 years) to have government-issued identification if they wanted to leave the country. Agents of the Dominion Police (one of the precursors to the RCMP) appeared at the ferry crossing to intercept and interrogate men who might be seeking to evade service.[40] Windsor's City Council protested that these border security measures were objectionable in an area in which free and easy passage was a way of life. From forbidding the distribution of Sunday newspapers to prohibiting saloons, and finally to forced military service, the state had moved from voluntarism to compulsion. Now, instead of merely urging men to come forward, they were about to be forced to serve and possibly die for their country.

Local attitudes toward conscription became clear during the federal election of December 1917. The Conservatives put forward Lt. Col. Ernest Wigle. Five-time mayor of Windsor, a war hero, and representative of a Union Government of Conservatives and pro-war Liberals, Wigle promised to see the struggle through to victory. He reminded audiences that compulsory military service was the only way to keep faith with the boys who had gone before. His opponent was a rising figure in the Liberals, William Costello Kennedy. A shrewd businessman, Kennedy entered the oil and gas business in 1897 and from 1908 to 1917 was president of the Windsor Gas Company. As an English-speaking Catholic, he had feet in several camps, including the Board of Trade and St. Alphonsus parish. Kennedy supported Liberal chieftain Wilfrid Laurier and was a cautious critic of conscription. This was an essential position, for the French of the North Essex riding detested being forced to fight and die on behalf of a government that sought to deny them their language and culture. Kennedy's supporters were categorized by Wigle's men as disloyal, even traitors for their opposition to military service. But Kennedy understood the depth of French-Canadian feelings, and he was elected by an overwhelming majority. The only area that rejected him was the stoutly Anglo enclave of Walkerville. Looking at the massive number of Liberal votes, Kennedy mused that, "There are evidently a lot of traitors in North Essex."[41]

Once again, the area had proven itself to be an anomaly. English-speaking Canada overwhelmingly supported conscription and Borden's Union party won 74 of 82 seats in Ontario. But in the Border Cities, there was no great enthusiasm for the war, and considerable revulsion toward conscription. The order for all aliens to register their place of residence caused near riots when East Europeans balked at signing the forms. "Incipient Bolshevism" was the response of the *Evening Record* who considered it further proof of the untrustworthiness of the Poles and Russians who packed the boarding houses on Marion Street.[42] In contrast, the Chinese of Windsor quietly complied, and would likely have enlisted, had they been permitted.

By November 1917, the government was desperate for funds. A huge "Victory Loan" demonstration in Windsor featured the band of John Philip Sousa and an emotional plea by the Scottish entertainer Harry Lauder to support the war effort. By 1918, there were difficulties sending food supplies to Britain, and there were even food shortages in Canada. Farming had become a strategic factor in the war and for once, the interests of rural and urban residents coincided. Yet, mobilizing agriculture was not easy. Five hundred acres of unused Essex County land was leased to urban manufacturers and fifty men from the Canadian Bridge factory were sent out in the spring of 1918 to commence cultivation. Gordon McGregor reportedly offered to close his plant so that his men could help take in the crops. The gesture garnered publicity, but the factory remained open. Within the city, "war gardens" were laid out, and the commercial middle class was put to the unaccustomed task of weeding and planting. It is not apparent how successful all these projects were in increasing food supplies, but they did have the effect of involving the entire community in the war effort.[43]

In early August 1918, news reached Windsor of the breakthrough at Amiens and a fresh series of victories that seemed to be the prelude to German defeat.

But it was not until October that the cost of these victories became evident when reports of area men killed in the offensive began to flood in. Each newspaper carried stories of local boys who had died at the front. On October 19, it was reported that Stan Reaume, a popular athlete and son of former MP Dr. J.O. Reaume, had been killed. The same edition noted that Percy Jacques, a Ford worker, had died: "His mother had a premonition of his death and refused to go out." So it went for edition after edition, the roll call of death effectively dampening any enthusiasm for the victory that finally seemed within grasp.

At least the conscripts were filling out the ranks and even more men were coming forward. In the spring, three young men from Windsor's Jewish community enlisted in the Jewish battalion bound for Palestine. Union Jacks and Zionist flags were on display as they were given a send-off by Windsor's *Bnai Zion*. Poland had struck out for its freedom and Windsor's Poles also enthusiastically rallied to the cause and volunteered for the Polish brigade. Forty-two recruits attended a farewell Mass at Holy Trinity and were dispatched to a training camp at Niagara-on-the-Lake.[44] No one anticipated the tragedy that would result from this move.

Plague

Sporadic news had been arriving about a strange new disease that was killing thousands in Europe. It spread almost instantly through the population and claimed its victims within a few hours. No one knew how it started, or where it came from, but its effects were lethal. The Spanish influenza allegedly entered Canada through the Polish military camp at Niagara-on-the-Lake and spread from east to west across the province. Furloughed or wounded troops returning from Europe may also have aided the spread of the disease. One in six Canadians would get the influenza and in roughly six months it would kill 10,000 Ontarians, almost as many as had died in the war.[45] There was no treatment or vaccine, and the only preventative measure was to prohibit persons from gathering and thereby spreading the contagion.

When the Spanish influenza reached Windsor in mid-October 1918, it quickly filled Hôtel-Dieu with patients. Sixty-three Border Cities residents died that month, and public meetings were banned. By the end of October, the outbreak seemed to lessen and Mayor Tuson, in a remarkably reckless act, revoked the ban. While the number of new cases trailed off, the influenza returned with a vengeance in mid-November and new cases were reported at the rate of seven a day. While the ban on public gatherings had been lifted in Windsor, it was still in effect in Sandwich. Mayor Hoare of Walkerville gave up trying to control gatherings in his town when churches and theatres were all open in Windsor. The only way to control influenza was to try and prevent it being spread, and that meant limiting human contact. Far more people would die after the ban on public meeting had been lifted by Tuson than before.

In mid-December, the illness still raged along the border and was claiming an average of six lives a day. Hôtel-Dieu was filled beyond capacity; in one room, nine influenza patients filled a 15-square-foot space. The Great War Veterans' Home was turned into a temporary shelter and handled the hospital's overflow. In Windsor alone, there had been 109 influenza deaths during the first three months of the outbreak. Taking into account the additional three months of 1919 and fatalities in the other municipalities, the Border Cities must have suffered about 250 deaths in total. The failure of the various local Boards of Health to effectively deal with the emergency was glaringly obvious. The *Border Cities Star* (formerly the *Evening Record* and now under the ownership of W.F. Herman) signalled its support for a unified health board:

> In some of the Border Cities schools and churches and other public assembling places remained open while others continued closed.
>
> Yet the people of the various Border Cities continued to meet and to work together and to ride in the same street cars together.

This failure to co-operate left "a trail of victims on every street" and ought to have spurred action from higher levels of government.[46] In this case, it was. On July 1, 1919, the Province created a joint local Board of Health for the Border Cities and the adjacent developed township lands. The area comprised 19 square miles and took in 50,000 citizens. In some ways, the new board mirrored the Essex Border Utilities Commission. It covered almost the exact same area, was also headed by Gordon McGregor, and even shared the Utilities Commission offices. Much like the EBUC, the joint health board was also an early step toward a unified government.

Armistice

The war ended suddenly, not with victory or surrender, but with a temporary suspension of fighting, an "armistice." News of the armistice came shortly after 3:00 a.m. on November 11, and the city's fire bells awoke the citizens to announce the arrival of peace. Ferries and ships added a steady stream of blasts to the noise as people gravitated to the city's downtown. An estimated ten thousand Windsor citizens gathered spontaneously at Ouellette Square next to the armouries to pray and give thanks that the slaughter was finally over. There was no formal order to the proceedings, and a selection of clergy mounted a stand to lead the people in prayer. All day long the cheers continued, and impromptu parades filled the city's streets.[47]

In a few weeks, some of the married troops were released to go home and began arriving at the Grand Trunk station. Some jumped from the train coaches, others limped off. All were received by welcoming crowds and bands and paraded up Ouellette Avenue. Half of the first contingent to return were Detroiters, and they had to fight their way through well-wishers to get to the ferry to take them home. In January, one of the first big groups of returning men, 98 in all, arrived at the station. The men, some of them still wearing their trench helmets slung over their shoulders, were embraced by wives and families.

That sunny Civic Holiday weekend in August 1914 had been the end of an era. So many of the young men who had rushed to enlist in the euphoria of those early days were gone, never to return. Most had expected a short, glorious war in the mode of the South African conflict. None had anticipated the industrialized carnage that awaited them. The loss of so many of its youths would deeply scar the area's families and be the source of sorrow for years to come.

Thanksgiving service in Ouellete Square, November 11, 1918.

Chapter Four
The Thirst
1919–1921

After the trauma of the war, many people yearned for the old ways. When Edward, the Prince of Wales, came to Windsor in October 1919, it was a re-affirmation of the established British connection. As the future King stood to attention before the altar in All Saints' Church to dedicate the colours of the 99th Battalion, it was also a tangible recognition of the new status of the city. No longer a brief stop on the Prince's way to Detroit, as it had been in 1860, Windsor was now included in the Royal Tour as an important centre in its own right.[1] In other ways, the world was returning to its normal rhythms. Women were no longer being allowed into bank employment and only men were being offered staff jobs. But unquestionably, the world had been transformed.

Subscribers to the *Border Cities Star* regularly read about hirsute revolutionaries in Russia and Germany using the cover of labour strikes for what was really an attempt to overthrow capitalism. Was Windsor next? During the last year of the war, organized labour had grown increasingly militant and in the spring of 1918, Windsor's Trades and Labor Council called for the "complete organization of Windsor as an out-and-out union city, with an eight-hour working day." To deal with this incipient revolution, Ottawa enacted several War Orders in Council which suppressed freedom of the press, and banned certain organizations dominated by foreign immigrants. It was feared that much of the radical agitation had its origins in the Russian enclave that existed along Drouillard Road. In the summer of 1918, a small gang of Russian men in Ford City were accused of belonging to a seditious organization, the "Union of Russian Workmen" and charged with "holding a meeting at which a foreign language was used" contrary to the recent War Orders to halt bolshevism. Furthermore, they had in their possession "literature in the Russian language which is thought to be of a seditious nature." With limited translation services, no one was too sure if it was actually Russian; nor would they ever find out as the accused Russians skipped bail and fled. In any event, prosecutions were vigorous, and Windsor trailed only Toronto in the number of charges for violations of the War Orders in Council.[2] By the spring of 1919, the city was in a state of deep unrest.

At the war's end, Canadian industry had finally geared up for war production and wages were on the rise. Unfortunately, the cost of living was increasing even more rapidly due to runaway inflation, and for many workers, this resulted in real wages going down. They had seen a business elite make obscene fortunes during the war, and many working people linked the inflation to war profiteering. Added to this was the outrage felt by returning soldiers who could not find work while "alien enemies" were still in the factories. The veterans' organization, The Great War Veterans' Association, was already a powerful political lobby and one of their leaders, "Comrade" Carrick lectured a Windsor Chamber of Commerce audience that "It was the poor man who fought in that war" and now they wanted their due. Employers hastened to assure veterans that foreigners would be fired and their places taken by returned men. Pearson Wells of Ford's labour department promised to get rid of twenty-five foreigners in the heat treatment section and replace them with returned soldiers. The problem was that only east Europeans would work there, where the excessive heat and gas fumes rendered it "not a white man's job."[3]

Union membership had swelled in the last two years of the war and sixteen unions now numbered over 3,000 members. Before the war, Windsor's carpenters' union numbered 100. By 1919, it had 400 members. The Windsor branch of Local 718 of the International Association of Machinists represented workers on both sides of the river and with almost 900 members in the machine shops of the Michigan Central, Grand Trunk, and Canadian Pacific railways, it was the largest labour organization in the Border Cities. With this powerful base of members, four labour leaders were elected to Windsor's City Council in 1918. Archie Hooper, one of the most bombastic of the new members, was the leader of the local machinists. English by birth, Hooper had arrived in Windsor in 1896 and carried the enthusiasm of the English working-class struggle with him. He warned his members that the bosses were planning to cut wages and "blamed the capitalists for all the strife and destruction in the world." A workers' revolt was simmering in many urban centres across Canada and "It grew out of a newfound confidence in working-class power, a profound sense of injustice and a determination that society could run differently."[4] As for Windsor, the discontent did not arise out of any revolutionary impulses, but rather out of specific grievances from stagnant wages.

Among the worst paid workers were the recently unionized motormen of the SW&A street railway. Due to the varying demands of the public, a shift on the streetcars could last 14 or 15 hours for which the men were paid far less than a factory wage. The union had finally achieved recognition in April 1918, but a year of negotiations had failed to secure any wage increase. Finally, on Saturday, May 3, 1919, the men went on strike. According to Alderman Hooper, a strike was the only way to force the owners of this "junk line" to see reason. Moreover, as the streetcars were owned by the Detroit United Railway, the men would not return to work until they were paid at the same rate as their Detroit compatriots. A reporter described how "The crash of wheels on steel and the purr and spark of the electrically charged trolley poles" had given way to the quiet tramp of men walking to work. It was the first major labour confrontation in Windsor's history, and radicals were determined to make the most of it. Hooper vowed that all the other unions would support the car men rather than "pander to the capitalists." The strikers were widely supported, as the public largely agreed that the men were underpaid. As for the employer, the SW&A, with its poor service and refusal to develop its lines unless its franchise was extended, was one of the most detested institutions in the Border Cities. The strike went on for a week with no solution. By the second week, the SW&A brought in several motormen from Montreal and Toronto and sent them out with the streetcars on May 12. The cars were instantly surrounded by strikers who dragged out the replacements and roughed them up. One of the apprehended strikebreakers was brought before Mitchell Bell, the president of Windsor's Trades and Labor Council, and told him that they were hired to "smash a bolsheviki movement that had tied up the street railway." Bell assured reporters that the streetcar workers were not Bolsheviks and that they were simply fighting for a fair wage. Nevertheless, several streetcars were vandalized and one strikebreaker was badly beaten up.

W.F. Herman's *Star* categorized strikers as either lazy, foreigners, or both, as shown by this cartoon from 1919.

This display of violence was enough to trigger a request for military support from Crown Attorney J.H. Rodd, and 180 soldiers from the London garrison were sent to preserve order. On Tuesday morning, May 13, 1919, soldiers with fixed bayonets manned Windsor's streetcars. The streets were crowded, but an eerie silence prevailed and no attempts were made by customers to board the cars. Only weeks before, the sight of uniformed men marching through Windsor's streets would have brought applause and cheers. Now, a sullen crowd watched as soldiers moved two heavy machine guns toward the car barns. There were murmurs that strikebreakers were running the motors, but the mounted troops who moved through the crowd dissuaded any attempts at violence. The streetcars made two loops on the beltline between Windsor and Walkerville, their only passengers being the soldiers protecting the motormen. Once the soldiers reached the car barns, many of the strikers (veterans themselves) began to mingle with the troops and explained to them the purpose of their struggle.

This appearance of armed force brought the situation to a dangerous new level. One of the labour aldermen proclaimed that, "It is organized labor against capitalism and now it has come to a showdown between them." There were threats by some unions, notably the machinists, to widen the strike and call in a variety of trades to support the streetcar workers. The notion of a general strike brought with it European notions of political upheaval, and the secretary of the machinists' union warned that, "The whole labor situation on the continent is sitting on a barrel of dynamite waiting for a spark."[5] That spark might have gone off in Windsor. Instead, it ignited in Winnipeg. Only two days after soldiers were dispatched to Windsor, a massive general strike broke out in Manitoba's capital. In some ways similar to Windsor, Winnipeg had endured the pent up frustrations of the war years, and a series of labour disputes burst out in a general strike of 22,000 workers on May 15, 1919. The strike paralyzed the city and closed down factories, streetcars, telephone exchanges, and fire stations. Unions assumed the power of the civil authorities and began issuing permits for essential services.[6] Unlike the Windsor streetcar strike, the Winnipeg General Strike had a drastic effect on every aspect of ordinary life and it was perceived by those in authority as an attempt to take over the government. While in Windsor there was a precise, limited objective and a good deal of public sympathy, in Winnipeg there was only an ambiguous hope to improve conditions by bringing everyday life to a halt. Winnipeg's general strike ended in violence, death, and the repression of the strike leaders. The Windsor strikers were more pragmatic, and ultimately more successful.

This was especially thanks to the leadership of Mitchell Bell who avoided pressure from hotheads such as Hooper to call a general strike and instead focused on the immediate wage dispute and how to resolve it. The company and the strikers reached a temporary settlement in late May that was based on the public accepting a fare increase. Even though the strike erupted again in July when voters rejected the rate hike, the confrontation was confined to the affected workers. Ultimately, the provincial regulatory body, the Ontario Railway Board, had to briefly take over the SW&A and impose a settlement with limited gains to the workers. The spring and summer of 1919 proved to be a season of labour ferment in Windsor with additional strikes by municipal garbage men and by women at a local cigar factory. Still, these were isolated struggles and they demonstrated that Windsor labour leaders were not partial to the "One Big Union" concept that all unions should strike on behalf of one of their members. All would be represented in the broader labour organization, but in the last resort, each union was on its own.

Six-Dollar Daydreams

The origins of the workers who made up this expanded labour movement was another measure of how the Border Cities were changing. Returning veterans who had previously spurned factory work eagerly lined up for well-paying industrial jobs. And jobs were plentiful. By 1917, there were 1,730 labourers at Ford and 190 office staff. Ford was so dominant that it was having a ripple effect on the rest of the Border Cities' economy. Nine out of twenty local parts makers were Ford suppliers. Dominion Forge doubled its building space in 1917 to cope with increased orders for auto frames. Menard Truck, the all-Canadian manufacturer, received a capital infusion from Maple Leaf Manufacturing of Montreal and expanded its Windsor operation. Exciting news from W.C. Durant, the president of General Motors, came in the spring of 1919 that the company (through its Canadian subsidiary, "Canadian Products") would spend $6 million to build a new plant along Walker Road that was expected to employ 2,000. Gangs of men had already moved in to tear down old houses and prepare the site for construction.

As for the Border Cities (and the British Empire's) largest manufacturer of automobiles, Ford of Canada production declined slightly in 1917–1918 from 46,914 automobiles from the previous year's 50,827. The wartime demand for steel appears to be the principal cause of the downturn. The loss of sales was somewhat offset by an increase in the price of the Model T and the sale of Ford trucks.[7] Gordon McGregor carefully avoided labour disruptions by timing wage increases such as the "$6 Day" in May 1919 to impress upon his workforce that they were already among the highest paid workers in the Border Cities.[8] Similarly, Studebaker announced a profit sharing plan and engaged a clergyman as chief of their employee welfare department.

Windsor was defying the national trend, for in other parts of the industrial economy, the war had distorted production and recovery was difficult. "Firms such as Canadian General Electric and Canada Cement... have devoted the war years to forging artillery shells... the savings that were available to the economy were diverted to tool up munitions production."[9] In Sault Ste. Marie, Algoma Steel had supplied huge amounts of *matériel* for the war effort but had lost money. The vigorous growth that had characterized Canada before the war cooled. But, in contrast to the rest of the country, civilian production continued unabated in Windsor. By the end of the war, the *Border Cities Star* noticed that while most other Canadian cities were stagnant, in Windsor "the manufacturing expansion has been more or less phenomenal." In 1918, at least one new industry was locating in the Border Cities each week. During the war, Gordon McGregor had no compunction in seeking out energy and steel resources that might otherwise have gone into war production to keep his civilian vehicle production lines running at full capacity. Other than heading up Victory Bond campaigns, McGregor avoided involvement in the Canadian war effort. Even one of his competitors, Russell Motor Car of Toronto, had retooled for munitions production. But this was not McGregor's way, and while hardly patriotic, it was certainly lucrative. Ford was making so much money that the wartime excess business profits tax required it to pay $150,262 in 1916 and $785,181 in 1917. Conscious of any accusations of being a war profiteer, McGregor simply paid the taxes and avoided any controversy.[10]

The war years had been ones of phenomenal growth. Windsor's pre-war population of 22,077 had grown to 31,629 by 1919, making it the fastest-growing city in Canada. By the time of the 1921 census, Windsor had 38,591 residents, an increase of 116.5% over the course of the decade. This impressive increase did not include the even faster growth rates in Walkerville and Ford City, which was making the Border Cities into a true metropolis. When taken as a unit, by 1921, the Border Cities had a population of 57,000, making it almost tied with London as the sixth-largest city in eastern Canada (see Appendix B).[11] The city was even physically expanding. On January 1, 1918, it annexed 99.3 acres from Sandwich East, north of the CPR tracks, and the following July, 54.2 acres from Sandwich West also north of the rail line.

This post-war boom came at a price, for the city was unable to house the sudden influx of workers. By late 1918, it was estimated that Walkerville alone needed 500 new houses. Clients would regularly drop by real estate offices in the vain hope that some housing had become available. The housing shortage became so acute that by August 1919, W.E. Gundy, the housing commissioner, found that many people were living in tents while their houses were being constructed. Gundy related stories of how returning soldiers were finding good-paying jobs, but were unable to even rent a house. Government loans were available to assist construction and the Border Cities had more applications pending than any comparably sized area in Canada. In 1915, Windsor had new building permits worth $229,950. In the first six months of 1919, $764,230 was spent on new construction, mostly housing. But it was in Walkerville that truly massive growth was underway. In 1915, $72,000 worth of building permits had been issued. In the first six months of 1919, the town issued permits for $1,223,000 of construction, almost double the value of the improvements in Windsor.[12] Clearly, the focus of growth had shifted to the east and the area's explosive growth would focus on Walkerville and Ford City.

Public services were soon unable to cope with the stresses caused by this expansion. There was discontent with the ferries which, in addition to a steadily increasingly flow of cross-border labourers, now carried scores of automobiles across the border. The ferries had not changed significantly since Victorian times, and knots of pedestrians and motorists jockeyed dangerously for space to pass through the antiquated ferry dock. But Walter Campbell, the irascible head of the Detroit and Windsor Ferry Company, refused to provide a modern dock or buy the land to accommodate vehicles for customs inspections. Instead, in 1919, he raised ticket prices. As a result, "the frustrations experienced by the city and the company seemed endless."[13] Politicians such as Mayor E. Blake Winter resented the increases and suggested that Windsor would be better off running its own ferry service.

Even after Campbell's franchise lapsed in 1918, he continued the service under the authority of the federal *Customs Act*. Some relief was provided by the launching of a new ferry, the *LaSalle* in 1922. With a capacity for 3,000 passengers and 75 automobiles, it was a fine addition, but the docking area was as congested and inefficient as ever. In 1923, the impasse was finally resolved and the company promised to build the new dock. Ferry service finally reached a degree of efficiency in 1924 with the *LaSalle* being used exclusively for vehicles while the *Pleasure* and the *Promise* provided rapid

The LaSalle, a Windsor-Detroit ferry, which served from 1922 to 1938.

passenger service across the river. After decades of controversy, an expanded dock facility finally opened for service in 1926. Four years later, the Detroit-Windsor Tunnel would render it obsolete.

The inadequacy of the ferry service was not the only difficulty afflicting commuters. Streetcars had long been a source of the public's anger and the company's insistence that they would do nothing to improve the service unless their franchise (due to expire in 1922) was extended only added to the public's wrath. In September 1919, the SW&A was given notice by Windsor to vacate the streets once its franchise expired. During the war, a strong current arose in favour of the government taking over the streetcars. The movement found its champion in the "Power Knight" himself, Sir Adam Beck, who frequently visited the Border Cities to preach the gospel of municipal ownership. After the streetcar strike, Beck directly entered into negotiations to purchase the SW&A, and in a Windsor speech in October 1919, he mixed military rhetoric with socialist aspirations to declare that the border municipalities "will form the battlefield for the last fight against corporate ownership of electric railways in Ontario."[14] The streetcar company yielded to the inevitable and in January 1920, the parent company, the Detroit United Railways, sold the system to the Hydro-Electric Power Commission for two million dollars and the assets vested in HEPC in trust for the municipalities of northern Essex County. Shortly thereafter, a new line was extended along Erie Street to serve the southern reaches of Windsor and Walkerville. In 1925, tracks were extended along Parent Avenue to the distant Tecumseh Road. Youngsters in South Walkerville could now take the streetcar downtown, although frequently they had to switch the trolley wires on the car so that the vehicle could go in the other direction. The streetcar was a fast, smooth ride and a "bogie" in the middle of the car allowed it to swivel. Commuters also had new options. The Windsor Bus Company was operating a bus up Lincoln Road through Walkerville. One bus patron recalled that the vehicle had solid tires and as a result "the ride was not exceptionally soft."[15]

The rapid increase in population created problems beyond the inadequacy of streetcars and ferries. Hôtel-Dieu was unable to deal with the numbers who needed care, and as a result, the task of providing a maternity hospital fell to the Salvation Army. Army members were no longer being pelted with dead cats as they marched on Windsor's streets (as had been the case in the 1880s) and were now widely respected for their humanitarian efforts during the war. If Dean Wagner, the pastor of St. Alphonsus Church, had been the driving force behind Hôtel-Dieu, the Salvation Army's inspiration came from Adjutant Fred Martin. It was Martin who approached "Squire" Ellis, the dean of Windsor's lawyers, and proposed the purchase of his soon-to-be vacated mansion at Crawford and London Streets. Martin first had to make his way past Ellis' giant police dog "Ripper" before entering the house and explaining his purpose. Ellis exploded, "I won't do it… I'll cut it up and sell it for building lots before I'll let it go to the city for a hospital." Martin calmly explained that the Salvation Army would own and operate the hospital for the public benefit. A placated Ellis sold the land, and a modest 28-bed hospital opened in the former mansion in February 1920 with Commandant Lavinia Wood as superintendent. The squire's stables at the rear became the nurses' residence. Martin continued to work for a more modern institution and enlisted Gordon McGregor to chair a campaign committee. At the urging of Essex County's medical association, the facility would be a general instead of just a maternity hospital. In December 1922, a proper hospital building was completed and the Salvation Army Grace Hospital provided an additional 120 beds for the expanding population.[16]

H.T.W. Ellis and his police dog "Ripper," 1929.

Another charitable organization, the Imperial Order Daughters of the Empire, had devoted themselves since 1909 to the treatment of tuberculosis. A diagnosis of "consumption" in the early 20th century remained practically a death sentence, so the IODE opened a sanatorium at Union-on-the-Lake near Kingsville in 1913. When this burned down in 1920, the chapter re-located to Prince Road in Sandwich. The new building opened in February 1923, and was steadily added onto. For thirty years, the Board of Directors of the Essex County Sanatorium, the "San," was completely female and composed of the leading ladies of Border Cities' society. Their philanthropy would save scores of persons and over time IODE Hospital would become far more than a sanatorium.[17]

Confrontation at Kenilworth

In the post-war world, Victorian values were being set against the more relaxed approach to life that emerged after the harsh years of conflict. All-night cafés sprang up in which young people, most noticeably young women, were conspicuous. One citizen wrote a warning letter to Mayor Tuson that "The young girls in Windsor and vicinity are going at a merry pace" in these cafés. By the fall of 1920, the Mayor was visiting Chinese restaurants where young ladies "who should be in their homes dining" were socializing and using the restaurant cubicles as "spooning booths." The one public official who would be the face of an invigorated morality was Crown Attorney J.H. Rodd. He had already demonstrated his vigilance early in the war by helping to suppress the Sunday Detroit newspapers. A vigorous defender of the Lord's Day, he tolerated no baseball or other games on Sundays, and he promised that there would be no wagering on boxing events or unauthorized spooning.

One aspect of vice even Rodd could not stop was horse racing. Based on the notion that it improved breeding stock, racing had been legal in Ontario since the early 19th century. Yet many Victorians condemned it as a denial of the honesty of industry and it was banned in several states, including Michigan. For that reason, horse racing in the border area ballooned in popularity and the 26 racing days offered by the Windsor Jockey Club in 1910 grew to a combined total of 42 days in 1916. These races were now split among the Jockey Club and two new tracks located just outside the city, Devonshire and Kenilworth. On race days, punters from Michigan, as well as Ohio and New York, flooded into the area in order to enjoy the extended season unavailable to them in their states. Provincial authorities seemed intent on stopping this proliferation of racing and a Royal Commission warned that the easy availability of tracks and wagering had

Man o'War racing against Sir Barton, October 12, 1920.

a bad influence on the young.[18] Even while the moral authorities were forming a rear guard to make any form of gambling illegal, the Border Cities were about to become the site of arguably the greatest horse race ever run.

It was all the brainchild of Abe Orpen. The Irish entrepreneur and owner of several Ontario racetracks, including the Kenilworth Jockey Club three miles south of Windsor, realized that ever since the chestnut colt Sir Barton had won the first Triple Crown of racing in 1919, it was only natural to feature him in a head-to-head race with the big red thoroughbred who seemed invincible, Man o' War. To the chagrin of the New York promoters, Orpen secured the right to the race and a new grandstand was built at Kenilworth as well as special stalls for the celebrity horses. Reporters who crowded into the Border Cities for the race on October 12, 1920, were struck by the track's obscure location "on a prairie out of sight of any habitation" as the stage for one of sport's greatest events. However remote the area seemed to American reporters, race fans thronged to the border and the *Border Cities Star* described a crowd of over 35,000—a "colorful picture" in which "Women presented a large portion of the crowd... attired in all the latest fashions." Man o' War won easily and cemented his legend as possibly the greatest racehorse of all time. During the race, men and boys wiggled under the rail and invaded the track, forcing Man o' War to go wide, and preventing him from setting a record for the ten furlongs.[19] Aware of the significance of the event, Abe Orpen filmed the entire race (to be shown at cinemas across North America), which clearly showed in the backstretch the flat prairie and farm fields of Sandwich East Township.

Border Cities Wet

One unwelcome change that struck the men returning from the war was that it was almost impossible to get a drink. Temperance had become law while most of them were overseas and many were taken aback to find their favourite taverns closed down. The law did provide one loophole: the prescription of alcohol for medicinal purposes. As New Year's Day 1919 neared, one practitioner, Dr. G.N. Gardner, was particularly attentive to his patients' needs. Men with stricken looks lined up outside his office verandah on Lincoln Road as the doctor ground out prescriptions (222 in one day) for whisky.[20] He was charged with abusing his position, and at his trial, it became apparent that Gardner's medical practice was almost entirely restricted to issuing prescriptions for hard liquor. He was fined $200 and costs.

Later that year, on August 18, 1919, the almost-forgotten aroma of whisky permeated the air of downtown Windsor. A curious crowd gathered to inhale the scent and watched as five policemen unloaded a huge cache of liquor (marked "apples") and secured it in the downtown vault of Inspector M.N. Mousseau. For weeks there had been rumours that there existed a "cornstarch trail" of Quebec liquor labelled as food products being shipped by rail to Windsor for distribution to Detroit and beyond. Mousseau had been watching the train depot and his patience bore fruit with the seizure of 1,032 quarts of fine whisky. The Inspector believed it to be a notable success, and that the river of supply that "has almost continuously flowed in some mysterious way eastward from Quebec into the deserts of Windsor and Detroit" had been dammed. The following day, a local hotelman, Louis Kirsch, appeared before a magistrate, took responsibility for the illegal shipment, and cheerfully paid the $1,000 fine. Kirsch was a front man for others higher up for whom the fine and the loss of one shipment was a small price to pay in a larger and more lucrative enterprise.

The *Ontario Temperance Act* of 1916, the OTA, was originally a temporary war measure which closed the bars and only allowed 2.5 percent "near beer" and liquor to be sold for medicinal purposes. The following year, the federal government enacted regulations prohibiting the manufacture or importation of liquor anywhere in Canada. As a result of the provincial and federal restrictions, Prohibition effectively descended on Ontario. As promised, when the war was over, the provincial government called for a referendum to determine whether or not the OTA should continue. In retrospect, it may be difficult to grasp how the question of whether or not a person should have the right to drink was such a vital issue which so dominated public attention. But it did, and the ensuing referendum was as passionate as any fought in Ontario. Flamboyant evangelist Billy Sunday packed the Toronto Arena to give a hell-fire and damnation sermon against demon rum and even against near beer. In Windsor, the rhetoric was very different. At the Collegiate Institute, a pro-temperance speaker, Hughson Johnstone, addressed a large crowd (many of them returned soldiers) just days before the referendum. The meeting turned into a free-for-all as the veterans made it clear that they wanted liquor to flow again. One ex-soldier called out: "We won the war on rum rations, not on 2 ½ percent beer."[21] Windsor, Walkerville, Sandwich, and northern Essex County voted overwhelmingly to scrap the temperance laws and reopen the bars. As usual, the area was out of step with its God-fearing neighbours and temperance was supported by wide margins in almost all other Ontario districts.

Nevertheless, the strict limitations on acquiring alcohol came to an end on January 1, 1920, when the federal regulations prohibiting interprovincial sale of liquor were revoked. It thereby became permissible to stock one's cellar with alcohol mailed in from a "wet" province such as Quebec or ordered from outside the country. Ironically, as Canada was easing controls on liquor, the United States was imposing a national ban on all alcoholic products. In 1916, Michigan enacted a constitutional prohibition amendment that went into effect on May 1, 1917. Detroit Police Commissioner James Couzens announced that his department would rigorously enforce this new law and make Detroit "a better town."[22] The impact of state laws was overshadowed by the passage of the Eighteenth Amendment in 1919, which prohibited intoxicating liquors. The subsequent Volstead Act effectively banned the manufacture and sale of alcoholic beverages across the U.S. In theory, Detroit became absolutely dry. The actual effect of these enactments was to create an illegal economy, one of whose distinctive features would be smuggling liquor across the Detroit River.

In January 1920, the month in which the Eighteenth Amendment came into force, the people of the Border Cities rose almost as one to the challenge of supplying Americans with alcohol. "Rum-running," a term that had never been heard before, became a mass participation, get-rich-quick scheme. The *Border Cities Star* described the "sweet, demure little maid with a bottle tied under her skirts, the cripple with liquor hidden in the rubber tires of his wheel chair" making tidy profits on each bottle smuggled across the border. The *Detroit News* carried reports of speedboats carrying whisky loads from the Canadian shore to roadhouses in Grosse Pointe, Michigan.[23] The resale value in Michigan was enormous. A $1 bottle of Canadian liquor could sell for $10 to $13 on the Detroit side, and the only thing separating retailers from customers was an eight-minute ferry ride. During the winter, larger scale smugglers simply drove cars across the frozen Detroit River. This could have disastrous results, and in 1920, many rum-runners and their cargo disappeared under thin ice. On February 14, 1920, barely a month into the Prohibition era, Windsor's Police Magistrate Miers expressed his exasperation at the tide of liquor charges that overwhelmed his court: "From all the cases of breaches of the Ontario temperance act that have been up before this court recently, the rest of Canada is beginning to look upon this community as a lawless centre..."[24]

By April 1920, Mayor Winter was denouncing "the intolerable conditions created by such illegal traffic" and the horde of bootleggers who had descended on the district. License Inspector Mousseau was the only official enforcing the OTA and the local police appeared to be either hostile or uninterested. In Toronto, Premier Ernest Drury's United Farmers of Ontario government desperately wanted to return Essex County to respectability. The premier's chosen instrument in the enforcement of the OTA was a fervent temperance man, his attorney general, William Raney. Raney possessed the certainty of the pure of heart, and for him "the war on liquor constituted the keystone in the arch of social rejuvenation." He was convinced that decisive action had to be taken in that part of the province that defied temperance.[25]

Confrontation at the Chappell House

The backbone of the dry movement was Protestantism, especially the Methodist Church. One of the firmest believers in pure Methodism was the Rev. J.O.L. "Leslie" Spracklin. The younger brother of the famous boxer Willie, Leslie had undergone a profound religious conversion after his brother's sudden, violent death in 1907. He left his job as a machinist, returned to school to study for the ministry, and was ordained in 1916. In 1918, he became pastor of the Sandwich Methodist Church.[26] A short distance from this church was a popular roadhouse, the Chappell House. Located in townships or towns where few police were at hand, roadhouses had a reputation for paying little attention to the liquor laws. Mrs. Francis Chappell, the proprietor, routinely flouted the temperance [rules] and served hard liquor. She sold out to Beverley "Babe" Trumble in 1918. The Trumble family had a reputation as hellraisers, and the father, Hamilton "Ham" Trumble, was one of the most controversial Windsor aldermen of his time. He regularly got into spats with his colleagues and in 1910 was arrested for pulling a fire alarm to test the readiness of Windsor's firemen. His son Babe would prove to be no less controversial. Ironically, Leslie Spracklin and Babe Trumble had grown up together. As a youngster, Leslie led a gang at the Cameron School while Babe was the chief at Central. "Both boys were good fighters" one contemporary recalled, the difference being that "Leslie never knew when he was licked" and that "Trumble wasn't what you would call a fighting kid, he could fight hard when pressed, but Leslie seemed to love to fight."[27]

For once, the border had attracted the attention of the Toronto press, and journalists descended on the infamous roadhouses to report on just how lawless the area had become. A *Toronto Daily Star* reporter spent two days among the rum-runners and filed an adventurous account of bootleggers dodging river patrols, sudden gun fights, and thrilling escapes. The border area was portrayed as a dangerous, lawless frontier and an editorial in the Toronto *Telegram* concluded that the Border Cities had become the "plague spot of Canada." Even W.F. Herman's *Border Cities Star* regularly featured editorials which denounced the border lawlessness as "a stench in the nostrils of decency." An editorial in the Toronto *Globe* titled "The Scandal of the Border" conceded that fines were of little use when there was so much money to be made. Nevertheless, the newspaper urged that the "Essex frontier" be brought to order.

On Saturday evening, June 19, 1920, one individual, Rev. Spracklin, decided to take action. He posted himself discreetly outside the Chappell House at 9:30 and watched as taxis and streetcars deposited scores of men and women at the establishment's doors. Those exiting had obviously not been consuming near beer, for they were heavily intoxicated. And where were the police? As it turned out they were on the scene. Sandwich's Chief of Police, Alois Master, was sitting on the Chappell House's front steps. One young lady exiting the premises was so drunk that she paused for a few moments on the Chief's knees. About 10:40 p.m., the Chief went into the house and emerged fifteen minutes later. Spracklin concluded that Trumble was breaching the OTA and that the police were a party to this lawlessness. He duly reported this to the next meeting of the Sandwich town council. However, the response from the Sandwich's Mayor Ed Donnelly was to deny that anything was amiss. The council ignored Spracklin's report and whitewashed his accusations. But Toronto was listening, and a month after Spracklin's charges, the reverend met with Attorney General Raney to discuss the border situation. A week later, Spracklin was appointed a provincial license inspector with instructions to clean up Essex County.

The "Fighting Parson," as he was called by his supporters, assumed his duties with gusto. The new inspector patrolled the Detroit River in a speedboat provided by the attorney general and used it to seize bootleggers before they could deliver their products. He was also assisted by a hastily recruited group of "specials" (inspectors) who appeared to be ambivalent as to which side of the law they were on. This was especially true of two of his men, the Hallam Brothers, who were quick to fire on whomever (even other license inspectors) attracted their suspicion. Raiding premises without warrants, Spracklin's men

J.O.L. Spracklin (at far left) and his squad of liquor inspectors, circa 1920.

wreaked havoc along the border and gunfire became a regular feature along the riverfront. It even came home to the inspector on October 5, when five shots were fired at Spracklin's house.

Three months after his appointment, the situation along the Detroit River border seemed to be spinning out of control. There were calls for an investigation, and the Ontario legislature created a special committee to look into the operation of the OTA. While the committee's mandate covered the province, it was apparent that its focus was on Essex County.[28] At the committee's meeting held on November 2, 1920, Windsor lawyer Frank Healy testified that Spracklin and his armed men regularly invaded private property without warrants and threatened citizens. Worse, the inspectors accepted bribes and confiscated liquor only to sell it themselves. The previous Sunday, Spracklin's men stopped fifteen cars as they left the parking lot of Assumption Church after Mass and with no legal authority, searched each car. The enforcement of temperance had become the excuse for an inexcusable erosion of civil liberties. At the end of Healy's comments, one MPP casually observed, "This man Spracklin is a fool." The following day, Spracklin defended his actions, claiming that it was impractical to get search warrants for liquor that would vanish across the border before it could be secured. Just before the committee adjourned, J.D. Flavelle, the chairman of the Ontario Board of License Commissioners, bestowed a glowing tribute that "Extreme measures were justified in Essex" and "I think Mr. Spracklin has been doing exceedingly good work."[29] Within 48 hours, these assurances would be undone.

Spracklin was back in Sandwich the next day, and in the early hours on Saturday, November 6, he and his men stopped outside the Chappell House to find a man who had apparently been beaten. According to Spracklin's account, Babe Trumble was there as well. When Spracklin inquired about the trouble, Trumble ran inside his premises and locked the doors. The inspectors gained access through a window and found Trumble demanding to see their badges and waving a gun at them. As Spracklin's men backed off, Trumble advanced, pushing his weapon into the minister's stomach and growling "damn you Spracklin, I am going to shoot you." Spracklin hesitated a few seconds, then deciding that "it was either him or me," fired his revolver. After shooting, Spracklin and his men fled.

At the inquest held that evening, Trumble's wife Lulu offered a very different version of the events. She had been ill that night and her husband had been attending to her when they heard a commotion downstairs. Holding a hot water bottle and a cigarette, Trumble went down to confront the intruders. Moments later, Lulu heard a gunshot and her husband cry out "You dog, you have shot me!" Together with another man, Lulu helped Trumble into the bedroom where he died a few minutes later. When asked if her husband had a gun, she replied that the only thing he held was a hot water bottle. The inquest was conducted by Crown Attorney Rodd who proved to be far from a neutral figure. Not only was he a leader of the local Methodists, he had frequently worked with Spracklin on temperance enforcement. Under Rodd's skilful direction, the inquest jury found that the minister was only fulfilling his duty and that the killing was justified.

It took substantial prodding from the Trumble family for the attorney general to actually press charges. Finally, Spracklin was charged with manslaughter and tried in Sandwich in February 1921. Despite the fact that Trumble's alleged revolver was never found and several witnesses testified that he was unarmed, the jury accepted Spracklin's plea of self-defence, and he was acquitted. When news of the acquittal was relayed to the Ontario legislature, a congratulatory clapping on desks broke out among United Farmers members. At a prohibition rally at Massey Hall, the participants were in the middle of a hymn when news of the acquittal was suddenly announced. The hymn of praise was abruptly cut short as the crowd shouted out "three cheers and a tiger" for their champion.

While Protestant Ontario rejoiced, the reaction in the Border Cities was significantly different. Less than two months after Spracklin's acquittal, a public meeting was held to hear speeches concerning the proposal to ban all alcohol imports into Ontario. The Windsor armouries were packed on the evening of April 11, 1921, and an array of Protestant clergymen were there with their supporters. A banner proclaiming "'Dry' Clean the Border Cities"

SECOND EXTRA

The Border Cities Star

CIRCULATION YESTERDAY 19,955

FORD, WALKERVILLE, WINDSOR SANDWICH, OJIBWAY

VOL. 5. NO. 142 — 20 PAGES — WINDSOR, ONTARIO, THURSDAY, FEBRUARY 24, 1921 — PRICE THREE CENTS

SPRACKLIN FREE; JURY OUT 59 MIN.

SANDWICH CLERGYMAN "NOT GUILTY" IN DEATH OF BEVERLEY TRUMBLE

No Demonstration As Famous Case Comes to End—Judge Sums Up Evidence After Addresses by R. L. Brackin and A. M. Grier

BRACKIN SCORES MRS. TRUMBLE'S STORY

"She Stood There and Lied and Lied and Lied," Lawyer Tells Jury—Defends Action of Pastor-Inspector—Criticism of Ontario Government

Rev. J. O. L. Spracklin left Sandwich court this afternoon at 3.20 a free man, five minutes after members of the jury filed into the crowded court room and announced, amidst impressive silence, that they had found a verdict of "not guilty," after 59 minutes consideration of the evidence. The climax came unexpectedly in the middle of the examination of a witness in the case against Vincent Masse. Court officials, evidently laboring under suppressed excitement, hurried into the room and informed Sir William Mulock that a verdict had been reached.

Reinstatement of Spracklin May Be Asked If Acquitted

RELEASED FROM LONG STRAIN

REV. J. O. LESLIE SPRACKLIN

STATES WANT DIVISION OF WAR SPOILS

Equal Interest in Disposition of German Possessions?

NOTE BEING DISCUSSED

Members Claim U.S. Forfeited Rights by Withdrawing

Helping Pastor

MR. J. WALTER CURRY, K.C., M.L.A.

CATTLE BAN IS ISSUE RAISED IN POLITICAL FIGHT

Lord Beaverbrook Replies to Charges of Minister of Agriculture

ALLIED OFFER ACCEPTED BY TURK PARTIES

Unexpected Turn Comes When All Demands Agreed To

BODIES ACT AS ONE

Premier Briand Declares Conference Now Nearing Settlement

Headline from Border Cities Star declaring J.O.L. Spracklin's acquittal, February 21, 1921.

was hung from the main platform. The Rev. Oaten, a representative of the Dominion Alliance, had a band in attendance which struck up several hymns and the ladies in the audience added their voices. They were all waiting for their star performer, William E. "Pussyfoot" Johnson to begin his address. As a law enforcement officer in the American west, Johnson had earned his reputation by his cat-like stealth in creeping up on and raiding saloons. From there he had gone on to become one of America's foremost temperance advocates and had been making a swing through Ontario in support of the cause. However the majority of the crowd, particularly the men in the gallery, seemed to be in no mood to listen to a temperance sermon. They kept up a cacophony of noise and refused to let any of the clergymen be heard. Windsor's Police Chief Daniel Thompson mounted the stage and pleaded with the crowd to at least listen to a local preacher. They refused.

Dry Crusader William "Pussyfoot" Johnson, 1920s.

Nevertheless, Johnson climbed the platform and began his address. He seemed to take the hubbub good-naturedly and smiled to his few supporters in the audience. Unable to be heard, he unfurled a large version of the referendum ballot with the "X" marked over the "yes" for the ban on imports. A reporter described the following scene:

> Again the sound waves burst over the heads of the crowd louder than a battery of artillery, but when the famous prohibitionist calmly poured himself a glass of water from a pitcher which stood upon the table and drank it for the crowd's benefit all the noise ever produced in the world before paled into insignificance.[30]

This last demonstration of water-drinking was too much for the crowd, and men surged forward to seize Johnson. Chief Thompson and the few policemen present managed to grab him and squeeze him out one of the armouries side doors. The police ran down Ouellette Avenue with their charge in a direct line toward the ferry terminal. They were closely followed by a mob that had lost none of its enthusiasm for ripping Johnson limb from limb. Rocks and bottles rained down on the retreating officers and the prohibitionist until they arrived at the ferry. The police immediately shoved Johnson onto a boat and barely succeeded in holding off the crowd until the gangplank was raised and the vessel was safely on its way to Detroit.

That a large number of Border Cities residents were so exercised about Prohibition that they were prepared to lynch a prominent advocate of that cause was a demonstration of the depth of public feelings. The searches, the questioning, and daily irritants thrust upon them by inspectors from Toronto seemed to be reaching a breaking point. They further registered their anger in the referendum of 1921, by overwhelmingly rejecting (in Sandwich by a vote of 650 to 161) the measure to prohibit liquor importation into Ontario.[31] Inevitably, the proposition was hugely approved of by the rest of the province. The Toronto *Telegram* was one of the few newspapers to suggest that perhaps the problem did not lie with the attitude of the people of the Border Cities, but rather with the foisting of a moral law on a population that did not respect it. In a bitter editorial against attorney general Raney, the *Telegram* suggested that "It was Raneyism that shot Beverley Trumble. It was Raneyism which went buccaneering on the Windsor river."[32]

A New Industry

In the wake of the Spracklin debacle, a few more liquor inspectors were sent to the border. But these paltry efforts would have little effect. After the spring of 1921, when the importation of liquor from Quebec was banned, the supply issue became even more acute. The *Detroit Free Press* reported that armed gangs were combing the downriver area looking for caches of liquor to sell and that "Citizens in the west end of Windsor are in a state of semi-panic at the failure of the police department to check the bold operations of the daring gangs of thieves." Lawlessness had reached the state that "The residents are discussing the formation of armed civilian patrols to protect their homes."[33]

Whatever the difficulties, the enormous potential for profits from illegal sales to Americans would, in time, attract sophisticated business networks. Until then, some of the most unlikely individuals became tycoons. Cecil Smith was a portly cab driver who made a modest living until he smuggled a few bottles of whisky to Detroit and realized the enormous profits to be had. Smith expanded his operations to include train cars filled with liquor and made huge returns until October 1921, when he was convicted of bribing a policeman. At his trial, Smith noted that in the past two years he had paid $96,000 in fines.[34] To him this fortune was nothing, merely the cost of doing business. On the morning he was shipped off to the penitentiary, Smith ordered a fine hot breakfast for himself and his jailers. The Toronto *Globe* took note of Smith's bravado and a journalist dispatched to the border reported that: "In Windsor bootlegging apparently has been raised to the dignity of a profession and it is probably the only city in Ontario where it may claim to figure as one of the basic industries."[35]

Rum-running was one of the few bright spots in the local economy. By late 1920, a brief post-war downturn in automobile demand hit Windsor and plants were letting men go. Hundreds of returned soldiers were put to work with pick and axe to clear land for the first provincial highway from Windsor to London, and to dig the foundations for the new police station.[36] While factories were idled, the smuggling of liquor continued and even gained momentum. American enforcement authorities were taking note that liquor from the Border Cities was supplying speakeasies across America. As one writer observed, at the height of Prohibition, it was impossible to get a drink in Detroit "unless you walked at least ten feet and told the busy bartender what you wanted in a voice loud enough for him to hear you above the uproar."[37] These American tipplers rarely paused to reflect that their favourite speakeasies relied upon liquor supplied by the diligent bootleggers and pliable enforcement officers of the Border Cities.

Chapter Five
Miracle Years
1922–1926

The rise of the Border Cities was largely attributable to one man, Gordon McGregor. It was McGregor who conceived the plan to transfer some of Henry Ford's assembly operation to Canada, and over the years he had supervised the orderly expansion of this subsidiary. His administrative skills made the Canadian branch plant wildly successful and resulted in Ford of Canada supplying automobiles across Canada and the British Empire. To a great extent, he had transformed a collection of sleepy Victorian towns into an industrial dynamo. By the early 1920s, McGregor was still fully engaged with business, but was also prepared to enjoy his wealth and dominant position in local society. A gregarious man, he enjoyed a good game of golf with friends and colleagues at the Essex County Golf and Country Club (of which he was a director) and handing out trophies to the winners of various Ford sports teams. But McGregor had not been well, and in early March 1922, he travelled to Montreal for an operation. He died there on March 11, 1922, at the age of forty-nine.

His death shocked Windsor, and was reported in the *Star* with banner headlines usually reserved for the passing of a sovereign. Always a huge backer of McGregor's projects, the *Star* would be unstinting in its praise after his death. The newspaper felt that the wheels he had set in motion were operating to perfection as a result of his "wisdom, foresight and personality." On the day of his funeral, the Ford world stopped in respect, and all the Border Cities' plants, as well as the Highland Park and River Rouge factories in Detroit, halted production. Both Henry and his son Edsel Ford were present for the service, as were scores of workers. The *Star* would later boast that while Henry Ford had solved America's transportation problem, "the late Gordon McGregor solved it for Canada." Even accounting for hyperbole, there is considerable merit in the claim.[1] While they mourned his death, the machinery McGregor had started now had an impetus all its own and the loss of one man could not slow it down.

Juggernaut

> To the average visitor, the sight along the river front from Ford to Sandwich is an inspiring one. Tall factory smokestacks tower toward the sky, and by day and night huge black clouds of smoke are seen issuing there from and these smoke stacks belong in a large measure to the motor factories.[2]

By the 1920s, automotive production in Canada was being consolidated and the days of the lone innovator had passed. For a company to survive, it needed "sizable markets, technological prowess, immense capital, and massive economies of scale."[3] Gordon McGregor had instilled these key ingredients into Ford of Canada's fabric. He also left a company that operated with a striking level of independence from its American parent. While General Motors of Oshawa (formerly the McLaughlin Motor Works) was a branch plant operated by its American parent, Henry Ford had such confidence in McGregor that he largely allowed the Canadian affiliate to make its own decisions. At the Canadian Tariff Commission inquiry of 1920, Ford of Canada's representative insisted that the company was not a branch plant, but rather, "an entirely distinct corporation." Moreover, it was an increasingly profitable and powerful one. After the pulp and paper industry, the automotive sector emerged in the 1920s as Canada's fastest-growing industry. During that decade, auto production went from eighth to fourth place among Canadian manufacturers as Canada became (after the United States) "the most motorized country on the globe."[4]

Wallace Campbell, McGregor's secretary, was named the company's new vice president two days after his predecessor's funeral. Windsor born and raised, Campbell had started with Ford in 1905, the year after its incorporation. While he lacked McGregor's flair for salesmanship, Campbell was a dedicated company man, and he would implement his fallen chief's plans to spur production. Even before McGregor's death, huge expansion plans were underway. The riverfront was too cramped for major volumes of production, and the company looked inland. Just south of Sandwich Street, Ford constructed a huge new power plant. Along the riverfront, a series of immense wharves were completed in 1924. With an eye toward expansion, McGregor cultivated a business relationship with the Reaume family (Ulysses Reaume being Ford

City's mayor) which enabled Ford to buy 175 acres of land south of the Grand Trunk Railway. By early 1923, residents were amazed to see a massive 12.5-acre machine shop arise on the new site. Designed by Albert Kahn of Detroit (also Henry Ford's preferred architect), it was the largest factory built in Canada up to that time. Moreover, it featured the most modern industrial construction available. The Canadian Bridge Company, located less than a mile away on Walker Road, was supplying tons of girders that supported a light, airy structure. Trussed Concrete, operated by Kahn's brother Julius, supplied reinforced concrete and the C.M. Bennet Company of Walkerville, the glass. While Kahn had already designed more traditional buildings in Walkerville, such as Willistead Manor, by the early 1920s he was designing "the prototypical 20th-century factory, a monumental steel-framed, glass-skinned enclosure that solved all the classic needs for light, air, strength and big open spans—all on one level." While the new Ford plant was intended to be functional, "modernists saw beauty in his work."[5]

Wallace R. Campbell, 1922.

This vast new plant was essential for Ford production to remain on an upward trajectory. At the riverfront facility, Ford produced 74,315 vehicles in 1923. When the machinery was moved to the new plant in December 1923, production capacity more than doubled. Ford could now manufacture more than 500 vehicles a day. It was the economic lifeblood of the community and by 1924, Ford's yearly payroll of over eight million dollars supported more than 20,000 (or one in three persons) in the Border Cities. By 1926, the Ford auto assembly plant was not only the largest in Canada, it was the largest in the British Empire. Even though the sales of Model Ts began to decline in the United States in the 1920s, they remained strong in Canada. Ironically, their best sales year was 1926, the year before production was discontinued.[6]

Ford Motor was the dominant, but by no means the only, industry in the eastern part of the Border Cities. By February 1920, spark plugs for engine assembly were being provided by Champion Spark Plug (the only spark plug manufacturer in Canada) at the corner of Howard and Hanna Streets. Many of the parts suppliers existed solely to supply the Ford assembly lines. In addition to getting wheels from Kelsey and auto cushion springs from L.A. Young Industries, Ford also used the body painting facilities supplied by the American Auto Trimming Company. That company opened a small Canadian branch on Walker Road in 1911 so that they could paint and enamel Gordon McGregor's vehicles. The company's owner, Benjamin Gotfredson, was a keen observer, and he noticed that Henry Ford did not permit his Canadian subsidiary to manufacture trucks. For that matter, no Canadian firm had stepped forward to manufacture larger vehicles in quantity. Gotfredson recognized an opportunity and seized it. By 1919, he had gained enough mechanical knowledge to convert part of his Walkerville paint plant over into truck and bus assembly. The results were a strong, reliable vehicle that sold well across Canada. In its first four months of 1926, truck sales were $800,000. It was reported that some municipal bus fleets in Ontario were entirely Gotfredsons. In the final result, "the Gotfredson was a Canadian-built truck launched by American capital and enterprise." In an unusual turn of events, Canadian production was so successful that the company set up a branch truck plant in Detroit.[7]

Ford's insatiable need for parts suppliers extended deep into Windsor's industry. Dominion Forge had been stamping parts from metal sheets since 1910. However, the company failed to make the transition from war production back to civilian contracts and had to sell out to Ford in 1919. Stamping operations came to an end and instead the factory concentrated on drop forging crank and cam shafts for Ford engine assembly lines. In the forging process, red-hot metal would be beaten into a steel die by steam-powered hammers. A *Star* reporter toured Dominion Forge in 1925 and saw pieces of metal being cut into the required size and heated into a near-molten state:

> Then, when properly heated, each piece goes under the hammers. These range in size from great steam hammers that strike a blow of tons to the small "rapid fire" hammers… the visitors watches the hammers crashing down and the sparks flying about, directed by expert men who go about their duties cheerfully and readily.[8]

It may have been questionable how cheerful they were after a nine-hour shift handling red-hot metal, with only goggles for protection. To a visiting reporter, the sight was exhilarating, but the constant noise, vibration, and danger made work at Dominion Forge hard to endure—an ordeal that only the toughest could handle for an extended period. Moreover, even those who lived in the area had to reconcile themselves to the ever-present din of the drop forges.

Studebaker Assembly Plant, Walkerville, circa 1923.

A few of the new manufacturers were independent of Ford, but were still outgrowths of plants that had existed in the area for years. The Globe Furniture Company, originally one of the Walker family's plants, was sold in 1910 to the Everett-Metzger-Flanders auto company, the manufacturers of the "E-M-F 30." The Globe plant gradually changed production and in its first year, assembled both living room furniture as well as cars from parts made in Detroit. In 1913, the U.S. division of Studebaker purchased E-M-F, and the plant thereafter became the "Studebaker Corporation of Canada." In contrast to Ford's hands-off style of management, Studebaker Canada was directly operated out of South Bend, Indiana, and the company's directors made no attempt to hide the fact that they had bought the factory in order to beat the tariffs and sell in the Canadian and Empire markets.

American investment was so vital that the area's Member of Parliament, W.C. Kennedy, warned Prime Minister Mackenzie King in December 1922 that local Liberals opposed any moves toward free trade. Kennedy had been overwhelmingly re-elected in 1921, and King rewarded him with the cabinet position of Minister of Railways and Canals. Many considered that this popular and capable man might eventually become Prime Minister. However, he died suddenly in January 1923, at the age of 54. His funeral Mass at St. Alphonsus Church was almost a state affair, attended by both the Prime Minister and the Leader of the Opposition. Significantly, Kennedy's last communication with King had been a plea to uphold the tariff barriers.[9]

It was a measure of the growing technological sophistication of the area that one small group of talented tool and die men moved from Detroit to Windsor in 1920 to found Canadian Engineering and Tool. William Tregenza had already worked as a tool foreman with Packard, Maxwell, and General Motors in Detroit. While Tregenza brought a wealth of experience in the tool and die trade to the business, finances were handled by Percy McConnell, formerly of Ford.[10] The major companies were spinning off these smaller enterprises which could supply them with technical pieces that might otherwise cost them too much to produce.

One prominent newcomer to the auto scene had firm foundations in Detroit, but no Canadian roots. In 1916, Chalmers Motor of Detroit established a branch plant in Walkerville in order to access the Canadian market. Shortly thereafter, another American company, Maxwell Motor, opened up in Windsor. When Chalmers floundered, it was taken over by Maxwell and operated as Maxwell Motor Company of Canada. When it too came on hard times in 1921, Walter Chrysler came to the rescue. A designer and innovator, Chrysler came out with a popular new model, the "Chrysler 70," a six-cylinder quality product that was available at a price slightly higher than the Model T. Walter Chrysler incorporated the Chrysler Corporation of Canada in June 1925, and converted the Maxwell plant on Tecumseh Road into an assembly facility. In August of that year, the first Chrysler 70s came off his Windsor line.

The Chrysler vehicles were a huge success in Canada, although almost all of the parts were shipped over from Detroit. However, the demands for assembly soon dictated that more parts be made in the Border Cities. In early 1927, Chrysler bought the empty Fisher Body factory on Edna Street in Walkerville and reopened it for assembly. In announcing the purchase, Chrysler's president, John Mansfield, predicted that it would triple Chrysler Canada's capacity. He also noted that it marked the beginning of the local production of

Original Chrysler of Canada plant at McDougall and Tecumseh roads, 1925.

axles, transmissions, and wheels to feed the new assembly line and "thus, the car will be practically all manufactured in the Border Cities." In a move that would have a profound impact on Windsor's future, in 1928, Chrysler management announced the purchase of a 78-acre site on Tecumseh Road, just west of Drouillard. A new five-million-dollar plant would assemble Desoto and Plymouth cars as well as Fargo trucks. While it had started more than a decade after Ford Motor, Chrysler was rapidly making strides to catch up to its rival auto maker. This new assembly plant on Tecumseh Road would be expanded over the years until it would eventually become the heart of Windsor's industrial complex.[11]

One factor assisting this unprecedented surge in industrial activity was the prevailing labour peace. After the unrest following the war, there was little agitation in the early 1920s. This was especially true in the auto industry. It was reported in 1920 that a union, the United Automobile, Aircraft and Vehicle Workers of America Local 28, had been established in Windsor and that it had 40 members. Two years later it had ceased to exist. Management had its ways of dealing with union leaders; in January 1921, Archie Hooper was fired by the Grand Trunk Railway for his outspoken views. Early attempts at unionization had proven futile and "for Canadian workers, organized and unorganized, the twenties turned out to be a decade of torpor and defeat."[12]

Dodge truck main assembly line, circa 1930.

The People of the Border Cities

The Border Cities were filling up and many of the newcomers were veterans who were at loose ends after the war and looking for a place to settle. One Canadian veteran, who had moved to several places after his discharge, settled on Windsor as "it was a boom town—things were going like crazy there."[13] English-speaking Canadians, as well as British immigrants,were making their way to Windsor in huge numbers. British immigrants were being encouraged by both government and press to come to Canada, and census records indicate that the British population of the Border Cities rose from 35,791 in 1921 to 62,689 in 1931 to make up over sixty percent of the area.[14] Many of the Anglo-Protestant newcomers were attracted by the professional opportunities the growing area offered. The legal profession was booming, and by 1929, sixty percent of Windsor's lawyers were of British stock from other Ontario communities. All Saints' Anglican Church, the spiritual home for many of these new arrivals, was expanding and had established three local missions. One of the Church's officers, Deacon John Tully, was a former British soldier who ministered to the veterans who lived in the missions. Both Methodists and Presbyterians were also forming new congregations in the expanding neighbourhoods.

One issue that had an impact on the British population was the Church union of 1925. In that year, the Methodist, Presbyterian, and Congregational denominations came together to form the United Church of Canada. The imposing "Central Methodist" in Windsor's downtown became "Central United." Ironically, the Methodists of south Walkerville had been in the process of building a new church. When it was opened for worship on June 11, 1925 (the day after church union came into effect), the Ottawa United Church on Lincoln Road became the first United Church in Canada taken in under the amalgamation.[15] But not all members of the former congregations agreed. In Windsor, St. Andrew's and Knox Churches voted to remain Presbyterian. This may well have been due to the influence of church leaders. Rev. Hugh Paulin, St. Andrew's pastor from 1915 until 1952, was a hugely popular preacher and was so successful that by 1925, St. Andrew's became the largest Presbyterian congregation in Ontario.

In contrast to the British influx, those who identified as French Canadian were a diminishing percentage of the urban area's population. From 1921 to 1931, French Canadians declined from 23 to 17 percent of the city's population, and many of those who described their ancestry as French no longer spoke the language. In many ways, this was out of necessity, as factory instructions were given exclusively in English. But not all the French Canadians who had migrated to the city ended up as factory hands. Eugene Mailloux, from the village of Pointe-aux-Roche, had come to Windsor in 1904 and built up a nest egg. Together with Ernest Parent, he found the "M & P" grocery store on London Street and McEwan in 1913. One of its initial innovations allowed customers to use a bag to go up and down aisles and collect their purchases instead of bringing them individually to a counter. By 1935, M & P would have 32 grocery stores spread across southwestern Ontario, making it one of Canada's first chain stores. Of course, their business was conducted exclusively in English.

The decline in the use of French in the city was apparent. The pastor of Immaculate Conception parish noted that even in francophone families, the children spoke English in the schoolyard. This was hardly surprising, as none of Windsor's three public and three separate schools offered any French instruction. While leaders from previous years, such as Gaspard Pacaud, grudgingly accepted Regulation 17 and its limitations of French in schools, one nationalist firebrand, Joseph de Grandpré, kept up the struggle for French identity. De Grandpré had been in the front ranks of the Ford City riot in 1917, and in 1922, he broke with the staid St. Jean Baptiste Society to form the more radical *Ligue des Patriotes*. In that same year, he founded an independent bilingual school, Jeanne d'Arc. Ultimately, it was a futile struggle as "local francophones manifested indifference to nationalist maxims and many even preferred to embrace the majority English culture around them to open doors of economic opportunity for their children."[16] Jeanne d'Arc closed in 1927.

One of the area's oldest racial groups was also becoming increasingly hard-pressed. In the 1864 census, Windsor's 570 black residents made up 22% of the town. Yet the white population grew immensely until by 1931, the 1,000 black citizens comprised fewer than one percent of the Border Cities. Segregation was the order of the day and blacks could live only in the McDougall-Mercer Street area. As Jim Watson, a black resident of the 1920s politely put it, "This particular location seemed to be a favorite one for Negroes to locate in." Less polite were clauses in deeds that specifically excluded blacks from buying lots in new subdivisions. A large number of immigrant Jews also lived in this district, and Watson recalled playing with their children and acting as the *shabbes goy* and lighting candles and stoves on Jewish holidays. Black residents knew that they could not go to a white barber, be served in most restaurants and hotels, and their employment prospects were limited.[17] One of the few positions open for black men was working as waiters and porters on the trains. When the Canadian National Railways threatened to remove them, the Windsor branch of the Canadian League for the Advancement of Colored People met to protest. The railways relented, and at least these jobs remained available.

There were a few exceptions, and one individual successfully defied racial barriers. Cornelius Langston Henderson was born in Detroit and grew up in Georgia. He obtained a degree in civil engineering from the University of Michigan in 1911, but despite his qualifications, no American firm would hire a black engineer. He turned to Canada and was hired by Canadian Bridge where he provided design and engineering on their upcoming projects, most notably the Ambassador Bridge.[18] Henderson defied the odds. More typical was a black lawyer who tried to buy a house on Askin Street in Sandwich in 1925 and found the neighbourhood united in its determination to block the sale.

Other newcomers to the Border Cities were desperate for work and were prepared to take on the dangerous and difficult jobs in the factories. An example was the Scislowski family from Poland. They arrived in the 1920s and the husband worked in the Ford foundry, a place his son described as a "tough, dirty, hot and stinking a job as any could be and most foundry workers were Polish, Hungarians or Ukrainians… and it was a miracle that they lasted on the job as long as they did." The elder Scislowski did not last, and he died (likely of silicosis) in 1932. The family had no workplace benefits and had to go on relief.[19] As a result of the restrictive American immigration quotas of the early 1920s, many central and east European immigrants such as the Scislowskis were being diverted to Canada. Canadian organized labour resisted this influx and tried to block new immigration schemes. Nevertheless, between 1921 and 1931, the number of east Europeans in the Border Cities rose from 1,758 to 5,800 and now made up almost six percent of the urban area's population. There were almost 1,000 Ukrainians in Ford City alone, and in 1924, the United Hetman Organization, or Windsor "Stitch," established St. Vladimir and Olga Ukrainian Catholic Church.

With the help of Rev. Paulin of St. Andrew's, Presbyterian Hungarians formed a church in 1927. Lutheran Hungarians followed shortly thereafter. For immigrants, it was not only religion, it was language that was central to their community. Catholic Hungarians found that speaking their tongue during services was "a privilege which has been denied to them in the English and French-speaking Roman Catholic churches."[20] In reaction, under the leadership of Fr. John Matty, they formed the parish of St. Anthony of Padua in order to hear Mass in their native language. For a generation at least, the Border Cities, its peoples and churches, would be divided among a cosmopolitan variety of languages.

Many of the Slavic arrivals had rudimentary English at best. To improve their language skills, the Ford City branch of the IODE sponsored English classes taught by Ada C. Richards at the Belle Isle School.[21] Language was such a barrier that William Englander, one of the area's oldest Jewish residents, spent his time at the courts translating a variety of languages into English. A reporter noted that Englander was indispensable in Windsor's police court as a large percentage of the people who took the stand were unable to understand English. The Anglo majority recognized the need to teach the newcomers English and saw the opportunity to make them into "proper" Canadians. In 1925, Methodists established a mission to the Ukrainians to encourage them to become decent, English-speaking Protestants.[22] While Ukrainians made every effort to adapt to their new land, most remained attached to their Catholic or Orthodox roots. Still, many clergymen realized that thanks to the influx of workers, a large, rootless population existed. A few denominations were determined to capture them. Rev. O.E. Chapman of the Bruce Avenue Baptist Church hired the downtown Allen Theatre early in 1924 to provide an entertaining Sunday service that included musical numbers and recitals. He attracted a large congregation of "roomers"—young people "who have no place to go other than their rooms."[23] There was such a transient population of young men that the Albert Residence for Men had been set up in 1914 to provide them with a bed until they could find work and their own place. Like all other social institutions of the time, it relied on charity.

The draw of the Border Cities' factories was reaching across the world, and a new ethnic group appeared after the war. Before 1920, few Italian families had made their way to the area. The Ferraris operated a grocery store from 1903 to 1910, and Louis and Paul Merlo and John Ray had founded a construction company in 1913. But after the war, there were enough Italian residents in Windsor to form a cultural union, the Dante Aligheri Society. The *Star* smugly noted that Windsor's Italians were "entirely different" from their feuding American cousins, for they were drawn from a "very high grade, being mostly recruited from the Northern provinces."[24] During the 1920s, more than 2,000 Italians came to Windsor in search of work. In January 1925, a small group established the Border Cities Italian Club which became the organizer for the community's dances and picnics. The club also established a mutual benefit fund and, in 1928, the "Border Cities Italian Club Band."[25] In time, members linked the name of their club with the Italian explorer Giovanni Caboto. While east Europeans and Italians were becoming significant factors in the community during the 1920s, the area remained indelibly British.

Building the Metropolis

With this surge of people coming to Windsor, the housing market was red-hot. The *Star* looked at the value of building permits and estimated that there was twice as much building activity in the area than any other municipality in

Canada. Windsor trailed only Toronto and Hamilton in the value of new buildings. When considered from its modest beginnings, the population growth rate and building in the Border Cities was the fastest in the country.[26] In 1926, the *Star* reported that not only was the per capita value of building permits in the Border Cities the highest in the country, in 1925, it was double that of Toronto and almost three times that of Montreal. The value of new building construction permits issued by the Border Cities stood fifth in Canada and only trailed the much larger and established metropolises of Toronto, Montreal, Vancouver, and Winnipeg. A reporter found that "An automobile trip around the Border Cities amply confirms the figures. The most striking feature of such a trip is the large number of new houses under construction… one sees whole blocks of houses being erected at once."[27] The Border Cities was becoming a metropolis and extending into new areas. While prior to the war, Hôtel-Dieu hospital had been on the city's southern edge, by the 1920s, the hospital was surrounded by residential neighbourhoods and was considered to be in the downtown.

"Peter Osterhout, home-builder!" was the simple but emphatic title given by the *Star* to the man who, more than any other, facilitated this residential development. Since he came to Windsor in 1906, Osterhout had thrown himself into construction. In twenty years it was estimated that he had built from 3,500 to 4,000 houses, and that one-sixth of Border Cities residents lived in homes he had built. Many of these were outside the immediate core in areas where his business competitors thought he would fail. But Osterhout was willing to take chances, and had even built homes along the "Grand Coulee," later Giles Boulevard, the former drain along Windsor's south side.[28] Thanks to the work of Osterhout and a partner, A.A. Little, Giles Boulevard became a beautiful, tree-lined street in 1919. The city was now rapidly moving away from the river and developing the east-west streets that would form its future

Homes built by Osterhout and Little on Elm Street, looking north, 1913.

transportation network. Erie Street was paved in 1917. In 1922, the Windsor end of Ottawa Street was completed and the Walkerville part paved the following year. Only ten years before, Ottawa Street had merely been an open field that Hiram Walker's staff used to play golf. By 1928, little vacant land remained in the city proper to be developed.

The dedication of the Essex County War Memorial, the cenotaph designed by Masson, on Giles Boulevard, November 11, 1924. The guest speaker was Major-General Sir Archibald Macdonell; his father had been Windsor's mayor in the 1860s.

In addition to the lines of workers' houses, imposing new structures were going up on Ouellette Avenue. One of them included the Prince Edward Hotel. By September 1921, Canadian Bridge had completed the network of steel girders for this six-storey structure, the largest hotel in Ontario outside of Toronto. It was a measure of the area's increasing wealth that money was being spent on larger and architecturally significant structures. James Pennington, the dean of local architects, had been practising since 1909. Influenced by Louis Sullivan, he used carved stone detail in his work on the Hôtel-Dieu addition and Walkerville Collegiate. The sudden need for educational space was a boon to architects and a Scottish immigrant, David Cameron, designed Windsor-Walkerville Technical School, Kennedy Collegiate, and the School of Business in the popular "collegiate gothic" style of the times. The pride of Sandwich was General Byng School on Felix Street. Opened in 1923, it had amenities which were unknown in previous schools, including a gymnasium, auditorium, and a swimming pool. In addition to the school expansion, there was a need for accommodation in the central city, and Guy Butler Colthurst designed many of Windsor's downtown apartment buildings.

A few architects were starting to test new waters. George Y. Masson created the Essex County War Memorial in 1924 using a simple granite shaft with thrusting, straight lines. Masson, a Detroiter and graduate of the University of Pennsylvania, partnered with Windsor's Hugh Sheppard in 1924. For his part, Sheppard had no academic training but his work with Albert Kahn gave him a solid foundation in modern building techniques. Together Sheppard and Masson would design the new YW-YMCA building, the John Campbell School, as well as the beaux-arts style federal post office in 1932. The YW-YMCA building on Pelissier Street (opened May 1, 1926) was a beautiful North Italian Renaissance structure and was especially significant for being the first such facility in Canada to provide recreational opportunities for both males and females. Perhaps the only drawback was that the young men of Windsor continued the tradition of nude bathing, for one participant admitted that "us guys just went in unadorned when it was our turn to use the pool."[29]

The most innovative builder to arrive in the Border Cities was a young Scot, Arthur Lothian. After service as a dispatch rider in the Canadian Army, he had, like many British emigrants, been drawn to the Windsor area. Several of his buildings in the 1920s, such as Dillon Hall for Assumption College, were elegant, but conventional structures. However, by the later part of the decade he began to challenge accepted forms and inserted modernist Art Deco motifs into his work. His St. Bernard School used a series of angles and lines to create distinctive geometric forms. The Catholic Church enabled Lothian to create his most significant accomplishment. Father Edward Doe, the pastor of St. Clare of Assisi Church and a highly respected chaplain, approached Bishop Fallon on building a new facility which reflected modern tastes. The Bishop was not known to be partial to modernism, but he was persuaded by Doe to hire Lothian to create a unique house of worship, possibly the only completely Art Deco church in the country. St. Clare's was later described as:

> A rare and beautifully realized Art Deco style church rising above the traffic on Tecumseh Road West… From a distance, its tall, slender steeple suggests Gothic affinities… but zigzag contours and angular recesses speak the language, not of the 12th century, but of the frenetic Machine Age of the 1930s.[30]

Essex Border Utilities Commission in Action

The Border Cities would be hard-pressed to contain this surge in growth. Children had to attend school on a platoon system as there was not enough room to take them all in at one time. Some relief was provided when Walkerville no longer sent its secondary students to Windsor, for in 1922, it completed a continuation school that two years later became Walkerville Collegiate. Local impetus for a modern industrial trade school came from the principal of this Collegiate, W.D. Lowe. Arriving in Windsor in 1908, Lowe taught classics, but was aware of the needs of industry. His views coincided with the desire of the provincial government to provide trades education for young men and domestic training for women.[31] At a 1920 speech to the Chamber of Commerce, he noted that while some argued against technical courses at the high school level, he felt that a school dedicated to industrial education was essential to train the modern workforce. Initially, Walkerville balked at joining with Windsor on this project. But in a December 1919 mass meeting to discuss the future of Windsor's education, the Rev. J.C. Tolmie passionately argued on behalf of a new approach, and he urged voters to support the concept of "one big school" that offered modern technical training. Tolmie won over the doubters and a joint school was undertaken by Windsor and Walkerville. When the technical school opened in August 1923, it offered an impressive array of metal and woodworking shops as well as a model housekeeping suite for female students in the domestic science department. This advanced facility required a provincial statute for the school boards of both Windsor and Walkerville to finance its construction. The technical school was also a reflection of the fact that major projects could only be accomplished when the Border Cities worked together.

The same dynamic was true when remedying the antiquated sewer and water systems. Walkerville and Ford City were still discharging waste upriver of Windsor's water inlet. The Windsor waterworks were old, in constant need of repair, and not able to meet the increasing demand. Walkerville's plant was newer, but was designed for a far smaller community. However, instead of collaborative remedies, the municipalities that made up the Border Cities were focused on their individual problems. The one institution that could provide a unified response to the infrastructure dilemma was the Essex Border Utilities Commission. Even so, the EBUC found it almost impossible to overcome the petty rivalries that dominated the area. Sandwich, afraid that it would be the site of the pest (isolation) house, refused to join the health board. Windsor objected to a joint water project if it meant supplying water to new suburbs. By the end of 1920, Windsor's mayor was urging the city to withdraw from the EBUC.

Despite this opposition, the EBUC would take major steps to provide a unified system. This was in large part due to the leadership of Gordon McGregor. In his final years, McGregor devoted himself to the utility and was regularly returned as Ford City's Commission representative. The provincial government agreed that the area badly needed central direction on health issues. In the summer of 1919, the special act creating one health board had effectively granted authority in health matters to the EBUC. It appeared that "McGregor wanted to use health as grounds for taking over the individual water systems..." as well as town planning, parks, and sewers. One of the EBUC's first accomplishments was the construction in 1920 of the East Interceptor sewer from Pillette Road to Parent Avenue. Instead of eleven drains emptying raw sewage directly into the river, sewage now flowed from Ford City, Walkerville, and eastern Windsor into one outlet away from Windsor's water intake.[32]

The preeminent problem remained the quality of the water supply. In March 1920, it was agreed to refer the issue to an expert panel of three engineers. Their report recommended that water be drawn from the main channel of the Detroit River at the end of Strabane Street.[33] At that point, a new filtration plant could be built and the purified water pumped through Windsor and Walkerville's existing systems. In December 1922, the "Water Question" came to a vote with the medical and most of the business community backing a joint filtration plant. Naysayers such as ex-mayor E. Blake Winter denounced it as just another government extravagance. To the surprise and relief of many, the project passed by a mere 300 votes. The scheme would ultimately be implemented in 1925 with the construction of the filtration plant and additional pipes to carry water to Sandwich and LaSalle. The problem with tainted water that had cost so many lives since the 1880s had at last been resolved.

It would take one final tragedy to highlight the urgency of united action. In the middle of February 1924, smallpox was detected and the Medical Officer of Health, Dr. Fred Adams, began to mobilize a vaccination campaign. With one Board of Health taking the lead, free vaccinations were mandated across the Border Cities. In marked contrast to the Spanish Flu epidemic in 1918, there was a unified, coherent response to this outbreak. The entire community was vaccinated almost within hours and affected families were quarantined. As a result, what might have been a major disaster (thirty-two victims did succumb to smallpox) was controlled. Some noted that this was the result when the Border Cities acted effectively as one unit.[34]

Yet, the EBUC was constantly finding itself having to fight off the criticism of one disaffected municipality or the other. Much of the wrath against the EBUC was directed against its chief engineer, Morris Knowles. One newspaper termed Knowles, an American from Pittsburgh, a "Master Manipulator" who was an overpaid autocrat. Later analysts concluded that "The E.B.U.C. as an area wide planning agency proved quite incapable of acting as a restraining influence" on its constituent parts.[35] To its credit, the Commission had a string of notable accomplishments. Residents drew their water from one well-regulated intake which water was processed by a single filtration plant. Sewage disposition was now handled in a more responsible manner and, as a 1934 report boasted, no longer was "the whole waterfront polluted by reason of the free and unrestricted discharge of sewage."[36]

Much of this was thanks to the young chief engineer who replaced Knowles in 1921. J. Clark Keith first worked in Moose Jaw, Saskatchewan, but was lured to Windsor by the prospect of higher pay and interesting challenges. He supervised the construction of the interceptor sewer and the water intake on Strabane Street. Keith took an aggressive approach and sought to use the EBUC to achieve community results. One of his first projects was to get approval for a series of neighbourhood parks. However, it was not approved by the voters, and an outgoing Knowles noted "the feeling of depression upon [Keith's] part" but consoled him that an "enlightened public opinion" would eventually back such projects.[37]

Within Windsor, the pressures of dealing with this unprecedented growth fell on Chief Engineer, M.E. Brian. He oversaw the reconstruction of Ouellette Avenue when the streetcar tracks were doubled to enable cars to go up and down the street simultaneously. Ouellette Avenue was widened and paved, and finally took on the appearance of a proper main street. Brian's task was aided by Windsor's acquisition of an asphalt plant which enabled engineers to reface streets as required. Thanks to Brian, Windsor took on "an orderly appearance in keeping with the city's progressive era."[38] But there was a cost, and in 1924, the city spent $634,500 on sewer and roadworks. It was a significant financial burden, but to keep up with the pace of growth there seemed no other choice. In the December 1923 municipal election, E. Blake Winter ran for office on a promise that he would continue the Civic Income Tax to raise additional revenues. He lost. His opponent, Frank Mitchell, the popular sales manager at Gotfredsen's and pillar of the Chamber of Commerce, promised to get rid of the tax. Yet by 1925, even Mitchell was aware that Windsor faced a debenture debt of $10 million dollars and that "retrenchment" was a necessity. His response was to close the Howard Avenue Mission to the Poor ("Mitchell explained that the city's relief policy provided for work only") and delayed proposals for a new city hall.

Just before Christmas 1926, the Church of the Ascension on London Street was gutted by fire. The Rev. H.B. Ashby managed to save some of the vestments and communion vessels, but the building was destroyed. Windsor's grizzled Fire Chief, Clarence DeFields, described as "lean, tall and tough-fibered…the most colorful, cussingest character in town" pointed out that during the fire, his undermanned department had to depend on neighbours to carry hoses and ladders. The city had simply grown beyond the capacity of the present force to provide adequate protection. When Mitchell was replaced by Cecil Jackson as mayor in 1927, the new administration expanded the service and built a new fire hall in 1928. As well, Mayor Jackson announced bold plans to acquire the Jockey Club for a public park and to make significant street improvements.[39] These projects were welcomed at the time, but in short order the spending spree would lead to disaster.

Even if infrastructure was gradually catching up to the expanded urban requirements, the underlying problem for the Border Cities remained its division. Each municipality was competing against the other to draw in more industry, and as a result, there was a jumble of development without any plan or thought. The primary issue, the one that was so often debated but not resolved, was the failure of the border municipalities to amalgamate. In the fall of 1922, Ford City and Walkerville negotiated amalgamation, but the project floundered when neither would accept the other's name as the title of a joint municipality. In October 1926, the Chamber of Commerce advocated for a plebiscite to test whether residents of the Border Cities favoured a preliminary survey on amalgamation.[40] When this tepid proposal was put to a vote the following December, it was seen by many as a vote on amalgamation. Windsor and Ford City residents voted enthusiastically in its favour. Sandwich, and especially Walkerville, remained adamantly opposed.

The provincial government was becoming concerned and in 1928, J.A. Ellis, the Director of Municipal Affairs, was delegated to look into border affairs. He was surprised to uncover a situation in which five municipalities "are to all intents and purposes one community and one city in everything except municipal government." There were five public school boards, five separate school boards, five fire brigades, and so on. Ellis estimated that the Border Cities population at 115,000, and based on its rate of growth, it would soon be the second-largest urban centre in Ontario behind Toronto. It was absurd that the area's governance should continue to be conducted by a multitude of warring villages. "What I have in view," he concluded, "was the working out of a partnership between the five municipalities rather than a merger of them."

The response was immediate. J.H. Coburn, a Walkerville lawyer who spoke for the vast majority of the town, wrote to Ellis denouncing his proposal. It was a matter of class. Walkerville was the home to executives and managers. Being lumped in with the dross of Windsor or Ford City was simply out of the question:

> The fact of the matter is, that we regard the municipal government of Windsor, Ford City and Riverside to be far inferior to our own; and we realize, notwithstanding your attempt to give a representation to each municipality which will prevent any one dominating the others, that the amalgamated municipality could be dominated by Windsor and would get the same kind of government that Windsor has had for many years.[41]

In light of this opposition, the Province would not act and any prospect of amalgamation was quietly shelved.

Yet More Border Cities

Instead of joining together, in the early 1920s, the border community splintered into additional, independent boroughs. Moreover, these new neighbourhoods insisted on ethnic and racial separation. The only area where Walkerville could expand was to the south, and in 1920, an order was issued by the Ontario Railway and Municipal Board permitting the annexation of the lands south of Tecumseh Road and north of Grand Marais to Walkerville. In the "out-south," as its residents called it, fine new subdivisions were built. Restrictive covenants in deeds prevented sales to blacks or Jews and as a result, South Walkerville was almost exclusively a white, Anglo-Saxon enclave. In the 1920s, developers could openly boast about ethnic and racial exclusivity.[42] Typical clauses in deeds required purchasers to be of "Caucasian descent" and that occupation or ownership by persons of "Semitic, Negroid or Asian races" was forbidden. The Remington Arms company had planned for a 100-acre cartridge assembly site in Windsor's south-central area since 1913. After the war, the area became Remington Park and the northern section "Pacific Park" was developed in the mid-1920s. Ads for Pacific Park boasted that it was reserved for "English-speaking people."[43]

Even in Sandwich, which had retained some of its French heritage, the forces of Anglicization were succeeding. French children were no longer speaking their parents' language and one nationalist sadly remarked that in Sandwich's public schools "le français y est très peu enseigné" (very little French is taught there).[44] English was the town's language and there was an increasing flow of English-speakers into the community. The population in 1919 of 3,448 would almost quadruple to 11,331 by 1929. The 78 acres of the original Essex County Golf and Country Club were sold in 1928 for residential development. Sandwich's Canadian Salt plant was thriving (even if most of the salt was mined in Windsor) and additions were being made to the chemical processing facilities. Impressively, the town's rate of growth in the late 1920s was even greater than that of Walkerville, and its solicitor, John Sale, bragged that Sandwich was no longer the "Sleepy Hollow" of the border.

On the fringes of the existing urban area, new border cities were popping up. The push for development reached south far beyond the river and the tiny settlement at "Jackson's Corners" (roughly the area of Cabana and Howard Avenues) was emerging as a separate community. Originally a black settlement where refugees could easily buy or simply squat on farmlands, the area was so remote and distant from water that it was ignored by other settlers. Jackson, the original black pioneer in the area, lent his name to what was a picturesque stage-coach stop on the way between Windsor and Leamington.

By the mid-1920s, it was discovered by the newly wealthy, and land was being bought up for mansions such as those of Dr. Raymond Morand and Windsor Lumber baron, James Scofield. By November of that year, it became a police village and its original rustic name was discarded in favour of the more marketable "Roseland."[45] Roseland Golf and Country Club was laid out in 1926 by Donald Ross, the leading golf architect of the period, in the centre of the project with housing development surrounding it. Planners presumed that a golf course would spur interest in this neighbourhood so far removed from the city. Developers further economized by using black earth removed for the roadworks to build up the greens. By 1928, Gundy and Gundy real estate were ready to market the area, and the golf course became its central feature. "Roseland Park" would be a sinuous lay-out of streets bordered by high-quality houses and available only to "exclusive purchasers."

The main push in development was away from the smoky factories and farther along the Detroit River toward cleaner residential areas. To the southwest, on the southern part of "Petite Côte" the oldest European settlement in Ontario, the new municipality of LaSalle was created in 1924. The incorporating statute described it as a place suitable for "summer residences." In reality, its sole manufacturer was Hofer Brewing and LaSalle's only reason for existence seemed to be its splendid location from which to conduct bootlegging. Leading the charge for incorporation was local hotelier Vital Benoit. Benoit's Wellington House was already well connected by ferry service to Ecorse, Michigan, and much like the Trumbles, he took advantage of this facility to export alcohol. The most easterly of the Border Cities was the recently created (incorporated, 1922) town of Tecumseh. Focused on the farm lot patented to the Lesperance family, Tecumseh developed as a separate community during the war. However, it had limited connection to the other municipalities through one streetcar line, and it remained set apart.

The one area to the east that promised to become a major suburban complex was (as it was called by statute) "River Side." Dissatisfied with the Township of Sandwich East's indifference to the infrastructure needs of a residential population, the area seceded and was incorporated in 1921. The new town's distance from industry ("Riverside Ozone Has No Smoke Zone," developers bragged) became its main selling point. Yet, for many years Riverside remained a distinctly French enclave. The founding families, the Janisses, Reaumes, and Baillargeons still worked their narrow farms. Early in the 20th century, Joseph Janisse recalled going back into the rear bush to clear trees where "he could remember well hearing the wolves howling." Local characters abounded, such as Paul Le Duc, a massive hunter and farmer, who ran the dock at what is now the foot of Reedmere Road and provided wood to the cross-river ferries.

"Noble Beasts" Paul Le Duc of Riverside and dog Gordie circa 1933; The Le Duc grist mill, that stood at the end of Reedmere Road.

Keeping up with the traditional ways, Le Duc also operated an old grist mill on the river and farmers still stopped by to gossip as their grain was ground into flour. William St. Louis, the first mayor and the donor of land for St. Rose Catholic Church, would see Riverside's population grow from 1,500 to 5,000 by 1930. But times were changing, and after William's death, the St. Louis homestead was sold off and divided into building lots. While several streets were built in the 1920s, development followed a stately pace. As one resident Evelyn McLean recalled, even by the 1940s, there were few big houses along Riverside Drive and many vacant spaces between them. There was so much riverfront left that "Everybody swam in the river, we would wait for one of the big side-wheelers of the D&C [Detroit and Cleveland Steamship Lines] to go past and then body surf in on the rollers… it was the most exciting thing then to do in little Riverside."[46]

Flash of Colour, Glimpse of Ankle

The 1920s began in Windsor in a blaze of light and colour. Loew's Theatre opened on December 31, 1920, and with its vast art nouveau interior and magnificent chandelier, it was the most splendid display the city had ever seen. However, it was not a business success and in 1923, it was taken over by Simon

Interior of the Tivoli Theatre, circa 1930s.

Meretsky and Ed Glasscoe and renamed "The Capitol." In 1920, Meretsky also opened the Walkerville Theatre (after 1930, the Tivoli) on Wyandotte Street. Straddling the border between Windsor and Walkerville, this new show house could seat over 1,000 patrons and featured a technical marvel, a combined heating and cooling system.[47] No longer did residents have to go to Detroit to see the latest films. The public's appetite for entertainment was proof that they had money to spend and leisure time to enjoy it. The same applied to sports.

It was a youthful population and the area was sports mad. In 1922, teams from Windsor Collegiate won the western Ontario championships in basketball and soccer. There were amateur teams in abundance and the Walkerville "Chicks" baseball team frequently led the local league. In 1926, the Chicks gained (according to the *Star*'s sports page) "lasting fame" by not only winning the local championship, but marching through the playoffs until they faced the Toronto Oslers in the provincial semi-finals. At the opening game of their series played at Stodgell Park (the only border park other than the Detroit Tigers' Navin Field to be fenced in), one overzealous fan entered the field with a pig and a sign urging locals to "Root Against Hogtown." It was not enough, and the Chicks were overmatched by the Toronto club.

While baseball was the preeminent game on the border, golf was gaining in popularity. A municipal golf course was laid out at the Devonshire Race Track in 1924, and for the first time, people of modest means were able to play a round. Lacrosse and even cricket were still played, but one sport in

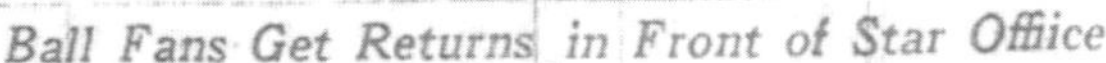

Fans gather to listen to the Star broadcast of the Walkerville Chicks semifinal game against Toronto, Border Cities Star, October 4, 1926.

particular was rapidly gaining new fans. Hockey made a dramatic comeback in the Border Cities and the Assumption College club, as well as the Windsor Monarchs, played in area leagues. The sport's popularity was enhanced when the Border Cities Arena was completed in November 1925. This solid brick structure (soon nicknamed "The Barn") was extolled by an adoring reporter as "a vast monument of concrete and steel dedicated to the greatest athletic pastime in the captivity of sportdom." To have such a major facility, with artificial ice and seating for 6,200 fans was uncommon in the 1920s, and a tangible sign of the area's wealth.

The arena was also fortunate to have Percy Le Sueur, one of the canniest men in early hockey, as its first manager. A former star goalie for Smith's Falls, he had played for that team in the Stanley Cup challenge of 1906. With his extensive contacts, Le Sueur arranged for some of the premier teams of the day to play at the Border Cities Arena. In late November 1925, Le Sueur organized a match between the Victoria Cougars, the reigning Stanley Cup champions, and the New York Americans of the NHL. An overcapacity crowd of 7,000 jammed the arena and 3,000 huddled outside as two of the best hockey clubs battled it out that night. It was a great spectacle, and the fans clearly wanted more. Having the Cougars visit the Border Cities was no coincidence, for Le Sueur was acting for Detroit interests in getting an NHL franchise. Having a quality team at hand was crucial, and Le Sueur played a key role in buying the Victoria franchise which became Detroit's entry into major league hockey in 1926.[48] Detroit had no arena so the Cougars, (to be renamed the Falcons and in 1932, the Red Wings) would play their first season in Windsor. Capacity crowds filled the arena to watch the finest players in the world faceoff against each other. Local pride was reserved for the Windsor Hornets (who had a far better winning record than the Cougars) of the Canadian Hockey League.

The Charleston and Starbeams

After the trauma of the war years, society was moving away from its Victorian moorings into fresh new waters. Young girls with bobbed hair discarded their corsets and were smoking in public. For the first time, men were putting their ungloved hands on the bare skin of dancing partners in backless dresses. When the Masonic Temple opened in February 1920, it became the site for dancing for years to come. At the opening, Morgan's orchestra played syncopated steps, interspersed with more stately quadrilles and waltzes. Public dancing was increasingly the way in which young people could socialize apart from supervision by their families. On occasion, this "so-called 'tough' dancing involved close body contact, a fast pace, and various shakes and shimmies that strongly hinted at sexual intercourse."[49] Dance halls such as the Masonic Temple became the place where working-class women could exercise some control over their social lives with young men. As historian Craig Heron observed, it was the female equivalent of the "male-dominated space, the saloon."

In September 1925, the latest dance craze, the "Charleston," hit Windsor. E.J. Zimmerman promised that while his dance school would teach this new

Windsor quartet tries out 'The Charleston' while an amused crowd looks on, Border Cities Star, September 1925.

step, all "immoral phases" would be omitted. He was only echoing the senior generation who thought that perhaps the Twenties were a bit too roaring. Once he assumed office in January 1924, Mayor Frank Mitchell made it clear that Windsor's prime problem was the "pool rooms and gambling places." He further warned that "many of our young ladies frequent dance halls and associate with men of questionable reputation." One evening in late 1924, Mayor Mitchell personally apprehended a group of teenage boys and girls engaged in a "nude bathing revel." After investigating accusations of beachfront liaisons and "petting parties," Mitchell drove the girls back home where they were "Questioned by the mayor… the girls revealed a condition of affairs that requires a rigid probe, the mayor said."[50]

Good times meant that a rising middle class was beginning to demand quality. Drawn by the prospects of growth, an experienced retailer, Clarence H. Smith, came to Windsor in 1914. His 1920 expansion on Ouellette Avenue was a magnificent limestone facade with an interior of bevelled glass, walnut panelling and brass fittings. It was an ambience that drew in well-heeled consumers, offering them styles not usually available. In 1926, C.H. Smith expanded again and offered even more luxuries including a beauty parlour where seven male barbers who were "adept in the art of 'bobbing' and 'shingling' are in attendance."[51]

However, for many women, especially those of the upper class, morals and society had not appreciably changed. The social columns of the *Star* were filled with the society weddings of the season where the "smartest and prettiest" brides vied for the most attention. One of the brightest younger stars was Camilla Stodgell, who had entertained the Prince of Wales during his Windsor visit on her harp, and who had danced with Henry Ford's son, Edsel. Her marriage to John Wigle was the social event of 1923, and united two of the most prominent families of the border. Further sophistication was provided in 1919 by the organization of the Border Cities Symphony Orchestra under the baton of Henry McCaw. The symphony became a cause of the wealthy, and Mrs. A.D. Bowlby, the wife of the area's leading car dealer, was a leading symphony officer. Urbane residents also gravitated to the "Arts and Letters" club of Walkerville which provided showings of modern art, and readings from prominent writers. The smart set frequently met at the Walkerville Boat Club. Since its opening in 1909, the Club (located just to the west of Strabane Avenue in Ford City, but still preferring the panache of the Walkerville name) had become a favoured social spot. Crowds of the well-to-do packed the verandahs which opened onto the river to watch competitive rowing or sail racing. In 1925, for the first time, women abandoned the Club's bridge tables and took an active part in the annual regatta.[52]

The working-class had much more limited and dangerous access to the Detroit River. The best they could hope for during the summer was a dip in the small public beach at the foot of Bridge Avenue. Not only was the water highly polluted, there was a thick growth of weeds that entangled swimmers, and a few feet from shore there was a sudden drop-off into deep waters. In 1920, a returned soldier drowned, and an enraged resident pointed out that the soldier was the eighth person in the last eight years to drown at the beach. The resident also pointed out that the bathhouse offered no privacy, and that after dark the place was "worse than a brothel."[53] City aldermen shrugged, and concluded that they had to provide some place for youngsters to swim "and that this is the only available spot. All other points along the river are taken up by the railways and the ferry company." If the classes were unfairly divided according to their recreational choices along the river, there was a good deal of mixing at the one pastime that captivated all strata of society. Both high and low were enthralled by the horse races.

Camilla Stodgell and John Wigle on their wedding day, 1923.

During the horse racing season, everyone with the price of admission could attend the meets. For those with more funds at their disposal, an appearance at the Jockey Clubhouse was a must. The *Star* described the clubhouse as "thronged with smartly gowned women, affording a veritable fashion parade." During the two weeks of the summer racing season, the Women's page and the Sports section of the newspaper almost melded together. In 1926, a throng of 16,000 "turf followers" watched the champion "King Nadi" win the Frontier Handicap.[54] As the punters surged near the track, the clubhouse was filled with demure society ladies from both sides of the border. To be described in the next day's newspaper as wearing a fine French crepe scarf could be the supreme moment for any Border Cities matron. Whichever horse won the race was, to the ladies, decidedly irrelevant.

For women at the other end of the class spectrum, life remained far less agreeable. Women still worked on the bottling line at the Hiram Walker distillery,

A postcard from Border Cities Bathing Beach, looking north towards Detroit, circa 1924.

and others in the sub-assembly of auto parts or manufacturing spark plugs at the Champion plant. But opportunities were limited. Desperate women would do whatever it took to survive, and sometimes that meant participating in the latest craze. In 1928, the Windsor Arena, as it was now called, hosted a marathon dancing competition where exhausted couples clutched each other and tottered around a dance floor. Respectable society was appalled, and Rev. J.W. Magwood of Lincoln Road United Church demanded that this "revolting" display be outlawed. It was little noted at the time that several of the women participants were trained secretaries who took part as the only way to make a little money. One of the dancers, Mary Young, was described by her mother as "an expert typist and stenographer, but although she offered to work for $5 a week no one would give her a job."

Magistrate W.E. Gundy was shocked to discover that a few women had come to play a leading role in running "blind pigs," the unlicensed taverns that spawned around factory gates. Liquor laws strictly limited hours of operation and licensed premises were frequently closed when men coming off shifts at the factories were looking for a drink and something to eat. Women were competent at running small places where they could get both. However, to Gundy it was a great evil and it was a disgrace for women to be profiting from bootlegging.[55] A typical operator was a widowed mother, Mary Ostopovitch, who used the earnings from her blind pig to raise three children. The magistrate said that he had "no alternative" but to give her a month in jail. But whether he liked it or not, times were changing. A columnist for the *Star*, R.M. Harrison, wrote irreverent articles in his *Starbeams* column in which a tolerance of liquor, and an open approach to sex, were accepted. A whisky drinking, cigar smoking *bon vivant* Harrison was far more in touch with the changing times than those magistrates and matrons who still dominated Border Cities' respectable society.

"A Little Kingdom of Our Own"

The Border Cities underwent an astounding transformation during the Twenties. Starting as an insignificant, semi-rural community, it emerged as one of Canada's largest urban centres with a technological capacity as sophisticated as anywhere else in the industrialized world. Automotive production had been soaring in the Border Cities since the brief setback of 1921–1922, and the demand for workers was relentless. In 1923 alone, Windsor's population increased by twelve percent. It was an unprecedented expansion, and would be sustained throughout the decade.

The use of electricity was a strong indicator of the rate of growth. Windsor's modest consumption of hydropower in the war years changed markedly in the 1920s. The huge increase in electricity use peaked in 1929 (Appendix C) at the same time that population growth also reached its zenith. This was not surprising as (thanks to Sir Adam Beck) the availability of cheap hydro power encouraged industry to expand. The average cost of electricity to factories was 1.4 cent per kilowatt hour, a figure which "agreeably surprised" American manufacturers.[56] In comparison to Windsor, Walkerville did not significantly increase its power usage during the 1920s, nor did its population experience anything like Windsor's growth. It was apparent that the town's size limited its potential. On the other hand, Ford City (after 1929, the city of East Windsor) did have the space available and both its population and power usage doubled between 1923 and 1929. By the end of the decade, East Windsor's population of 16,203 significantly exceeded Walkerville's.

Starbeams

Fun for the Kiddies!

THIS, of course you know, is a back view of Miss Sadie Shortskirts in her ½-piece bathing suit. But what about a front view? Ah, that's the game.

Gather around Uncle Ignatz's knee, children, and you shall hear. In order to obtain a front view of Sadie, simply turn to The Third Page. Having mastered this simple movement, hold The Third Page up to a strong light—the headlight on a Michigan Central locomotive will do. And there you will have a front view of Sadie! Such fun!

If the light you use will not shine through the paper, wet the paper slightly with Papa's gin. Papa won't care.

Run home and try it now, children. After you have got the hang of it, surprise Papa with this fascinating new game. Once he sees how simple it is he may decide not to go out to the "board of directors' meeting" this evening.

* * *

R.M. Harrison's unconventional wit on display in this Starbeams column from 1926.

In 1900, Windsor was an insignificant city of 12,000. Thirty years later, the Border Cities, with Windsor at its core, was the centre of an urban complex of 102,000 people, and the fastest-growing municipality in Canada. The Border Cities had far outstripped London in population, and had emerged as the fourth-largest urban complex in Ontario. It was now challenging Hamilton and Ottawa to become Ontario's leading municipality, second only to Toronto. This was due in large part to its favoured position, with access to major sea and rail transportation routes, and vast quantities of low-cost power. The labour force was largely quiescent, and additional workers were readily available from other parts of Canada and Europe. It also had a corps of established industries, especially in metal fabrication, which would supplement the emerging auto giants. But other Ontario centres, notably Hamilton and Toronto, also had many of these features. Why Windsor?

The answer was clearly in its relationship with Detroit. The Border Cities were an adjunct to what was not only the fastest-growing industrial area in the United States, but a phenomenon the world had never seen before. What had been a moderately prosperous city in 1900 (285,000 people, 13th in size in the U.S.) exploded into a major metropolis of over a million by 1920. By 1930, Detroit's one and a half million people would make it the fourth-largest city in the United States. The wealth it generated was also phenomenal. In 1912, Ford made a profit of $13.5 million and in 1916, $57 million. Detroit had become an industrial dynamo where huge, integrated assemblies mass-produced consumer products. The scale and efficiency of these new assembly processes had never been dreamed of at the turn of the century. Henry Ford had created an industrial complex on the River Rouge near Detroit that consumed raw materials at one end, and turned out automobiles at the other. River Rouge was unprecedented, an entire conglomeration of coal processors, foundries, machining plants, and electrical power facilities. By 1926, it had 75,000 employees working in 93 buildings and producing 4,000 cars a day.[57] Nothing in the Border Cities, nothing in the world, could compare with this. This mass of production needed consumers, and there was bound to be spillover as American factories used the border area as their base to mass-produce for Canada and the British Empire, thereby avoiding tariffs and gaining access to a lucrative market.

Testifying before the Dominion Tariff Commission in 1920, the heads of Studebaker, Fisher Body, Parke-Davis, and Canadian Products (General Motors) of Canada insisted that tariffs were essential to their industries, and that without them, the parent company would instantly relocate all production to the United States. Backing them up was the Chamber of Commerce's spokesman, F. Maclure Sclanders, who told the committee that there was a definite cause and effect between the tariff and the border's remarkable growth. It was "to protection we therefore owe all the wonderful prosperity and general expansion." Sclanders instructed the commission that the area had developed its own distinct relationship between parent and branch plants. "It would almost seem that we are here in a little kingdom of our own and to some extent apart from the outer world."[58] When the restrictive American immigration law of 1924 threatened to end the free flow of workers and managers, the Detroit Board of Commerce lobbied Washington to exempt the Detroit-Windsor area as:

> The business men of Detroit consider the border as merely an imaginary line. Because they are so closely related to the business life of Canada, they would hesitate to see anything… that would interfere with free and uninterrupted flow of commerce and labor between the two countries.[59]

By the end of the 1920s, Americans owned 136 of the 260 companies located in the Border Cities. The protectionist policies initiated in 1879 by Sir John A. Macdonald were still seen by many as essential to Windsor's industrial development.

The tariff barriers that protected industry also raised prices, and were a divisive political factor. In 1925, the Liberal government of Mackenzie King considered lowering tariffs to stimulate trade and reduce consumer costs. King wished to appease western Canadians who were upset that the cost of vehicles was artificially high to protect Ontario industries. Dr. Raymond Morand, the Conservative candidate in Essex-East (which included Ford City and Walkerville), warned that King's policies "would result in all factories in the Border Cities being closed."[60] While Morand was narrowly elected, the Liberals won the country, and one of their first steps in 1926 was to reduce the auto tariff from 35 to 20 percent for all cars under $1,200. As warned, after the tariff changes, Ford of Canada's market position deteriorated from 43.4 percent in 1920-26 to 23.2 percent for the remainder of the decade.[61]

One of the few positives to the local economy was tourism. In the auto age, more and more Americans were exploring by car, and one of the most interesting, unexplored territories was Canada. The Chamber of Commerce was aware of the possibilities, and brochures extolling Essex County were circulated in Michigan. On the 4th of July weekend of 1926, it was estimated that a record 75,000 Americans crossed the border to holiday in Canada. But the area fell victim to its own popularity, and the outdated ferry system was pressured beyond its capacity. At weekend's end, 500 American vehicles were stranded on the Windsor side when the ferries stopped running. The Detroit-Windsor region was operating economically and socially almost as one. But it would take imaginative engineering solutions to overcome the physical barrier of the river, and truly unite the border region.

Chapter Six
Bridged And Tunnelled
1927–1929

The Border Cities would never boast an Empire State Building nor an Eiffel Tower. Its two monuments would be equally impressive works of engineering, but they would be eminently practical, and one would be almost hidden from view.

Stranding hundreds of autos on the Canadian side was only one instance of the inadequacy of the ferry system. While the Michigan Central had shown since 1910 that the river could be tunnelled, this facility only benefited rail traffic. As the new automobile capital of the world, it seemed that the Windsor- Detroit area should take the lead in providing rapid car transit across the border. In 1919, Charles Evan Fowler, an American bridge designer with several successful projects behind him, stepped forward. Together with another engineer, Gustav Lindenthal, Fowler proposed a massive bridge supported by two huge towers that combined railway and vehicular traffic on two levels. Neither of them could

Postcard showing the proposed bridge design by Charles Fowler, circa 1923.

envisage a structure without 19th century railway and streetcar features. The cost was enormous, and ultimately Fowler was unable to finance the scheme.[1]

Still, the concept was sound and if successful, a bridge could serve a growing volume of traffic. Detroit businessman James Austin took over the project at the end of 1923, and met with officials of McClintic-Marshall, one of America's premier steel fabricators. They were excited, and introduced Austin to the man who would become the key behind the Ambassador Bridge's creation, New York financier, Joseph A. Bower. Bower had previously lived in the Detroit area for twenty years, and he seized on building a cross-border bridge with a passion. From the start, he eliminated any rails or streetcars and proceeded with an exclusively vehicular structure. Financing became the principal hurdle, and beyond his connections with New York capitalists, Bower looked for government support. Detroit and Michigan made it clear that they would not contribute, so together with Canadian Transit Company (the corporate entity for the Canadian side), leading corporate lawyer Charles McTague, and Ford's Wallace Campbell, Bower began to work the political process to raise a five-million-dollar guaranty in Canada. One of his challenges was to win the support of Windsor's mayor, Frank Mitchell. Mitchell had become popular by being the gadfly of public services such as the ferry, and he was initially opposed to a privately owned bridge until he realized that any publicly funded bridge would require an enormous tax hike. The various councils of the Border Cities also voted in favour of the project, and it was approved by plebiscite. Despite this support, neither the provincial nor the federal governments would guaranty bonds for a privately owned bridge. Bower forged on anyway, and in March 1927, he announced that his consortium would proceed with construction without government aid.

The bridge's design had to satisfy a number of factors. It would be located at the narrowest part of the Detroit River connecting the town of Sandwich to 19th Street in Detroit. The bridge would be of suspension design and supported by cables from two main towers. The Lake Carriers Association was concerned that it might impede shipping, and an officer of the U.S. War Department eventually decided that the height of the bridge at its centre had to be 152 feet with 135 feet at the harbour line. This ensured that the structure would have the graceful arch that became its hallmark. Leon Moisseiff, one of the most distinguished bridge engineers of the day, did the mathematics and calculated the stresses and loads the cables would have to bear. By using high-strength silicon steel, Moisseiff gave the bridge a much more slender appearance, while still building in ample strength. Overhead bracing would be eliminated so motorists could drive much like on an open road.

Before going up, the bridge had to go down. On Thursday, September 22, 1927, work began on the Sandwich shore for the main pier. Concrete caissons were sunk below the river 250 feet from the shore until they reached bedrock. "Sandhogs" working below the river faced the dangers of depressurization and only a crude repressurization chamber reduced the dangers. No men died from the "bends," but two were killed in accidents. Once the piers were completed, the towers rose and steel cables could be strung across the river. Galvanized wire was spun out and compacted into the two main cables that supported the roadway. Much like a giant knitting project, wire was passed back and forth across the river until the strands could be collected and compressed. Bower was always on the lookout for ways to promote the works, and on September 15, 1928, James Austin's sixteen-year-old daughter Helen braved the footbridge between the main towers to become the first woman to walk from Detroit to the Canadian shore. By April 1928, construction had reached the stage that the bridge needed a name. Bower rejected the prosaic "Detroit-Windsor International Bridge" and decided on "Ambassador Bridge" as he later explained, "I thought of the bridge as an ambassador between the two countries, so that's what I called it."

Helen Austin, the first woman to walk the Ambassador Bridge, 1928.

Tunnelled

When Fr. Louis Hennepin first navigated and described the Detroit River in 1679, the waterway was in its natural state, the geological result of the previous Ice Age. There were shoals, islands, and sandbars that impeded the passage of large vessels. By the early 20th century, the strait was being tamed and reshaped for the smooth flow of commerce. Built between 1907 and 1912, the Livingstone Channel eliminated treacherous crossings downriver and provided safe and efficient passage for freighters. Windsor's first Mayor, Oscar Fleming, spent the early decades of the 1900s looking after his business interests. In 1919, he reinvented himself as an advocate for the deepening of the St. Lawrence waterway to provide ocean-going ships with access to Great Lakes ports. That same year, he instigated a conference on the issue in Windsor and the result was the creation of the Canadian Deep Waterways and Power Association. The Association proposed a massive scheme to dredge the seaway, eliminate the rapids that blocked shipping, and harness the waterway for hydroelectric power.[2] While it would take several more decades for this project to proceed, what was technologically feasible in 1927 was a vehicular tunnel under the Detroit River. The driving force for this tunnel would come from an unexpected source.

Salvation Army Captain Fred Martin had spearheaded the drive to finance and build Grace Hospital on London Street, and this success gave him an appetite for greater schemes. Even though he did not have an engineering background, Martin was convinced that a vehicular tunnel could be laid under the river to connect the downtowns of Windsor and Detroit. He took leave from the Salvation Army and began to court partners in Toronto. On some of these business trips, he was reportedly so short of funds that sometimes he slept in his car. Two powerful allies joined him. F.G. Engholm, a prominent engineer, drew up plans for two tubes, one for vehicles and another for an electric subway, and lawyer Charles Miller worked on getting a charter and municipal approval. It was left to Martin to plead his case before a group of New York bankers on December 22, 1926.[3] He convinced Chase National and several Chicago banks to supply the capital. It was a worthwhile risk, for potential revenues were substantial, and the recently completed Holland Tunnel under the Hudson River had shown the

A sand hog working on the Detroit-Windsor tunnel, circa 1928.

project's feasibility. Parsons, Klapp, Brinckerhoff, and Douglass, perhaps the premier tunnel engineering firm in America, would head up the construction. The second tube for streetcars was dropped and only one tube for cars would be built.

The first step was dredging, and in the summer of 1928, huge machines dug an enormous trench on the river bottom for the tunnel tube. The construction of the tunnel was proof that the Border Cities made things. The nine steel sections that made up the underwater tube portion of the tunnel would be fabricated only a short distance away from the tunnel site at Ojibway by the Canadian Bridge Company. On the Detroit side, a giant shield backed by hydraulic rams was moved into position to eat through the earth and excavate the Detroit connection to the tube. As the shield moved forward, the spoil it generated had to be rapidly removed by hand. "Sandhogs," working under enormous pressure, shoveled the earth back from the excavating machine. It was exhausting, nerve-wracking work that advanced until the connection was made to the underwater tubes. On the Canadian side, the tunnel started at the site of St. Mary's Academy. According to contract, this venerable institution could remain until the end of the school year of 1929 when the Sisters of the Holy Names would have to relocate to a new site.

On the morning of December 21, 1928, diver Louis Florent was walking along the bottom of the Detroit River trying to solve what had become a major delay in the tunnel project. The first of the steel tubes, 500 tons of metal, had tumbled off its launching ways at Ojibway and become stuck on the river bed. Florent reported on how the fins surrounding the tube had become caught in the launch ways. The obstructions were cleared, the tube refloated, and the next day it was dropped into the correct position and the cement covering poured around it.[4] Throughout the winter, ice permitting, the tube at the bottom of the river began to take shape.

Taking Off

As a direct result of the prospects created by the bridge and tunnel, the lands south of Windsor were being groomed for development. The Detroit realty firms Kinsey-Doyle and Allan S. McNeil had already bought up hundreds of acres of farms in Sandwich West Township. They felt that the rapid progress of the bridge "coupled with the beginning of construction work for the Windsor-Detroit tunnel have given the necessary impetus on which to launch their activity." The focal point of their development in rural South Windsor (elegantly named "Windsor Manor") would be the new St. Mary's Academy. This splendid, Gothic-styled structure would be surrounded by handsome houses for the well-to-do.[5] It was the automobile that made this dispersed form of residential development possible. Developers even hoped to induce Detroiters to move to the district, which would be only minutes away from the cross-river transportation routes. Internal combustion engines were revolutionizing how cities were laid out, enabling commuters to go from door to door far beyond the confines of fixed streetcar routes to live in spacious areas far removed from the blight of factories.[6]

Despite the impact of automobiles, not to mention the presence of massive auto factories in their cities, authorities persisted in the belief that existing technologies would continue into the distant future. Windsor's first planning report, issued in 1929 by renowned urban planner Thomas Adams, proposed the extension of street railways for "there is no indication that the streetcar will ever be displaced by the motor bus for local street transportation." It was also assumed that county residents would never rely on cars or trucks for transport. In 1928, the municipalities of Essex County banded together to buy the cross-county electric railway, the WE & LS system. Its superintendent promised that "the people will never regret their decision."[7]

However, the onslaught of new technologies could not be avoided. On a sunny Saturday afternoon, September 8, 1928, a crowd of about 2,000 gathered near Windsor's new airport to see eight airplanes lift into the air and race around Essex County. Only seventeen years previously, in 1911, an airplane had first flown over Windsor. Now, crowds of ordinary people jammed the airport and jostled for rides on the blimp, the "Puritan." The border was machine-mad and aeronautics was the latest sensation to join fast cars as a local passion. Ever since the founding of the Border Aero Club in 1920, a nucleus of flying enthusiasts sought to bring flight to the border. Lindbergh's daring crossing of the Atlantic sparked further interest, and the Chamber of Commerce sponsored the "Royal Windsor" to fly to the sister city of Windsor, England. Even though it never completed the trip, the stunt stirred further interest in aviation. The problem in building a flying facility near Windsor lay in the increasing price of land caused by speculation and the divided political interests of the municipalities. The answer came from the Walker family. Edward and Hiram H. Walker had retained much of their father's farmlands that lay to the south of the urban area and they offered to lease a portion of it for minimal rent and contribute $10,000 for a hangar. In recognition of their contribution, the facility was known as the "Walker Airport."[8]

In addition to the airport, the Walker family also made another major contribution to the community in the 1920s. The Medical Officer of Health, Dr. Fred Adams, had exposed the glaring inadequacy of hospital facilities. While the provincial standard was six beds per thousand citizens, and most Ontario municipalities exceeded this level, the Border Cities rate was 2.5 beds per

Postcard showing Walker Airport, circa 1930.

thousand. In 1920, the National Council of Women took up this cause, and found a patron in J. Harrington Walker who left a bequest of $25,000 toward a new hospital. The Walker distillery added a further $75,000. In 1924, the Walkers pledged their ongoing support on the condition that the hospital serve the entire district, and that an equal amount be raised by public subscription.[9] Oscar E. Fleming stepped forward yet again to head the fundraising, and his business skills and contacts were invaluable in raising a further $140,000. When the cornerstone was laid in March 1927, the Walkers had contributed half the cost of the hospital and the municipalities and public the remainder. Unlike its predecessors, Metropolitan General Hospital was a product of the modern age. It had no religious affiliation, and it provided the first isolation unit for infectious diseases. As further proof that it was a municipal institution, it would be under the control of J. Clark Keith of the EBUC.

A major new institution such as Metropolitan Hospital was a mark of the growing maturity of the Border Cities. But it had not been a smooth ride. In 1927, the area experienced mass unemployment when Ford retooled from the Model T to the Model A. Layoffs reduced the total industrial workforce to 12,744, one of its lowest levels. However, by the spring of 1928, 6,500 men were back producing 300 Ford vehicles a day. By the end of May, the layoffs were over and the total Border Cities workforce of 20,000 was the highest on record. While Ford still dominated the manufacturing scene, Chrysler now had 1,200 workers making 140 cars a day, General Motors had 575 workers, and Gotfredson 325. Even while so many worked in the factories, it was the underground economy that caught the public's attention. Because of its unique location, the Border Cities remained the focus of the international uproar over the illicit cross-border liquor trade.

Metropolitan General Hospital, circa 1930.

Gentlemen Rum-runners

"Canada is the enemy" proclaimed the U.S. prohibition commissioner in 1929, "of the social and economic benefits which prohibition has brought to this country." And the enemy's main front was the Detroit-Windsor border, which was the principal entry point for alcohol into the American heartland.[10] Since the haphazard days of cab driver Cecil Smith, rum-running had moved on to become a large-scale, more industrial operation, and two Windsor men, whose careers followed strikingly similar patterns, would characterize the new business age.

Harry Low was born in Ottawa, but came to Windsor as a young man to work as a toolmaker. Moving on to run a pool hall, Low was exposed to criminal circles, and like many others, he was taken in by the profits to be had in the liquor trade. But smuggling one or two bottles in a prosthetic leg was not his style, and he invested in a speedboat to export cases of whisky from Windsor's export docks to Michigan. In due course, he bought two ships, the *Vedas* (a former World War I minesweeper) and the *Geronimo* to handle large shipments. By the early 1920s, his export firm of Low, Leon and Burns all but controlled liquor export on the Windsor waterfront. The former toolmaker's web expanded to include Montreal connections and a vice-presidency in Carling Breweries. On rare occasions, the public caught a glimpse of Harry Low's operations. The 1927 Royal Commission on Customs and Excise investigations found that Low possessed export seals that enabled him to seal his own cargoes. Shiploads full of Carling Beer would be labelled "milk" or "canned goods" and leave Windsor docks for distant ports and return in less than a day. The Royal Commission exposed only a portion of the corruption on the Windsor export docks. William

Ford Model A parked behind the Harry Low house, 1929.

Egan, a former lawyer, was the "boss" of the riverfront who organized the bribes and illegal shipments. When one customs officer, L.J. Lafferty, refused to take bribes or give out seals, Egan "approached him to accept what was going on... that there was nothing wrong in the practice." The resulting profits were enormous and they demanded display. Harry Low built a mansion in Walkerville that became a local landmark and the symbol of his wealth.[11]

Much like Harry Low, Jim Cooper came from out of town (London) and also started out in a menial position; in his case, working for the railways. Around 1910, he moved to Detroit and operated several saloons until Prohibition shut them down. But if one door closed another opened, and Cooper became a Detroit agent for Hiram Walker distillery. The law in the early 1920s permitted Ontario residents to order liquor from another jurisdiction, so as Walker's agent, Cooper "simply walked into his Detroit office in the morning, picked up the Ontario orders and cheques on his desk, and came back across the river to leave them at the distillery. The firm would then make deliveries in Ontario..." It was easy, lucrative, and even legal. When this loophole was shut down, Cooper broadened his export business into less legal areas. Much like Low, he had a huge interest in Windsor's export docks and the easily bribed customs officials who ran it. As the Royal Commission would show, Cooper had freighters taking huge shipments of liquor to Michigan. Walker's distillery was quite aware that Cooper was falsifying bills of lading, but they made no inquiries.

Much like Harry Low, Cooper appreciated that great wealth deserved to be displayed, and his 1924 Walkerville mansion, "Cooper's Court," was one of the grandest to date. It was lavish, took up an entire block and featured a huge organ. Despite his occupation, Cooper and his wife were prominent in society, and in 1926, they entertained British statesman Sir William Glyn-Jones and Lady Jones at Beach Grove Country Club. Moreover, his bootlegging fortune enabled Cooper to indulge in his main passion: farming. He bought up several hundred acres in Essex and Kent, and pioneered deep plowing methods as well as the use of tiles to drain fields. But both Jim Cooper and Harry Low were products of the Prohibition era, and neither of them would survive it. Although he did not lose his money in the stock market crash, Cooper lost his health, and on a trip to Europe in 1931, he went missing overboard. The cause of his death was never confirmed.[12] Harry Low's fortune dissipated during the 1930s in a series of legal actions. In 1939, he was wanted under a US indictment and skipped back to Canada. Sneaking back into Detroit, he returned to tool making until he was caught and deported in 1954. He died in Windsor the following year.

Starting from the same level as Low and Cooper, Harry Hatch and his brother Herb got into the bootlegging business in the Belleville area by buying speedboats to carry illicit cargoes. "Hatch's Navy" became famous and gave him the capital to buy the Toronto firm of Gooderham & Worts in 1923. In early 1927, the Walker family sold their interests to Hatch and their distillery passed into the hands of this former bootlegger, now a corporate mogul. It was the end of a dynasty, but Hatch was a capable businessman who would see that the firm would emerge even more powerful once Prohibition came to an end.[13]

In the meantime, the violence attributed to the liquor trade grew. Under diplomatic pressure, the Canadian government began to assist US authorities in curbing liquor smuggling. In the summer of 1926, a detachment of RCMP officers swept down on the Detroit River border and effectively took over the customs docks. While exporters could still load shipments to the US, they could only leave during daylight, and after the Mounties had alerted the American Coast Guard. Beer exports, which had previously totalled 2,000 cases a night, trickled to practically nothing. During the summer of 1929, a

"Cooper's Court," Jim Cooper's mansion in Walkerville, 1925.

small naval war was being fought across the river where American excise craft, guns blazing, pursued their quarry into Canadian waters. The wounded were treated at Hôtel-Dieu and fresh rum-runners took their place.[14] New breweries sprouted up, including the Riverside Brewery, located far from other producers but directly on the riverfront close to its intended market. Riverside Brewery was controlled by Detroiter Joe Moceri whose "River Gang" was supplying beer to Detroit's east side. When Moceri was implicated in the attempted assassination of Detroit Police Inspector Henry Garvin in 1929, and Moceri henchman Roy Pascuzzi (the treasurer of Riverside Brewing) was indicted by a federal grand jury, the gang wars that marked the Prohibition era had come uncomfortably close to the Border Cities. After being implicated in the murder of a Detroit policeman, Thomas Licavoli, the brother of mob boss Peter Licavoli, was found hiding in the Prince Edward Hotel. The rest of Canada was beginning to wonder at the violence that pervaded the frontier and *Maclean's Magazine* attributed it to spillover from the "overcrowded, cosmopolitan metropolis of Detroit."[15]

On a less-threatening level, many women entered the bootlegging industry simply to survive. Bertha Thomas, an enterprising widow from Detroit, was a prime example. Her Edgewater Thomas Inn, a roadhouse to the east of Windsor, became popular among Detroiters and was celebrated both for its "shore dinners," hot jazz, and obliviousness to the liquor regulations. Her place was honeycombed with secret places or "hides" where liquor was stashed. When discovered by the police, she explained that the hides were merely places where she chilled her private stock. Although she was frequently before the magistrates, the flamboyant Bertha Thomas stayed in business until the 1950s and amassed a fortune, much of which she spent to help the unfortunate. She was a fixture at Sunday Mass at St. Rose de Lima Church in Riverside where she appeared in "fox furs, lots of rouge, lots of gorgeous blonde hair, and when the collection plate was passed, she would drop all her silver dollars from great heights."[16]

In the years following Babe Trumbell's killing, the people of the border had become even more incorrigible in their drinking habits. In the provincial election of 1923, Windsor returned an avid anti-temperance Conservative, Frank Wilson. Speaking from the balcony of the *Star* building on election night, in the pre-television era, thousands gathered at the newspaper's office to watch the election returns, Wilson proclaimed that his triumph was "a repudiation of the iniquitous clauses in the Ontario Temperance Act." It was a law that was certainly ignored by most. A police crackdown in 1924 revealed that at least one hundred blind pigs served liquor at all hours in unlicensed premises. The response of Conservative premier Howard Ferguson in May 1925 was a halfway measure to license the sale of 4.4 percent beer. On May 21, "Fergy's

Foam" went on sale, and huge crowds jammed the lobbies of Windsor's "beverage rooms." But it was a tepid drink, and one brewer offered a prize of $100 to anyone who could get drunk on 4.4. No one won.

Bertha Thomas in the 1940s.

W.F. Herman's *Border Cities Star* was even leery of this measure, for they had always supported the OTA. But the Windsor public had enough of mandatory temperance and in the 1926 provincial election they voted overwhelmingly for Ferguson's Conservatives and (to the *Star*'s dismay) the "crumpling of the O.T.A." By the summer of 1927, Windsor was a city of contrasts. The law strictly controlled the issuance of licenses, the hours of operation, and permitted only the most inoffensive of beers to be sold. In reality, the city had a web of unlicensed clubs which dispensed liquor, wine, and real beer at hours when working men wanted them. The police were well aware of the situation, and for the most part ignored it. W.F. Herman was resolved that all this would change.

Before taking over the Windsor newspaper in 1918, Herman had made a name for himself building up the Saskatoon *Star* and publishing more news reports than his contemporaries. He was determined that the *Border Cities Star* would also stand out. One rival, the Ottawa *Journal*, conceded that Herman "put out a big, expensive paper with page after page of almost solid reading

Locals try out "Fergy's Foam" (4.4% beer) at a Windsor Hotel, 1925.

matter set on his own linotypes, filled with magnificent cuts and costly features- and made it pay." Above all, his paper "was always at the service of movements and policies he thought for the public good."[17] In 1927, Herman initiated a crusade that would severely shake up Windsor law enforcement.

Blow-Up

Daniel Thompson was every inch the perfect police chief. His 6 foot 2 inch height and 270 pound bulk made him a dominant figure both before City Council and on the streets. Lured away from Peterborough in 1920 to assume the top position in Windsor, Thompson introduced a series of innovations. Traffic fatalities were rising and he introduced automatic traffic signals and a system of violation "cards" for offenders. One of his new officers was James Wilkinson, a precocious Englishman who had studied the latest identification techniques at Scotland Yard, and brought modern forensic techniques to Windsor. Thompson helped Wilkinson establish an identification branch that provided fingerprinting and a cross-indexing system of criminals. The system was so advanced that the FBI's J. Edgar Hoover became one of Wilkinson's colleagues, and the two occasionally exchanged ideas.[18] Despite these modernizations, controversy followed Thompson throughout his career. In 1922, there was an accusation that a constable had badly beaten a suspect. The police commission took no action. In 1925, Alderman Archie Hooper charged the police with tolerating a red-light district, which resulted in Windsor having the highest venereal disease rate in Ontario. The newspaper reported that Chief Thompson "dismissed the story with a laugh."[19]

James Wilkinson with two assistants in the Windsor Police Identification Branch, circa 1945.

Laughter came easily to Thompson, and he was a popular, gregarious figure. The *Star* regularly praised him and his department's occasional show of force in closing down bootleggers and gambling dens. The 1927 International Association of Police Chiefs convention held in Windsor was a most convivial affair, and Thompson hosted receptions for visiting Chiefs at his headquarters where free liquor was served by constables acting as waiters. Perhaps as a result of the convention's success, Thompson was elected first vice-president.[20] A *Star* editorial that June boasted that he was well qualified for the office for "Long years of experience in police work, a proven administrative capacity, speaking ability and other assets are his." Rarely was the press to turn on a public figure so quickly and with such vehemence as occurred a few weeks later.

In September 1927, editorials in the *Star* such as "All Citizens, Attention!" and "Alarming" instigated a sense of outrage that the blind pigs (which had existed for years) were suddenly a great source of public danger. Laxity in enforcing the law could no longer be tolerated, the editorialists wrote. The front page of the *Star* featured an open letter from "A Responsible Citizen" who proclaimed that in four blocks of the downtown core, some 29 blind pigs and gambling joints were operating and that "quite a number of these are run by women." The moral crusade was on, and in a community that was so dominated by one news source, few doubted that stern measures were needed. Mayor Cecil Jackson knew enough to join the parade and by mid-September he was praising the *Star* for its "courageous stand." Other politicians also got on board, and at the Council meeting of September 26, Alderman Clyde Curry harangued a packed chamber with demands to establish a Royal Commission.

One of the first victims of the *Star*'s morality campaign was a single woman, Ida Wild, who ran a blind pig and had committed the offence of selling three glasses and two bottles of beer. To the presiding magistrate, W.E. Gundy, it was apparent that "if one may judge by the newspaper" that what only a few weeks previously would have been considered a trifling offence was now the equivalent of manslaughter. Moreover, he did "not like to see a woman the first convict as a result of the agitation" given a severe penalty. For daring to oppose the *Star*, Gundy was denounced in its editorial pages and on October

This cartoon was part of the Border Cities Star's campaign against Windsor's vice trade, October 8, 1927.

12, he was granted a leave of absence. This was not a time for questioning. Moreover, the crusade was great political fodder, and Alderman C.R. Tuson was rapturously received by a packed Council Chamber when he gave an extended address demanding that Windsor's name be cleared and that "these cheap, rotten bootlegging and gambling joints" be run out of town. Curry formally filed complaints against Thompson, and Police Commission chairman Judge J.J. Coughlin promised an inquiry.

Stephen's Inn, a blind pig on Sandwich Street, 1927.

Occasionally, the hypocrisy that underlay this moral panic shone through. One alderman noted in passing that Curry had served as the bartender at the last real estate convention and that another alderman had drunk "plenty" of liquor at the recent police convention. Some of the alderman who were condemning the sale of a glass of beer were heavy imbibers themselves, but were clearly afraid to take a stand against the *Star*. The one person who stood above the fray was Judge Coughlin. His inquiry began in late October and was conducted with thoroughness and fairness to the accused. It came out in evidence that a number of downtown "clubs" offered after-hours drinking and gambling. These clubs varied from plush establishments to Stephen's Inn on Sandwich Street. A witness recounted "I have been in tough places on the Barbary Coast... but there is not a place on the Barbary Coast to compare with Stephen's Inn. It's a tough place." Another witness, a downtown businessman, confirmed that this was nothing new and that such places had been operating for at least the past ten years.

Still, it was apparent that Thompson was doomed. He admitted to taking fees and gifts instead of returning them to the general revenues. Only a half hour before the police commission was to return with its report on November 19, 1927, Thompson handed in his resignation. The overflow crowd in the council chamber sat in disappointed silence as Judge Coughlin read out the resignation letter and advised that as a result, the investigation would not be made public. Nevertheless, the Judge unburdened himself of his thoughts on recent events. He felt that the failure to enforce the law was not necessarily the result of poor policing. It was a consequence of the government enacting a legal code that had little public support. The temperance law "had so much public sentiment against it" that there would have had to be a massive police presence to make it effective. He hoped that Premier Ferguson's recent liberalizing of the liquor laws would be seen by the public as more acceptable, and that it would be honoured.

While probably wetter than other areas, Windsor was not unique. The temperance law was disrespected in most urban centres, and it was observed that there were "... widespread gestures of disrespect for the OTA. Liquor flowed freely at Toronto hotels."[21] But the agitation had raised the *Star*'s profile and editorials in the Montreal *Gazette* and the Toronto *Globe* praised its moral stand. Moreover, the *Star* had won and Thompson (as well as Gundy) were removed. Yet, it is questionable whether anything had really changed. Crime statistics showed that between 1925 and 1926, there were an average of 411 liquor arrests per year. Thompson's men had obviously been trying to enforce the law. In the three years after Thompson, there were 619 arrests per year.[22] The tempo of enforcement had increased somewhat, but not to a major degree. The continuing high volume of arrests also proved that the blind pigs were not going away, but remained an enduring feature of the Border Cities.

An Era of Marvels

While the newspaper fixed public attention on scandals, the enduring achievements of the late 1920s were being built by brave men working hundreds of feet over the Detroit River and others deep underground.

By March 1929, Joseph Bower could bask in the knowledge that the Ambassador Bridge was fourteen months ahead of schedule. The cables were all in place and the main span was under construction. Bower was attending a dinner to celebrate his accomplishment in New York that month when two engineers took him aside: the metal used in the cable wires, a new type of heat-treated, high-carbon steel wire, was defective and had to be replaced. As Bower later recalled, "The whole thing would have to be torn down and replaced... I didn't want any more food that night nor wine either."[23] There was nothing for it but to reverse the order of construction, dismantle the cables, and build new ones. Nevertheless, Bower and his men persevered and by August 15, 1929, new cables were in place. The main span was rebuilt and a dedication ceremony was scheduled for November 11, 1929.

In keeping with the usual formalities, politicians and businessmen presided and made their speeches. But it was the enthusiasm of the public that overwhelmed the officials; fifty thousand people gathered at the Canadian side and double that number on the American. The crowds broke through the rope barriers; thousands of ordinary citizens from both sides rushed onto the bridge and some even climbed the catwalks to the top of the piers. The Ambassador Bridge was the greatest structure the people of the border had ever seen and they had no interest in speeches; they wanted to walk on it, to see the river from its height, and to simply be awed by it. The *Star* recorded that "No ceremony could have been half so impressive as the unbridled, uncontrollable rush of thousands of people, turning out to see this new engineering marvel of the world."[24]

While this dedication was ongoing, the final push was on to complete the tunnel. Most of the tube sections were laid out and joined on the river bottom. The only thing that remained was a short stretch of 1,250 feet from the Windsor entrance to the underwater connection. Unfortunately, it would be one of the most difficult portions, as the hydraulic shield would have to dig through clay beyond the shore and 250 feet out from the harbour line. Once it was in place, it bore its way down to the river while sandhogs worked feverishly to remove the spoil. Behind them, an erecting crew put up the steel rings which lined the under land portion of the tunnel. It was a carefully choreographed process, all conducted under compressed air, in which one crew conducted the "shove" and the followers fitted the lining ring into place. It was "fast, accurate and well-timed work on the part of gangs that took a pride in just such performances."

Once the connection with the tube was made, the sections were pumped out. After that, it still took months to fabricate the roadway and install the electrical and ventilation systems. Ventilation towers with 12 fans on each side of the tunnel drew out car exhaust and pumped in forty complete changes of the air every hour. The tunnel's dedication on November 1, 1930, was an international affair. President Hoover in Washington pressed the button to actuate the gongs signalling that the tunnel was open. Windsor's Mayor Jackson strode across the bottom of the river and shook hands with Detroit's Mayor Frank Murphy at the international border line. *Popular Mechanics* wrote that "every foot of the $25,000,000 submarine mile reflects the romance and daring of engineering."[25]

Opening of the Ambassador Bridge, November 11, 1929.

Exuberance and a sense that the good times would flow on forever marked the end of the Twenties.

In addition to the ever increasing production from the car plants, Canadian Bridge could barely keep up with demand. Steel transmission towers to carry electricity across New Zealand, the vertical lift bridge for the Welland Canal, and even the steel frame for the roof of the new Union Station in Toronto were all fabricated from their Walker Road factory. American speculators bought up hundreds of lots in the Ojibway area in the certainty that their value would escalate. In this super-heated economy, downtown land prices skyrocketed. An Ouellette Avenue site that sold in December 1926 for $59,000 was resold barely two years later for $209,000. The Labelle Building on London Street sold for the phenomenal price of $350,000 in March 1929.[26] It was a free-wheeling market based more on wild enthusiasm than reality.

Despite this surging economy, the Border Cities remained vulnerable to outside events. No one could conceive that the international financial system, and the Border Cities along with it, was about to fall off the precipice.

Windsor Mayor Jackson and Detroit's Mayor Murphy (left) shake hands at the international boundary at the opening of the Detroit-Windsor tunnel, November 1930.

Chapter Seven
Surviving Hard Times
1930–1934

Farley Mowat, later to become one of Canada's most popular writers, was a youngster when his family moved to Windsor in May 1930. In his explorations, he was struck by the absence of activity, by the "factory dumps, and the big patches of 'waste' land which had been cleared and surveyed by speculators… during the boom years, but had been abandoned and were now returning to wilderness." When the city stopped growing, "Rabbits, foxes, raccoons, and other wild creatures were recolonizing these regions although they had to share space with unemployed and homeless men who had nowhere else to go."[1]

The economic disaster that young Mowat witnessed had begun even before the stock market crash of October 1929. Employment in the car factories peaked at 15,157 in March 1929, only to average half of that for the last six months of the year. It picked up briefly in early 1930, but overall employment was well below 1929 levels. The Depression hit Canada hard, and the secondary manufacturing sector was especially vulnerable. Vehicle output in Canada, which had reached almost 190,000 in 1929, fell to barely 48,000 in 1932. This collapse in demand was especially hard on auto cities such as Windsor and Oshawa. The Border Cities population shrank from 109,384 in 1929 to 96,199 in 1932. In the worst years, 1931 and 1932, the population fell by 5,400 residents each year. By early 1930, many of those families who remained were seeking "relief" or welfare from the municipalities. Responsibility for those in need was still considered to be a local problem, and the councils did what they could. Often, that was very little. In May 1930, the Windsor relief budget was already exhausted and Mayor Jackson ordered those on assistance to "get out and get work at once."[2] It was a ludicrous suggestion when there was no work to be had.

The provincial Department of Labour was monitoring the situation and reported in 1930 that the temporary closure of the auto plants was causing significant unemployment. Matters did not improve in 1931, and a government labour report noted that "the majority of plants only worked part time during the whole year and many hundreds of men did not even get part time work."[3] In May 1932, the Chamber of Commerce released a report outlining the confluence of events which had led to economic disaster. First was the explosive growth of the Twenties. From 1921 to 1927, cities such as Montreal had grown by 28 percent, Vancouver by 21.5 percent. In Ontario, Toronto had grown by 8.5 percent and Hamilton by 7.5. The Border Cities had grown by a phenomenal 85.5 percent. Unfortunately, this rapid expansion came at a price, as the Border Cities borrowed heavily to finance schools, roads, and sewers. If the pace of growth had continued, it could all be managed. But the sudden halt in auto production and employment led to massive losses in tax revenues and the border municipalities were left with huge debenture costs, and no way to finance the repayments.

The border was especially vulnerable to changes in American policy, and in 1924, the American *Immigration Act* all but closed the U.S. border to immigrants. To accommodate American industry's insatiable demand for labour an exception was provided, and Canadians were permitted to work and live in America. The Chamber of Commerce report noted that "the Border Cities in a sense consisted of a city within a city, one really substantial city composed of workers who worked in the Border Cities area" while the other "consisted of 15,000 workers who were employed in Detroit, and their dependants." This city within a city could function well so long as the door was kept open. But beginning in 1927, and increasing in intensity after 1930, Washington closed the door. Canadian workers were being steadily deported from Detroit until by 1932, the number of commuters was reduced to 1,500 (see Appendix D). Similar retaliatory restrictions were enforced by Canada and those Americans who had always worked at the Windsor racetracks found themselves being turned away at the border. The closing of the border and the loss of some ninety percent of the commuter jobs left thousands destitute. In December 1930, a deputation from the Chamber of Commerce met with Prime Minister Bennett to plead with Washington to open the border. He promised to do what he could, but American authorities were unmoved.[4]

Trade War

As if the Depression did not bring enough misery, American politicians were determined to make the situation even worse. Two congressional Republicans, Smoot and Hawley, introduced legislation in 1930 which drastically increased

U.S. tariffs against foreign products. As the purchaser of 18 percent of American exports, Canadians were aghast that the Americans had effectively barred them from selling in their market. Yet, without any comparable Canadian tariffs, American manufacturers could still sell in Canada. The obvious move was to consolidate operations. The Studebaker plant in Walkerville considered closing its doors and shipping completed cars into Canada from its American factory. It was an infuriating situation. "There is one thing to be said for the Hawley-Smoot tariff bill" the *Star* editorialized, "it has solidified and concentrated national sentiment... the Canadian people to a man resent the selfish tariff attitude of the American politicians."[5]

One of the first victims of the ensuing tariff wars was the Canadian Steel plant at Ojibway. After so many false starts, a development had finally started in 1927 and blast furnaces were built. At first, the plant produced wire and then shifted to tinplate. After 1930, Ojibway was supplying half of the tinplate used in the Canadian canning industry. However, when Ottawa finally enacted countervailing tariffs on U.S. natural products, it resulted in the plant being deprived of its American raw materials. In 1933, the Ojibway steel plant shut down and 500 men lost their jobs.[6]

On February 20, 1931, the Bennett government retaliated against the American auto sector by imposing prohibitive tariffs on American imports. Border Cities car producers and their employees were ecstatic. John Mansfield of Chrysler hailed the new protectionism as "an act of justice toward manufacturers" and two new assembly lines started up to produce Dodge trucks and Chrysler Imperials.[7] In April 1932, Chrysler put its assembly lines on display for "prominent Borderites." Most of the visitors had never set foot inside a factory, and they were impressed by the 3,000 foot long assembly line where chassis came in at one end and completed Dodges and DeSotos rolled off the other. The plant's special feature was the "floating power" Plymouth. Designed to capture the low-priced market, the Plymouth featured a new engine design. Four cylinder engines of the day invariably transmitted substantial torque to the rest of the car. But the floating power design let the engine rotate slightly as it was mounted on two rubber blocks which absorbed vibration. The technology may have been lost on the visiting society matrons, but they could not have missed the several hundred women working in the Chrysler trim department, using electrically driven knives to cut out 20 thicknesses of material at a time. From there, the women handled sewing the pieces into the interior upholstery of the vehicles.[8] It was impressive proof that with adequate tariff protection, some industries were prepared to expand, develop new products, and re-employ workers.

As further result of Bennett's higher tariffs, Studebaker shelved its closure plans and started a new truck line in Ford City. The *Detroit Free Press* recognized that the new rules "will serve effectively to bar American-made machines from Canada." If not bar, they drastically reduced American auto exports to Canada. In 1929 and 1930, finished American cars had averaged 20 percent of the Canadian market. In 1931 and 1932, they were reduced to 8.1 percent. The Detroit-Windsor area, which increasingly saw itself as a unified region, had been abruptly reminded that it was separated by an international border and that the residents of one were not necessarily welcome in the other. Commercial and personal cross-border traffic fell steadily after 1930.

Within the walls erected by the reinforced tariffs, American branch plants increased production in order to sell in the Canadian and Empire markets. One auto manufacturer, Graham-Paige Motors, opened up a small plant on Wyandotte Street in 1931. In the same year, Packard Motors set up a plant downtown. By the spring of 1932, Packard made its production even more Canadian by adding 21 men and four women to a body and axle-building department. While Packard's output was modest, it promised "A big jump in production… if, as expected, the coming Imperial Economic Conference increases intra-Empire preferences at the expense of the United States. This would probably mean transfer of all Packard's Empire market to the Windsor plant."[9] The Ottawa Agreements, a series of 12 bilateral trade agreements negotiated between Britain, Canada, and other dominions and British territories, provided for mutual tariff concessions. They were so advantageous that in January 1935, Ford announced that "In South Africa, Ford sales made an all-time high record this year; in Australia and New Zealand, sales were nearly double the 1933 figure." Empire sales were so good that Packard moved to a larger facility on St. Luke Road and by 1937, it was producing 2,566 four-door

The first Packard made in Canada rolls off the line in Windsor, 1931.

sedans. Canadian car manufacturers were successfully making up for the loss of the American market by cultivating markets in Britain and the Empire. Ford of Canada, for example, boasted that their sales throughout the Empire were increasing during the Depression years.[10] But as far as American-Canadian trade was concerned, the border had hardened.

To Be on the Dole

The massive loss of commuter jobs was compounded by the losses of 7,000 jobs in local industry. While most of these were in the auto plants, the five railways that operated on the border also shed hundreds of workers. The lack of money affected the entire economy; construction came to a halt and the building trades were thrown out of work. Much of the distress was attributable to the fact that the municipalities had little revenue available to them to cope with the crisis or keep up payments on their debts. Without jobs, residents could not pay property taxes, and the arrears mounted as the Depression deepened. By 1931, "Windsor had the highest percentage of unpaid taxes in any municipality in Ontario." The sudden drying up of revenues also meant that the Border Cities did not have the resources to fund relief for the indigent. The hopelessness ground on year after year and by 1934, an average of 28,636 people, almost thirty percent of the total population, was on relief.[11]

Putting unemployed men to work on public projects was considered to be one stop-gap measure to deal with the crisis. By the late summer of 1930, Windsor initiated a major sewer project, and Fire Chief DeFields was drafted to help organize hundreds of hopeful men who registered to work on the project. East Windsor capitalized on the pool of available men to build the Wyandotte-Drouillard subway. In April 1932, Ottawa authorized the payment of $100,000 to enable the construction of a subway under the Pere Marquette tracks to make Wyandotte Street a main thoroughfare to the east. Even the fine new federal post office built downtown in 1931–1932 was intended to revive the construction trades. Yet, it became clear that public works were no solution. Ford of Canada Chairman, Wallace Campbell, advised in the fall of 1931 that "It would cost the various municipalities much less to keep these people than to provide costly projects just for the sake of providing work."[12] The only solution was recovery, and that was a distant chimera.

Beyond the statistics was the harsh reality of desperate or destroyed lives. With the loss of employment, many families faced the immediate need simply to feed themselves. Men who had previously held regular jobs now struggled to find anything. Bert Brightmore, an English immigrant, found half-day work every other week. He considered himself lucky. Armand Paroain, an Armenian immigrant who had worked 12-hour shifts at a foundry in the 1920s, found himself out on the streets in 1931. Survival became the sole objective, and for the next few years, Paroian would walk the Essex County roads doing any agricultural work he could find and carrying home produce culled from the fields. One desperate individual made meals out of the small birds caught in the ivy on the Metropolitan Hospital walls.[13] As the catastrophe worsened, the human toll became more apparent. By the end of 1930, the Medical Officer of Health warned that the low standards of living were responsible for tuberculosis becoming widespread in East Windsor. Conditions were "especially bad in the west side of the city [East Windsor], where large numbers of people are huddled together in structures not fit for human habitation."[14] A sliding scale of provisions was made for indigent families. A family of four received 7 portions of milk and 10 of bread a week. Vegetables were not provided and meat was a rarity. The end result was, if not starvation, then poor health and high infant mortality. Often, the fatal victims of malnutrition were mothers who sacrificed food so that their children could eat.[15]

Those who swallowed their pride and applied for relief faced the ignominy of being interrogated by suspicious welfare officers. Walkerville officials were especially wary of requests for clothing for "One has to go into the home, look into every cupboard, closet and drawer, and even inspect the garret" to see if the indigents did not already possess clothing. Officials monitored applicants as to their moral lives, whether they drank or smoked and what they owned. Stan Scislowski, whose mother was raising seven children alone in East Windsor, recalled a relief inspector who "came around to periodically check on our larder to make sure we didn't have more extras than was allowed. What a crime! They took the attitude that it was their job barely to keep people alive—not one morsel more."[16] License plates for cars had to be surrendered and radios and telephones were forbidden luxuries. Depending on which Border City a person lived in could make a significant difference in how much relief they received. Poor people were moving into Walkerville and renting a room for the required three months in order to become eligible for the higher rates of relief available there. As a result, the chairman of the Welfare Board warned that the town's resources were becoming stretched and that it might "be reduced more to be equal with East Windsor and Windsor."[17]

Even while workers were leaving the Border Cities for better prospects elsewhere, county residents, whose municipalities had few resources, were flocking into the city where the relief benefits were higher. By the end of 1933, the Border Cities Relief Board was protesting to Amherstburg about giving money to its citizens for the sole purpose of leaving their community and becoming a burden in Windsor. In East Windsor, one alderman complained that "Every rat-hole and hovel in the city is being filled up by the steady influx of families from other municipalities."[18] Some thought that the unemployed should return to the farms, and a back-to-the-land movement in Essex County, *L'Union des Cultivateurs d'Essex et Kent*, urged young men to stay on the family farm instead of going to the cities in search of meagre wages or relief.

As part of the indignity of applying for relief, men had to report to the municipal offices for work. Usually, there was nothing for them to do, and the experience was "organized time-wasting." A special insult was the clothing which marked those on relief. An unemployed Windsor man wrote to Prime Minister Bennett politely inquiring if he could have a proper pair of pants, as "They give pants here all right but they are made of bran sacks" which identified the wearer as one of the outcasts. School boys on relief wore brown corduroy trousers and muslin shirts. One East Windsor lad recalled that "some of the kids would tease us about our welfare clothes" but after a while, there were so many children wearing the same thing that the joke paled. While police statistics showed that crime was down (there was little to steal) suicides were up. "To be on the dole," as a third of Border Cities residents were, "was to be something less than human in the Canada of the 1930s."[19]

In the first years of the Depression, the Chamber of Commerce played a leading role in trying to cope with the situation. An offshoot of the Chamber, the Border Citizens' Service Committee was a group of civic-minded citizens who tried to raise funds from private sources for relief. Formed in late 1931 and headed by Ford Chairman, Wallace Campbell, the Committee was a temporary organization intended to coordinate private efforts. In six months, it raised almost $200,000 and its contributions made up almost 20 percent of Border Cities relief. Employers raised money from their own workers by compelling those who still had jobs to aid those who had none. This service supplemented the various Welfare Boards of the municipalities, as well as private agencies like the YMCA. Even so, the ability of local Welfare Boards and private funds to cope was limited. By the spring of 1932, resources were exhausted and the Chamber of Commerce concluded that "It is idle to discuss a crisis next winter because the crisis in the acutest forms is now upon these municipalities."[20]

The following year, 1933, would see the worst days of the Depression. The Essex Border Relief Board, the provincially mandated authority that took over from the overwhelmed municipalities, controlled most assistance in the Border Cities. Local officials could not touch welfare allowances without the approval of this Board. This meant that in Riverside, the 320 families on relief received a three-cent allowance per meal. This was barely enough to get by on in 1932. By 1933, food prices had gone up and a town councillor complained that the existing allowances would condemn many of them to a slow death: "The people are not getting enough and they are starving."[21]

The Croll Years

The man who would guide Windsor through its most desperate times was a most unlikely looking leader. With his pudgy figure, dark complexion, and natty mustache, David "Dave" Croll, the boy who had arrived in Windsor from Russia in 1906 at the age of six and ran a newsstand and polished shoes, looked more like an aspiring young lawyer than a dynamic social reformer. Yet more than anyone else, he would become a voice for the poor, and a pragmatic leader who would do his best to alleviate their suffering.

"Joiner" would be the best word to describe Dave Croll. An active, if not necessarily devout member of his congregation, Croll, David Meretsky, and David Kaplan became the "Three Davids" who spearheaded the drive to build the grand Byzantine synagogue, Shaar Hashomayim, on Giles Boulevard. He liked to be with people and joined the Masons, the Goodfellows, and the Maccabees. While he studied law at Osgoode Hall in Toronto, he joined Pi Lamba Phi. Called to the bar in 1924, he joined a local firm, then opened up on his own in 1927. The next organization he joined, the Essex-West Liberal Association, would have a decisive impact on his future. "I had a feel for politics" he later recounted "that was my tradition and my upbringing." He also attracted useful friends, including the *Star's* proprietor W.F. Herman and Mayor Cecil Jackson. After assisting fellow Liberals in their campaigns, Croll decided to strike out on his own and run for mayor of Windsor in 1930. He gathered the support of union stalwart Archie Hooper who brought along the Trades and Labor Council. Being seen as the labour candidate did not hurt, especially when so many union men were looking for a leader. Neither was being Jewish necessarily a liability in a community which was now so diverse. Croll later recalled that his religion was not very important for "Windsor was more of a cosmopolitan city. There were a great number of ethnics and when you attack one ethnic, you attack the other ethnics and they don't like that one bit!"[22] On December 1, 1930, David Croll, a Russian-born Jew, was elected to a mayoralty which for almost forty years had been the preserve of the Anglo-Saxon, Protestant elite.

One of his first acts was to appoint an advisory board composed of prominent members of business, but which also included a Ukrainian, Martin Maleyko, an Italian, Caesar Saccaro, a representative of the black community, I.C. Parker, and even two women, Mrs. W.R. Whiteside and Mrs. C.C.

Chauvin. The world, or at least Windsor, had changed and there would be a broad new group advising the mayor. Yet Croll was hardly a naive idealist, for he thought it essential to stop all capital spending. The city's resources had to be focused on paying off the debentures and relief for the unemployed. The first resolutions of the new council in May 1931 were to call upon the federal and provincial governments to assist with relief payments.[23] Pressure from many municipalities eventually prevailed, and shortly thereafter Ontario and Ottawa agreed to pay two thirds of the relief cost. In 1932, the Henry government in Toronto even called on Windsor's Wallace Campbell to head a committee to investigate welfare reform. The committee's report recommended that relief should no longer be strictly a local matter, but should be administered in a non-political way with fixed standards applying across the province.[24]

By 1932, Croll was well aware that there was nothing the municipality could do to provide jobs. But, at the very least, it had to sustain its most vulnerable residents. "We must not build a community of shallow-eyed youngsters and withered adults" he stated in his 1932 inaugural address, "That is neither right nor humane… Human life is sacred and we must spend the people's money for the people's benefit." The city's Welfare Commissioner Clyde Curry (a persistent critic of Croll) responded by compiling a list of indigent aliens and directing that they be deported from Canada. To Curry, the problem with the poor might be solved by simply getting rid of them. At a rally at the Allied War Veterans' Hall in June 1932, the two men confronted each other. Curry stoutly maintained that "I am out for the true Canadian, the one born and raised here and I am proud I was born on Pitt Street." Croll shot back that "I have no apology to make because I was born in Russia, and Commissioner Curry can't deport me to Russia." He vowed that no man who was legally in the country would be sent out of Windsor and that any politician who insisted on pinching pennies "out of the bones and sinews and broken backs and empty stomachs of the unfortunate is bound to go to his doom." Thunderous applause greeted Croll and Curry disappeared under a torrent of catcalls and jeers.[25]

When Croll ran for re-election that November, he dismissed comments that he was a "Red," pointing out that he had run a financially conservative administration which had partially paid down the city's debt. Moreover, he had sponsored the *Moratorium Act*, a progressive piece of legislation which gave a province-wide extension on mortgages, enabling the unemployed to stay in their homes. As a result, there had been little social unrest in Windsor because, as Croll observed, "the people know that there is some sympathy for them in the mayor's office." In the resulting election, Croll received a massive 72 percent of the total votes cast and decisively humiliated his closest rival, Commissioner Curry.

As the Depression carried on into 1933, Croll became even more directly involved in the relief efforts. Together with a Conservative Commissioner, Harry Gignac, Croll trekked out to the land settlement of 28 Windsor families in Kapuskasing district. Under the Ontario Relief Land Settlement Program, poor families were sent up north to clear and farm vacant lands in "New Ontario." Croll and Gignac were aghast at what they found there. The lands were barren swamps, and long-time settlers were already on relief. Many of the Windsor families were near starvation, forced to eat groundhogs and roots. Croll gave a vivid description of the squalor and misery in the north and demanded that the government either terminate the program or properly look after the people. His account of this disaster was widely publicized across Ontario and *Saturday Night* magazine declared that Croll was no longer just a local politician; rather he had "become a national figure."[26]

Despite his recent notoriety, there was little that Croll could do to mitigate the financial consequences of the Depression. The Border Cities were finding it increasingly difficult to cover the debenture costs of their utilities. Riverside and Sandwich had made it clear that they could no longer pay their share. By the winter of 1932, all the Border Cities surrounding Windsor and Walkerville were effectively bankrupt. The provincial government was becoming increasingly anxious about municipal defaults, and one official was carefully monitoring the Windsor situation. H.L. Cummings was a legal advisor to the Province, and in a memorandum of October 31, 1931, to the attorney general, he castigated the Border Cities for their previous rash spending and that "in their private and public undertakings [they] have given full reign to their imagination and fancies..." Cummings felt that the continued friction between the municipalities was intolerable and that the border area desperately needed one body which could deal with the financial morass. Should the Border Cities default, it would badly reflect on Ontario's credit and provincial intervention was justified:

> The importance to the Province of having the disastrous state of affairs now prevailing in the Border Cities district, which is having a very bad effect upon every municipality throughout Ontario, cleared up is one which justifies the Government participating in every way possible.[27]

In response, the provincial legislature passed a bill in 1932 to remove spending powers from municipalities which threatened to become insolvent, and vest their budget powers in a provincially appointed Board of Control. Dr. Paul Poisson, the member from North Essex, was a principal architect of this bill. Speaking in the Assembly, Poisson admitted that "This act may appear drastic" but that "Essex County, unfortunately, has now several municipalities in financial difficulties." Shortly after the passage of this act, seven border municipalities—Riverside, Sandwich, Tecumseh, East Windsor, LaSalle, Sandwich East, and Sandwich West—were put under the direction of Boards of Control, and they effectively ceased to control their own finances.[28]

Magistrate David "Six Months" Brodie was appointed chairman of Windsor's Board of Control, 1932.

Windsor resisted the imposition of a Board of Control until November 1932, when it appeared that the city would be unable to make the interest payments on its bonds due December 1. Cummings hurried to Windsor and delivered an ominous speech, warning that the situation was critical and that turning the city's finances over to a Board of Control was essential. Croll hugely resented his interference and drafted his own emergency plan to spread out principal payments to bondholders. Chairman McKeown of the Ontario Municipal Board liked Croll's plan, but Cummings dismissed it as impractical. Shortly before December 1, a majority of City Council voted to submit to the rule of a Board.[29] Croll fiercely resisted this usurpation of local democracy, but in the end it was futile. A Board of five businessmen (two from outside Windsor) were appointed to supervise the city's budget. Unquestionably, the Board was an elite institution, for at its head was a formidable figure of law and order, Magistrate David "Give Him Six Months" Brodie. On December 1, Windsor met its interest payment, but fell into default on the principal payment of its bonds.

Resentment against the Board of Control came largely from the left. Socialist leader George Bennett pointed out that the Controllers were the chiefs of insurance and banking concerns who were solely intent on securing their clients' investments rather than helping the public. The Controllers were, according to Bennett, "the big men of the financial world who are stripping you bare naked." Yet, the Board of Control would do what the elected Council had resisted: it cut municipal wages and laid off staff to balance budgets. Whatever their conduct, Croll continued to rail against this elitism. "The special interests are in the saddle of this city," he grumbled.[30] Yet, to some the Mayor was seen as too moderate, and too willing to compromise with the special interests. An energized minority was eager to confront the forces of capital head on and create a radical new order in Windsor.

Reds

Lanspeary Park in East Windsor was intended to be a place of contemplation and relaxation. Instead, by the early 1930s, it was a haven of radicalism where communist agitators held rallies and gave speeches to try and convince the east-European residents in the adjacent neighbourhoods that revolution was the only alternative to the misery of the Depression. Under a huge red banner (later banned by by-law), communist leaders would preach to increasingly receptive audiences.

In the 1920s, labour organizations were largely moderate and limited to the skilled trades. The first attempt to organize the mass of men in the auto plants came in 1928, when James Simpson of the Dominion Trades Congress (an offshoot of the American Federation of Labor) came to Windsor. He bragged that the union had achieved notable success in Oshawa organizing a GM plant and that they could do the same in Windsor. Communists disrupted Simpson's organizational meeting, and succeeded in convincing some workers to form a more radical union, the Automobile Industrial Union of the Border Cities. The *Canadian Unionist* proclaimed that "the men of the Border Cities… are asserting their claim to freedom and to better conditions of work and wage." However, the union's existence was brief and by late 1929, it had ceased to operate.[31]

The mass unemployment of the early 1930s discouraged attempts at labour organization as workers hung on to whatever jobs came their way. Communist activity shifted toward organizing the unemployed and clandestine attempts to infiltrate work groups. "The [communist] movement in Windsor was highly developed," historian John Manley observed, "capable of working immediate issues such as evictions and relief payments as well as conducting mass public agitation." He estimated that by the spring of 1933, fourteen shop groups had been infiltrated by Communists who engaged in political discussions "with occasional forays into Marx, Engels, Lenin, and Stalin."[32] The public face of the Party was Tom Raycraft who, as leader of the Marxist "United Front," was elected to the city council of East Windsor in 1931. With almost a quarter of that city's population being east-European born, East Windsor was fertile ground for communists. The following year, Raycraft was joined on the council by two comrades and the three communists made up a significant voting block on the city council. The RCMP was keeping a close eye on East Windsor, and their weekly summaries detailed the 1934 celebration of the Russian Revolution at the Empire Theatre by a Ukrainian choir singing "The Internationale." Police agents also infiltrated Lanspeary Park where communists, as well as fascist elements, argued the merits of their respective ideologies. The newspaper described a typical evening:

> Fascism collided with Communism in Lanspeary Park last night. Admirers of Hitler and Mussolini argued it out under the trees with disciples of Marx and Lenin as police mingled with the warring groups, strained ears to a babel of tongues and probably wondered what it was all about.[33]

Communist rallies occasionally met with open hostility. On May Day 1930, students from the Tech school occupied Lanspeary Park and burst into "O Canada" whenever Red speakers tried to give an address. The Catholic Holy Names Society was fervently anti-communist and their processions were both religious and political denunciations of "the Godless social system." Alderman Leo Laurendeau of East Windsor (the majority of its aldermen were French-Canadian) condemned the communists for circulating seditious literature in the schools. The Windsor Trades and Labor Council would not tolerate communists and fired those it found in its ranks.[34] The reaction to communism even spawned a local Fascist group, the "Blue Shirts of Canada." Ever-vigilant Mounties were watching this "curious society" that had attracted 700 young men to its ranks and paraded through Windsor's streets in steel helmets and blue shirts. The RCMP was not sure who was behind the group, but in the end they posed no threat to the public peace.[35]

The greatest enemy the communists faced came from the political left when socialists and Christian reformers organized in 1932 into the Co-operative Commonwealth Federation. While it favoured public ownership of key industries and universal healthcare, the CCF never advocated the revolutionary changes to restructure society as advocated by the communists. Ben Levert, a Windsor dentist, was one of the first local organizers of the movement, which attracted some moderate labour leaders, as well as religious support. Reverend Calvin McRae of Riverside Presbyterian spoke publicly about the legitimate rights of the labour movement as expressed through the CCF. The street railwaymen's union severed all connections with "the red movement" but remained comfortable with the CCF platform. Others were not so sure. In September 1933, James Simpson led delegates to the Trades and Labor Council meeting in Windsor in the hope of tying local workers to the CCF. A proposal to do so was not even put to a vote.[36]

As the Depression deepened, even the middle class began to feel its effects. Many lawyers left the profession and tried to find manual labour. One of Croll's initiatives was to hire a few law students such as Leon McPherson and Larry Dezeil at minimum wage to provide free legal services for those on relief.[37] As the City Solicitor observed, "the big idea was to reassure most of these people as to what their rights were." Likewise, there was a proposal to take doctors who were on relief and have them provide clinics for the poor. One unforeseen impact of the Depression was a movement toward providing government-supervised legal and medical services. Socialism was arriving without the socialists in power.

A photograph of Sophie Kornacki that was printed in the Border Cities Star, the winner of "Miss East Windsor" in 1931.

Getting on with Life

The "Hard Times Hop" was the main event at the Walkerville Boat Club in January 1933. Partiers arrived in ragged skirts, swallow-tail coats with shorts,

Partiers at the 'Hard Times Hop,' 1933.

and other "hobo" attire. However amusing this was to the social set, it was all too real to the one-third of Border Cities residents who lived on relief. The moneyed class took in the Harmsworth speedboat race off of Belle Isle in the fall of 1932. Lounging on their hired yachts, well-heeled local socialites watched as Gar Wood piloted *Miss America X* to the trophy. Afterwards, the *S.S. Manitoulin* hosted a party on Lake St. Clair where couples danced through the night.

In contrast, the working class had to be content with more common pleasures. East Windsor constructed a public beach and bathhouse at the foot of George Avenue where the public could cool off in the highly polluted waters of the Detroit River. Every May a civic party was held at the beach, and Miss East Windsor (in 1931, Sophie Kornacki) was crowned. Pleasures were simple and had to be found close to home. The main celebration of the summer was the Firemen's Field Day held at Jackson Park. The parade to the park gave ordinary people a chance to try on homemade costumes and decorate a car as a float. The field day featured races, sports, vaudeville shows and the crowning event, the "Miss Western Ontario" beauty pageant. In an increasingly celebrity conscious era, assessing and crowning women had become a major pastime. Even the CCF summer festival featured a beauty pageant to select an attractive representative of democratic socialism from an array of working women.

One release that was still available to most people was sports, and during the grim days, sports took an even greater significance in public pride. The Windsor Bulldogs already had a place in the community's heart with their victories against the odds. In 1929, the Bulldogs made the finals of the Canadian Professional League, but faced the Detroit Olympics, a team to whom they had lost every regular season game. Yet, stars such as "Happ" Emms rose to the occasion, fought the Olympics to a draw, and forced a deciding game on April 11, 1929, in Fort Erie. Hockey fans jammed Ferry Street to listen to the broadcast of the game from the *Border Cities Star* building. As freezing gusts blew up the street, crowds cheered as Mickey Roach's goal defeated Detroit and gave Windsor the Professional League title. The following year the Bulldogs moved to the International Hockey League where they again won a championship. Local pride was further buoyed by swimmer Ruth Kerr of Kennedy Collegiate, who swam for Canada in the 1932 Olympics in Los Angeles.

Day-to-day sports were dominated by baseball and Walkerside Dairy was the Border Cities' team in the Essex County League. It took little equipment to play baseball and, in lieu of work, hundreds of young men spent their days playing ball.[38] It was a situation that began to concern the bureaucrats, and in 1933, the Department of Labour reported that a generation of Windsor youth were growing up without the discipline of regular labour. As a result, "it is

Members of the 1933-1934 Windsor Bulldogs hockey team.

scarcely to be expected that these untrained and inexperienced persons can be readily adjusted to industrial life."[39]

The Depression also threatened to destroy the lives of women just as it did men. While female employees did have access to minimum wage regulations (men did not), their wages were meagre, and the regulation was frequently ignored. The Women's Section of the Chamber of Commerce felt that government programs had focused on men at the expense of women:

> ... no effort had been made to care for the girl who was broke or homeless on account of unemployment. It was pointed out that the psychology of girls was different from that of men in that unemployed men group together and make their wants known while unemployed girls keep to themselves and hesitate to make their situation known... they were generally in very desperate straits before they would ask for assistance.[40]

Women were about to come forward to make their situation better known. In 1923, Mrs. L.A. Killen was the first female to run for elected office in Windsor. She headed the polls in the race for the Board of Education, a victory attributed to the "hard work of the women" in the Home and School Club. In 1930, Mrs. W.C. Kennedy carried the Liberal standard in the federal election in Essex West. While she lost, she tallied more than 10,000 votes. Women were regularly elected to the school boards and in 1933, Emily Lynch, an active young lawyer, was elected to the East Windsor city council.

Above all, it was the rise of Olive Jane Whyte that shook the male establishment. After graduating from the University of Toronto social services department, she came to Windsor in 1930 as a United Church missionary. Once the church administration opened up to admit women, she became the first female elder of Giles Boulevard United Church. Whyte combined her religious duties with a fervent social conscience, and she identified closely with the CCF and the labour movement. In the 1933 municipal race, she impressed union leaders with a brief, intelligent address. Still, she was a woman and news report concluded by critiquing her attire and the "close-fitting brown jumper" she wore to the meeting. She narrowly missed being elected. In the provincial election in the summer of 1934, Whyte was nominated by the CCF. During the course of a speech at Clay Park on the crisis of youth unemployment, a rock was thrown at her and struck her just below her glasses. After a brief pause, and with blood still trickling down her cheek, she continued her speech. Onlookers were struck by her courage. Nevertheless, her Liberal opponent was the hugely popular Mayor Croll, and he was resoundingly elected to the provincial Assembly and left the mayor's office. Undismayed, Olive Whyte ran again in 1934 in the last municipal elections ever held in the Border Cities. This time she was elected to Windsor city council and declared that "It is an honor to be on the city council, its difficulties and trials should be shared by women."[41]

East Windsor Is Red

In the absence of David Croll, the political landscape on the border veered significantly to the left. George Bennett, the head of the streetcar workers' union, and an avowed socialist, announced that he would run for mayor of Windsor in November 1934. As well, five communists, including the female firebrand Georgina Ketcheson, would run for council or the school board in Windsor. But it was in East Windsor that the communists hoped to leave their mark. The RCMP closely followed events and reported with some understated horror that the communists had entered a full slate of candidates in the 1934 election. Their campaign slogan was "A majority in the City Council." The prospect of a Canadian city under communist control alarmed the establishment. Alderman Dr. P.N. Gardner warned that "East Windsor will become Communist headquarters for Canada" should they succeed.

The subsequent campaign was one of the most raucous ever held. At the nomination meeting held in East Windsor, the city clerk commenced the proceedings with a singing of "God Save the King." Hundreds of communists looked on in stony silence. Silence was anything but the rule at most political meetings, where hoots and catcalls greeted opposing speakers. Meetings frequently dissolved into bedlam as police had to be called in when heckling turned into fisticuffs.[42] Early on in the campaign, Bennett struck a deal with the communists whereby in return for increased relief rates they would give him their support. Bennett's opponent, Clyde Curry, pointed to this deal as proof that Bennett was little more than a Red himself. In the following days, Bennett distanced himself from the communists and stressed instead that he was just a true-blue union man. In East Windsor, the pressure intensified and a slate of anti-communists was put into the field. Local clergy came to their aid, and Rev. F.H. Paull at St. Aidan's Anglican and Monsignor F.X. Laurendeau of Our Lady of the Lake openly urged their congregations to vote for the anti-communists.

In the end result, the communists were thoroughly trounced and one clergyman, Rev. Harry Merifield, the rector of St. Mark's Anglican, was elected to the Windsor school board. Merifield had spent the campaign denouncing the communists, and they had repaid his attention by disrupting his meetings. Rev. Merifield topped the election poll of 1934, and Georgina Ketcheson was defeated. The bright side for the left-faction was George Bennett who became the city's first socialist mayor. Still, the Reds were decisively vanquished in East Windsor and the anti-communist slate overwhelmingly elected. The communist journal, *The Daily Worker*, reported on the "bitter fight" in East Windsor and the "gallant stand" made by their comrades who had been sabotaged by the "vicious campaign… by the reactionary election machine thru the press and church." The Toronto *Globe*, on the other hand, congratulated the good people of East Windsor and smugly declared that "The solid common-sense elements of every community will not, for long, put up with the impudent activities of the 'Red' fellows."[43]

On the same day that revolutionary Marxism was repudiated, the provincial government issued a remarkable piece of news. On December 4, 1934, Premier Mitchell Hepburn's government unexpectedly announced that on July 1, 1935, the border cities of Windsor, Walkerville, Sandwich, and East Windsor would be amalgamated into one "City of Windsor."

The *Border Cities Star* proclaimed in exultation "Amalgamation, at Last!"

A crowd listens to returns outside of the Border Cities Star on election night, 1934.

Chapter Eight
City United
1935

The problem with the Border Cities, according to H.L. Cummings, Croll's nemesis and now a member of the Ontario Municipal Board, was that "There are still too many 'parish politicians'… too many raids on municipal treasuries" that rendered their finances "a complicated mess." During a speech at Windsor's Rotary Club in May 1933, he hinted darkly that unless the municipalities put aside their pride and started to co-operate, the province would be forced to step in and make "a decision." Cummings' warnings drew an indignant response from Mayor Croll who demanded action rather than threats: "Mr. Cummings knows perfectly well that amalgamation or anything approximating it cannot be achieved in the Border Cities voluntarily. Yet he comes around hinting about a decision having to be made… If the government intends to put through amalgamation, for goodness sake why don't they put it through?"[1]

The increasing urgency of amalgamation originated both in the financial crisis created by the Depression and the Canadian constitutional system that made addressing that crisis next to impossible. In the United States, the Roosevelt administration transferred half a billion dollars to state and local authorities under the Federal Emergency Relief Administration, and bought local bonds at low interest rates to shore up municipal finances. However, in Canada, there was no federal role in supporting municipalities and the government of Prime Minister R.B. Bennett was reluctant to create one. As a result, municipalities across the country were falling into debt and collapsing into bankruptcy.[2] The only hope was the province. Ontario cities and towns had been created and regulated by provincial statutes since the 1840s, but there had been a laissez faire approach in which the municipalities were at liberty to run their own finances and make their own decisions on amalgamation. Prior to 1934, it was unthinkable that the province would force one municipality to amalgamate with another.

This lack of support from senior levels of government was especially of concern to the Border Cities as their separate finances were spiralling into a pit of insolvency. The "complicated mess" Cummings referred to had many origins, including the loss of property taxes, the coming due of payments on the debentures, and the burden of relief. In the 1920s, the Essex Border Utilities Commission had incurred a huge debenture debt to construct sewers and water facilities. By 1932, only Windsor and Walkerville were still maintaining their payments to the EBUC.[3] This was not a sustainable situation, and in January 1933, the EBUC went into default. The streetcar system was also a persistent drain on resources. With the loss of jobs, ridership on the system declined and revenues dropped from $1.2 million in 1929 to less than half a million in 1933.The provincial hydroelectric company, which had encouraged streetcar expansion and profited from the sale of power, suddenly dropped their involvement in 1933. Even so, the streetcars were efficiently run, and the operations showed a small profit. The unsustainable losses were attributable to the SW&A's ongoing interest payments. The $6 million spent to purchase and rehabilitate the system had grown to $7.5 million in 1934, and the company concluded that the repayment of this debt was "an absolute impossibility."[4]

In addition to the insolvency of the utility and transit agencies was the municipalities own failure to meet their financial obligations. In 1931, East Windsor, and in 1932, Windsor and Sandwich, went into default on their debenture payments. With an enormous debt and few sources of revenue, Sandwich's plight was hopeless. Proud Walkerville, on the other hand, remained technically solvent. Solvency, however, came at a price as it had to borrow extra funds and give a lien on the town's revenues in order to meet its debenture payments. One Walkerville councillor objected that this method "of supposedly maintaining our independence" was simply postponing the inevitable.[5]

The province was funding relief in all border communities except Windsor and Walkerville and administering it under its own agency, the Essex Border Relief Board. No local politicians were allowed on the Board and it effectively operated as an arm of the provincial government. Even with this help, the burden of relief payments was proving to be too much. In October 1934, Windsor gave up and admitted that it could no longer support its citizens. All further relief would have to come directly from the province.

The Board of Control—that had been created amid such controversy in 1932—had actually succeeded in creating some stability. In the seven border communities surrounding Windsor and Walkerville, the Board directed by Thomas Bradshaw had balanced the budgets and made limited headway on debt reduction. In the two years since 1932, Bradshaw, an unassuming actuary from London, was probably the most powerful man in the Border Cities. A recognized authority on municipal finance (praised even by David Croll) he had reduced East Windsor's debt by seventy percent.[6] LaSalle had a credit balance. But a plan for the eventual repayments of all municipal debts was beyond Bradshaw's mandate, but could not be put off indefinitely. A new body resulting from the amalgamation decree would have to resolve all these problems.

The Coughlin Commission

No one was prepared for the sudden amalgamation announcement of December 4, 1934. Premier Hepburn gave a short address that the present operation of the Border Cities was "like chain-stores at a busy corner" and it had to stop. A Royal Commission was appointed to determine how to implement the union, and above all to find a way to refinance the new city. To many, amalgamation acknowledged the failure of local democracy. Area politicians simply could not put aside their petty differences, and instead, solutions had to be imposed from above. The Border Cities were far from the only municipalities in this predicament, and Oshawa and Hamilton were also teetering on default. In January 1935, Hepburn's government announced that no municipalities would be permitted to default. Local councils were ordered to tighten controls, collect tax arrears and, above all, they were prohibited from any further borrowing.[7]

Standing just behind the Premier at this announcement was his Minister of Municipal Affairs as well as the Minister of Public Welfare, David Croll. Croll had a close relationship with the new Premier, who (despite Prime Minister King's misgivings) had no hesitation in appointing Croll as Ontario's first Jewish cabinet minister. The new minister heartily endorsed the Hepburn plan—even though it was a flagrant breach of the campaign promise he had made to Walkerville that there would be no amalgamation without a public vote. He awkwardly explained that amalgamation was the only solution to an intractable problem, and its time had come. Croll unveiled the personnel of the Royal Commission who would oversee the process. Judge John Coughlin, one of the most respected figures in the Border Cities, would chair the Commission.

When the judge called the Commission to order on December 12, 1934, Mayor Russell Farrow of Walkerville began by restating his community's unalterable opposition to joining with its neighbours. He pointed out that in the last municipal election, Walkerville voted by a four-to-one margin against any form of amalgamation. Farrow was instantly silenced by H.L. Cummings, the Province's representative on the Commission, who bluntly informed him that amalgamation was a fact and that the Commission's sole purpose was to put it into effect. At hearings in March 1935, Windsor City Solicitor B.J.S. Macdonald presented a situation that was even bleaker than they feared. Macdonald, an Albertan who had studied at Harvard Law School and was drawn to Windsor in 1927 by the area's opportunities, had been the City Solicitor since 1930. A tough, determined administrator, Macdonald addressed the problems of amalgamation and re-financing the bankrupt municipality.[8] In addition to the city's inability to pay the interest owing on its debentures, its relief costs, and the bankrupt streetcar system, there was also the "dead horse" (as Macdonald called it) of the Windsor, Essex & Lakeshore Railway. The area municipalities had been induced by the hydroelectric commission to purchase this county-wide rail service in 1929. It had been an unmitigated disaster, losing money from its inception until it ceased operating in September 1932. Macdonald concluded that the hydro commission had cleverly transferred a $450,000 liability onto the unsuspecting Border Cities.[9]

The Coughlin Commission found that the case for amalgamation was overwhelming. Local politicians, afraid of disappointing voters, had been afraid to take any meaningful steps to confront economic realities. The result was a disaster that left the Border Cities in financial ruin. "Unless the situation is dealt with in some manner," the Commission concluded, "the pyramiding debt structure will, in all probability, within twenty-five years exceed the fair market value of everything in the area." The only solution was an end to local control and the submission of all spending to a provincially appointed Finance Commission.[10]

Even before the Commission's report was tabled, Croll and Hepburn were determined to act. On April 11, 1935, Croll moved first reading of the *Amalgamation Act* whereby Windsor, East Windsor, Walkerville, and Sandwich became the City of Windsor.[11] The school boards were also amalgamated, while the statute abolished the EBUC and created a new "Windsor Utilities Commission." Over all of them was the provincially appointed Finance Commission which would put the amalgamation into effect and deal with the financial morass. There was little

A thinly veiled anti-Semitic attack on David Croll, seen here as 'Judas' beating Walkerville into submission from *Walkerville News*, 1935.

opposition to the bill; however, some members were uneasy that if Queen's Park could do this to the Border Cities, then other municipalities might be next. In Croll's view, "It is our duty to see that not only the Border area but any other district is saved." The Border Cities mayors went to Toronto just before the bill was finalized and requested several amendments, including a provision that any amalgamation be approved by the people, that the legislature wait until the Coughlin Commission's Report was available, and that the authority of the Finance Commission be limited.

Croll ignored them.

While he may have been popular elsewhere, in Walkerville, David Croll was considered the devil incarnate. The *Walkerville News* roundly condemned him for going back on his promise not to force amalgamation, and for "trying to deprive the Anglo-Canadians of the right to the ballot to defend their homes and town from being tied up to two municipalities (Windsor and East Windsor) which are hopelessly in debt..." While these decent "Anglo-Canadians" were being robbed and forced into a union with their unsavoury neighbours, there was clearly little they could do about it. The amalgamation bill was passed with no amendments and little dissent. On July 1, with a minimum of fanfare, the new City of Windsor, the eighth-largest city in Canada, came into being. A minority in Walkerville refused to accept amalgamation and challenged the measure before the Ontario High Court. A judge ruled in July 1937 that the Province was within its rights to alter municipalities as it saw fit. Nevertheless, in a futile and expensive crusade, Walkerville's elite appealed the ruling to the Ontario Court of Appeal and ultimately to the Judicial Committee of the Privy Council in London. They were defeated at all levels, and the amalgamation, a dramatic and unprecedented use of provincial power, was confirmed.[12]

Having flexed its muscle so impressively in the Border Cities, the Province might have turned toward Toronto where equally compelling problems were

An anti-amalgamation sign at the corner of Kildare and Tecumseh roads, still up in 1939.

apparent. Many of that city's suburbs were bankrupt and it would seem most efficient to annex them to Toronto. But fearing the political consequences, Croll and his associates held back and chose to reserve their powers for more malleable situations. The *Toronto Telegram* reassured its readers that there was little to fear. After all, the Border Cities were in such a dire state that all their relief obligations were now being met by the province. In the *Telegram's* view, the state of affairs in Windsor was entirely different from Toronto's, for all of the Border Cities were insolvent and they deserved to be subjugated to provincial authority. "Windsor, defunct itself, cannot complain that it is being loaded with defunct neighbours"[13] it smugly concluded.

In succeeding weeks, workers addressed the nuts and bolts of amalgamation. The three "Victoria" streets of the new municipality were reconciled so that only one bore that name. "John Doe" Street (nobody could think of an appropriate name) was added to College Avenue.[14] The four alarm systems used by the fire departments were rearranged into one. A unified Police Commission decided that there were too many officers and ten were laid off. In the daily effort to survive the Depression, the political and administrative impacts of amalgamation probably meant little to most people. The ability to get work at the factory gate was all-important, and in 1935, the prospects of work were, at last, starting to look up.

Limited Recovery "Gate" Bottles and the "V8"

As if business did not have enough challenges to deal with during the Depression, Ottawa decided in 1930 to cooperate with U.S. authorities and ban the export of alcohol to the states. On behalf of Windsor distillers, the area's Member of Parliament, Sidney Robinson, moved that the ban be set aside. The Bennett government opposed it, and Robinson's lonely "aye" was drowned out by a chorus of "nays."[15] Nevertheless, the distillery business, principally Hiram Walker, was highly resilient and their reaction to the loss of their principal market was a textbook example of corporate ingenuity.

By the late 1920s, Walkers had set up a system of surrogate companies who shipped their liquor to the French islands of St. Pierre and Miquelon and from there to U.S. dealers in the Bahamas or Bermuda. When dealers complained that the traditional long-necked bottles of Canadian Club were prone to break while in shipment by sacks, Walkers developed the squat, durable "Gate" bottle which could endure the rigors of bootlegging.[16] To cloak their shipments from the prying eyes of American customs agents, a system of codes was established between Walkers and their shipping agents that rivalled most countries' espionage networks. Even so, some shipments were apprehended during spirited sea chases. It was reported back to one of Walkers' surrogate companies in 1932 that only part of a British Honduras (Belize) bound cargo was unloaded "up north," the rest was captured and "our Chicago friends had consequently one hard luck after another."

Inevitably, this put Walker's agents into proximity with some hard cases. Walker's chief Harry Hatch was informed that one of their distributors had been captured by a rival syndicate. His men tried to ransom him back, but "the story is that he was put into an incinerator." The gangsterism that marked the liquor trade could be set aside once Prohibition was repealed in 1933. Hatch unveiled a plan for a massive expansion into the U.S., where the brand had retained its goodwill and "can step into the United States market when open entirely unembarrassed." This was because "we [Walkers] would not stoop to methods of using gangsters and hoodlums…"[17] While this was not entirely true, the company had used enough buffers to avoid direct contact with the underworld and it re-entered the U.S. liquor market as an upright corporate citizen. Breweries were the other beneficiaries of the end of Prohibition, and a "two-way golden flood beer from the Border and dollars from Detroit" swept across the border when experienced Canadian brewers were called on to end the thirst resulting from fifteen years of Prohibition in Michigan. While those who worked on the bottling lines at Walkers were happy to have their jobs and quite unconcerned as to where their product was headed, most Windsor workers still depended on the car plants.

By the mid-1930s, the auto plants were also on the mend. With Wallace Campbell operating the ladle, the new Ford Foundry opened in March 1935. The electric furnaces in the foundry were the latest technology and the carbon electrodes could reduce a ton of metal to a liquefied state in 82 minutes. Even more impressive, the molten metal would flow into a precisely aligned assembly of sand cores to produce the casting for a V8 engine. The V8, perhaps Henry Ford's last great mechanical triumph, was the product of an ingenious method of aligning 54 separate cores in a mold to produce an eight cylinder, 221 cubic inch engine that produced 65 horsepower. It was easily the most powerful, mass-produced car engine on the road, with unprecedented acceleration and performance. The V8s were the talk of the auto shows of 1934, and consumers also liked the new product. By early 1935, employment at the Ford plant had risen to near pre-Depression levels.

Perhaps even more revolutionary was the Chrysler Airflow of 1935. Discarding the standard box style of the 1920s, the Airflow was a sleek, futuristic model that was far ahead of its time. Assembled at Plant 3 on Tecumseh Road, the Airflows generated a huge initial demand and company President

John Mansfield kept the men at a standard eight-hour shift to spread out the employment. As a result, by March 1934, Chrysler was back to employing over 1,600 staff. Prosperity also returned to General Motors and its Walker Road plant was turning out engines for the Oldsmobile Six model.[18] As tariff barriers stopped exports to the U.S., Windsor industry turned more than ever to the British Empire. Campbell boasted that new records were being set in sales to Africa and Asia. Britain even reduced its "horsepower tax" to facilitate the import of V8s.[19]

However, to a great extent, the Canadian auto industry still remained at the mercy of the tariff system. Prior to 1926, Canadian car manufacturing largely consisted of the assembly of American-made parts into finished vehicles. After that year, lower tariffs reduced the price of U.S. cars and at the same time encouraged the production of Canadian auto parts. The Liberal government intended to reduce the consumer cost of vehicles, and at the same time to encourage Canadian component production. As a result, parts sales doubled between 1925 and 1929 and for the first time, many of the cars coming off Canadian assembly lines were more than fifty percent Canadian made.[20] Two Windsor parts plants, L.A. Young (seat cushions) and Bendix Eclipse (brake shoes), were both operating at near capacity. Bendix's plant manager boasted that "the 1935 automobile had greater Canadian content than any previously manufactured automobile."

Straightening Out the Mess

Before the new City of Windsor could make any plans, it had to regain financial stability. In January 1936, bondholders met with civic officials. At first, it seemed as if the creditors would accept the city's diminished ability to pay and extend the time period for repayment (the city hoped for sixty years) and lower interest rates. However, some thoughtless comments (that the city had plenty of money) by Walkerville alderman, Angus MacMillan, caused them to re-consider. The problem was referred to the Ontario Municipal Board. City Solicitor Bruce Macdonald recalled the magnitude of the problem; the city's debt, both principal and interest, was over $40 million. This constituted about one-third of the total defaulted municipal debt in Ontario. Moreover, there was no guideline to work with for "this too was the first large municipal debt refunding in the history of Canada… so we didn't have a great deal to go by."[21] Working with the counsel for the bondholders, as well as H.L. Cummings, an arrangement was finally agreed upon in April 1937 for a slightly lower interest rate and repayment extended over forty years.

The financial resolution was a huge benefit to the new municipality. Bondholders were guaranteed (eventually) their principal, but their returns were diminished. The bonds lost much of their value to the extent that the city was able to redeem some of them and thereby further reduce the debt. As Macdonald later recalled, "And it all worked out beautifully, and the debt [was] all rewritten and eventually it was paid off." Part of the cost of this solution was that Windsor's budgets were now under the review of the OMB, and any future capital expenditures would be under outside scrutiny.

As a final note to the proceedings, Bruce Macdonald, who had played a principal role in engineering the solution, was fired. As part of the settlement, costs were paid to the lawyers involved, and Macdonald was awarded $17,500. This was an enormous sum in 1937, and one member of the city's elected Board of Control took exception. Arthur Reaume, the tall, good-looking former mayor of Sandwich, thought that this payment to a civil servant was a travesty. With his trademark stutter, Reaume had made his mark as a populist much in the same mould as David Croll. Elected to Sandwich's council when he was just 24, Reaume became mayor at 26 and proceeded to work on behalf of the indigent. When relief men were sent out on a construction project in bitter cold, it was Reaume who sent them indoors until they were properly clothed.[22] After amalgamation, he continued to be Sandwich's man on the Board of Control and he raised the payment to Macdonald as an abuse of the system. While the legal bill was quite in order, Macdonald tendered his resignation. Reaume, eager to push the knife in deeper, insisted that the Board of Control formally fire him. The background had been laid for decades of enmity between these two men who would both be prominent in the city's public life.

Still, as a result of the financial settlement, a huge rock holding back the community had been lifted. As one of the accountants before the OMB had observed, "It is better that both creditors and debtor should give in somewhat in order to straighten out the mess." It was all the more important that they be flexible for "Windsor had been in default for four years. In that condition there was bound to be some loss of civic pride."[23]

Civic pride was about to be restored, and in the most unlikely of places.

The German airship Graf Zeppelin floats over the Detroit River, October 1933. The Nazi swastika (not visible) was located on the port fin. The newly completed federal post office designed by Masson and Sheppard is in the foreground.

Chapter Nine
New Confidence
1936–1941

Berlin, the capital of Adolf Hitler's Third Reich, had made every preparation for the 1936 Olympics. With its striking pageantry, the games became a grand display of Nazi efficiency and the renewed power of Germany. It would also be a stage where Windsor athletes would achieve remarkable distinction.

The one sport in which Windsor would field a legendary team at the 1936 Olympics was basketball. Young men and women in the city loved the game, and Windsor's basketball teams regularly won provincial and national titles at the collegiate and senior levels. This was due in part to intense competition with American teams, as well as the coaching of Fr. W.P. McGee of Assumption College. His "Five Fighting Freshmen" squad included Stanley "Red" Nantais, Gord Aitchison, Don Desjarlais, Irving "Toots" Meretsky, and the big forward, Willie "Moose" Rogin. That a number of Assumption's players, including Rogin and Meretsky, were Jewish did not disrupt the nominally Catholic squad. Winning collegiate titles was one thing. But in order to qualify for the 1936 Olympics, Assumption had to face national competition, starting with a Ford of Canada sponsored team made up primarily of ex-Assumption players.

Their confrontation in February-March 1936 was a classic matchup of the best basketball players in the country. For Assumption, Willie Rogin, described as the "huge and seemingly ponderous forward" was the dominant player.[1] But the Ford team, frequently called the "Ford V8s," had a number of stellar veterans including Julius Goldman and a fine coach in Gordon Fuller. While the games in the best-of-five series were all close, Assumption established a two-to-one lead by mid-February. Nevertheless, the Fords had great success on the smaller floor at the Assumption gym and evened the series. The deciding game was played on March 4 at the Kennedy gym where 1,600 fans jammed into the hall and hundreds more milled outside awaiting the outcome. In a clever, if suspicious, tactic, Coach Fuller used tape to crop four feet off each side of the playing area so that it replicated the surface of the Assumption floor. Father McGee countered by having his squad play a zone defence that, in the first half, stymied the Ford players. But in the second half, the V8s broke through Assumption's defences and won the city championship. That victory was essentially the national championship, for the Ford V8s cruised through the remainder of the national playoffs and won the Canadian title. The V8s (with three players from British Columbia) would represent Canada at the Olympics. While Fuller offered a position on the squad to Assumption star Rogin, as Ford would not pay the costs of non-V8s and his family could not cover the travel expenses, Moose Rogin was denied his chance at the Olympics.

At the Olympic opening ceremony, Windsor's basketball contingent was part of the Canadian team that gave the stiff-armed salute as they marched past Hitler's reviewing stand. The salute was actually the official 'Olympic greeting,' developed in 1924, but looked so similar to the Nazi salute that the British and French teams refused to participate. The crowd roared its approval, even though the move was widely condemned back in Canada. Windsor basketball player Tom Pendlebury later admitted that "As far as I could see it was the same as the German salute." During this first-ever Olympic basketball tournament, Canada easily defeated its opponents until it faced the United States in the finals. Germans had little familiarity with basketball to the extent that they were unaware that it was usually an indoor sport. Instead, they had cobbled together clay tennis courts and drew in

Windsor's Ford V-8 basketball team prepares for the 1936 Berlin Olympics.

makeshift lines. The gold medal game was played in the rain with a light, unbalanced ball that absorbed water and had unpredictable bounces. The horrific conditions threw off both teams, but the Americans adjusted better and took the gold with a 19–8 win.[2]

Another Windsor athlete achieved unexpected glory at the 1936 Games. John Loaring was just a skinny youngster at Kennedy when track coach Hec Creighton saw something in him and urged him to take up track and field. Loaring was a natural sprinter and soon excelled at the 440 yards. As well, he was especially agile and could easily handle sprints over hurdles. He first caught the public's attention by winning an Intra-Empire event in Australia in 1934. From that point on, he specialized in the hurdles and set up his own course on a Lake Erie beach where he raced against his dog. While not given much of a chance of even making the finals, Loaring went into the final heat in Berlin and won the silver medal. It was one of Canada's finest performances of the games. Despite the enduring political controversy of the 1936 games, Windsor's athletes had made their mark. Nevertheless, the background of the Berlin games was inescapable. Windsor's Irving Meretsky, a basketball silver medal winner and a Jew, ventured out of the Olympic compound and into the Jewish commercial district of Berlin. There he found an eerie sight with stores closed and counters stripped bare. The few residents who peered out appeared downcast—"you could tell they were scared," he later recalled.[3]

Getting Back on Your Feet

In 1935, the Chamber of Commerce reckoned that Windsor was at last emerging from the Depression. They attributed this revival to the imperial preferences agreed upon at the Ottawa Conference of 1932. As a result of these agreements, Canada's trade with Britain and the Empire now exceeded its trade with the United States. The Chamber boasted that "Windsor has become an attractive locality for American firms desiring to expand their export business in the British Empire." It was estimated that by the mid-1930s, "of the 260 companies located in Windsor, 136 of these are American." National automobile production was recovering. From a low of 61,000 cars manufactured in 1931, in 1935 production had tripled to 180,000. Chrysler was feeling confident enough in 1935 to build a major extension to No. 3 plant. However, the revival of the branch plant economy was threatened by the return of the free-trading Liberals to power in 1935. Conservative MP, Dr. Raymond Morand, warned that "abolition of the tariff on automobiles would wreck the manufacture of automobiles in this community." Nevertheless, a young Liberal, Paul Martin, was elected for Essex East in 1935, and Mackenzie King formed a Liberal government.

True to Morand's warnings, tariffs were reduced and the number of imported cars rose from 4% in 1935 to 7.8% in 1936. Wallace Campbell published a booklet in 1938 decrying the auto tariff reductions of 35 to 17.5 percent and that "any further reduction would jeopardize employment." But Liberals were determined that any remaining shelters would be stripped from the auto industry. In 1939, as part of the previous year's trade agreement with the U.S., the excise tax on imported cars was revoked. This time, labour unions joined with management in a chorus of protest. Leading socialist George Bennett argued that "the government should give it [auto industry] every protection possible."[4] That was clearly not the intention of King's government. In 1939, Hudson Motors in nearby Tilbury moved all of its production back to Detroit and threw 500 men out of work. As the last car rolled off the line, men placed a placard on it reading: "The Last Supper From King."

In March 1939, the *Detroit Free Press* published an extensive report on tariff reductions and reported that two of the three principal auto plants in Canada were planning to repatriate all assembly operations to the United States. The loss in employment would be catastrophic. Even Norman McLarty, the Liberal MP from Essex West, had to admit that between 1937 and 1938, exports to the United States fell by 26 percent. During the same year, employment in the auto industry fell and wages declined by seven percent.[5] "The new Canada-United States treaty is responsible directly for the critical situation," declared the *Free Press.* Paul Martin, the Windsor MP whose party had caused the situation, rose in the House of Commons but was unable to provide any justification for the job losses. He meekly suggested that perhaps a system of unemployment insurance was called for.[6] Yet, the long-term impact of King's trade policies would never be known. With the disruptions to production as a result of the Second World War, the effect of Liberal free-trade policies would never come into full force.

Nevertheless, Windsor workers had done well during the high tariff period, and the after-glow continued for at least a short while. In 1936, Chrysler offered a bonus to its employees, and that December, Ford announced that they would build an additional assembly plant to increase their production by another 25 percent. The new plant, located south of the existing Ford works, was yet another example of the city expanding away from the Detroit River, as Windsor industry increasingly depended on rail instead of water for the transport of its goods. By the spring of 1937, Windsor's employment increase of 46 percent over the 1926 rate eclipsed the rate of three percent in Vancouver and

Toronto. Banks were now confident enough to lend out money for residential construction. The value of buildings erected rose from $703,000 in 1936 to over $3.5 million in 1937.[7] As a measure of its confidence in the future, Ford established its own trade school in 1936, building on the success of the three-year apprenticeship program that had been offered at Windsor-Walkerville Technical School since 1925. The new school was in a building, separate from the factory, where young men had access to a welding shop, an electrical laboratory and were instructed by senior tradesmen. Ford Trade School became an elite institution, and its graduates were a steady source of highly skilled workers.[8]

Another tangible sign of better times was slum removal. While the old residential area east of the downtown had poor housing, and Remington Park south of the central city was largely composed of simple one-storey homes, the worst housing in the area was located in Sandwich West Township along Dominion Boulevard just outside the city limits. Known as "Tin Can City," it was, according to geographer J. Lewis Robinson, "a real slum area. Here, houses were actually constructed of cardboard boxes and tin cans as the full weight of the depression struck the automobile industry."[9] By the end of the 1930s, with better housing available and the township starting to enforce by-laws, most of the shacks were torn down or replaced by proper structures. It was time to get rid of the relics of the Depression.

One of those relics was the reliance on relief instead of work. Provincial Minister of Welfare, David Croll, was aggressively pushing municipalities to weed out ineligible recipients. This was of particular concern as other cities were beginning to complain that too much was being spent on Windsor. The *Hamilton Spectator* pointed out that while Woodstock received $1.25 per head in relief and Toronto $9.26, Windsor was getting $37.00 per capita. The *St. Catharines Standard* questioned why Windsor should receive this largesse and wondered whether it was a case of "Mr. Croll playing Santa Claus in Windsor." Croll was sensitive to these accusations, and warned Windsor's council that they would have to live within their means.[10] The response from socialist mayor George Bennett was a demagogic "I don't care if there are five overdrafts on the bank" and he threatened to spend Windsor back into bankruptcy. Fortunately, finances remained firmly under the control of the provincial Department of Municipal Affairs, and the city continued to meet its obligations.

Another way of reducing welfare was to require the unemployed to participate in public work-projects in return for relief payments. The Windsor official in charge of this program was another one of the dynamic female figures to emerge during the 1930s. Nell Wark, one of six girls raised in a pioneer cabin in Manitoba, worked her way up from being a teacher in a one-room school to studying social work at the University of Chicago. In 1926, she became the first head of Windsor's Social Services Commission. She later set up welfare departments in Hamilton and St. Catharines. By 1935, she was back in Windsor as an officer of the provincial Department of Welfare and the city's acting welfare administrator. Beginning in 1935, able-bodied men who sought relief were required to report to a city yard for work. In July 1935, Wark arranged for 128 relief men to work at the Drouillard Road Woodyard. Charles Newbury (a communist agitator), Alderman Raycraft, and an estimated mob of 500 protestors tried to stop them from getting in. Wark, with a police escort, opened the gates and personally "supervised the work of getting men started at their jobs."[11]

While business in Windsor dipped slightly in 1938, perhaps in response to the greater imports from the U.S., a general recovery still seemed to be the trend. That year, Ford's new assembly plant came into operation and the Mercury 8, a mid-sized car with a V8 engine, was introduced. Canadian Automotive Trim bought a surplus Ford building and expanded its supply of parts to the assembly plants. Perhaps the most impressive statistic was the decline in the number of persons on relief. Croll was right that work was available and that the welfare rolls could be reduced. From 25,000 in February 1936, the welfare number dropped to 17,630 one year later. In the summer of 1938, for the first time since the start of the Depression, the city's relief roll declined to under 10,000.[12]

The United Auto Workers Arrive and Sit-Down

Better times also meant the unleashing of demands that had been pent up during the wilderness years. In 1934, there were a series of strikes at Windsor Bedding, Auto Specialties, and Canadian Auto Lamp by the communist Workers' Unity League. These strikes achieved some wage gains, but no union recognition. Thereafter, union activity was sporadic and largely ineffective. Yet, a new force was rising in Detroit. While the American Federation of Labor (AFL) represented the traditional craft unions, under John L. Lewis, the Committee of Industrial Organization became a reinvigorated branch of the U.S. labour movement and broke from the AFL in 1935. The following year, Lewis's group formed an alliance with a newly chartered union, the United Auto Workers, and formed the Congress of Industrial Organizations (CIO). By the fall of 1936, the CIO and the UAW were actively targeting General Motors facilities in southeastern Michigan. While their focus was on organizing American workers, UAW officials could not ignore the benefits of joining forces with Canadians. Even if the tariff system and immigration laws had divided American and Canadian business, the labour movement had no hesitation in dealing with the Detroit-Windsor region as if it was one.

James Napier, a Scottish immigrant and one of the most militant workers at Kelsey Wheel, had been keeping track of events in Detroit. He began at Kelsey in 1930 at age 19, but was laid off during the Depression. Upon his return in 1936, he was appalled by the company's attitude. Efficiency experts were looking at ways to speed up the assembly line while wages were constantly dropping. Anyone who dared complain would be replaced by one of the thousands of men who were still desperate for work. Napier would stop by the tool crib to chat with an old hand, and from him "I got a steady dose of communism." In late 1936, Napier crossed the river and met with Walter Reuther and Richard Frankensteen, the UAW leaders at the American Kelsey plant. They explained that their men were about to go on strike and that it would be a morale booster if their Windsor comrades would join them.

Deciding to cast their fate with the UAW, Napier and a few other men chartered the first Canadian UAW branch, Local 195, on December 9, 1936, at Kelsey Wheel. A week later, Napier and four other union organizers were fired. Kelsey went on strike, and sixty men conducted a "sit-down" occupying the factory floor. Occupying a plant had become a new method to keep employers from using outside workers, but it failed to work at the Windsor Kelsey plant as there were so few men that the police could easily dislodge them. Kelsey President Malcolm Campbell flatly announced that he would not recognize any unions. Tom Parry, an American communist from the UAW, arrived to help organize while Napier supplied the muscle. That is, he personally administered beatings to men who tried to cross the picket line. As Napier recalled,

Pickets at Kelsey Wheel, 1936.

"The next morning at 6:00 a.m., about fifty or sixty of us turned out to see that no one went in to work... I was pounding the hell out of a scab between some parked cars in the lot" and later "Ken Clark and I were sent out to Remington park to take care of a guy. We decided just to scare him, just to put a brick through his window." When this failed to deter, Napier concluded: "he was stopped, however. Other means were used."[13] Still, Kelsey continued production, and on December 20, Frankensteen came to Windsor and exhorted the men that "no one goes into that damned plant tomorrow." The following day, picketers tried to stop cabs carrying employees from entering the factory. "As each taxicab arrived, pickets swarmed around and endeavored to hold the cars back... Police armed with batons mixed it freely with strike pickets."[14] It was no use. The police were prepared to use the force necessary to keep the factory operating even at a reduced rate. After the Detroit workers settled on December 22, the steam went out of the Kelsey strike and they settled on December 29 for a five-cent-an-hour increase. Local 195 did not gain official recognition. It was a disappointment to many, and Napier concluded "Reuther sold us out."

While it was an important step in union activism, the Kelsey Wheel strike was about to be overshadowed by events elsewhere. In the winter of 1937, UAW activists targeted the General Motors plant at Flint, Michigan. A massive sit-down strike and subsequent confrontations with police were won by the union. GM was forced to recognize the UAW and the floodgates were opened to union mobilization. Canadian activists had anxiously monitored the Flint strike and understood that the same pressures could be brought to bear against GM in Oshawa.[15] The CIO was well organized among the 4,000 workers at the huge GM plant in that city; however, management was adamant that they would sign no agreement with them. In the ensuing strike, Minister of Labour David Croll emerged as a voice of moderation who was prepared to deal with labour representatives. However, Premier Mitchell Hepburn feared that the CIO was a subversive front for communism, and he was determined to use as much armed force as he could muster to quash it. He had no use for moderates such as Croll, who along with Attorney General Arthur Roebuck, were dismissed from cabinet. In response, Croll explained that the workers were acting lawfully and responsibly, and concluded with the phrase that would resonate long after the strike: "my place is marching with the workers rather than riding with General Motors."[16]

Even if he was now out of cabinet, Croll's point had been made. The Oshawa strike had established that mass production industries could organize, and their unions were a force to be reckoned with. As for Croll, he was rapturously received back in Windsor, and Liberal and even Conservative spokesmen lauded him. His city, however, remained a hotbed of labour unrest. During the Oshawa strike, 500 Windsor GM workers were laid off and in solidarity with their Oshawa brothers, pickets were raised along the Walker Road plant. Napier and a fellow communist, William Emery, were determined to raise union agitation to a new level. As Emery phrased it, "It is our objective to unionize this city."[17]

Strikes broke out in May 1937 at the spring factory of L.A. Young and at Walker Metal. The Young plant had a substantial female workforce in their auto trim department and many of them confessed to "having to use their bodies to get their jobs." Contracts were signed at both plants, but still there was no union recognition. 1938 would see even more union activity and Windsor endured five strikes between August and October. "The struggle was intense," historian Louis Veres observed, "and often the real issues were overshadowed by the tactics used."[18] Walker Metal again went out, and this time, there was a series of attacks against non-strikers and constant picket-line violence. Napier, one of the principal assailants, went to jail for thirty days. A bomb capable of destroying a house was placed at the home of a non-striker and only failed to detonate due to a defective fuse. But the escalating violence only seemed to harden management's resolve to resist. The ultimate settlement at Walker Metal, after three months, again failed to achieve union recognition.

The agitation of the late 1930s had shown that unions, largely communist-led, had an impressive ability to organize workers. Along the way, communist agitators were prepared to use whatever force they deemed fit. Frequently, as in the Kelsey Wheel and GM strikes, they had achieved limited results. But the series of strikes also showed that most workers in Windsor were still leery of becoming allied with such radical forces. In any event, the violence had not achieved its main objectives. By the end of the 1930s, there were no effective laws requiring collective bargaining or compelling workers to join a union. Union activity could, and frequently did, result in workers being fired. Perhaps there was another way.

Other Options

The non-communist response to Jim Napier came from an unexpected source. Edwin Garvey had worked at the Oshawa GM plant in the late 1920s, then joined the Basilian Order, and was ordained a Catholic priest in 1932. He began teaching philosophy at Assumption College in 1937 and offered an open class to workers on social justice issues. These classes eventually grew into the Pius XI Labour School where Garvey "advocated the rights of workers to organize and criticized reactionary groups opposed to unionization." To some extent, the popularity of the school was due to Windsor's religious makeup. If the city was forty percent Catholic, the factory floor had a similar, if not slightly greater, composition. It was found that "Many Catholic workers were hesitant to have anything to do with unions, particularly if they were perceived as radical, as the CIO certainly was. In Windsor, a particular complication was that workers were drawn from the surrounding farming country and carried a rural suspicion of unions."[19]

Due to its diverse ethnic mixture, Windsor had many denominations, but religion remained a significant factor in most people's lives. Every summer the city's Protestants got together for weekend outings at Bob-Lo Island.[20] Up to 2,000 members of All Saints' Anglican, Central United, Temple Baptist, and Westminster United chartered the S.S. *Columbia* in 1939 for a day at Bob-Lo. Marxism and revolution was not in the cultural makeup of these congregations. Moreover, they remained unabashedly patriotic. Anglican parishes conducted special services in 1937 to mark King George VI's coronation. Also in that year, both Catholic parishes and the Windsor Council of Churches sponsored two full boxcars of foodstuffs to be shipped to suffering families in Saskatchewan. Submitting to communist leadership was abhorrent to those who still treasured their spiritual life and traditional ways.

Father Garvey's classes offered open discussions in which workers of any religious or political affiliation could voice their opinions about the future of the labour movement. Garvey's labour school was home to an increasingly powerful vanguard of labour activists who dissented from communist leadership. But for communists such as Napier, to whom Marxist principles had assumed a quasi-religious status, Fr. Garvey was the enemy. Napier devoted a chapter of his recollections to denouncing the priest and the group of union leaders he encouraged. To Napier, it was the communists who had inspired the union activism of the late 1930s. Yet, it was the "fireside philosophers" of the CCF (whom he detested in equal measure to the Catholics) and Catholic activists who eventually came to lead the labour movement. It was a cruel trick, he thought, for "behind the mask of religion was the ugly face of the capitalist class."[21]

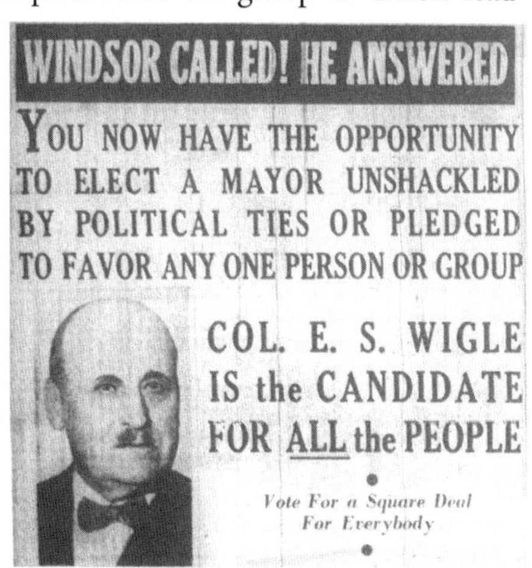

Campaign advertisement in the Windsor Daily Star for Ernest Wigle, 1936.

Even local politics took a turn to the right with the election of Ernest Wigle as mayor in 1936. In the most surprising comeback in Windsor's political history, Wigle, a five-term mayor in the first decade of the century, came back in its fourth at the age of 76 to again run for chief executive. After service at the front as commander of the 18th Battalion, a fruitful career in the law, and a legacy as the founder of Windsor's parks, it might have been assumed that Wigle's day had passed. But the Chamber of Commerce wanted to put a solid businessman forward, and Wigle accepted the challenge. At first glance, the decision appeared to be pure folly, for the incumbent mayor, George Bennett, had been elected by a huge plurality in 1935 and the area was seething with anti-business sentiment. Nevertheless, Bennett's bombastic style, combined with the insults he hurled at anyone who questioned him, alienated all who crossed his path.[22] Wigle was narrowly elected and proceeded to give the newly united city an efficient government. The city's finances were put in order and on June 25, 1937, for the first time in years, the Council passed a by-law authorizing new debentures. Tax revenues were now flowing at a reliable rate and more than 80 percent were collected in 1937.

One of Wigle's most difficult assignments was to reduce Windsor's relief rate to the provincial average. He accomplished this in May 1938 by forcing a 20 percent reduction in welfare allowances. During the council meeting on May 17, communists responded by mobilizing a mob that surrounded City Hall. Heedless for his own safety, the 78-year-old mayor marched out of City Hall, "through the surging crowd the broad-shouldered figure of the mayor stepped off the paces that separated him from the safety of his car. He never faltered."[23]

Neither was Wigle some kind of heartless ogre. At the same time he was reducing allowances, which the province would have forced Windsor to do in any event, Wigle convinced Toronto and Ottawa to grant $50,000 to the municipality to finance riverfront improvements. Even with the addition of the wooded space of Memorial Park in 1926 and Jackson Park in 1929, Windsor still had a paucity of parklands. In 1929, an ambitious plan to join with the County and beautify the Essex County waterfront had fallen apart.[24] Within weeks of the 1938 welfare reductions, scores of unemployed men were hired to landscape riverfront lands. Thanks to the bridge and tunnel, these lands were no longer needed for commercial purposes and scores of workers groomed terraces and planted shrubs along the frontage from the Ambassador Bridge to Bridge Avenue. It was a first step in the long-term objective to develop the riverfront for the people.

As for David Croll, by late 1938, he was languishing on the provincial backbenches. Before his summary dismissal from the cabinet, Croll's stature had grown to the extent that he threatened to overshadow Premier Hepburn.

His bill to provide a minimum wage for men was popular, and as the prime supporter of another bill to share corporate taxes with separate schools, he was admired by Catholics. Still, he missed the challenge of executive office and decided to run for mayor in November 1938. Despite an acrimonious campaign—and accusations that since he was supported by the communists he was one—Croll was easily elected, and Colonel Wigle sent back to retirement.

Modern Times

While the 1930s might be dismissed as a static period, where survival was the only objective, it was a time in which much of our modern world emerged. Windsor's first radio station, CKOK, opened on June 1, 1932, with a broadcast of "God Save the King."[25] The following year, it merged with a London station to become CKLW. Describing itself as a Windsor-Detroit station, CKLW appealed to Detroit advertisers and drew the ire of WXYZ in Detroit, who thought the station should keep to its own side of the river. But radio waves were impervious to geography and CKLW started to gain an audience across the Midwest.

Yet, it was in the area of transportation that truly significant changes took place. Windsor's streetcar system was old and tired. The replacement of cars and the refurbishing of tracks would require a significant capital investment. A far cheaper alternative was simply to rip up the tracks and replace them with trolleys or buses. By early 1938, W.H. Furlong, the SW&A's chairman, announced a plan to phase out streetcars and replace them with buses. On July 7, 1938, the last streetcar rolled up Ouellette Avenue and on May 8, 1939, the remaining cars were pushed into the barns for the last time.[26] The streetcars, the popular mode of travel for almost 70 years, ceased to run.

An even more dramatic transformation was the end of the ferry service. With the tunnel carrying hundreds of cars across the river at all seasons with little or no delay, the economic rationale for the ferries had long ended. Still, the ferry company was bound by various contractual obligations, and the ships continued to sail across the river even after they ceased to be profitable. Finally, in 1938, the service was due to end, and on the evening of July 18, the *Cadillac* left the dock for the last run across to Detroit. Hundreds of citizens jammed the boats all afternoon to be a part of the end of an era. As the *Cadillac* left the shore, a spontaneous party broke out. People stormed the captain's bridge and girls planted kisses on his cheeks. It was "hilarity mixed with sadness" as the exuberant crowd that packed the ship "came to bid farewell to the service that carried them to their daily labors for decades."[27] Other changes, not nearly so dramatic but far more profound, defined the late 1930s. Until that time, diphtheria, rickets, and typhoid were regular visitors to Windsor's families. But public health was now a major government priority, and regular inoculations of schoolchildren and inspections of milk and water radically reduced child mortality. At the Capitol Theatre, a free chest clinic detected tuberculosis cases and sent them on for an X-ray at Metropolitan Hospital. After amalgamation in 1935, free child welfare clinics were offered across the metropolitan area. Infant and mother mortality declined to a third of what it had been in the 1920s. As for diphtheria, the 400 to 800 cases a year in the early 1920s declined to fewer than ten a year.[28] At last, the hospitals caught up to the greater population, and with the addition to Hôtel-Dieu, there was ample capacity. By 1938, Metropolitan Hospital had a cancer clinic in 1938 and Grace Hospital a "shock-proof" X-ray table.

One positive outcome of the Depression was to open up the doors for medical coverage to everyone. The Medical Officer of Health, Dr. Fred Adams, explained in 1937 that the 25 cent per month stipend that the government provided to each welfare recipient for medical costs was sent to the Essex County Medical Association. Local doctors provided services to all indigents and were paid from this fund. Adams explained that the Rockefeller Foundation was intrigued by this arrangement and provided a grant to develop this plan which was "unique and has drawn international attention." Former Conservative MP, Raymond Morand hoped to build on this by creating a co-operative system of pre-paid medical services. Morand proposed that a similar scheme be extended to those working in the factories. Small monthly installments would enable workers to buy medical insurance and the Essex County Medical Association would oversee the implementation of the plan. A pioneering start was made on Morand's idea when Windsor Medical Services began in 1939. Under the plan, workers paid a monthly fee and received coverage for specified medical services. The program appealed to workers who had a regular income and whose families needed protection against unexpected medical expenses. Six weeks after its July opening, 1,000 workers had enrolled. While its secretary, Dr. M.S. Douglas, conceded that it was "socialized medicine," the plan was effective and would grow in popularity during the 1940s.[29] Whatever hardships the 1930s had brought, Windsor emerged as a community that put a premium on the health and welfare of its citizens.[30]

Low Life and High Society

Still, Windsor was not a genteel city. Workers emerging from the factories were frequently covered in oil and dust, and they were expected to clean up on their own time. Nevertheless, they could still use a drink after a nine-hour shift. But the inspectors who monitored the "hotels" where limited drinking was permitted after 1934 were anxious to preserve middle-class propriety. Frequently, this was just not possible in Windsor. Inspector U.G. Reaume kept an eye on the American Hotel in Sandwich which served men coming off shift from a foundry:

> It is very difficult to keep this place clean because of the smoke, dust and soot from the foundry… Men go into the beverage rooms and their clothes are greasy and it necessitates washing the furniture every day, sometimes more often during the day. Yet as other hotel owners explained to Reaume, this place renders quite a service because workmen would not feel like going into the other [hotels] in their working clothes."[31]

An exception was made for the American Hotel. However, for other licensed premises, patrons were expected to be clean and proper, to drink quietly, refrain from playing cards, singing or making too much noise. Closing time was 11:00 p.m. Regulations required women who wished to drink in public to be accompanied by a male escort and sit in a separate part of the tavern. In other words, drinking spaces had to comply with Victorian dictates of middle-class respectability. This was becoming increasingly difficult to enforce when those laws had lost their moral authority during the rum-running years. It was especially challenging as Detroit clubs, only minutes away from Windsor, regularly offered dancing and music until two in the morning. Why did Canadian establishments have to be so dour while their American competition was so lively?[32] Ontario's Chief Inspector surveyed the state of hotels in Windsor and ruefully observed that "some are trying to emulate the American ideas with Music and Entertainment." Some roadhouses, such as Bertha Thomas's Edgewater Inn, simply ignored the rules and offered music, dancing and bottled beer—all in contravention of the LCBO regulations

Victorian morality never had any appeal to the non-British population. Inspector Reaume was aghast to discover at Windsor's Ostschwaben Alliance a "place filled [with]… approximately, 40 women and about 100 men… singing German songs… to music from a five-piece orchestra accompanied by a piano." The operator of the city's Hungarian Club was of the view that women "have the same rights to enjoy the privilege of having beer as the men members." Worst of all, an inspector at the Polish War Veteran's Association of Windsor found "men and women drinking with babes in arms not over three or four months old." The ethnic clubs functioned as social centres "along the lines of the norms of the host country, where this communal beer-hall configuration presumably contradicted Ontarians' sense of respectability."[33] While the rest of

Ontario seemed content with the moral laws of the 1880s, Windsor was set apart as a community of defiant imbibers.

At least controlled drinking was legal. Gambling, by contrast, remained an inexcusable vice. But with the return of limited prosperity in the late 1930s, the public's appetite to gamble was apparent. On March 1, 1937, it was reported that the "Michigan Club," a large-scale gambling emporium on the top floor of the Davis Block, had been raided by Windsor police. Upon breaking in, the police discovered a well-appointed, fully equipped casino with the latest gambling tables, chip racks, and dice sets. While 129 persons were arrested, few of them were from Windsor. Significantly, almost all of the Michigan Club's patrons came from Detroit while a few were from Toronto and Montreal.[34] Nevertheless, respectability was making a stand in a few well-heeled bastions.

During the bleaker years of the Depression, many members of the middle class had flirted with disaster and had joined the ranks of the workers or even sought relief. Now, with the return of limited prosperity, society was recovering. Beach Grove Golf Club formally opened the 1937 spring season with a sumptuous gala. The Windsor Yacht Club opened in the summer of 1938, and in recognition of the changed times, Commodore Villeneuve explained that the financial background of members was no longer relevant. The club was 'organized along democratic lines [and] is open to those who are that way about boats." There was nothing democratic about the "Royal Air Force Ball" in the spring of 1938 in which Mayor Wigle led the most prominent members of society at the Prince Edward Hotel. Tickets to the event were coveted by the elite in Detroit as well as Windsor, and resplendent gowns were the order of the evening for the female members of the cream of cross-border society.

None of this could match the festivities that were scheduled for June 6, 1939.

King George VI and Queen Mary arrive in Windsor during their royal tour of Canada, 1939.

In 1938, it was announced that King George VI and Queen Mary would tour Canada. Windsor was not included on the itinerary. While the royals would stop at rural areas on the Prairies, the agricultural and industrial heartland of southern Ontario was largely ignored. Liberal members from the area, who had been strangely quiet while auto tariffs were reduced, howled in protest at this insult and the itinerary was hastily redrawn to include a brief stop in Windsor. The royal visit was an opportunity to renew the Anglo-Canadian connection, and those of British stock planned to be in the forefront. They were not alone. UAW Local 195 offered to supply a guard along the five-mile train route, while Chinese restaurants hung up lanterns along Goyeau Street and the Italian Club held a formal Royal Visit Dance.

The trip also attracted some unwanted guests. The day before the King's arrival, Sean Russell, the chief of staff of the Irish Republican Army, was arrested in Detroit. It was a mere coincidence, he explained, but officials were not so sure. Late in the afternoon of Tuesday, June 6, the blue and silver train carrying the royals edged along the tracks through a five-mile-long throng of flag-waving enthusiasts. The immense skyline of Detroit was outlined against the setting sun, and the river was filled with a flotilla of vessels. Prime Minister King, who had appointed himself Their Majesties' constant companion, thought that the Windsor welcome was "easily the finest display of the whole tour."[35] The only regret was that since the Windsor stop went over schedule and darkness was falling, the train did not stop at the children's grandstand on the way out. Thousands of youngsters who had waited in the heat were bitterly disappointed.

The royal visit also stirred other feelings. It was the first time that many Windsorites had seen their riverfront as something other than a grimy railway yard. Many suddenly appreciated that with the trains gone, the riverfront was a splendid natural vista. Even Prime Minister King, who had little familiarity with the area, was struck by its beauty. "With the river on one side and the people between the train and the river… skyline of Detroit visible on one side" the entrance to the city was spectacular. The editorial in the next day's *Star* noted that "Thousands of Windsorites saw their riverfront in a new light on Tuesday evening… it made one really begin to appreciate what possibilities

Crowds throng at the riverfront during the royal visit, 1939.

our riverfront holds."[36] For the moment, there was no prospect of the trains moving elsewhere and the riverfront being returned to the people. But the seed had been planted.

A Different City

Whether the royals knew it or not, Windsor was markedly different from the other stops on their tour. For one thing, it was far less British than other Canadian cities. At 59 percent British stock, Windsor stood in stark contrast to London, which was 89 percent and Toronto and Hamilton which were 78 percent. Windsor also had a strong French minority of almost 20 percent whereas comparable Ontario cities had a minor French presence. While the number of non-British Europeans was also high (19 percent) in growing cities such as Toronto and Hamilton, in Windsor this rate was even higher and 21 percent of residents were from eastern or southern Europe.[37]

Some came from even farther away. Windsor had a Middle-Eastern community of Lebanese (usually referred to as "Syrians") of almost 250. Similar to most ethnic groups, their head was their religious leader, Msgr. Peter Farah, who established St. Peter's Maronite parish in the early 1920s. While to outsiders, the ethnic groups appeared to be cohesive blocks, there were always tensions within the communities. In 1933, the Hungarian Presbyterian Church erupted in a dispute and dissident members broke away to form the Hungarian Reformed Church. The following year a "Church War" divided the Russian Orthodox neighbourhood on Drouillard Road and led to the creation of a new parish.[38] While Windsor ethnic groups remained distinct entities, usually under the banner of their local church, there were signs that they were melding into a larger community. When basketball star Red Nantais got married in the late 1930s, he chose as his best man Willie Rogin, even though it required a papal dispensation for a Jew to assist at a Catholic wedding. It was also a sign of the times that the grandson of a Yiddish-speaking Jew from eastern Europe was the best friend of a descendant of French-Canadian farmers.[39]

Windsor's Italian community, almost ten times the size of the Lebanese, also looked to their spiritual head, Msgr. Constantino De Santis. Almost fifty years old when he came to Windsor, De Santis was sent for the specific purpose of organizing a church to serve the city's Italian immigrants. Many of his congregation had little to live on, and nothing to spare to build a church. So as well as routine parish work, he focused on his people's needs. Many mornings, the Monsignor could be found at plant gates, seeing if the foremen could use another hand. Men who had nowhere else to stay could find a place at his rectory.

In gratitude, De Santis could rely on men donating their work to the church, and on skilled men working at less than scale. It all added up until St. Angela Merici began to take form. In December 1939, the Monsignor said Mass in the basement of the still unfinished (and freezing cold) church.[40]

Bishop Kidd and Monsignor De Santis bless the cornerstone at the new St. Angela Merici Church, 1939.

While still a much smaller group than the East-Europeans, the Italians had begun to make their mark. Mariano Meconi ran a prosperous winery in Sandwich West, and in the early 1930s, was elected reeve. Like many prominent Italians, Meconi was a member of the *Loggia General Umberto Nobile*, a patriotic club which emphasized the comradeship between Italian and British veterans. Having fought in the same cause, Italian veterans were prominent during all Remembrance Day ceremonies. Even in the 1920s, Italians began to establish construction companies. Antonio Colautti settled in Montreal in 1913, where his first work was tunnelling under Mount Royal. By the 1920s he, along with his brother John and brother-in-law John Costaperaria (Costa), formed Colautti Brothers Construction and moved to Windsor where expansion created so many opportunities. By 1929, resentment against Mussolini's dictatorship caused the Colauttis to change the company's name to the neutral "Keystone Construction" and retain lawyer Charles Clark as their spokesman.

While the rise of Adolf Hitler and the international tensions of the late 1930s were just newspaper headlines to most Windsorites, for many immigrants, these events affected their friends and relatives back home. While most Canadians followed the British example in condemning Italy's invasion of Ethiopia in 1935, one group of Windsor Italians met at St. Alphonsus Hall in January 1936 to hear the vice-consul, George Tiberi, praise Mussolini and ask for money to assist the invasion. In response, several women donated their gold wedding rings.[41] Luigi Meconi, who had business contacts back in Italy and was a well-known Fascist supporter, chaired the meeting. The Italian club on Brant Street favoured Mussolini and gave out Fascist garments. During the Depression, some men took the offer of a free shirt and pants simply to get the clothes; it was a good deal "so long as you liked the colour black."

Still, other local Italians detested Mussolini and made it clear that they favoured democracy over Fascism. One was Angelo Zamparo, who came to Windsor as a young man of 20 in 1919. Despite having no formal education, Zamparo was an intelligent and energetic leader who mobilized the Italian community around the Liberal party. He became a principal lieutenant of David Croll, and at election times, he could be counted on to deliver the Italian vote as a block to the Liberals. After a trip to Italy, Zamparo assured the *Star* that many Italians secretly disliked Mussolini and prayed for the end to his dictatorship.[42] He emerged as a spokesman for Italians and defended their club on Wyandotte Street against Anglo critics who considered it a way of keeping immigrants apart. Zamparo argued that instead it helped to gradually integrate immigrants into the broader society.

As the world crisis mounted in the late 1930s, one group that was particularly concerned was Windsor's small Chinese community. Newspaper stories on the Chinese were rarely complimentary, and it was continually reported that they were either operating opium dens or threatening white women. This was in the face of evidence that they were hard workers and largely self-sufficient. Nevertheless, when an American Chinese athlete in transit to Boston was refused entry at the Windsor border in 1937, it only served to underline the laws which forbade any further Chinese immigrants. When Japan's aggression against China accelerated in August 1937, the community met at the Chinatown at the foot of Goyeau Street where Lee Dean, the head of the Chinese Society, appealed for funds to send humanitarian aid.[43]

Even more concerned were Windsor's Jewish citizens. In January 1939, much of the congregation of Shaar Hashomayim gathered to hear Irma Ehrlich describe her experiences in Vienna. After the Nazi annexation of Austria, her husband had been taken to a concentration camp where he was beaten to death. The situation was beyond desperate, and families were "putting their children on trains hoping to get them out of that dreadful country." Rabbi Nahum Shulman added "We dare not waste a day. We must rescue the Jewish children from the hell of Europe."[44] Funds were raised to send ten children to Palestine, but it seemed a small response to such an overwhelming problem.

"This Is not Our War"

The summer of 1939 was filled with anxiety as the outbreak of war seemed imminent, and no one followed events closer than the men of the Essex Scottish Regiment. The regiment had been formed in 1927, largely as a matter of attire. The new Scottish regiment sported the McGregor tartan, for it was presumed that highland dress was just the thing to draw in fresh recruits. To be an officer in the Essex Scots was a mark of social distinction and the officers were invariably drawn from members of the professional, British elite. Nevertheless, like all militia units, the regiment suffered from a lack of resources. When Germany invaded Poland on September 1, 1939, the commander, Lt. Col. Arthur Pearson, was instructed to raise 845 officers and men for a full strength battalion. Despite the outbreak of war, there seemed to be little urgency and Pearson announced that recruitment would begin after the weekend.[45]

There was a huge difference in the response between 1914 and 1939. When the First World War broke out, there was unrestrained enthusiasm on the streets of Windsor, as crowds waving Union Jacks surged up and down Ouellette Avenue. When Canada officially declared war on September 10, 1939, it almost passed without notice. The Essex Scots stolidly kept on recruiting, but with no place to house the men, those accepted for service returned to their homes for the evening. This restraint was reflected in Prime Minister King's policy. He hoped that no large expeditionary force would ever be sent to Europe and, at a meeting with British officials, he blurted out that "this is not our war." Even though the Essex Scots were eventually brought up to full strength, it did not appear to be their war either. Close order drill and interminable training exercises seemed to be the extent of their war contribution. One highlight was the enlistment of Mayor Croll in the battalion. Signing on as a private soldier, Croll, almost forty and the father of three young children, cut an unusual figure in platoons made up almost exclusively of younger men. But he was sincere in his desire to serve and, along with his comrades, moved into the military camp at the former Packard factory on St. Luke Road.

Mayor David Croll enlisted in the Essex Scots in 1939.

While the King government was reluctant to send troops overseas, the one area it was willing to participate in was air training. During the initial phase of the war, Ottawa looked upon the British Commonwealth Air Training Plan as "the most satisfactory vehicle for their principal war effort." Of course, the plan needed extensive access to airports. Since 1938, the federal government had been negotiating with Windsor over transforming the Walker facility from a short airstrip used by casual enthusiasts into a functioning airport. Mayor Croll balked at the city taking over the expense of running the service. But with the growing prospect of war, Ottawa gave in, and in the summer of 1939, it agreed to build an airport. While the army was in no hurry to mobilize, the Royal Canadian Air Force wasted no time, and the training school was scheduled to open on October 9, 1939. In July 1940, the No. 7 Elementary Flying Training School, a centre for the training of pilots from the Commonwealth and Allied countries, was inaugurated at the airport that only a few months before was farmers' fields.[46]

The city's indifference to the war was shattered in the spring of 1940 by Hitler's blitzkrieg across northern Europe. By the end of May, the French army was destroyed, the British trapped on Dunkirk's beaches, and on June 10, Italy entered the war against Britain. Windsor' reaction was nothing short of hysterical. All civic employees of Italian or German birth were suspended and City Council ordered that all church services be conducted in English or French. Jack Palmieri, the City's superintendent of construction and the city's only Italian policeman were fired. The most radical action was the immediate purge launched against Windsor's Italian population. More than 100 officers raided the homes of Italian families and scores of men were arrested. While it was no surprise that Fascist leader Luigi Meconi was one of those taken away, many others, such as Antonio Colautti, who had no known connection to any subversive organization, were also seized. Mounties also interrogated several German-born residents; however, none of them were arrested. As a *Star* editorial concluded, while Germans were a risk, "the menace from the Italian residents was even greater."[47] Scores of Italians, many of them patriotic Canadians who were the subject of malicious gossip, were headed for internment camps.

As they were leaving, another group was on its way. With the increased bombing of British cities, children were being evacuated and Wallace Campbell contacted his counterparts at Ford of Britain to bring children over to Windsor. The first group of "little war guests" arrived in early July. Most of the evacuees were the sons and daughters of British Ford executives, and Wallace Campbell arranged for Windsor Ford staff to take them in for the duration of the war. Another consequence of the blitzkrieg was to add greater urgency to the deployment of the Essex Scots. With Britain now alone and facing imminent invasion, reinforcements were desperately needed. On Saturday evening May 26, 1940, the battalion moved out by train for final combat exercises at Camp Borden before being shipped to Britain. Prior to their departure, they conducted a route march through the city as onlookers, many of them the families of the troops, sang songs and cheered them on. As best they could, families shared a few private moments before their husbands, fathers, or brothers boarded the train.[48] It would not be until July 23, 1940—eleven months into the war—that the regiment actually sailed to England.

The change in venue did not halt the regular dose of training, and more training. The regiment shuffled between various bases in Britain, but for them the war seemed to be nothing but an endless stream of exercises. To the Scots, and their families back in Windsor, it was almost as if the war was elsewhere and affecting other people. That was all to change on August 19, 1942.

Local Italian men line up before being sent to internment camps, 1940.

Chapter Ten
Making A People's War
1941–1944

Addressing the House of Commons in August 1940, Winston Churchill warned that Britain faced an imminent Nazi invasion and that the nation's survival hung in the balance. Sitting in the visitor's gallery was a private from the Essex Scottish Regiment. "It was a great moment," David Croll wrote back to Windsor, "it was the united voice of Britain, clear proud, unyielding."[1] But if prospects in Britain were grim, they had never been rosier in Windsor.

The spring blitzkrieg dispelled the prevailing inertia and impressed the need for action upon Mackenzie King's government. Yet, it seemed that there was little that Canada could contribute. Britain had not placed factory orders in Canada and Ottawa did not see any need to provide its forces with Canadian-made equipment. Still, there was one ray of light for "The only strong industry capable of moving fairly quickly into full-scale production for the war effort was the automotive industry."[2] By the summer of 1940, inaction turned to action and millions of dollars in contracts were flooding into Ford and Chrysler to provide military vehicles, mostly trucks. In contrast to the First World War, the major auto industries quickly retooled to meet the military's needs. Beyond trucks, Ford expanded in July 1940 to provide a facility to build the Universal (or Bren Gun) Carrier. Minister of Munitions and Supply, C.D. Howe promised that the emergency "will send Canadian wartime production into a crescendo of production." Windsor had never witnessed such an abrupt change in its prospects. As a watime measure, consumers would be prohibited from buying foreign products. The free-trade policies of the Liberals were hurriedly scrapped and heavy excise taxes imposed that prevented the sale of American cars in Canada.

One of the first Windsorites drafted into war service was Ford's Wallace Campbell. As the head of one of the country's most effective industries, he seemed the appropriate person to be the interim head of the War Supply Board. In short order, it became apparent that he had little understanding of national mobilization, and was described as "autocratic and indecisive." In April 1940, he was replaced by C.D. Howe.[3] Howe was ruthlessly efficient, and by the end of 1940, over $11 million in contracts had been allotted to Windsor factories. The impact on the community was dramatic. After a decade of young people sitting idle, now there were not enough hands to do the work. By September 1940, employment reached a zenith of 23,484, higher than it had ever been in the 1920s. By the following month, Ford alone was employing 8,900. Kelsey Wheel was put on a continuous shift basis, and at Auto Specialties, truck frames were being poured from molten metal day and night. A reporter looked in at Auto Specialties, "as muscular men with a minimum of clothing toil in the heat. Sparks fly in all directions as drops of fiery liquid are spilled so that the entire building is aglow." At the Gar Wood plant, the roar of riveting was heard day and night, as truck bodies were manufactured. All parts suppliers had to do their bit and Essex Wire, whose workforce was predominantly female, produced the wiring needed by the hundreds of trucks rolling out from the assembly lines.[4]

Reporters inspecting the four-ton Universal Carriers that were rolling off the Ford assembly lines found these "nimble little war machines" to be lightly

Artillery tractor being tested near Ojibway, 1942.

armoured, but versatile. By the end of May 1941, it was reported that of 115,000 Canadian vehicles supplied for the war effort so far, 75,000 came from Windsor. Campbell boasted that as a result of having "a well-established automotive industry," local factories were able to divert production to the military with a minimum of delay. Even if the Allied forces in North Africa had no Canadian troops, the British Eighth Army was riding in Canadian trucks and carriers, most of which had been made in Windsor.[5]

The Windsor Daily Star decries the eviction of military families in this cartoon from 1941. Mayor Reaume found a solution to this problem.

Reaume in Command

The war had also brought the city an invigorating new leader. David Croll's absence overseas (despite his service in England, he remained *in absentia* Windsor's mayor until 1940 as well as the Windsor-Walkerville MPP until 1943) left a void which was filled by the "golden boy" of border politics, Arthur Reaume. The tall, elegantly dressed former Sandwich mayor was remembered by one of his staff as "unassuming and pleasant under all circumstances. His morning greeting was always accompanied with a pleasant stutter. The Reaume stutter was his trademark." He had frequently filled the position of acting-mayor, and was elected mayor in his own right in December 1940. One of Reaume's first acts was to telegraph Croll and pledge to continue his programs. But Reaume was also determined to make his own mark, and he seized on the dilemma that affected so many families: the housing shortage.

The economic rollercoaster that had suddenly returned the good times to Windsor created an acute supply and demand problem. Hundreds of workers were now able to pay for houses, but were unable to find any. In something of a publicity stunt, Reaume announced in February 1941 that he could build a house for $3,000. Despite the mayor's bravado, city council shied away from proposals to incur debt and enter the construction business. But senior levels of government saw the need, and by the spring of 1941, 150 houses for war workers were being built by a federal body, Wartime Housing Limited. The houses were Spartan, being made up of pre-fabricated sections with a total dimension of 24 by 28 feet and mounted on cedar posts. A four room dwelling rented for $22 a month, well within a worker's budget. Private interests were also building houses, but not in Windsor. To avoid municipal taxes, most construction was going up in Sandwich East Township on the farmlands adjacent to what had been East Windsor. Identical rows of wartime houses filled in the blocks between Central and Aubin roads. The cost of these prefabricated houses was minimal and buyers with young families "like the open country." By the summer of 1943, the wartime housing program was the "acknowledged salvation of Windsor… 2,050 individual dwelling units have been erected. The small frame dwellings are now to be found in every ward in the city."[6] Mayor Reaume ensured that everyone knew who had inspired the plan.

As well, Reaume was successfully putting Windsor's financial house in order. A 1943 special provincial statute enabled the city to retire its debt even faster than planned. The SW&A was making more money than ever before, with its growing number of riders. The only obstacle to even greater revenues was that after 1941, no non-military vehicles could be manufactured and it could not increase its fleet. Bus ridership more than tripled between 1939 to 1943 to reach 32,000,000 riders-a-year. With rubber restricted to military use, new tires were unavailable and many cars were up on blocks for the duration of the war. Factory workers, school students, and office staff, all rode the buses.[7] The bus system was bringing in so much revenue that Reaume wanted its debt cancelled to reduce the municipal arrears by 20 percent.

The dynamic young mayor was an avowed populist in the mold of Dave Croll. By the spring of 1941, when the blitzkrieg hysteria had subsided, he proposed that a number of the "enemy aliens" get back their jobs. Nativists stoutly demanded that any civic jobs be reserved for those of British origins. But Reaume was determined that even ethnics should get a chance to be heard. City Council listened as Frank Sasso, a suspended city worker, explained how he came to Canada from Italy in 1907. He was hired by the city as a garbageman in 1927, when few people wanted such a hard, dirty job. During the Depression he was laid off and lost his house. Now, because of his Italian origin, he had again lost his job and the means to raise his five children. "I'm as loyal as you are," Sasso pleaded, "I would like to go to work." As a result of Reaume's efforts, a few Italians were put back on the job. The Utilities Commission restored four Italians (one of whom had fought in the Canadian army for two years in the First World War) to work. However, many more remained in internment camps far away in Petawawa. Antonio Colautti served six months in a camp on suspicion that he was pro-Fascist. When the rumours proved groundless, he was released. Two of his sons would serve with the Canadian Army, and one would be wounded in Belgium.[8]

Transnational Arsenal of Democracy

Across the river, Detroit had also been undergoing changes. While it also suffered through the privations of the Depression, it still possessed a huge reservoir of industry. But unlike Windsor, where municipal consolidation had been forced by the province, Michigan discouraged annexation and thereby limited the city's expansion. There were also significant demographic shifts. While in the 1920s, Detroit could be described as a city of European and Canadian immigrants, the immigrant exclusion laws had stemmed the flow and forced industry to draw labour from the American South. Large numbers of blacks began to populate the segregated slums on Detroit's east side and by 1940, Detroit's 150,000 black residents (out of a total population of 1,623,452) outnumbered all of Windsor. War production further stimulated Detroit's growth, and an additional 450,000 whites and 50,000 southern blacks flooded into the city to send its population to well over two million.[9]

While industry and commerce continued to expand, the border region failed to regain the level of interconnection that had existed in the 1920s.

An American solider, at left, and a Canadian soldier guard the Ambassador Bridge the day after the attack on Pearl Harbor, December 8, 1941.

Greetings From the Irving Berlins

To the people of Windsor —

"May all your Christmases be white"

Irving Berlin

Ellin Berlin

During his 1942 stop in Windsor, Irving Berlin autographed a sheet of music at the Officer's Mess at St. Luke Rd Barracks.

The line was firmly drawn by American law, and became even more fixed in June 1940. New border regulations went into effect which, for the first time, labelled Canadians as "aliens" and required them to have special permits to enter the United States. A *Detroit Free Press* reporter joined a confused crowd at the US customs exit where commuters tried to understand the new rules that "makes Canada a foreign country in reality as well as geographically."[10] But after the Japanese attack on Pearl Harbor on December 7, 1941, the two countries were suddenly allies in the war against the Axis. Early in 1942, both governments agreed that war matériel could pass duty free between them. The flow of matériel was further facilitated in October 1942 when the duty-free haulage (no border inspections) of war components was approved. To a degree not usually acknowledged, Ford of Canada's massive output of military vehicles was largely dependent upon its access to parts from its American parent company. In November 1941, when Canadian labour organizers threatened to involve the American UAW in a Windsor dispute, materials from Detroit's River Rouge plant were suddenly stopped. The effect in Canada was instantaneous, and production halted in a few hours without the necessary parts crossing the border.[11]

The American entry into the war inevitably had a social impact on Windsor as well. American propaganda films such as "Atlantic Convoy," featuring "a dramatic story of Uncle Sam's flying Marines" would play for weeks at the Vanity Theatre. In December 1942, American songwriter Irving Berlin brought his travelling show "This Is the Army" to play at the Vocational School. Part of the sense of shared sacrifice between Windsor and Detroit arose out of the fact that so many Americans had volunteered to serve in Canada and many Windsor residents, for a variety of reasons, were serving in the US forces. Still, one of the main differences between the countries after Pearl Harbor was that the US had wholeheartedly entered into the conflict.

The American economy, already gearing up for war, was completely turned over to military production. All men were subject to the draft and to possible service overseas. In contrast, the Canadian commitment to the struggle remained ambivalent.

'Stamp out Hitler' was one of many campaigns to raise funds for the war effort, 1940.

Jitterbug Heroes

After the first rush of volunteers for the Essex Scots in 1939, there was little interest in further enlistments. Windsor lagged in meeting its quotas and it was only the number of American recruits that kept up its numbers. By the summer of 1940, a quarter of the new recruits for the Essex Scots were Americans. Officers regretfully reported that the request for volunteers for the Essex Tank regiment "has brought little response to date." In September 1940, a company of the tank regiment that had been called into local service was demobilized. Perhaps this was just as well, for their commander, Lt. Col. D.C. Warnica, had been unable to obtain any tanks and the men did their best to train on an armoured truck. By the spring of 1941, Ottawa was issuing new demands for troops, but men in Windsor were reluctant to respond. Recruiting officers conceded that the "stream of applicants has been thinner". This lack of enthusiasm is not surprising when memories of the slaughter of the Great War were still fresh and there were so many opportunities to make good money at the factories. Windsorites even seemed reluctant to support the war financially, and Victory Loan Campaigns were met with indifference. The *Star* hinted that the city "fell down on its patriotic duty."[12]

As for industry, Wallace Campbell was able to report to shareholders in 1941, that Ford's 13,188 employees were working at full capacity and the company was making record profits. While military production reached new levels, Campbell claimed that "this was effected without a material lessening of production for civilian requirements." It was not until the last quarter of 1941 that the King government finally ordered drastic cuts in the production of consumer goods, and imposed wage and price controls. As the

Prime Minister told the House, "We have no choice but to reduce our consumption of consumer goods. To us, too, has come the choice between guns and butter."[13] But it was obvious that war workers in Windsor could afford a good deal of butter, and in the fourth wartime Christmas of 1942, retail sales were as heavy as ever, and far better than the previous decade. A *Star* reporter found "most gift shops were thronged with shoppers, toy stores were particularly busy... Increased circulation of money is generally credited with the increased business."

In order to stimulate Windsor's involvement in the struggle, on September 30, 1941, the Canadian Army Demonstration Unit staged a mock assault on the city. Units swept down and captured the tunnel and bridge, and soldiers with fixed bayonets captured and locked up customs officers. Other bands whipped through residential districts "with machine guns and rifles blazing and laying a smokescreen for following units." But other than terrorizing several housewives and a busload of American shoppers, the raid seemed to accomplish little. That was until Mayor Reaume had an idea. The mock invasion coincided with public concern over the pending eviction from apartments of the families of men serving in Europe. A soldier's pay was not enough to keep a family in Windsor's overheated rental market and several families were about to be put onto the street. It seemed unconscionable that these families who were already sacrificing so much should have to suffer further privation. Reaume had pleaded with the federal government to make some wartime houses available to military families, but Ottawa ruled that these houses were intended exclusively for armament workers. So before the demonstration unit packed up, Reaume had a word with their commanding officer. Before the end of the day, army trucks, escorted by motorcycles with screaming sirens, were on their way to two of the soldiers' homes where "they conducted a veritable blitzkrieg on the erstwhile residence of the two families. The soldiers formed a chain up to the second storey and handled down chairs, tables... carpets, infants' wear, toys" and installed everything into two prefabricated houses. Safe in the knowledge that Ottawa was unlikely to expel a soldier's family, at least two of them had a secure place to live. Moreover, Art Reaume had demonstrated that he was not only a man of the people, but a man of action.[14]

Occasionally, a bizarre incident could bring the war home. In April 1942, a German pilot, Hans Peter Krug, broke out of a prisoner camp and made it as far as Windsor. Skulking around the Riverside waterfront, Krug stole a rowboat and crossed the river to Belle Isle. Once in Detroit, he was entertained by sympathetic Germans and almost made it to neutral Mexico before being recaptured. Krug's escapade was a small, but telling incident that brought the war's reality to Windsor's attention. To try and run down characters such as Krug, civilians could participate in the Windsor Civilization Defence Committee (otherwise known as the "Air Raid Precautions" or ARP), which patrolled the municipality. This was especially urgent in Windsor as authorities stressed that "There are many subversive elements and underground organizations here which are only awaiting favourable opportunity."[15]

Peter Krug, 1942.

While other Allied nations were bearing the burden of casualties, Canada, as a result of King's demand that the army only be used to reinforce Britain, had not sustained major losses. In the first war years, Windsor's casualties were largely limited to the Air Force and the Navy. The first Windsor boy lost was Jim Cody, a popular Walkerville student, who was killed flying for the R.A.F. in October 1939. Several of the sailors recruited at the Howard Avenue barracks had also been lost at sea. One of the first to see action was the Olympian, John Loaring. Serving on a British destroyer late in 1940, Loaring's ship came to the aid of a sinking "mercy ship" of British child evacuees. He attended to five of the children pulled from the sea and managed to save two of them.[16] There was also the novelty of the air war. News of the bomber campaign against Germany was front page news, and RCAF casualty lists inevitably followed. Cliff Chappel, a popular youngster, went overseas in March 1941 and was killed on a bombing run in September 1942. Many families suffered more than one loss. The Riddells of Windermere Road had one son, James, killed in Egypt, followed a few months later by his younger brother Robert lost flying a bomber escort over Germany.

While the list of area men killed in the expanding bomber campaign was increasing, to many the conflict remained someone else's war. Columnist R.M. Harrison ironically pointed out that "Canada has a large number of young men under training of sorts—including a very large number still training in poolrooms, in handbooks and on street corners. Obviously, recent appeals for recruits have left a lot to be desired."[17] In March 1942, unmarried men between the ages of 21 (later reduced to 19) and 30 who were not engaged in war work were subject to conscription, although they could not be forced to serve outside Canada.

When the government conducted a plebiscite in April 1942 to release the government from its pledge not to send men overseas, the results in Windsor were equivocal. While a majority voted for overseas service, a substantial minority (especially in French-Canadian areas) voted against it. In the summer of 1942, Windsor's second active service unit, the 30th Reconnaissance Battalion (Essex Regiment), tried to recruit men, but did not get many takers. By the summer of 1942, it was reported that the Mounties were looking for 400 Windsor draft evaders. Controller Ernest Atkinson complained about the lack of interest and especially about those "jitterbugs that drink up beer and dance all night." These shirkers "laugh at men in uniform. They're having a good time spending more money than they ever had before."[18] Windsor was about to get a tragic introduction to the true cost of the war.

No Jubilee: Dieppe, August 19, 1942

By the summer of 1942, the Essex Scots were trained to a fine edge. Older men had returned to Canada, or as in the case of David Croll, were assigned to staff work.[19] As the regiment conducted exercises throughout southern England, there were rumours that they might be in the thick of some assault on occupied France. When word came through that they had been picked for an operation, Fr. Mike Dalton, the regiment's Catholic chaplain, accompanied the troops on the assault ship and said Mass at the bow. Many of the unit's Protestant men and officers attended. "I didn't know till they told me later" he recollected. This particular mission was cancelled. Dalton had been a curate at St. Alphonsus church downtown and had joined up when war broke out in September 1939. So many of the parish's young men had enlisted that Dalton felt that "I had to go with them."[20]

Father Mike Dalton performs mass for Essex Scots, circa 1942.

Unknown to Fr. Mike and the rank and file of the Essex Scots, high-ranking strategists had been making plans for the regiment's first combat. As part of the 4th Infantry Brigade of the Canadian Second Infantry Division, the Scots were selected for the assault on the French port of Dieppe, a renewal of the operation that had been cancelled a few weeks before. Captain Walter Donaldson (a nephew

Weary soldiers return from the Dieppe Raid, 1942.

of the Ford of Canada founder) was dismayed that after so many men knew of the raid that a similar plan (now called "Operation Jubilee") was back on. While the assault seemed fine on paper, much of it was questionable. While Dieppe was supposed to be a limited commando raid, General Montgomery insisted on a full infantry attack on the port. Vice-Admiral Mountbatten, the director of Combined Operations, approved the plan even though he knew that the naval and air support that was crucial to an amphibious assault would not be provided. A senior naval officer warned that, without large-scale air and naval bombardments, failure was inevitable. He was replaced.[21]

Just before dawn on August 19, 1942, the Essex Scots landed on "Red Beach" fronting Dieppe, while the Royal Hamilton Light Infantry attacked the remainder of the beach on their right. After a perfunctory naval and air bombardment, the men of the Essex Scots could see the coast in front of them as the morning sun rose. In the last moments of quiet, two of the men, Pvt. Tom McDermott and Lt. Jim Palms, both Americans, shook hands just before the landing craft hit the shore. Enemy defences were practically unscathed, and the guns mounted in headlands overlooking Dieppe were capable of repelling any attack. Nevertheless, led by their Colonel, Fred Jasperson, the Scots came roaring out of their transports. One company was halted by a huge roll of concertina wire, and would have all been massacred, if not for McDermott who threw himself onto the wire, creating a human bridge for his comrades to race over. Some of them made it as far as a seawall several metres up from the landing area. But that was as far as they could go as the wall was covered by yet more wire, and the intensity of the fire made it impossible to advance farther. Jim Palms, exposing himself to the fire, tried to cut a way through the wire and was killed. The long hours of that morning would see countless incidents of courage and self-sacrifice such as that of McDermott and Palms.

Lt. Col. Jasperson tried to organize assaults across the seawall and its obstructions, but those attempting to cut the wire were quickly killed. One intrepid section of fifteen men led by C.S.M. Stapleton did manage to get into Dieppe and caused significant damage before they retreated. Otherwise, the battle dissolved into chaos with small groups acting independently to try and stave off annihilation. Landing craft sent to extricate the remaining troops at Red Beach were destroyed or landed elsewhere. The aftermath was beyond belief. In England, Fr. Dalton searched in vain for his men, and out of the 553 who were sent to the beaches, he counted only 44 returning. In the final tally, the regiment suffered the worst losses of any of the attacking battalions. A total of 121 men were killed or died of wounds, and 382 were captured. The Essex Scottish Regiment was effectively destroyed. The following Sunday, Dalton tried to preach a sermon but was emotionally overcome, "so many empty seats… when we enlisted we bargained for hardships of war but we didn't realize we would miss our pals so much."

The reaction in Windsor was one of confusion followed by disbelief. At first, there was a measure of pride that the Essex Scots had been selected for the raid, but it was mixed with anxiety over how many had been lost. It was not until five days after the attack on Monday, August 24, that the enormity of the tragedy became apparent. "It is doubtful if the people of this city have ever spent such a weekend of nerve-wracking tension as that just passed" the *Star* reported and that "nothing comparable to the weekend casualties that poured into the city was experienced in Windsor during the last war."[22] When the massive list of hundreds of men "missing-in-action" came in, there was pure shock. A few of the men were known to be dead, but it was apparent that almost all the others were either killed or were still somewhere behind enemy lines, their fate was simply unknown. Elizabeth Murphy, the mother of four sons in the regiment, received four telegrams from Ottawa regretfully advising her that all her sons were missing.

As the weeks passed, uncertainty persisted about the men's fate. It was not until December that official notices were received of who had been killed and who was in captivity. For many, it was grim news. It seemed that in each day's edition of the *Star* there were more and more photographs of smiling boys who had died on Red Beach. Each report listed the boy's high school and the parents who survived him. Detroiters remembered the lads in the jaunty kilts and pristine gaiters who had marched up Woodward Avenue to St. Paul's Cathedral for evening worship. It was hard to think that so many of them were dead, and as the *Detroit Free Press* added, many of them "were Detroit's boys in fact. All were ours by ties of neighborly affection." Moreover, the casualty list had an impact on all ethnic groups that made up the area. Many of the names were French-Canadian. The St. Louis family had four sons serving overseas and two of them had been on the raid. Maurice died at Dieppe and his brother Milton was captured. A requiem Mass was held at Our Lady of the Lake for the brothers Alphonse and Leon Rivait, both killed at Dieppe. Roy Wigle, a descendant of the Loyalists, died on the beach shingle, as did Sam Berger, a Polish-born Jew who had come to Windsor in 1935.[23] Many of those killed, such as Richard Podger and Gordon Barrett, had lived most of their lives in Windsor. Other fatalities included Henning Calberg, a patriotic Danish seaman who had rushed to Windsor to volunteer when his country was invaded. With the uncertainty dispelled, the families of the dead were left with their grief.

Home Front

Even before Dieppe, the pace of war production had been accelerating. By 1942, Windsor's industrial production had tripled since 1939, and almost all of it was war matériel (see Appendix E). Civilian car production was suspended early in 1942 and industry had to adapt almost overnight to new demands. Canadian Motor Lamp, which had been manufacturing auto lights before the war, was now making precision shell casings. The brass shells were calibrated by a small army of female inspectors while "all types of machinery are now being operated by girls in overalls." Before the war, Truscon Steel made construction frames. Now it produced hundreds of parts for military vehicles, as well as metal ammunition boxes. Ford's use of centrifugal casting to produce lighter, more durable parts was one wartime innovation. Parts that had formerly been forged were now made in spinning moulds. The resulting casts were stronger and could be produced faster than by older methods. As the war progressed, Windsor industry moved beyond vehicles. In July 1943, the tanker HMCS Dundalk was launched from Canadian Bridge's Ojibway shipyard.[24] At Canadian Bridge, and other factories, men and women were working one (and sometimes two) full shifts a day. The demand economy imposed by the war achieved what the free market could not; it brought prosperity, and a highly paid workforce that more than doubled during the war years.

The trauma of the Dieppe raid certainly spurred enlistments. At the St. Luke Road barracks, recruiters remarked that volunteers were coming in asking to be taken "as reinforcements for the Windsor unit." The process of leaving civilian life and going to war followed a similar pattern for many Windsor youngsters. First, there was the farewell. Before leaving the factory floor or the office, there would usually be an impromptu ceremony in which the recruit would shake hands all around and be wished the best of luck. At the auto plants, he would be told that should he return, his job would be held for him. One of those getting the call-up was Stan Scislowski from the Chrysler loading dock. On his final day of work, Scislowski filled out the paperwork and said farewell to his mates. His first day in the Canadian army was a mix of endless waiting and novel experiences. He recalled the St. Luke Road Barracks as an old factory which "reeked of pine oil disinfectant" and was held up by ancient wood staircases that made a din as hundreds of young men charged up and down all day. A bored documentation clerk filled out his attestation papers and inquired as to Scislowski's hobbies and beliefs. Years later, he would find out that the clerk categorized him as "a Polish lad of average foreign appearance." The highlight of the process was getting military kit including webbing, gas mask, and helmet. The recruits, most of them like Scislowski barely more than teenagers, tried to fit on the gear amid "shouts of laughter and outrageous comments as we slowly transformed ourselves into reasonable facsimiles of what should be soldiers."[25]

Recruits could shop around as they examined the services and selected which branch to enter. Early in the war, volunteers for the RCAF required at least Grade 13 education. With mounting casualties, the standards were lowered until they waived education requirements. Paul Laforet, who had left Windsor Vocational School, did not like the idea of being in the mud with the army but also feared seasickness. After working briefly, he noticed that "all my friends and buddies were going to war and I thought, Paul, why don't you join the service?" So it was off to the Canada Building where he enlisted with the RCAF and was dispatched to the Toronto manning depot. Likewise, Bill O'Neill talked it over with his pals and considered joining the Air Force. After a shuffle between air and ground crew, he grew frustrated: "So I went down to the Armory, and bang, no problem at all and they signed me up right away. That was the beginning of my Army life."[26] Impulsive decisions such as this might determine whether they lived or died. Laforet would never fly in combat while O'Neill would see heavy fighting across northwest Europe.

As opposed to the detachment that many had felt in September 1939, "By late 1941, most Canadians believed they were involved in a total war. To a degree unimagined in the earlier war, men and women as well were directed, regulated, rationed, and exhorted."[27] From schoolchildren collecting cans and bottles for reuse to the Victory bond drives at the factory gates, it was now everyone's war. Leon Paroian was a boy growing up on Parent Avenue, and he recalled that "during the war there was a great effort on to have all of this material recycled and indeed the whole philosophy of the community was to waste nothing." Old newspapers were burned in furnaces as fuel and the ashes were strewn on icy sidewalks. Pop bottles were hoarded and cashed in to supplement the grocery money. Parent Avenue, like most Windsor neighbourhoods, was a close-knit community and everyone knew which families had boys serving in the war. "They were fiercely patriotic" Paroian remembered, "and fiercely proud of their families." Whenever the dreaded word arrived that one of the boys had been killed overseas, "an entire pall fell over the neighbourhood and we young kids were warned on pain of physical harm to recognize the grief these people were in and to make sure that we didn't make a sound or play "kick the can"... each of the families made contributions to the food of the family that had lost the boy."[28] Nor was it just a British war.

Unlike the First World War, which had been largely a concern of the Anglo-Protestant community, this conflict would engage everyone in Windsor. When Hitler's forces invaded Yugoslavia in March 1941, Peter Bulat led a group of Serbs, Croats, and Slovenes in support of the Allied cause, and bragged to the press that seven Yugoslavs had recently joined Canada's active military. That spring, Windsor became the site of the first recruiting post for the Polish Legion. The Legion headquarters became a magnet for American Poles wanting to free their homeland and under Captain Michael Aer, veteran Polish soldiers came to Windsor to act as instructors. Even Windsor's sixty Lebanese families came together to raise money for a "much needed tea-wagon" for the troops.[29]

Still, one ethnic group remained apart. Windsor's black population, as patriotic as ever, were relegated to secondary positions. In the war's early years, no applications from black recruits were accepted by the RCAF. The army deliberately kept black recruits in the lower ranks. Windsor's Jim Watson had graduated from Osgoode Hall in 1937 and became one of Ontario's few black lawyers. While all of his fellow lawyers were commissioned, Watson found that his race precluded him from any leadership position in the army. Despite passing several gruelling training courses, he only advanced as far as Lance Corporal. Eventually, he transferred to the RCAF where he was commissioned and made a bombardier. Still, blacks and whites served together in Canada's forces, and unlike the First World War, there were no segregated units. At Windsor's Emancipation Day celebration in 1943, civil rights advocate and future congressman, Adam Clayton Powell lauded Canadians as being relatively more tolerant, noting that as Canada's military did not countenance segregation—"You have democracy marching." He contrasted Windsor with the tensions existing in Detroit where a race riot had exploded in June 1943 that left 34 dead and the city torn along racial lines.

Windsor, with a far smaller black population, did not suffer from these extreme stresses. But injustices were apparent, and factories, which might have welcomed black labour kept up racial barriers. Chrysler adamantly refused to hire blacks. A small staff of about 200 black men were working at Ford, mostly in the worst jobs in heat-treat or the foundry where "along with the Armenians, they typically performed the least desirable job of iron pouring." Black women would not be hired in industry at all.[30] But Windsor's black community was able to exert some pressure and under Mayor Arthur Reaume, they had a welcome ear. In September 1942, Alton Parker became the city's first black policeman. But there was a long way to go. Fire Chief DeFields adamantly refused to appoint any blacks to Windsor's Fire Department.

Every segment of society was becoming increasingly drawn into the war effort. At Windsor's high schools, war news became part of the curriculum. A Walkerville student described the "defence course" as "learning home nursing and internal combustion engines." Every Friday, a man in a uniform would address the students and give them a rousing speech followed by songs such as "A Wing and a Prayer." The pressures of war certainly added to the incentive to apply oneself to school work. At a Walkerville Collegiate assembly in late 1942, the principal advised that "all boys over 18 who fail any exam will be subject to immediate draft, otherwise they are exempt."[31] Victory Gardens, small intensively cultivated plots, were planted at any available space, even school grounds. At Sandwich Collegiate, assemblies would be called by a weeping Principal J.L. Forster whenever there was an announcement that a former student had been killed in action. One Sandwich student recalled a teacher being told that her fiancé had been killed and watching as she fled the school in tears.

The war years were remarkable times for many young people. One girl recalled that while some foods such as sugar and butter were rationed, people would exchange coupons to see that others got what they needed as "everybody was for everybody else." Fred Sorrell recalled the sense of belonging in those days; of the numerous paper drives, of collecting huge balls of tin foil and jars of fat taken to butcher shops for further use. A female student recalled "They always told us to write to the boys. We went to the dances and knew the boys who were leaving for the war." And she did more than just write. "We used to meet the train and say goodbye to one soldier at the same time the incoming train was bringing in more men, and say hello; it was fun!" Another student recalled that from her high school windows they could peer at the recruits at St. Luke Road Barracks and "all the girls looked them over." By the summer of 1941, female High School students, "Farmerettes," were spending summers on farms adding to crop yields. At Kennedy Collegiate a labour representative asked for twenty students to work on the farms and got over 100 applicants.[32]

The war effort involved everyone at every level. Eleanor Barteaux, the assistant librarian at Carnegie Library, held lectures on salvaging, urging her listeners that "substantially everything you don't need can be transferred into munitions and weapons of war... bones yield glue which is needed for airplanes." The "Miss Canada Girls" sold tickets at a war stamp rally at the Norton Palmer Hotel. While the girls wore "their red pinafores over their pretty dresses, their jaunty blue forage caps set at jaunty angles," they were not identified. Much as in the military, the Miss Canada Girls were part of a corps, and had surrendered their individuality. Many groups came together to donate to the war effort. Windsor police Detective James Wilkinson headed fundraising efforts to buy a Spitfire for the Air Force. The plan worked and the aircraft, named "The Canadian Policeman," was dedicated in April 1942, and flown by an RCMP officer, Gordon Hoben. As for the Windsor Police, seven officers had volunteered for military duty and one, Alfred Green of the RCAF, was killed in action.[33]

The authorities were doing their best to encourage the public to get involved in the war. Victory Bond Drives, as well as contribution campaigns for the "Smokes Fund" were regular features of city life. A new naval installation, the HMCS Hunter, served as a basic training facility for new inductees into the Navy. Formerly the Marketorium Building, the Hunter opened up on Ouellette Avenue in December 1943, and started training men "who had never been on anything larger than an excursion boat in their lives." As did all major cities, Windsor had a civil defence committee that coordinated public safety. On Tuesday evening August 11, 1943, they tested Windsor's response to an air attack by sounding the sirens across the city and posting Civil Defence wardens to direct the public to shelters. To add to the simulation, the American Civil Air Patrol conducted mock dog fights over the skies of Detroit and Windsor and flew bombing runs (with bales of paper) over Detroit targets. The result was not quite what officials had hoped for, as hundreds of Windsor residents stood in the centre of the streets, necks craned to take in the air show, and all but ignored the CD officers who tried to shoo them into the shelters.

In a way, the public reaction to this civil defence drill illustrated the disconnection between civilian and military life. While in Windsor, the war was simply distant, in the skies of Europe, it was all too real. Throughout 1943, almost every day brought a new report of another Windsor airman killed in action. A typical casualty was John Gubb, an only son, who had been born in Windsor, educated at Walkerville Collegiate, worked at Chrysler, and had qualified as a bombardier. Assigned to Bomber Command in late 1942, he was shot down and killed a few weeks later. Sgt. Gubb was just one of a generation of airmen who were being lost before they had a chance to gain experience in the war.[34] By August 1943, the head of Windsor's recruit depot warned that air schools were on the verge of closing due to the lack of new volunteers. While to those remaining in Windsor, the war brought prosperity; to those fighting it and their families, the war had become a grim daily encounter with death.

Female Machine Gun Factory

Women, who in the Great War had been little more than darners of socks, now emerged to play a major role in the war effort. While the conflict brought tragedy to so many, to scores of Windsor women it was a godsend. One widowed mother of three children found factory work at SKD Manufacturing and was soon making $45 a week, far more than a widow's allowance. A Rumanian widow with four girls got on at Gotfredson's, and the job held her family together for the duration. Introducing women into the workforce was by no means a speedy or easy process. The Eaton-Wilcox-Rich factory resisted hiring females, but was forced by necessity to hire 25 women. Soon thereafter, most of their drill presses were operated by women. Chrysler hired 40 women, but only as inspectors. By the summer of 1942, neither Ford nor Chrysler had switched to female factory workers. The example of Willow Run in Michigan was inescapable. In the huge bomber plant, 25 percent of the assemblers were

A female worker making shell casings at Canadian Motor Lamp, 1940s.

women. "While industry in Windsor is going cautiously and timidly about hiring women," the *Star* observed, "experience at the Willow Run plant speaks well for the women."[35]

Despite the reluctance of the major factories, by 1942, it was apparent that much of Windsor's war production depended on women. At Canadian Motor Lamp, shell casings were being manufactured by women operating a number of precision instruments. As the casings had to be made to exacting standards, it was no easy business, and the final products were carefully examined by (usually female) government inspectors.[36] One young man at Truscon Steel observed in early 1942 that the plant had just begun to hire women. By the time he left in late 1944, the factory had a 75 percent female workforce. A Truscon executive conceded: "we'll have to do a lot of things we never did before." This included looking after the children of working women. In December 1942, the first child care centres opened up in Windsor to take in the "war orphans" of working mothers. Working women raised other concerns. A controversy broke out in the letters column of the *Star* in February 1943 between store clerks and women war workers. Salesladies were aghast that some of their customers appeared in public in their lumpy, oil-stained coveralls just before closing time. For their part, female factory hands made no apologies for their attire. "War Worker" responded in the letters column, "Yes, you stand behind a counter and laugh at a girl who walks in, her coveralls all dirty and so on… I'll work 24 hours if necessary, but the store should stay open at least one night a week and co-operate with the war workers."[37] It was a small but telling incident in the culture clash between former standards of female respectability and an emerging consumer society.

So many trained mechanics had been called into service that industry had to look toward women. Ford sponsored the "Women's Auxiliary Motor Service" that trained women in repairing and servicing vehicles. The program was so successful that in May 1941, a surprised Wallace Campbell found that "women of Canada have shown themselves highly adaptable to mechanical work."[38] Some women even took military training in the Women's Volunteer Reserve Corps or in the Women's Auxiliary Air Force. One of the city's major new industries was largely dependent on female staff. Border Cities Industries, a plant owned by both the Canadian and British governments but operated by General Motors, built a massive new plant just south of Kildare Road to produce Browning machine guns. The Brownings were precision instruments and had to be manufactured to exacting standards. Even before the plant went into operation in December 1941, hundreds of Windsor women were trained at the Vocational School on the operation of the equipment. Two deaf women were employed on the testing range preparing the guns for firing.[39] It was the first major step beyond vehicle assembly and a vote of confidence by Ottawa that Windsor could also produce armaments. That the machine guns would be turned out by a largely female staff was also a measure of their competence on the factory floor. Still, the role of women in the factories remained controversial, and was also about to play a key role in the coming labour unrest.

Chapter Eleven
Sacrifice And Victory
1944–1945

In late 1942, a Windsor skilled worker wrote to one of his three sons in military service and expressed his outrage that "this hole [sic] town is on strike over wages and girls working for 50¢ an hour."[1] Despite the wartime economy that created full employment, there was seething discontent throughout Windsor's workforce. Wage controls limited salary increases and kept them below inflation levels. In 1939, the federal government invoked the *War Measures Act* to assume control over all war-related labour relations, and the *Industrial Disputes Investigation Act* regulated military plants. However, the law did not provide for union recognition, and mandated a lengthy conciliation period before a lawful strike could take place. This was an inadequate framework for Canada's burgeoning labour movement, which grew from 359,000 unionized workers in 1939 to 832,000 in 1946.[2] The labour movement itself was changing and increasingly unions were not divided into trades, but were based on the total numbers of workers in a plant. This shift became important in Windsor, where vehicle assembly required massive numbers of workers.

Discontent among workers had been simmering since the 1930s, for life on the assembly line could still be precarious. Men who had worked at a plant for fifteen years could suddenly find themselves replaced by a younger employee. Currying favour with bosses was still expected, and slipping them a bottle or cutting their grass could be the price of keeping a job. When a factory shut down to retool, the staff was simply let go with no income or any guarantee that they would be called back. While the rhetoric of war-sacrifice had become pervasive, workers only saw wage controls and a labour system that was designed to prevent strikes but did nothing to protect their employment.[3]

Especially in Windsor, the Canadian UAW would use the leverage of the wartime labour shortage to fight for union recognition. But it would require a leader with extraordinary ability to steer the movement through this conflict.

If it had not been for the Depression, George Burt would likely have become a conservative small businessman. The son of a carpenter, he was born in Toronto in 1903 and apprenticed as a plumber. He hoped to work in his trade and perhaps have his own shop. But when work dried up in the 1930s, he was lucky get a spot at General Motors in Oshawa. An early member of the UAW, Burt took part in the groundbreaking strike of 1937. He was also caught up in the union's internecine struggles of 1938–1939. Homer Martin, a spellbinding Baptist preacher and UAW president, was an ineffective leader who divided the various factions that made up the union. One Windsor branch, Local 502, completely collapsed. At a special convention held in March-April 1939, Canadians resisted attempts to impose the CIO candidate, Charlie Millard, as their region's director. Instead a "unity" group of Canadians, made up of communists, nationalists, and left-wing CCFers, preferred George Burt. Burt's election as regional director signalled a change in direction of Canada's UAW-CIO, which would now benefit from the organization and commitment of its communist core. But this influence was not absolute, and other non-communist forces would be factors in the UAW. As a result, Burt "walked a fine political line, sometimes protecting communists from attack, and at other times aiding their opponents."[4]

One of Burt's first tasks was to transfer regional headquarters to Windsor in 1940, in order to spur the organization of new locals. He stayed at the Wyandotte Hotel until the proprietor discovered that he was a union organizer and threw him out. One of the few to befriend him was Fr. Garvey, who welcomed Burt to meetings of his labour class at Assumption College. Burt's first target was Chrysler and when the company resisted, he organized a picket line of 45 union men who paraded slowly in front of the plant. Police moved in and charged the picketers and Burt with loitering.[5] The arrests garnered national attention, but the 3,500 men in the plant paid scant attention to it and work continued without interruption.

From this, Burt learned that small steps were the best. At Ford, a number of skilled tradesmen formed a "Ford Club." As a social group it appeared to be harmless; one of its chief recreations was conducting drinking contests. But it served a greater purpose, as members of the Ford Club "talked union" on the shop floor and signed up UAW members. The Ford Club was elated when, in April 1941, the UAW won recognition in the Detroit Ford plants. While previously an intractable foe of the unions, Henry Ford's opposition collapsed and he agreed to union demands for a closed shop (that is, all workers had to belong to the UAW) and mandatory check off of union dues. The company would deduct dues from paycheques and automatically remit them to the union. Windsor labour leaders were energized and in September 1941, a committee of Ford men headed by Roy England resolved to seek the same contract.[6] A month later, the UAW was having mass rallies at the only building in the city big enough to accommodate them: the Windsor Market. Burt recalled that "We'd get about 8,000 of those guys and we'd have no chairs for them. They had to stand up. There's such an excitement in that kind of meeting. The union officers, we'd be on a raised platform. We'd have 1,500 workers behind us and the rest out there in front." Burt exhorted his men, "this is the biggest union drive in Canada's history." Ford workers were out to get a contract, "And by God we're going to have it."[7]

Ford's president, Wallace Campbell, had other ideas. He mounted a vigorous counter-attack and sent personal letters to every employee warning of the union's strong-arm tactics. He further condemned the UAW for hindering the war effort and proposed that the workers would be better off with their own union outside of the CIO. Burt decried these "Hitlerite tactics" and threatened to bring the Canadian labour troubles across the river. Fearful of any interruption to production at River Rouge, Detroit Ford stopped the shipment of parts to Windsor in November 1941. This caught Ottawa's attention; Burt and UAW Local 200 president Roy England were instantly flown to meet with the federal labour minister (and Windsor MP) Norman McLarty. "We depend on that plant" McLarty lectured them, "We've got a war going on and that plant is supplying the 8th Army." Without any legislative authority, he directed both sides to hold a vote on union recognition. It was not lost on union leaders that the final decision was being made in the Minister's office in Ottawa and not in some corporate boardroom. In this new demand economy, business decisions were ultimately political ones.

The union recognition contest was on, and both sides mounted vigorous campaigns. Workers were treated to the unlikely sight of Wallace Campbell standing on a truck, microphone in hand, exhorting them to vote for a non-UAW-CIO local. He also took out newspaper and radio ads warning his staff against the union and its communist element. The final result was surprisingly close with 6,833 votes for the UAW-CIO and 4,555 for a company union.[8] Nevertheless, the UAW had prevailed and in January 1942, a contract, which still did not include two of the union's main objectives, a closed shop and mandatory check-off of dues, was signed. In March 1942, a federal labour board recognized the UAW at Chrysler, and other companies followed thereafter.

Having achieved recognition, the UAW was ready to use its new-found power to protect its contract. When Ford hired 37 women in the plant and paid them 50 cents an hour instead of the man's hourly rate of 75 cents, the workers struck. On November 24, 1942, the 13,500 Ford workers of the largest single vehicle assembly plant for the British and Canadian armies put down their tools. The walkout stunned the country, for not only was it illegal (it failed to comply with the required conciliation steps) coming just three months after the Dieppe raid, it seemed to be exceptionally reckless. Refusing to produce war matériel in a dispute over 25 cents for 37 women seemed unpatriotic when so many were sacrificing their lives. Wallace Campbell, never at a loss for hyperbole, proclaimed that the Windsor strike was "making headlines in Berlin."[9] But it was the union's tactics that surprised many. In a carefully planned maneuver, mass pickets blocked the entrances to the factory and offices. Wallace Campbell was no longer in control of his own plant. "The situation this morning is badly out of control" he cried to Mayor Reaume. Yet when commanded to do so, the pickets opened up and permitted office workers to enter. The women of Local 200 supplied men on the picket lines with coffee and soup. It was peaceful, impressively well organized, and effective.

As the union wished, after a week the complaint was sent to arbitration. In the end, the arbitrator, Justice C.P. McTague, ruled that the women were not doing union work and were therefore not eligible for the higher wage. As the UAW insisted that all workers be paid at this rate, the dilemma was resolved by simply firing the women. This worked to everyone's, except the 37 women, satisfaction. The UAW newspaper *Ford Facts* applauded the settlement for having made "men's rights more secure." The incident highlighted that "It was obvious that the men were protecting their standards and did not want women in the industry."[10]

The role of women in heavy industry became even more controversial in the summer of 1943, when Ford got more military contracts and considered hiring up to 750 women to work directly on the assembly line. Even then, Ford could not conceive of paying women at the same rate as men and they proposed to the War Labour Board that the women get 80 percent of what the men were being paid. The UAW would not stand for any erosion in existing wage rates and they vigorously opposed the idea. Despite the fact that the company was already installing washrooms for the incoming females, the proposal for women to work at a lower rate was not approved and Ford never hired any women to work in the production area. This was in the face of government figures that showed that there were 4,300 vacancies in Windsor and 860 unemployed women available to fill them. But women would not be called upon, and as late as October 1943, the *Star* noted incredulously that "there are no women doing factory work in the large industries."[11]

The year 1943 would be one of the most confrontational ones between labour and management in Canada's history. In Windsor, walkouts and

This photograph of female workers assembling Browning machine guns at Border Cities Industries was accompanied by the tagline, "Happy working girls glad to help fighting men."

sit-downs became commonplace. All factories were affected and in January, 300 women at the Browning machine gun factory sat down and stopped production. Not all women joined in, and the strikers called out profanities to those who failed to stop work. When peace was reached with their union, three women were among the six signatories to the collective agreement. In April, work stopped at Ford plant No. 2 for a week when men refused to stop booing one supervisor. Minor disputes triggering work stoppages were a frustrating experience for both union leaders and management. Even the secretary-treasurer of the UAW, Nelson Addes, pleaded for an end to the stoppages: "No organized body can long exist without discipline within its own ranks."[12]

The Political Front

However disruptive the strikes were to the war effort, there was no doubt that public sympathy was with the growing labour movement. Incidents such as the Kirkland Lake gold miner's strike of 1941–1942, where the owners manipulated the law to delay any effective union pressure, had shown that the system was designed to frustrate workers' attempts to gain union recognition. In Windsor, support of labour was widespread. Early in 1943, the Rev. A.E. Millson of St. Paul's United Church proclaimed that even though most of his congregation was rural or professional, they admired the unions and looked forward to the occasion when "a representative of the CIO is in the pulpit."[13]

Early on, George Burt appreciated the power of numbers. Addressing a mass rally in September 1941, Burt exhorted his members to stand together for "a powerful Ford union would not only be a benefit to workers but would be a political power in Windsor." He foresaw the day when they would "elect representation on the city council who would have labor's problems at heart." One politician, Arthur Reaume, was quick to capitalize on this new power base. Burt and Reaume instantly hit it off, and as Burt later recalled, "Art became our champion at Ford. He'd come to our meetings to speak… It was a terrific shot in the arm for the union." Reaume often acted as a union spokesman, and during the sit-down at the Browning machine gun plant, the workers refused to negotiate without him. In the coming conflict between the rights of property owners and the aspirations of the unions, Reaume would be a voice in favour of the latter.

In a belated move to recognize this swing in opinion, the Ontario government introduced a bill in April 1943 to legitimize collective bargaining. Appearing at the debate on the *Collective Bargaining Act* was the soldier-member for Windsor-Walkerville, Major David Croll. Taking two days furlough from his military duties, Croll appeared in the Assembly and was instantly met with applause from all sides. He praised the bill, felt that it was long overdue, and mentioned in passing that he had proposed a similar statute four years previously. "I did not think at the time that I was ahead of public opinion, but in any event I was ahead of my colleagues in the government."[14] At last, organized labour had achieved compulsory collective bargaining and the recognition of unions as exclusive bargaining agents in Ontario.

Union power became dramatically apparent during the provincial election of August 1943. Described as "a watershed in the politics of labour," the campaign demonstrated that despite the continual strikes, the CCF was emerging as a mass movement.[15] Their popularity was augmented by support from all left-wing groups, including the communists. Even though they had been banned since 1940, communists were still well organized, and had a political front through the "Labour Progressive Party." Now they quietly threw their support behind the CCF. Directed by Moscow to support war production, Windsor's communists detested the Liberals and Progressive Conservatives who were "anathema to all communist supporters; only in the CCF was there a hope for electing a unified reform group dedicated to a strong war effort."[16] Other parties tried desperately to compete. The Progressive Conservatives under Col. George Drew were known to be partial to labour. It helped that their Windsor-Sandwich candidate, Mayor Reaume, was a darling of the unions and was even nominated by a UAW official. The Liberals of Windsor-Walkerville put forward the ever-popular Dave Croll. Eager to undermine the left, the *Star* published stories that communists had infiltrated the CCF, and that communist alderman, Tom Raycraft, was urging his comrades to vote for the socialists. Even with this help, the old-line parties had to deal with an invigorated labour movement. UAW leader Roy England encouraged his members to support the CCF as "only a strong and unified labor movement can effectively combat the pro-Fascist clique which is seeking not to unite with labor for the most forceful prosecution of the war against Hitler." The end result was a tidal wave of support for the CCF that overwhelmed the old parties. Croll was defeated by Bill Riggs, a *Star* printer and long-time unionist, while former mayor George Bennett turned back Reaume. It was a thunderous victory for socialists, and proof that a united left was a potent political force.

Faced with a growing and popular union movement, Mackenzie King's government realized that something had to be done to smooth out Canada's troubled labour situation. One person he turned to was Charles McTague, a Windsor lawyer and an innovative thinker on the management side of the table. Before the First World War, McTague was a star baseball pitcher as well as an instructor at Assumption College. During the First World War, he distinguished himself in France and shortly after his return was called to the bar. He established himself as a leading corporate lawyer, and Paul Martin, who was eager to work for him, recalled that, "From the seventh floor of the Security Building, Charles McTague, K.C., directed Windsor's most promising firm." His ability was recognized in 1935 when he was appointed to the Ontario High Court and four years later to the Court of Appeal. As a Catholic, McTague's prominence was all the more surprising since Catholics were rarely found in Ontario's high judicial circles. His legacy might have been limited to a brilliant, but not terribly noteworthy, legal career had it not been for the Second World War.

Early in the conflict, McTague reduced his judicial duties to act as a conciliator in labour disputes. Even though he was a Conservative, McTague struck Mackenzie King "as a fellow spirit, and labour remembered his sympathetic if unavailing report at the time of the Kirkland Lake gold miners' strike."[17] McTague was one of the few individuals who was trusted by both labour and management. In February 1943, King appointed McTague to head the National War Labour Board, describing him as "the best person who could be found to fill this very important position." Ultimately, McTague conducted a countrywide examination into labour relations, and his majority report, filed in the fall of 1943, recommended a national labour code as well as family allowances. King was uncertain as to what to do with the report but finally, in February 1944, cabinet approved Order in Council P.C. 1003. At last, Canada had a national labour code which recognized the legitimacy of unions and made collective bargaining compulsory. One historian concluded that, "McTague could take whatever private comfort he could that his ideas had finally been implemented, without credit, by a Liberal government… by the end of 1944, unions had access to formal certification procedures in virtually all sectors of the economy."[18]

Government support for collective bargaining could do little to tame an irascible anti-unionist such as Wallace Campbell. By 1944, Canadian Ford workers still had not achieved the goals reached by their American counterparts in 1941: being the exclusive bargaining agent and having mandatory check off of union dues. For that matter, Campbell was more interested in turning the clock back to the era when he had complete domination of the workforce. It guaranteed that the years 1944 and 1945 would be ones of confrontation.

Sacrifice

With the start of land campaign in Sicily and Italy in the summer of 1943, the Canadian Army started to take substantial casualties. The effect on those left behind in Windsor was heartbreaking. In December 1944, Pte. Ken Adair was reported killed in Italy. One other brother had already died there and another had been lost in the air war. Among Windsor's Chinese youth, Joe Hong was listed as killed-in-action with the RCAF, and his brother George was killed in Italy. Just before Christmas 1944, Mrs. Homer Rivait, who had lost two sons at Dieppe, was notified that a third son had been killed. Such sacrifices were not unusual, and many families lost more than one of their members. Occasionally there were reprieves. Windsor's Thomas Brannagan, an ace fighter pilot awarded the Distinguished Flying Cross, was shot down in August 1944. His family knew nothing of his fate until a card arrived just before Christmas 1944 announcing his capture. "It was the best kind of Christmas present" his mother confirmed.

After Dieppe, the Essex Scottish Regiment was recreated and hundreds of new recruits and men from other battalions filled their ranks. While this meant that the regiment effectively ceased to be an Essex County unit, many of its officers still came from Essex. Bruce Macdonald, the former Windsor city solicitor, led the Scots into battle in Normandy in July 1944. Unfortunately, at Verrières Ridge, their first action since Dieppe, the battalion lost almost half its men and Macdonald was relieved of command. The battle also led to fresh reports of casualties, including Chaplain W.L. Brown, the assistant-rector of All Saints Church. Remembered fondly by his parish and regiment, there was bitterness when it was learned that he was killed while trying to surrender.

"The Cost of War": Cameron Myers, graduate of Walkerville Collegiate, enlisted with the RCAF in 1941. Reported missing in action, his body was recovered in June 1943.

After the Canadian armies broke out of Normandy, one of the first objectives of the Essex Scots was Dieppe. On September 3, 1944, it re-entered the city and Fr. Mike Dalton said Mass at the Canadian cemetery that held so many Essex County boys. Larry Deziel, a former Essex Scot and now a staff officer, wrote to Bruce Macdonald that "the graveyard is in excellent shape and has been beautifully tended by the French people." He went on to note that "The defences are fantastic. I believe that 500 men could have held off a division."[19]

Back in Windsor, social groups did their best to encourage patriotic involvement in the war effort. The Rotary Club sponsored a naval vessel, the minesweeper HMCS Border Cities (there was already a "Windsor" in the Royal Navy) and paid for the crew's amenities. In May 1944, Squadron Leader Bert Houle, the commander of the City of Windsor fighter squadron, visited the city and addressed a "Buy Victory Bonds" rally. At the Hadassah Theatre Night of 1944, a variety program hosted by Doris Adelman raised money for the war effort.[20] These events were essential because for Windsor society as a whole, the war remained a far-off event.

Open City

As a result of war production, Windsor was once again a wealthy city, and some of that wealth was being translated into culture. During the 1930s, the "Fakir Art Club" and later, the Windsor Local Council of Women, staged small art exhibitions at the Willistead Library. The women's group was especially keen to establish a permanent art gallery, an ambition that seemed to become more in reach during the 1940s.[21] Since 1941, the Windsor Art Association had been displaying the works of local artists and in October 1943, the Willistead Art Gallery opened to the public. In February 1944, the Association bought a landscape by Manly Macdonald as the first picture for its permanent collection. Over 300 people attended the Association's meeting at the Willistead Library to see the new painting and to preview the show "Twenty-Five Years of Soviet Union." Dr. C.S. Sanborn, the president of Windsor's art association, introduced the show to an eclectic crowd of art lovers, local Russians, and communists.[22] Another major feature of the city's intellectual life was the Christian Culture Series. The series was started by a Basilian priest, Fr. J. Stanley Murphy, who had been teaching at Assumption College since 1932. In 1934, he felt that the hunger created by the Depression "also described a hunger for culture." He organized the Series and brought notable lecturers to Windsor including the Catholic evangelist, Msgr. Fulton Sheen.[23]

For all its finer pretensions, wartime Windsor had taken on a rougher edge over the years. Early in 1943, police reported that illegal drinking and gambling was under control, but reality was that many after-hours blind pigs thrived. There were also at least 15 bookies operating in the city. That is, a discreet level of illegal activity was being quietly tolerated by the police. This was perhaps understandable, as the enforcement of morality laws in a raucous city of over 100,000 was entrusted to a squad of just two officers. Gambling and drinking were almost expected in these topsy-turvy times, where young men came and went and life was precarious. However, Windsor's vice scene caught the attention of the military when the rate of venereal disease among recruits rose in 1944. The Windsor Police Commission had already been warned that the bus terminal was "attaining the proportions of a resort for pimps and prostitutes." In January 1944, the community was shocked when two juveniles were apprehended in an Aylmer Avenue brothel. On the way to the police station, one of the accused operators asked "Why does Alex (Sgt. Innes, one of the two morality officers) have to pick on me? There are lots of other places in this city paying off too." It betrayed the common understanding that those brothels that paid their fees should not be bothered by the police.

Prostitution and other vices were so widespread in war-time Windsor that, for a brief period in early 1944, there was a public outcry. Dr. John Howie, the Medical Officer of Health, attributed the lawlessness to the good times that attracted a small army of French-Canadian prostitutes to the city from Quebec and northern Ontario. He urged Police Chief Renaud to expand the morality squad. The ever-vigilant *Star* warned in an editorial that the "loosening of morals is, of course, the breeding ground of venereal disease." Going even farther, Controller Ernest Atkinson warned that the problem went beyond the bawdy houses and that Windsor's youngsters needed careful watching "in the cheap restaurants where (they) are allowed to hang around till after midnight eating hotdogs (with everything on them) to the strains of 'Pistol Packin' Mamma."[24]

To anyone who paid attention, it was clear that Windsor's problems transcended teenagers eating hotdogs. It was apparent that a well-organized system of prostitution had been set up in the city to service factory workers in both Windsor and Detroit. Ever since the Detroit race riot of 1943, single white Detroit men found a trip to Windsor to be well worth the short drive. In effect, Windsor became the "border brothel" for Detroit. Pete Licavoli, the boss of the Detroit Mafia, found Windsor and its compliant police to be a welcoming place to conduct his gambling operations. Throughout 1943 and 1944, there were few arrests at bawdy houses. Officers came from the same working-class milieu as the shift workers who wanted a beer when the licensed hotels were closed and there seemed to be no harm in turning a blind eye to these places. Just for show, there were a few raids, but the vast majority of bookies, pimps, and blind pig operators paid their dues and ran their businesses. New officers on the morality detail were instructed on which businesses had paid up and were not to be troubled. Enthusiasm in pursuing the wrong operators could result in an officer being reduced to "polishin' them fucken doorknobs" at headquarters. One policeman remembered that, "Just in the immediate downtown there were six or eight bawdy houses. Some of them stayed put waiting for customers to come in; other pimps would work the nearby hotels. No question there was big money being made."[25]

By 1944, Windsor was not only an open city, it was a city on the cusp of exciting new projects. Some were legal, others marginally so. The "pinball czar" W.F. (Bull) Fielding had made a small fortune in his pinball and slot machines which were scattered across Essex County. They were, of course, illegal, but local police tactfully advised Fielding and his customers prior to any inspections. In May 1944, Fielding began work on a "super-roadhouse" just south of the city and intended it to be a dining and entertainment centre. This Elmwood

The Elmwood Casino under construction in April 1944.

Hotel would be a major attraction, able to accommodate 1,200 persons in its main dining room alone. Despite government restrictions, Fielding had somehow gotten his hands on structural steel to build his "fun palace." When this was made public, work on the Elmwood was temporarily halted. But it proceeded to completion after the war, as would a huge new Metropolitan Store planned for Ouellette Avenue.[26] In January 1945, the block to the southwest of Ouellette and Wyandotte was sold for a phenomenal $350,000 and the new owner promised that as soon as the war was over a major new retail store [the Metropolitan] would be opened.

A new era of expansion was imminent and the question arose as to where and how. The war years had reintroduced the prospect of growth, and there were hopes that development would now follow on a rational, planned basis. Moreover, now that the area was no longer plagued by the divisions imposed by the Border Cities, all of Windsor could look to the future as one entity. Windsor's sad, grimy waterfront was the leading argument for greater controls, and a *Star* editorial argued that: "Windsor can do even better. Simply because we have not a ready made beauty spot along the river, there is no reason to presume that this district is doomed to warehouses and railway terminals."[27] A metropolitan planning authority was established in August 1944, under the chairmanship of Controller Mrs. Cameron Montrose. Elected in 1943, Montrose had a history of community activism. But the leading figure in post-war planning was an internationally renowned expert, Dr. E.G. Faludi. A graduate in architecture from the University of Rome, Faludi had extensive experience in town planning in Italy in the 1930s. Leaving Italy before the war, he assisted Toronto's planning board, and was hired by Windsor in November 1944 to prepare a zoning by-law. One of the by-law's first provisions was to freeze existing uses. As the city's lawyer explained, the temporary freeze "would facilitate later zoning under a city-wide plan."

The following year, Faludi identified the problems Windsor faced. Many of them were the residue left by the Border Cities era, such as industrial areas scattered indiscriminately through various parts of the city. Residential blocks were near commercial areas, and the resulting traffic led to a high death rate among children due to accidents. Separate playgrounds had to be set out where children could play off the streets. Older parts of the city had been developed on 30-foot lots, and those areas were now congested slums. Between Pierre and Windsor Avenue, hundreds of children were growing up with no playground but the streets. Their only recourse was the baked clay field behind Begley Public School. Faludi predicted that Windsor would soon grow to reach a population of 135,000, and plans had to be made to get rid of the slums and provide adequate parks for children.[28]

Victory

When news of Germany's surrender arrived in Windsor on May 7, 1945, the city erupted in jubilation. Downtown streets were jammed with horn-tooting cars and flag-waving children. Snake-dancing teenagers worked their way through the stalled traffic while noisemakers blared and confetti rained down. The Victory in Europe celebration was markedly less religious than at the end of the Great War. Partiers supplanted preachers as the focus of the occasion. Other celebrations followed. Shortly after the war's end, news arrived that one Windsor resident, Major Frederick Tilston of the Essex Scottish Regiment, would be awarded the Victoria Cross. Tilston had led his company through a series of German trenches during the battle of the Hochwald Forest, was wounded several times, and afterwards had both legs amputated. In July 1945, he was given a public reception at Jackson Park. With banks of wounded soldiers in attendance, and the proceedings recorded by the National Film Board, Tilston, the "Hochwald Hero" was saluted. Recognizing him was one small way of thanking all those who had sacrificed so much.

Now that the war was over in Europe, Dieppe survivors had first priority on repatriation. Late in the evening of June 10, the first group of Dieppe men arrived and an estimated 50,000 people jammed the CNR station to welcome them back. "Windsor had never seen such a display of unrestrained feeling," a reporter observed. "The fellows themselves wept unashamed as they took young sons and daughters into their arms, sons and daughters who were infants when their fathers left for overseas in May, 1940." Two weeks later, a larger contingent arrived and the city could barely contain its enthusiasm. As the train slowly pulled into the packed station, some men waved captured Nazi banners from the windows as thousands watched from the Sandwich Street embankment. Some on the embankment had loved ones who would never be on a returning train, but they came to witness those who had the gift of a reunion. Red Cross girls escorted men to their families, but most often the relatives simply broke through police lines in search of sons or husbands they had not seen in years. Returning soldiers and their families were then packed into cars for an impromptu parade up Ouellette Avenue headed by the Essex Scots pipe major Jock Copland. The last of the Dieppe prisoners, Major E.H.

Passengers on a SW&A bus read the extra edition: "GERMANY QUITS," May 7, 1945.

"Ted" Williams got back to Windsor on July 17. Like many of the men, he refused to talk about the battle, but the impact of it was far from forgotten. Underneath his battledress, Major Williams was still wearing the shirt he had on the morning of August 19, 1942.

Almost lost in the enthusiasm for the returning Essex Scots was the reality that there were other men on the incoming trains. Even though their reception was relatively subdued, many of the repatriated airmen, soldiers, and sailors had endured horrors as great as the Scots. Their reunion with their families was a more private affair. For these men, the fifty-mile stretch between Chatham and Windsor was the longest part of the journey, as it forced them to reflect on what they had endured and to confront the reality that for them, unlike so many of their comrades, there was a future. For the last stretch of the trip many of the men dozed off, but as they got closer:

> The lights of Belle River, then Tecumseh flashed past the coach windows and, like some fairy's magic wand, seemed to rouse the men out of their lethargy.
>
> Through smoke-begrimmed windows they recognized the outlines of the Ford Motor Company buildings—then the Hiram Walker structures—the Peabody Bridge—the Detroit skyline.
>
> They were home.[29]

Members of the Essex Scottish on the train home to Windsor from London, 1945.

Chapter Twelve
Ford Strike
August–December 1945

Over time, the 99 day Ford strike of 1945 would become a legend in Windsor. The story of thousands of men and women defying the power of the company and enduring privation and loss to overcome odds would become an epic. Labour historians would later reflect on the importance of the conflict. To David Moulton, it was "One of the most important strikes in Canadian working-class history" and to Irving Abella, "The [Ford] struggle was bitter and lengthy but the triumph of the union was complete." Subsequent historians have emphasized that "It set the tone of labour relations in the immediate postwar period… The Ford strike established both the basis for entente between industrial unions and large employers."[1] While much of this is true, the events leading up to the strike are hugely complex, the actual events chaotic, and the final outcome was very much in doubt.

Since signing a contract in January 1942, Ford's union stewards and company officials simply dealt with problems as they arose. However, when the contract expired early in 1944, Ford no longer felt itself bound to follow grievance procedures. When a union official was suspended, tempers boiled over, and without authority from their leaders, the 14,000 workers at Windsor's Ford plant walked off the job in April 1944. Both George Burt and Local 200 president Roy England pleaded with them to return. Even the communists in the Labour Progressive Party took out a newspaper ad requesting that the workers resume production. It took two weeks and a private meeting between labour leaders and management before the federal labour minister restored peace. Nevertheless, Wallace Campbell seemed determined to keep fomenting trouble. George Burt recalled Campbell's reaction to the resolution of the spring strike: "Campbell was a great big man over six feet tall. He drew himself up to his full height and said 'Mr. Minister, the company does not like your settlement at all but under the circumstances we have no other course to pursue but to accept it."[2] Even after the National War Labour Board approved one week's vacation for Ford workers in 1944, the company refused to pay until the union threatened legal action.

Ford's problems festered into the new year. The UAW was determined to get union recognition in its new contract. The company was equally determined to resist. A highly respected arbitrator, Louis Fine, was called in March 1945, and he reported that "an agreement was impossible and the situation was very complicated and difficult." Storm clouds were gathering, and union leaders were adamant that this time there would be no going back. They may have been of one mind, but their movement was badly divided. The UAW itself had split into the centrist Walter Reuther camp and a leftist group led by George Addes. As the Canadian region was suspected of leaning toward the communists, they were suspected by other unions and support was by no means guaranteed.[3] At an international meeting at Flint, Michigan, Burt made an impassioned plea for widespread support, asking that if Local 200 went on strike, Windsor's other big UAW local, Local 195, would join them and shut down all auto production in Windsor. UAW international president R.J. Thomas refused to grant permission and was leery of approving anything that gave the appearance of a general strike.[4]

Politically, labour had also lost much of its power. In the provincial elections of 1945, the left vote split as both labour leader George Burt and Mayor Reaume ran for the Liberal-Labour party. This drew enough support away from the CCF that its candidates were defeated in Essex County and three Progressive Conservatives were elected. While they may have ceased to exist on paper, the old political divisions of the Border Cities reasserted themselves. Burt was defeated by an Anglican minister, the Rev. M.C. Davies, who relied heavily on the Anglo-Protestant vote in Ward Two, the former Walkerville. The one bright spot for the left was the election of Alex Parent, the President of UAW-CIO Local 195, as the Liberal-Labour representative for Essex North. That union leaders such as Burt and Parent were supporting the party of renowned union-buster Mitchell Hepburn create much controversy and led to cries of "turncoat." Parent's winning margin was provided by Ward One, the red redoubt of East Windsor. Reaume narrowly carried Sandwich, but lost overall to businessman William Griesinger.[5]

Having lost their political clout and with wider union support in doubt, it might have caused Windsor's union leadership to question the wisdom of a strike. But to leaders such as Burt, England, and assistant regional director Tom Maclean, the lines were drawn. On June 23, Burt addressed the Canadian District Council #26 of the UAW and set out their objectives:

> We find in Windsor that the pattern set by Ford is being carried out in the smaller plants by the companies and we feel that it is necessary

> to break this pattern if we are going to be able to maintain our union. We have been negotiating a contract on behalf of Ford factory workers for nearly a year and during the last week the Ford Motor Company decided to declare war on the union... the outcome of the Ford situation and the situation generally prevailing in Windsor will affect not only the future of the UAW but also it will set a pattern for post-war labour relations in the Dominion of Canada.[6]

Already, Burt realized that this was not merely a local dispute, but one which would have national repercussions. In an attempt to reconcile the parties, federal labour minister Humphrey Mitchell appointed Justice S.E. Richards of Winnipeg to try and broker a deal. He too commented on the "bad feelings" between Ford and its workers. Wallace Campbell further poisoned the environment by sending out letters to the workers, urging them to override their union leaders and accept the company's latest proposals. At a mass meeting held on June 24, Roy England spoke to more than 8,000 members. "Since the defeat of the Facist foe," he read from a statement, industrialists were exploiting the peace to repeal the rights achieved by labour. "Using a false and hypocritical front of super-patriotism these industrialists hope to restrict, hamper and smash the labour movement." If ever there was a time for solidarity, it was now, and England urged that "the entire labor movement of Canada bring its full pressure to bear upon the federal government to amend present labor legislation so that Ford and Chrysler and other reactionary managements will be forced to sign proper contracts with the unions."[7] England had hit upon a sore point. Was the difficulty really with reactionary managers, such as Wallace Campbell, or with Canada's labour laws? The labour code provided grievance mechanisms, but was silent on the fundamental question of the union's right to be the sole agent for workers or its need for financial security.

Exasperated by the endless rounds of conciliation, Local 200 members approved a strike by over 90 percent in August 1945. The strike vote almost coincided with the last of the victory celebrations on August 15, over the surrender of Japan. As neighbourhood parties moved downtown, beer bottles in hand, there was a mob scene as the city heaved a sigh of relief that the war was finally over. But there was no peace in Windsor and the signs of a looming confrontation were ever more apparent.

On September 3, in a last-ditch attempt to avoid a strike, Ottawa appointed a conciliation board composed of Ford's lawyer Stanley Springsteen, union appointee Toronto law professor Bora Laskin, and Judge G.B. O'Connor of Alberta. However, almost simultaneously with the board's appointment, Ford announced that 1,650 men would be laid off. "This provocative act destroys the basis for any conciliation," declared the UAW's lawyer J.L. Cohen. For the first time, the hearings were held in public, and union members packed the City Council Chamber, applauding wildly when Cohen proclaimed that "a union shop is to collective bargaining what citizenship is to the citizen" and that the check-off of dues should be "as automatic as tax collections." There were other issues on the table—including two weeks' vacation pay, overtime for weekends, seniority for returning veterans, and better medical benefits. But the central union demand was for union security, and this was the demand that Ford adamantly refused to grant. While Laskin and O'Connor could agree to voluntary dues, the majority of the board would not recommend a union shop.[8]

The conciliation board report was handed down on September 11 and the following day, at the 10:00 a.m. break whistle, 10,000 Ford workers went on strike. Not all were UAW members, but those 1,300 who had not joined the union were firmly instructed to leave. C.G. Sampson, the superintendent of Plant 3, made no attempt to move, so he was picked up by the men and gently deposited outside the factory gate. That night, in one of the most emotional labour meetings ever held in Windsor, Mayor Reaume addressed 8,000 workers who filled the Windsor Market and milled about the outside streets. It was a serious occasion, and most of the men wore suits and ties. Reaume pledged his support to the strikers, guaranteeing that City Council would support their families and refuse to call in imported police. In the excitement, no one questioned how he could back up such assurances. The speaker of the hour was Local 200 president Roy England. Striding to the podium, England seized a copy of the conciliation board report, and proceeded to rip the document apart. "We're throwing this report back to [federal labour minister Humphrey] Mitchell!" he angrily shouted:

> We know we must fight Campbell to the bitter end. This city will not return to soup kitchens and breadlines of prewar years. When anyone proposes a voluntary check-off he is proposing we return to the days in the twenties when 500 workers were blacklisted by this weapon in the hands of the anti-union industrialists. We will not go back until we get a contract satisfactory to all members. The agreement will be written while you are on the picket lines.

It was militant rhetoric delivered to thousands of men and women who were more than prepared to respond. The Market crowd roared with cheers. The strike was truly on and no one could question their determination.

While England's dramatic gesture played well to the masses, it was less favourably received by the leadership of the Canadian Congress of Labour who accused England of "taking advantage" of the militant attitude of Windsor's workers and pre-emptively rejecting the conciliation board's report. The CCL was suspicious that the Windsor locals, under supposed communist leaders such as England and Alex Parent, the president of Local 195, were now seeking to stir up a wider conflict across several unions. No longer bound by their no-strike pledge to Moscow, communists were again the leading militants in the UAW structure.[9]

Yet Windsor workers were sufficiently militant without encouragement from anybody. The picket lines were compact, well-manned, and they effectively closed down the plants. It was the closure of the offices (whose workers were not on strike) that deeply offended Wallace Campbell. He wrote to the province's attorney general demanding that Windsor police "remedy this awful situation" by opening the picket lines so that his staff could pass through. When Campbell himself attempted to drive through the line, he was politely but firmly rebuffed. In response, he had the Windsor Police lay two charges of "besetting" against union officers who had dared to prevent him from entering his own office. Nevertheless, he had limited sympathy from the Police Commission. A new member, Magistrate Angus MacMillan, stated that the criminal laws should be vigorously enforced and that anyone who prevented a person from entering the plant should be arrested. However, for the moment, Judge Coughlin sided with Mayor Reaume, that discretion was the preferred route, and that the police should respect the picket line, even the one across from the office.[10] Ford was compelled to move its headquarters to a suite in the Prince Edward Hotel.

Peace seemed to be the order of the day, for on the picket line, there was little activity. The 245 acres of the Ford complex lay strangely silent with only "straggly lines of pickets in front of every gate." There was no need for a show of force, as the police had promised to respect the strike and not assist any Ford staff to pass through. Pickets received a steady ration of coffee and bologna sandwiches (called "picket-line chicken") from the Women's Auxiliary. While the plant was quiet, the focus of excitement shifted elsewhere. In Ottawa, Clarence Gillis, the fiery CCF member from Cape Breton Island, raised the Ford strike in the House of Commons. "We fought this war for something," he told the House. "Hundreds of men left the Ford plant to join the armed forces," and now "their employer is refusing them the rudiments of industrial democracy." CCF leader M.J. Coldwell called for the plant to be

Roy England, president of Local 200, tears up the conciliation board report during a fiery meeting, September 12, 1945.

run by a controller. Minister of Reconstruction, C.D. Howe, refused—it was about time the parties settled their own differences.

For his part, George Burt had the more articulate union officers fan out across Canada to stir up support and raise money. Ford worker Mansfield Mathias recalled Windsor strikers speaking in Hamilton and leading a parade to City Hall in support of the Ford strike. On October 3, Toronto labour packed into Maple Leaf Gardens for a Ford rally. Lyle Dozert, one of the Local 200 men that drove up in a squadron of cars, remembered parading onto the floor of the Gardens like a celebrity: "The applause was just fabulous. They almost lifted the roof off. That was a tremendous thing... the solidarity was tremendous."[11] The Toronto rally raised almost $15,000.

This was vital, for money was Local 200's Achilles heel. While Mayor Reaume had promised that City Council would stand behind the union, the financial reality was that supporting 10,000 families would quickly reduce the city to bankruptcy. After one week of providing relief, City Council reversed itself and discontinued benefits for strikers. There was no strike pay. The most the union could offer was a soup kitchen and some grocery vouchers. These meagre allowances were not available to the 1,300 men from the plant that did not belong to the UAW, nor to the thousands of employees from feeder plants that were being let go due to the Ford strike. Union squads began visiting local merchants and soliciting donations. Those that gave received a union card in the window, while those that balked were warned of a blacklist, or worse. After a month on strike, many families were beginning to feel the pinch and some feared they would lose their houses. The more prudent cashed in their Victory Bonds and others sought work elsewhere.

In contrast, Wallace Campbell did not appear to be perturbed by the stoppage. The plant needed to be retooled from war production and the company

The Women's Auxiliary prepare "picket-line chicken" for strikers, September 1945.

had already projected massive lay-offs. In any event, Ford had done very well during the war and was reported to have made $27,000,000 in profits and paid over $9,000,000 in dividends. If it had done any better, the additional revenues would have been scooped up by Ottawa under the excess profits tax. A month after the strike began, England wondered suspiciously whether Ford management was just as happy to let the strike drag on, as the company was "using what it would have paid in excess profits to starve the employees out."[12] Perhaps he should have considered that before ripping up the conciliation board report. But, by now, both parties were completely entrenched in their positions. Campbell insisted that he would not even consider negotiating until the union lifted their pickets from Ford's office. This would be an abject admission of defeat—and Campbell knew that it was never a serious prospect. He even rebuffed the government's initial attempt to seek a resolution. Local 200's only option was to increase the pressure, and this could only come from one source.

Powerhouse

The powerhouse was the heart of the Ford factory. Its large, coal-fired generators were powerful enough to supply all of Windsor's electrical needs and since 1923, they had been the sole source of power for Ford's machinery, water pumps, ventilation, and lights. Without this electricity, the molten metal in the foundry ladles would harden and the water in the plant's pipes would burst at the first frost. The powerhouse workers were members of the Local 200, but had not gone out on strike with the others. Instead, they had been instructed to remain on the job, as so much of the factory's infrastructure depended on the powerhouse. Nevertheless, "there was a lot of pressure on us too," Burt recalled. "People were starting to lose their homes. We didn't have enough money." Late on Sunday, October 7, the UAW played what it hoped was its trump card by calling out the powerhouse staff. For the first time since it had opened in 1923, the powerhouse shut down and the entire Ford complex sat silent and dark.

At last, something seemed to have stirred within Campbell. He agreed to meet in Toronto on October 15 with federal labour minister Mitchell, the union, and provincial ministers. Yet, after three days of negotiations, it was apparent that management had no interest in any resolution. Union leaders pointed out that they were only asking for the same deal that U.S. Ford had granted its workers in 1941. After a series of fruitless talks, Campbell invited the union men up to his suite in the Royal York Hotel. Burt recalled that Campbell produced a flask of whisky from which "he gave us a very meagre little shot and said: 'What do I have to do to settle it?'" Burt replied that he had to agree to union security.

Campbell refused, explaining: "I would have to get in wrong with all my fellow employers across this country." In passing, Campbell made one revealing comment: he indicated that if the government agreed that there should be union security and mandatory check-off, that they should legislate it.[13]

With the failure of yet another attempt at resolution, each side retreated deeper within its own lines. A fire broke out in the coal pile at the riverfront, but without electricity for the cranes to move the coal, it was left to smoulder. By the end of October, company officials seized the closed powerhouse as their key to breaking the strike. On October 30, G.G. Kew, Ford's secretary, wrote to the Police Commission that the closure "imperils valuable equipment which if damaged, might require months to replace and leaves all the plant without fire protection." The spectre had been raised of the loss of one of Canada's most productive industries. In another attempt to ratchet up pressure, Local 200 was severely limiting company access to secure the plant by prohibiting non-union watchman to cross the line. The protection of industrial property resonated with the judicial members of the Commission and they were prepared to take action. Judge Coughlin and Magistrate MacMillan agreed that the company needed between 100 and 115 security staff in buildings, not the five that the union permitted.

Yet, Ford management made no efforts to obtain an injunction to force the union's hand, nor did they attempt to land security men from the unguarded access points along the Detroit River. Instead, the company was eager to goad the police into directly confronting the strikers, and Windsor police were ordered by the Commission to take all necessary steps to see that the security men got into the plant. This infuriated the Commission's other member, Mayor Reaume, who engaged Judge Coughlin in a shouting match and as the newspaper reported, "Liar was a word fired between the mayor and the judge several times as the argument rumbled on."[14] But the majority of the Commission was convinced that the plant needed to be saved, and the police had their orders.

The following morning, Friday, November 2, a small squad of 15 policemen and 15 to 20 Ford security officers, led by Police Chief Claude Renaud, attempted to break through the picket line. At first, the intended target appeared to be the powerhouse and the picket line was reinforced around the building. However, they soon realized that Renaud's men were headed toward Ford's main office building. When a flying wedge of police tried to storm into the office, the pickets held them back and their lines were quickly reinforced by hundreds of men rushing in from other gates. A vigorous melee ensued in which the police tried to surge forward and the pickets pushed them back. No weapons were drawn by either side and only a few blows were struck. Nevertheless, in a pushing contest, the vastly outnumbered police were bound to lose, and they withdrew.

While the two sides eyed each other, many women seized the opportunity to join the picketers. Some were the wives of men on the line, while others came from neighbouring factories. As they fell into ranks, "the men would applaud and whistle." One five-year-old girl walked across the street to the line holding her father's hand. Deputy Police Chief W.H. Neale and another officer armed themselves with tear gas grenades and approached Chief Renaud about making another attempt. With the growing crowd, he decided against it, and the police packed up to leave. One picketer waved the headline from the latest *Star*: "Police to Take Ford Plant Guards Through Picket Line." A vehicle with a microphone mounted on its roof that had been directing the picketers' movements throughout the action asked the crowd for "A big hand for the Windsor Police Department." There was laughter and jeers for the departing officers.

Labour's Stalingrad

The Windsor Police Commission found nothing comical in their failure to preserve law and order. The following weekend was one of the most tense in the city's history as the Commission met to consider their response to this defiance. Once again, it was the majority of Coughlin and MacMillan who appealed to provincial attorney general Leslie Blackwell, declaring that a state of emergency existed in Windsor and local police were unable to restore order. Without power, the Ford factory would be severely damaged: "If the men on strike were to gather round the plant with sledge hammers and torches to do the same damage that the frost will almost surely do, there would be no doubt of the existence of an emergency requiring immediate action."[15] Blackwell

Windsor Police attempt to push their way through the picket line, November 2, 1945.

responded by immediately dispatching 125 OPP officers to Windsor—a move that Burt and union leaders promised would only result in violence. But Attorney General Blackwell, who had fought in the First World War and lost a leg at the battle of Cambrai, was not easily intimidated by anyone. If these reinforcements were inadequate, Blackwell pledged that more would be sent "so that law and order may be restored and maintained at Windsor."[16]

Ontario's Premier George Drew suspected that the UAW was only a cover for more sinister forces. During the evening of November 2, he had a lengthy telephone discussion on the Windsor crisis with the acting prime minister J.L. Ilsley (King was away in Britain). Wary of the significance of the Ford strike, Drew recorded his conversations with Ilsley as insurance against potential political disaster, as he was convinced that there were "probably two thousand active and vigorous communists at the core of this." He argued that even two hundred police were unlikely to restore peace and the government "should go to the other stage of relying on the militia." Ilsley confessed that "this burst on me with a little suddenness" and that the use of military force would require cabinet approval. Drew pressed him that it was a dangerous time, for "Windsor, right across from Detroit, is likely to present problems that wouldn't be presented in any other city in the whole of Canada." That is, communist thugs from Detroit were bolstering the ranks of local radicals, making the situation even more dangerous. But Ilsley remained cautious about the overt use of the military. Reporting to the House of Commons, he cited insurance reports that as a result of the withdrawal of power "a fire of calamitous proportions" could break out. While he would not send soldiers, he ordered a contingent of 125 RCMP officers to join the OPP in Windsor.[17]

Over the weekend, uniformed detachments of police began to arrive at Windsor's airport and were shuttled to the Navy's facilities at HMCS Hunter and the Burroughs Adding Machine building on McDougall Street. Horses were obtained for the RCMP, bringing back harrowing memories to many unionists of the armed charges the Mounties used against strikers in Winnipeg in 1919. Naval recruits were tasked with cooking and providing for the officers. Many of the young sailors had relatives on the picket line and they cheerfully reported every move of the police reinforcements to union leaders. Rumours were flying around Windsor: were tanks and troops about to occupy the streets? Everyone sensed that the climax was near—and union leaders knew they had to make a dramatic gesture to save the situation.

One step was to widen the strike and that weekend, Alex Parent's members in Local 195 defied the international union's cautions and joined the Local 200 fight. Chrysler, with its 3,600 employees, Gotfredson and GM each with 450, and 22 other plants voted to down tools. In total, it meant an additional 8,000 men and women were available to bolster the picket lines. Now, the greater part of Windsor's industrial labour force was out on strike and the police would face massive resistance. Added to this was another plan that would become the signature event of the great strike of 1945. While discussing what to do with Tom Maclean, Burt remembered an incident from an American labour struggle where workers had put up a barricade on Millar Road to enforce dues. "Get all the cars" he ordered Maclean. Starting with the union's vehicles, a blockade could be set up that prevented any police vehicles or mounted formations from approaching the pickets.

The following Monday, November 5, the city waited expectantly for the police or the union to make the next move. Even to a small boy such as Leon Paroian, these events were strange and perilous. He recalled his father, a usually quiet Armenian emigrant who was on the picket line "filling a rubber hose with lead... he stopped and told me that he was going to fight for his life. They had heard on the picket line that the next morning the military were going to come in and take over the Ford plant and take over their jobs… we would be destitute and so he was going to fight for our economic lives which he, at that time, correlated to our life in general."[18]

Yet instead of fighting, union leaders had their men commandeering and parking vehicles. Starting with union cars and a city bus, vehicles began to block Sandwich Street and then Drouillard Road. Strikers cordially waved oncoming vehicles into the lineup and then advised the drivers that their cars were going nowhere and that they should walk the rest of the way. Indignant motorists were told that there was nothing they could do and that the UAW, at least temporarily, owned their vehicles. One of the cars detained belonged to a senior police inspector, Albert Maisonville. "The barricade was formidable," Burt recalled. "We put hundreds of cars on her. Damn near the whole town was on strike now."

Within a short time, a massive barricade of cars had been erected that effectively blocked access to the Ford plant. No mounted police could approach it in formation and armoured vehicles would certainly destroy much private property in attempting to get near the plant gates. In addition, a union speedboat now patrolled the Detroit River, blocking any access from that front. Building the blockade was not always peaceful and one elderly man who objected was seen with a bloody face, and his car sustained a smashed windshield. On the whole, strikers remained solicitous, and guards were posted to see that private property was not vandalized.

Nothing like this had ever happened before and American news services were flying over the site to send pictures of hundreds of cars locked up in the blockade. At the time, few noted the irony that the product Ford manufactured was now being used to deny the company access to their own facilities. "The motor city today is like an armed camp," a *Toronto Star* reporter observed. Those strikers who had served in the military were instructed to wear their gear, and about 200 uniformed men joined the picket lines. Workers from Local 195 marched in military formation up to the Ford gates, led by a striker in an Essex Scots uniform who issued drill commands to the men and women who followed him. They were kept in step by a brass band playing "Rule Britannia" and "Solidarity Forever." Many of the marchers were carrying rubber hoses and several sported helmets. While the strikers appeared ready for action, the Toronto reporter did not see so much as one police officer. He did spy a little boy nearby who called out: "I hope daddy doesn't get hurt... A few people laughed at him but only for a moment as there was an earnest look on his face and a tension that no one could mistake."[19]

An aerial view of the blockade, November 1945.

The blockade created a furor that raised the Ford strike to another level of urgency. It led to another hurried series of calls between Drew and Ilsley in which the Ontario Premier insisted several times that "there is anarchy in Windsor" and that drastic measures were necessary. According to the Toronto *Globe and Mail*, the UAW was "substituting anarchy for reason" and that "in commandeering buses and forcing Windsor's citizens to conform to 'any' law they decree, they are lawbreaking and burning the fuse of provocation very low."[20] *Maclean's Magazine* ran an article titled "Strike Town," which portrayed Windsor as a hotbed of imminent revolution. According to *Maclean's* reporter Blair Fraser, "All the union's extreme measures were backed and probably initiated by the communists." Editorialists across the country feared that the worst was about to happen in Windsor. It was nothing short of "gang terrorism" and "organized hooliganism" spluttered the *Hamilton Spectator*, and the *Toronto Telegram* warned that "in Canada we have something called law—or did have." Editorialists in the *Windsor Daily Star* held that "mob rule has taken the place of law and order."[21] While it was provocative and certainly illegal, the blockade was seen by many labour supporters in Windsor and across Canada as a necessary reaction to prevent an imminent police assault to break the picket line. In their eyes, there was little violence, and private property, while taken from its rightful owners, was respected.

That night as moonlight shone on the 1,500 cars massed around the Ford factory, Parliament again debated the crisis in Windsor. For the CCF, Clarence Gillis called it a "little war," warning that if "someone is hurt in Windsor, you are apt to have a stand right from Vancouver to Louisbourg." He was followed by David Croll. After his discharge from the army, Croll decided to accept Liberal overtures to run in Toronto's Spadina riding. He won, and to the relief of Arthur Reaume, would focus the remainder of his political career in Toronto. Nevertheless, Croll spoke up in defence of the workers of his hometown and condemned Ford "which is built up on tariff walls" for its intransigence toward its employees. But as the evening wore on, it was the speech by Paul Martin, whose riding included the Ford plant, that captivated the House. As a junior cabinet minister, Martin had been constrained about what he could say, and for that he had been roundly condemned in Windsor. Now, as the commentator from "Today in Ottawa" noted, "his was one of the most moving addresses in the Commons in recent years." Martin declared that "The people of Windsor were not revolutionary thugs," but "law-abiding, as good citizens as one will find in any community in this country" who had been pushed beyond endurance by an unenlightened employer.[22]

The blockade had certainly energized labour and the following day, Montreal representatives of the Canadian Congress of Labour voted to increase their support to the Ford strikers. The Edmonton council of the CCL did the same the following day. At a labour rally in Winnipeg, one speaker felt that "the nation must make it clear that the strike area in Windsor is labor's front line in the

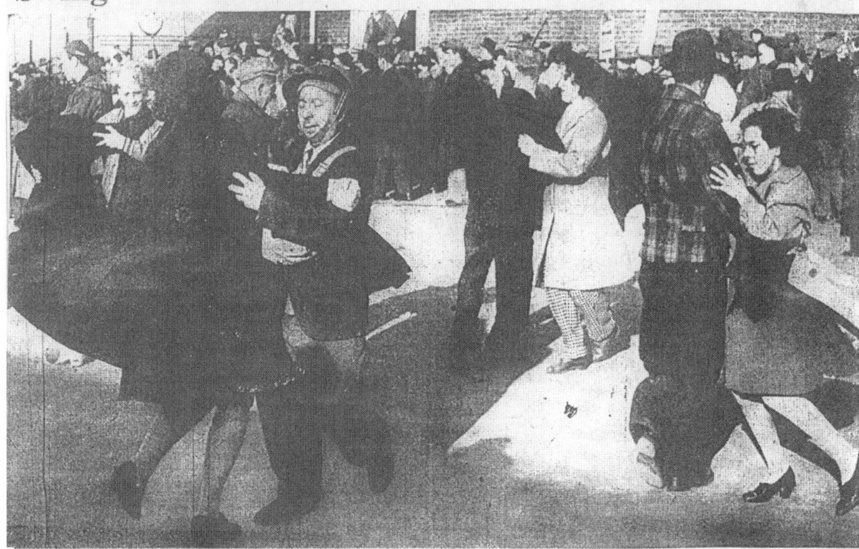
'Swing Your Partners'—Windsor Ford Pickets Dance

A ho-down on the picket line, as reported by the Detroit News, November 5, 1945.

fight for union and job security." Winnipeg unionists, armed with memories of police repression in 1919, warned that "If they get away with it in Windsor, they'll hound labor with police clubs in every similar situation." Industrial workers across Ontario recognized that the outcome of the Ford strike would have an impact on their contracts. Only two auto factories in Canada had a union shop and only one had mandatory check-off. Of the 240,000 persons employed in steel plants, only 2.1 percent worked in union shops. The national office of the United Steelworkers indicated "that many steelworkers' locals are just awaiting the signal from Windsor to stop work." The ramifications of the Ford strike would ripple across all industries and union leaders were fully aware of the consequences.

At McKinnon Industries in St. Catharines, 2,500 workers walked out in support of the Windsor strikers and one-day sympathy strikes were held in Kitchener and Sarnia. Westinghouse workers in Hamilton staged a one-day walkout in support of the Ford workers and promised that "they were prepared to back the Ford strikers to the hilt." The UAW-CIO had long been estranged from its competitor, the American Federation of Labor (AFL), but in the enthusiasm to support the Ford strikers, AFL Locals (such as Windsor's streetcar workers) signified their willingness to participate in sympathy strikes. News of the blockade had even spread around the world and the British Communist Party's *Daily Worker* hailed the fact that "The Canadian motor-car industry has been practically brought to a standstill as a result of the extension of the great strike."[23]

Enthusiasm for the Ford strike was now pouring in from unexpected sources. At the Carlton Street United Church in Toronto, 300 members and seven ministers urged the United Church to support the Ford strikers "both morally and financially." United Church ministers such as A.E. Wilson in Windsor and I.G. Perkins in Toronto became outspoken advocates for Local 200. More predictable support came from the Communist Party. The RCMP was closely monitoring communist involvement in the Windsor strike. They noted in their November report that "the Party in Windsor has enjoyed much publicity and has improved its position considerably" as a result of the confrontation. Ten days after the strike began, the communist newspaper, the *Canadian Tribune* published an editorial:

FORD STRIKE—FRONT LINE FOR ALL LABOR

> The strike at Ford's can become labor's Stalingrad in Canada. The 11,000 men and women who are picketing Ford gates in Windsor are not alone. Their demands are a summation of the demands of Canadian labor from Halifax to Vancouver.

> This must be but the first step in the rallying of a nation-wide action by all 700,000 Canadian unionists, by all workers, behind a battle upon whose outcome Canadian labor's entire future may hinge.
>
> As in Stalingrad, our slogan must be:
>
> "They shall not pass!"

In an addendum which he may or may not have resented, the *Tribune* dismissed Wallace Campbell as a representative of "that reactionary section of traditional union-busting monopolists."[24] J.B. Salsberg, leading Toronto communist and MPP, was seen encouraging workers and taking every opportunity to have his photo taken with them for the newspapers. The Party even sent the famous singer Paul Robeson to perform at a strikers' fundraising event at the Capitol Theatre. Certain union leaders, such as Roy England and Alex Parent, were widely suspected as being communists. While the acknowledged leader of Windsor's communists, Oscar Kogan, agreed that Parent "was pretty close to the LPP [communists]" and that meetings of Local 195 were dominated by Party militants, neither Parent nor England were actually members.[25]

After all the excitement of that Monday morning when the blockade was set up, an eerie quiet set in. While the *Globe and Mail* fretted that Windsor was on the verge of revolution, there were no subsequent acts of violence. The federal and provincial police confined themselves to their barracks and made no attempt to confront the strikers. Moreover, the government's response was surprisingly muted. While only a few days previous, George Drew had been urging the use of troops, he now suggested to the acting prime minister that "If, by any device that will find a possibility of settling the industrial dispute, we avoid the use of force... it's a matter of joint advantage to both of us." Drew went on to suggest that Paul Martin was the "best man" to bring the sides together. J.L. Ilsley hesitated to use Martin, but he agreed that a federal minister should go to Windsor to see if the situation could be defused.[26]

Seeing that the blockade had no appreciable effect on management and that many members of the public were outraged at the loss of their cars, Local 200 took pragmatic steps to reduce tensions. Windsor's City Council was outraged at the seizures, and Mayor Reaume held an overnight conference with Burt and England to restore the cars. The blockade had only been up for 48 hours when, on Wednesday morning, Burt ordered that it be taken down. In a sign of things to come, the pickets resented dismantling the blockade and it took some pleading from their leaders before they would cooperate with the police to restore vehicles to their owners. Shortly thereafter, the union offered to let the powerhouse men resume work. Campbell refused, much to the embarrassment of politicians who had been taken in by his woeful tales of his factory being destroyed by union recklessness.[27] Until all the picketing stopped, Campbell would rather that the powerhouse remain cold and silent. It must have made those politicians who had seen some merits in Ford's position question its credibility. Even C.D. Howe was becoming exasperated and he condemned the company for its delaying tactics and intransigence.

Ottawa had to take direct steps, and Labour Minister Humphrey Mitchell flew to Windsor on November 5 and spent five days meeting with all the principals. Perhaps the stress of the conflict had been too much, and Campbell was rumoured to have had a stroke. In any event, he was seriously ill, and Mitchell took the opportunity to go over his head and speak with the head of the international company, Henry Ford II. At first, the younger Ford (a vice-president of Ford of Canada) denied that he had any direct control over Canadian operations. But he admitted that he was monitoring events and was disappointed that the Canadian government was doing nothing to enforce the law. In reality, Ford knew he had the authority to order his Windsor staff as he saw fit. After a meeting with Mitchell in Dearborn, Michigan, he decided that it was time for the parent company to intervene. Late on Friday, November 9, Ford of Canada, as a direct result of Henry Ford II's talks with the Canadian minister of labour, released a radically new position. For the first time, the company agreed that it would submit the issue of union security to binding arbitration by an Ontario judge.

The Local 200 executive immediately dismissed the offer. They were now so entrenched in their position of winning the strike on the picket line that no other solution seemed viable. Without approval from the CCL or George Burt, telegrams were sent out by Roy England and Alex Parent urging other unions to join in a one-day national sympathy strike. This ill-conceived action was quickly rejected. The failure of the proposed mass walkout and its rejection by national labour leaders weakened the Local 200's position. Nevertheless, the strike ground on for weeks with no apparent end in sight. The fire in the coal pile burned on, and a pall of smoke hung over eastern Windsor. Ontario's Attorney General Blackwell was growing visibly impatient. He delivered a radio address warning the public that radical, communist elements were directing events and that "the present situation in Windsor was one of open insurrection against the Crown." This time, lawlessness

The Calgary Herald's editorial cartoon from November 7, 1945, blames both labour and management for the Windsor impasse.

such as a blockade would warrant "police or greater force."[28] None doubted that it was an idle threat. But unknown to the public, Paul Martin had become a key figure in fashioning a peaceful resolution.

Acting without the authority of the labour minister, Martin began to solicit "new faces" who might take a different approach. Pat Conroy of the CCL put Martin in contact with the international staff of the UAW. One of the strangest connections went through Assumption College's Christian Culture series to CIO head Philip Murray, who had won the Series Award only two years previously. He arranged for Martin to deal with the international's secretary general, George Addes. Working with Addes and Conroy, Martin hit upon the idea of using a Supreme Court of Canada judge to act as the decider. Senior cabinet minister C.D. Howe opposed Martin, and insisted that employers and employees should resolve their own problems. But in the end, Martin prevailed with the cabinet.[29]

On Monday, November 26, union and management representatives met with an array of government officials in Ottawa and for the first time, an agreement of sorts was beaten out. This was confirmed the following day, when Humphrey Mitchell and his provincial labour counterpart, Charles Daley, delivered what was effectively an ultimatum to union and management. A Supreme Court of Canada judge would be the arbitrator, oversee the negotiations, and render a final and binding decision. An umpire would also be appointed to oversee the implementation of the results. The strike would cease immediately and the workers return to their jobs.[30] Burt recalled that Pat Conroy of the CCL assured him that the arbitrator would be sympathetic and would give them a form of union security. But, for the moment, they had to keep it under their hats and not let the workers know. This was not what the union had hoped for, and in many ways, it was an admission of defeat. The new collective agreement would not be forged on "the picket line" as Roy England had promised. Once again, the union's fate was in the hands of a judge, a hand-picked member of the business class. But the union's resources were exhausted; it was close to Christmas, and their members had little enough money for food, let alone presents.

The vote on management's offer was held on November 29 at Windsor Arena. Those who attended appeared to be sullen and resentful: "'We have been out so long, we feel that it is foolish to go back without getting what we came for' seemed to be the consensus of opinion." The leadership, including Burt, England, and international head George Addes strongly urged the membership to accept the deal and move on. But communists circulated in the crowd, urging the men to keep fighting, and Tom Maclean, the fiery assistant director, gave a speech telling the men to stick with their demands. By a narrow margin, 52–48 percent, the proposal was defeated, and the picket lines, now very much diminished, remained up.[31] But the steam had clearly gone out of the struggle. Local 195 members went back to work and there was no further talk of sympathy strikes. It took another three weeks before the same proposal (with minor changes) was brought back, and this time, Ford workers voted by almost three to one to accept. They seemed to have little choice. In many ways, it must have been a huge disappointment to have made such sacrifices only to fail to get the contract they had been promised. The sense of defeat was palpable, and the resentment previously reserved for Wallace Campbell was being turned against the UAW leadership.[32]

Little did the strikers know that in the backrooms of Parliament, Paul Martin was making the arrangements that would bring the union its final victory. The carefully chosen judge from the Supreme Court of Canada was Ivan Rand. Born in New Brunswick, Rand had been a leading barrister in Alberta and later a corporate counsel for the Canadian National Railway. Prominent in Liberal politics, King appointed him to the Supreme Court of Canada in 1943. Described by his biographer as "self-centred, narrow-minded, intolerant, and bigoted," he nevertheless "rose above it all in a handful of key cases that defined not only his career but the court and an age."[33] Rand was sympathetic to labour's aspirations, and Martin calmed Burt and England with the assurance that Rand was likely to favour their position.

In early January 1946, Rand met with counsel for union and management and heard the extended story of the Ford dispute. On the afternoon of January 29, in the plush lobby of the Royal York Hotel in Toronto, Rand rendered his report which was to have such a dramatic impact on labour-management

Wallace Campbell (right, seated) and George Burt sign the collective agreement to end the Ford Strike, surrounded by members of the negotiation committees, December 1945.

relations in Windsor and ultimately, across Canada. The report was surprising—even shocking. The judge condemned the actions of the workers in the automobile barricade as "an insolent flouting of the civil order" and further considered that the actions of the strikers in shutting off power and risking plant property to be "a supreme stupidity." Neither would Rand order union security outright. This key union demand, which had been the spark for the entire dispute, was rejected on the basis that it violated a citizen's rights and "would deny the individual Canadian the right to seek work and to work independently of persons associated with any organized group." To that extent, Rand's award upheld traditional British freedoms in the face of collectivist pressure.

Yet, in the next breath, Rand acknowledged that the modern industrial workplace required a new attitude toward rights. Ford's insistence that it was their plant and that the thousands of workers who kept it running had no interest in it was "an absolutist concept," which was a "primary and essential error." He proceeded to require the company to oversee the check-off of union dues from every labourer who worked in the plant. "I consider it entirely equitable then that all employees should be required to shoulder their employment, the union contract; that they must take the burden along with the benefit." In so doing, he granted the essence of union security, whereby all persons who worked in a unionized factory had to contribute. The Toronto *Globe and Mail* recognized that the award "breaks entirely new ground, without precedent either in recognized contract procedure or labor law." David Croll declared that the decision was a "milestone" and that as result of the "Rand Remedy" a pattern had been formed.[34]

To those who had manned the picket line, it was clearly a victory. "It's the same thing as a union shop," one commented to a reporter. "You won't find many men who will not want to join the union when they have to pay dues anyways." George Burt reported that Rand displayed "a very surprising understanding of the problem which faced us" and he gave full credit to Paul Martin as "the most active supporter we had at Ottawa." There was further labour turmoil across Canada in 1946, but the results of the Ford settlement were felt across the country. "The Rand Formula became and still remains an integral component of Canadian labour relations."[35]

The finale of the great strike came as a relief to all. There was no major violence; there were no bloody confrontations. Leon Paroian remembered that his father returned to his family on the day of the blockade "by about 5:00… and we were absolutely joyous… the critical moment passed and there was no bloodshed whatsoever." He further recalled that it was "The stroke of genius [of the blockade] together with the courage of Art Reaume to talk down the militia that really saved the day." At least, that's what many people thought. Of course, no militia had ever been sent and Reaume never made any such heroic speech. But the Ford strike was quickly becoming the stuff of legend. In George Burt's memoirs, he recounted a chance meeting with Wallace Campbell at an airport sometime after the strike. "You beat me," Campbell confessed to Burt. "I wouldn't have put it that way" replied a modest Burt. "Oh no, you beat me," he insisted. "Very well," I told him, "if you want it that way. We beat you and we beat the hell out of you too."[36]

If this incident did happen as recounted, perhaps Campbell was being ironic? The Rand Formula also became a significant benefit to management, for it established a set of normative principles that, in return for union security, there would be labour peace. By relieving the union of the obligation to collect dues, the UAW became "financially independent of its members, [and] it became dependent on management." The Rand Formula rendered the unions part of the corporate bureaucratic structure, responsible for disciplining their members, thereby making "the union's role as the demobilizer of militancy in the workplace."[37] Certainly, the strike had been a costly battle. Ford workers had forfeited about six million dollars in wages and it would take many of them a long time to recover.

While the city had been captivated by the historic events taking place on its streets, the sacrifices of the recent past could not be forgotten. On November 21, 1945, The Essex Scottish Regiment arrived back in Windsor's CNR station. As the locomotive pulled in on a dour, overcast day, it carried a vastly different regiment from the one which had left from that same station in May 1940.[38] Only three men in the returning battalion had been with it at Dieppe. Almost all of the men came from across Canada and most had never been to Windsor before. Nevertheless, the city gave a huge welcome to the incoming troops. Pipers met them at the station and once the regiment had formed up, the men marched from the river up to Ouellette Avenue where they paraded in honour through the city's streets. Office windows were crowded with spectators who showered the veterans with confetti, and:

> Ouellette Avenue was a riot of color, hung with flags and draped in gay bunting, when the returned men got their first sight of it, as they turned the corner of Sandwich street and Ouellette avenue. And as far as the eye could see the street there were massed thousands, cheering wildly.

Whether the returned men were from Windsor or not, they deserved the welcome. It made up in small measure for those who would never return.

Epilogue

In early January 1946, bucketfuls of fiery coal were being dunked into the Detroit River from the Ford stockpile. Gouts of steam shot out from each glowing bucketful that was extinguished, and sodden loads of coal were dumped back on the shore for future use. The fire that had been casting a pall over the city for three months was gradually being put out. By the first week of January, all the men returned to work and Ford was producing its first post-war automobiles. The factory and the city were ready to resume their role as one of Canada's principal manufacturing centres.

In less than half a century, the border area had transformed itself from a collection of small, inconsequential villages into one of the Canada's largest industrial complexes. Based on the speed and scale of change, it was unprecedented. Especially during the 1920s, the Border Cities of Windsor, Walkerville, Ford City, and Sandwich had reinvented themselves as one urban metropolis based on automotive production. It had all occurred with incredible speed, and with little concern for the future. The road that led to this industrial transformation had not been smooth, nor was the city's post-war future clear.

At the root of the city's dramatic change was tariffs. This system, designed to keep out competitors and nurture a Canadian manufacturing sector, encouraged the blossoming of American branch plants in the Windsor border area. However, it would take the initiative of one individual to align the opportunities presented by the tariff system with burgeoning new technologies. Change is often triggered by individual inspiration and in Windsor's case, the spark came from that consummate salesman, Gordon McGregor. His idea to unite Henry Ford's genius for mass assembly with the opportunity to market automobiles across Canada and the British Empire led directly to the dynamic growth of the Border Cities in the 1910s and 1920s. McGregor not only saw the potential, he had the administrative ability to initiate the assembly program and create the sales system that would see the border area emerge, almost overnight, as one of Canada's major production centres.

Through this exciting period, it was protectionism that was the key to fostering the capital investment that was the lifeblood of the Border Cities and prevented American manufacturers from simply overwhelming the Canadian market. It was as a direct result of these protectionist barriers that American branch plants rapidly created an interconnected system of automobile assembly and auto parts production in the Border Cities. It was these branch plants that supported a rapidly growing and well-paid working class. Expanding faster than any comparable part of Canada, the Border Cities quickly outstripped its capacity to provide houses, roads, and schools for the thousands who eagerly came to work in its factories. It also became an international metropolis as workers flooded in, not only from other parts of Canada, but literally from around the world.

Even from its origins as a ferry stop across from Detroit, Windsor's ethnic and social structure was unique in Ontario. While the town was based on British settlers with an elite of Scottish merchants, the French settlers, who inhabited the Detroit River border since the mid- 1700s, remained a strong presence in the surrounding countryside. Still, in its first decades, the Border Cities were predominantly British and Protestant. To them, service in the First World War was the cost of membership in the Empire, and it would be largely fought by the area's British-origin men. What seemed at first to be such a gallant romp soon became a tragic, grinding ordeal that consumed hundreds of the area's sons. However, the region's economy was largely unaffected and for the most part, non-British residents did not take part. These ethnic "others" were to stand aside.

Yet, the demands of the factories were insatiable. More and more workers would be drawn from eastern Europe, diversifying Winsor's ethnic mixture as the population skyrocketed during the 1920s. More than comparable Canadian cities, Windsor became a polyglot of various cultures, and with such a diverse population, social conflict was inevitable. During the hard years of the Depression, many of the new arrivals seized upon the supposed benefits of communism as a solution. In the eyes of the Anglo majority, this made East-Europeans a group less than trustworthy. That they were clustered (or forced) to live in separate enclaves made them all the more suspicious, and to old-stock residents, they were not only alien but potentially subversive. In the end, assimilation was inevitable, and the ethnic divisions which may have seemed stark in the 1920s mellowed by the 1930s. The election of a Russian-born Jew, David Croll, as Windsor's mayor in 1930 was proof that the new arrivals could quickly take advantage of the opportunities available to them. By the Second

World War there seemed little distinction between the children of immigrants and those who had lived along the shore of the Detroit River for generations. The casualty reports that became depressingly common in 1943–1944 featured a variety of ethnic names that matched the community's composition.

Yet not all ethnic groups looked upon assimilation as an achievement. French-Canadians had hoped to preserve their language and culture, but they faced many obstacles, not the least of which was a hostile provincial government determined to stamp out French language education. As well, young French-Canadians migrating from the farms to the city found that the language on the factory floor was English and they, along with their Polish and Hungarian cohorts, were expected to learn it. Resistance to the elimination of French traditions came to a head during the Ford City Riot of 1917 when the French-speaking community united in a violent, but ultimately futile, confrontation with the forces of assimilation.

The ethnic diversity of the border set it apart from the rest of Ontario and this led, in part, to its estrangement from the moral laws that the rest of the province embraced. Most of Ontario was content with 19th-century restrictions on drinking and Sunday activities. The Border Cities were not. When issues such as temperance were put to a vote, the area consistently showed itself on the side of indulgence over restraint. The ethnic and religious mix of peoples on the border had a different and more relaxed approach to life. This distinction would break out into open conflict during the rum-runner years when so many border residents ignored provincial laws and became enthusiastic participants in the shipping and supply of liquor to the United States.

Ultimately, what marked the uniqueness of the area was its enthusiastic embrace of new technology and engineering symbolized by two monuments to the dynamism of the 1920s: the Ambassador Bridge and the Detroit-Windsor tunnel. Constructed almost simultaneously, they remain great works of engineering that exemplified the optimism of an early industrial age. They also reflected the period in which they were built, for their essential purpose was to move the cars and trucks built in the factories of Detroit and Windsor even faster and more efficiently. By the mid-1920s, there was such a sharing of capital that the industrial workforce of the Detroit-Windsor area operated almost as one in the great rush to prosperity. It is also significant that these structures were built by the people of the border. There was no need to import parts or labour for the standard of metal working available in the Detroit-Windsor area was the highest in the world, and fully capable of creating magnificent works.

The families of the young men working in the auto plants needed new houses, roads, sewers, and schools. Rapid growth required planning, and in Windsor, like the rest Canada, urban planning was still in its infancy.

Moreover, the rush to provide infrastructure would have to be hastily financed. The Border Cities was compelled to borrow against the future to build what it needed for the present; a policy which would have disastrous consequences in the 1930s. When the Depression came, the area was devastated as production fell to minimal levels. The American response of closing the border and forcing workers to stay on their respective side of the line was especially damaging to the Border Cities. The reduction of tariffs by Mackenzie King's Liberals in the late 1920s had already had an impact on production. Employment was already in decline before 1929 as capital returned to its American base. It was a further reminder that the international boundary was truly a dividing line and that what had seemed for a time to be one economic region could just as easily be divided back into two very distinct areas.

For most people the hard times of the Depression lasted an eternity. The building and growth that had seemed boundless only a few years previously now became a distant memory. The population declined and the cost of the infrastructure of the 1920s caught up to the Border Cities and bankrupted them. One of the few bright spots was the emergence of a communal feeling that resources should be shared and relief equitably allotted. Moreover, there arose the sense that public health services were for all. Hospitals controlled epidemics and provided the latest care for rich and poor. Still, the political divisions that divided the Border Cities only exacerbated their inability to deal with the financial and human crisis of the Depression. Ultimately, the provincial government had to step in and impose unity. The creation of a greater City of Windsor in 1935 at last ended the petty squabbling which had marred the community's development and enabled it to face the future with a more efficient administrative structure.

Yet, as always, Windsor's economy depended on the tariff framework for its existence. The reintroduction of tariffs in 1931 spared much of the area's industry from complete collapse and mitigated the impact of the Depression. But with the return of the free-trading Liberals to power in 1935, Windsor's advantage as a manufacturing area again diminished. All that changed with the coming of war in 1939. When the federal government initiated a massive program of armaments production, Windsor was one of the few areas that could be instantly mobilized to produce military vehicles in abundance. The city's industries responded with gusto to the demand economy and production expanded at a rate that matched that of the 1920s. Unlike the First World War, community leaders did their best to foster a feeling of home front camaraderie. From foil collecting to bond drives and "Miss Windsor War Worker," it was everyone's war. In reality, the war was a distant struggle and only those who had volunteered faced the danger of combat. For most, it was a golden time of unexpected prosperity, and the slight annoyance of sugar rationing.

With full employment, union leaders understood that their moment was at hand. A renewed sense of militancy seized workers, and there were wildcat strikes through 1943 and 1944. After the end of the war in August 1945, Canadian industrial workers realized that they stood on a precipice of either achieving union security or returning to the bitter conditions of the pre-war years. Windsor's Ford strike of 1945 became the national focus of this struggle. The strike captured the nation's attention as workers established, in dramatic fashion, their right to organize and agitate for a better deal. By far, the most mythic symbol of that struggle was the auto blockade of November 1945. The blockade became a symbol of community strength, of the willingness of men, women, and occasionally children to take direct action to secure their future. In the face of police and the threat of military repression, the ordinary people of Windsor compelled the owners to recognize and bargain with the union. The auto blockade became a glorious legend that would strengthen a confident and aggressive labour movement.

Yet, in many ways it was a myth, and indeed it is questionable whether the strike was necessary at all. But once begun, the confrontation quickly escalated beyond what either side anticipated. The infamous blockade, however lauded after the fact, was undoubtedly a violent assault on civil liberty. As one historian commented, "Stealing other people's property and then blockading the streets had nothing to do with the union's legitimate aims. The union was demanding its rights, but what about the rights of others—to their cars, to use the city streets…?"[1] Moreover, the existence of a line of cars would not have stopped the government from actually opening the factories. A military machine that had just hammered its way across northern Europe would not be impeded by a line of automobiles. What stopped the government in the end result was political expediency, not the blockade. Workers now had the weight of votes and influence that made it undesirable for the government to impose the settlements that had been accepted in 1919.

The more enduring impact of the Ford Strike was that workers now assumed some measure of property control of the plant. In the event of a labour dispute, union leaders could confidently depend on the co-operation of political authorities to deny the owners access to their factories. In so doing, unions had gained some measure of ownership, and the stake hold of the shareholders in their investment had been diminished. While capitalists had for decades adjusted their plans according to the prevailing tariff system, the triumph of collective bargaining had added yet another dimension to their long-term plans. Now, in addition to gauging market demands and imperial preferences, Windsor's manufacturers would have to factor in the demands of labour. As a result of the Ford strike of 1945 and the persistence of its legacy, Windsor was now indelibly a "union town."

Over time, myths can become more persuasive than facts. The Ford strike of 1945, which at the time of the settlement in December 1945 seemed to be an abject failure, would later be hailed as a great victory. It was the insertion of the Rand Formula which salvaged the reputation of UAW leaders and led to the institutionalization of labour relations. As the spark for the Rand Formula, the Ford Strike of 1945 would later be hailed as a significant breakthrough for labour. In much the same way, the Dieppe raid of 1942, a poorly planned debacle that needlessly resulted in the loss of hundreds of young men, would later be remembered as a glorious sacrifice on the path to victory. Its memory would remain so powerful that in 2010, a black granite monolith was dedicated in Dieppe Gardens to the regiment, and on every August 19, the sun's ray would pass through and shine on a stainless steel maple leaf. Both the auto blockade and the Dieppe raid had become part of the community's continuing past, part of a lived experience, not of the individual towns along the river, but of "Windsor."

With the end of the war, there was no guarantee that civilian production would resume as before. Future prospects were most uncertain, and many feared that another Depression was imminent. [2] The one bright spot was that the city had retained a core of experienced planners who would offer it a road-map to undo the chaos of the Border Cities period. In January 1946, E.G. Faludi's team unveiled a display at the Auditorium of C.H. Smith's department store on a thirty-year plan for Windsor's future. In a series of scale models, photographs and drawings, the public was invited to look at their city in the distant year of 1975. In that year, the city's population was projected to grow to 145,000 from the current 118,000. The monotonous gridiron street pattern would no longer dominate future residential areas and industries would be confined to separate districts. The decay along the riverfront would be swept aside and people would at last be able to appreciate the natural beauty of their surroundings. The Border Cities period was truly over, and the community was now planning to go forward as one metropolitan area. The *Star* urged the public to make every effort to see the exhibit, for those who saw it "will, in short, see what a fine city can be built up here."[3]

Appendix A

City of Windsor Growth Spurts

1895	11,549	
1905	14,007	Increase of 21%
1905	14,007	
1914	23,013	Increase of 64%

SOURCE: Windsor Municipal Archives, R.G. 3, EI, file 1/4, p. 18 Assessment Commissioner Annual Report, 1920

1921	38,530	
1929	70,031	Increase- 82%

SOURCE: Windsor Municipal Archives, R.G. 3, EI, file 1/13, p. 22 Assessment Commissioner Annual Report, 1929

Appendix B

WINDSOR: POPULATION AND ETHNIC ORIGINS
COMPARED TO OTHER MAJOR ONTARIO MUNICIPALITIES

1901:

	Windsor	London	Hamilton	Toronto
Population	12,153*	24,415	52,634	208,040
British	8,294	22,468	46,218	141,303
French	2,133	213	810	2,526
Black	930	200	450	592

*Windsor including Sandwich and Walkerville: 15,198
SOURCE: Fourth Census of Canada, 1901 (Ottawa: King's Printer, 1902)

1911:

	Windsor	London	Hamilton	Toronto
Population	17,829*	46,300	81,969	376,538
British	10,753	42,119	62,045	281,374
French	4,113	409	1,088	4,569
Black	1,018	213	292	468

*Windsor including Sandwich and Walkerville: 23,433

SOURCE: Fifth Census of Canada, 1911 vol. II (Ottawa: King's Printer, 1912)

1921:

	Windsor	London	Hamilton	Toronto
Population	38,591*	60,959	114,151	521,893
British	25,388	55,512	95,097	445,230
French	6,883	759	1,956	8,350
Black	1,028	209	375	1,236
Polish	752	173	1,478	2,380
Jewish	979	703	2,560	34,619

*Border Cities: including Windsor, Ford City, Walkerville, Sandwich, Riverside, Ojibway: 57,191

SOURCE: Census of Canada, 1921 (Ottawa: King's Printer, 1922)

1931:

	Windsor	London	Hamilton	Toronto
Population	63,108*	71,148	155,547	631,207
British	39,644	64,066	123,684	510,432
French	8,709	830	2,525	10,869
Black	(no longer specified in the census)			
Polish	1,495	688	4,362	8,483
Jewish	2,219	683	2,636	45,305

*Border Cities: 102,690

SOURCE: Census of Canada, 1931 (Ottawa: King's Printer, 1932)

Appendix C

Horse Power Units as billed by Hydro Electric Power Commission compared with Border Cities population growth

Year		Windsor	Walkerville	Ford City (East Windsor)	Sandwich	TOTAL
1915	H.P.	1,048	743			1,791
	Population	24,162	4,565	2,400	2,814	
1918	H.P.	1,590	2,211			3,801
	Population	29,334	5,725	3,138	3,334	
1919	H.P.	2,262	2,085			4,347
	Population	31,629	5,914	4,300	3,448	
1921	H.P.	5,397	3,722			9,111
	Population	38,530	7,469	5,860	4,153	
1922	H.P.	7,588	4,722			12,310
	Population	42,122	7,303	6,800	5,010	
1923	H.P.	11,033	4,955	1,276		17,264
	Population	47,177	8,088	8,000	6,056	
1925	H.P.	16,492	3,649	1,673	1,980	23,794
	Population	56,433	9,071	11,200	8,077	
1927	H.P.	22,145	4,811	2,829	3,026	32,811
	Population	66,893	10,208	13,531	10,258	
1929	H.P.	25,733	8,582	3,715	3,477	41,507
	Population	70,031	11,331	16,203	11,331	

SOURCES: University of Windsor Archives, J. Clark Keith Papers, Box 1, No. 95-007, Horse Power Statistics.

Border Cities population statistics from: Windsor Municipal Archives, R.G. 3, EI, file 1/13, p. 22- Assessment Commissioner Annual Report, 1929.

Appendix D

Location of Employment for Border Cities Residents

	Work in Border Cities	Commuters (approx.)	Total Employed
1927	10,332	15,000	25,332
1928	19,558	10,000	29,558
1929	22,501	8,000	30,501
1930	19,855	6,000	25,855
1931	15,040	2,000	17,040

SOURCE: University of Windsor Archives, Windsor and District Chamber of Commerce Papers, Box 3, file 20 "Observations in Regard to Employment" July 3, 1931

Population Decline of the Border Cities during the Depression

1927	100,890
1928	105,250
1929	109,384
1930	106,994
1931	101,557
1932	96,199
1933	97,472
1934	98,837

SOURCE: Windsor Municipal Archives, R.G. 3, EI, file 1/21, p. 27 Assessment Commissioner Annual Report, 1940

Appendix E

Industrial Production And Population Growth: War Years

Year	Factories	No. of Employees	Value of production	Windsor population
1939	222	17,729	$122,474,320	103,664
1940	215	20,916	$194,174,159	103,567
1941	223	29,486	$289,027,790	107,424
1942	233	27,057	$383,323,348	112,800
1943	229	38,516	$417,745,229	118,040

SOURCE: Windsor Municipal Archives, R.G. #, EI, file 1/26 p. 11 Assessment Commissioner's Annual Report, 1945 (Information provided by Windsor Chamber of Commerce)

Endnotes

Endnotes to Chapter One

1 *Windsor Evening Record*, "The New Armouries" January 31, 1902; on Queen Victoria's death, see *Evening Record* "Sincere Sorrow" January 23, 1901.

2 See discussion on this in Brandon Dimmel, "South Detroit, Canada: Isolation, Identity and the US-Canada Border, 1914–1918" 26 *Journal of Borderlands Studies* (2011) No. 2 at 199.

3 *Ibid.*, "Soul Battle Has Started" March 11, 1907; on All Saints' Church and the Imperial sermon, see "21st Regiment Attend Church" June 13, 1904.

4 *Ibid.*, "A Prosperous Congregation" January 10, 1901; on the Methodist Church, see *Evening Record* "Methodist Church in Ashes" January 4, 1904.

5 *Ibid.*, "New Chinese Leader" April 4, 1902; and also "Windsor's Chinamen" December 23, 1898.

6 On the Jewish community see Jonathan V. Plaut, *The Jews of Windsor, 1790–1990: A Historical Chronicle* (Toronto: Dundurn Press, 2007) Chapter Three "A Community Takes Root;" and see *Evening Record*, "The Jewish New Year" September 12, 1900; and see *Evening Record* "Windsor's Jewish Colony Prosperous and Law-Abiding" July 24, 1907—the newspaper recorded that Mercer Street was the centre of Jewish life in Windsor and stereotyped its inhabitants as—"There are some queer traits about the Jews. Energetic and personally ambitious, they never fail to take advantage of any opportunity that presents itself to make money." On David Croll, see R. Warren James, *The People's Senator: The Life and Times of David A. Croll* (Vancouver/Toronto: Douglas & McIntyre, 1990) 5- 11.

7 *Ibid.*, "Colored Trade" December 17, 1902; closing Lagoon Park, see *Evening Record* July 4, 1902; on the longshoreman relegated to the back of the Labor Day parade, see *Evening Record*, "How Labor Day Was Spent In This City" September 5, 1905.

8 Diocese of London Archives, Petition of the Board of Trustees of the Roman Catholic Separate School for the city of Windsor, presented on December 5, 1901; and see, Michael Power and Daniel Brock, *Gather up the Fragments: A History of the Diocese of London* (London: Diocese of London, 2008) 44.

9 Windsor *Evening Record* "Sandwich Public and Separate S." February 6, 1902; on the court order evicting Catholics from the Sandwich school, see *Evening Record* "In Again, Out Again" May 9, 1902.

10 *Ibid.*, "Pro and Con Arguments on Separate Schools" February 24, 1902.

11 Diocese of London Archives, Meunier to Bishop McEvay, February 23, 1904 and Justice Street's decision, February 10, 1904; on the statute that set up the Street inquiry, see *An Act Respecting the Property of Public and Separate Schools in the City of Windsor and other matters* (1903) *Statutes of Ontario*, c. 35; that the public board refused to part with the former Catholic schools even though they were hardly in use, see *Evening Record* "School Board in Quandary" March 5, 1902 and "Two Trustees Resign from School Board" May 10, 1902.

12 *Ibid.*, "Rev. Dr. Flannery" December 24, 1900; and see *Evening Record* "French Catholics" May 22, 1899—St. Jean Baptiste Society—"unanimously decided to ask that one French priest be stationed in Windsor, whose duty it will be to attend the spiritual welfare of the French, and to preach every second week." On the St. Patrick's dinner, see *Evening Record* "The Evening Was Spent in Feast, Speech and Song" March 18, 1903.

13 Windsor *Evening Record*, editorial "Le Progrès" April 16, 1901; and editorial "The Race Cry" February 25, 1902.

14 Power and Brock, *Gather up the Fragments*, 44-5.

15 The failed first start of the "Riverside Park" is described in the *Evening Record* editorial "River Front Park" October 9, 1912; "Riverside park became defunct and has been lying in the morgue during these years…"

16 Amherstburg *Echo* September 9, 1904; on the smoke over downtown Windsor see *Evening Record* "Time To Stop Smoke Evil" September 1, 1906, and see the lawsuit initiated by J.F. Hare against the Canadian Salt Company contending that "smoke and cinders from the salt company's plant pollute the atmosphere and otherwise damage his property." The company defended itself claiming that it was using the best quality coal and the best known engineering, in *Evening Record* "Test Case on Smoke Nuisance" November 18, 1903.

On the movement for a riverfront park, see *Evening Record* editorial "Our Riverside" June 16, 1903; after the small park was created, the newspaper published a further editorial "Beautify the City" May 15, 1905 urging the appointment of a board of park commissioners to consist "of gentlemen of taste and of some leisure."

17 Windsor *Evening Record* "Romance of Fourteen Years" July 12, 1904.

18 See the obituary of John Davis—*Evening Record* October 14, 1912 and the editorial "The Late John Davis."

What was called the "old macadam by-law" was passed by City Council—see Windsor Municipal Archives, R.G. 2, By-law 982, passed August 21, 1899; Macadam did not prove entirely successful. By 1902, the newspaper observed that "It is dusty and very injurious to the eyes, as well as easily cutup"—they recommended that waterproof asphalt be applied over the macadam.*Evening Record* editorial "A New Pavement" June 17, 1902.

19 See Appendix B; Not only were Windsor taxpayers unwilling to finance current debts, they sought to extend them well into the future. The one money-related by-law that was passed created a debenture of $20,000 to cover the "extra expenditures" over a period of twenty years—see *Evening Record*, "By-laws All Defeated with One Exception" May 13, 1905; on the bonus by-law rejection see editorial in *Evening Record* May 13, 1905—"A majority of the electors of Windsor are apparently opposed to any form of bonus to manufacturers."

20 *Ibid.*, "Windsor Is Improving" March 2, 1801; on Toronto industry see, Dean Beeby, "Industrial Strategy and Manufacturing Growth in Toronto, 1880–1910" 76 *Ontario History* No. 3 (September, 1984) 199-232; the Canadian Bridge Company, the "Manchester of Canada" was built deliberately to take advantage of Canadian tariffs by the operators of the Detroit Bridge and Iron Works, see *Evening Record*, "It Will Thrive" December 15, 1900.

21 Windsor *Evening Record*, "New Epoch of Sandwich" October 10, 1905.

22 Windsor *Evening Record* "New Civic Building" November 16, 1904; in 1901 the public school board was reminded that the title to the property was in the City's name and they were given notice to quit the site. When asked if this was short notice, one alderman reminded the public board that the Catholic children had withdrawn from their schools and yet the public board had retained all the property—"You will have schools to burn in a short while." He told them; on the editorial, see "Beautify the City" May 15, 1905.

23 Margaret Beckman, Stephen Langmead and John Black, *The Best Gift: A Record of the Carnegie Libraries in Ontario* (Toronto: Dundurn Press, 1984) 30-1; and see *Evening Record* "Arose From Bed And Went To Vote" February 18, 1902—Ald. N. A. Bartlet had to be roused from his sick bed in order to vote in favour of the library site.

24 Windsor *Evening Record* May 21, 1907; a comprehensive account of the acquisition of the SW&A by American interests is contained in Jack Schramm, William Henning, and Richard Andrews, *When Eastern Michigan Rode the Rails* (Polo, Illinois: Transportation Trails, 1994) see Chapter 5, "SW&A Division".

25 Windsor *Evening Record* "Battled Three Hours Over Ferry Question" April 26, 1907; and see William Oxford, *The Ferry Steamers: The Story of the Detroit-Windsor Ferry Boats* (Toronto: Stoddart, 1992) Chapter 9 "Fares and Franchises".

26 Windsor Municipal Archives, City Council Minutes, RG 2 A IV 1/8, June 25, 1906—Special Meeting of Council in which it—"discloses a desire to recover if possible the lease held by the city for 25 years prior to 1888... but failing that end to try and induce the company to make some concessions." 487.

Windsor *Evening Record* "Are Ready To Satisfy City" November 17, 1906—"Windsor has been crawling on its knees to the company which has a monopoly from the Dominion government. It is surely about time to try another company..."; on the franchise grant in 1908, see *Evening Record* editorial "The Ferry Franchise" March 3, 1908—that City Council, "went through the motions of doing something... the whole matter was definitely decided at Ottawa a long time ago" on the SW&A see—*Evening Record*, "Rapid Progress of Street Railway Line" August 19, 1905.

27 Windsor *Evening Record* "They Want the City to Help" February 3, 1903; on the belt line, see *Evening Record* "Belt Line About To Be Constructed" October 20, 1903.

28 James G. Snell, "The International Border as a Factor in Marital Behaviour: A Historical Case Study" 81 *Ontario History* No. 4 (December, 1989) 289-301; and Windsor *Evening Record* "Marriage Mills" March 20, 1901; and see Windsor Municipal Archives, City Clerk Letterbook, RG 2 B II/5, an exasperated Clerk Lusted writing to the Registrar General that local clergy "should be compelled to exercise sense" in recording the numerous marriages they were conducting and forwarding them to him April 11, 1900 p. 315-6; and see *Evening Record* "Popular as Gretna Green" July 6, 1907.

29 Melvin G. Holli, "The Impact of Automobile Manufacturing upon Detroit" 2 *Detroit in Perspective: A Journal of Regional History* No. 3 (Spring, 1973) 176-187.

30 Amherstburg *Echo* editorial, May 29, 1905.

31 Patrick Brode, "Robert Sutherland" vol. XV *Dictionary of Canadian Biography* (Toronto: University of Toronto Press, 2005) 988-9; few of the area's needs would escape Sutherland's attention. He lobbied the federal government for the Sandwich Post Office in 1904, the piers for Belle River harbour and even sent a letter of warning to the Windsor City Council when he discovered that Ottawa was about to enter into a new ferry agreement without local consultation, see *Evening Record* "Solons Left the Council" August 15, 1905—"Mr. Sutherland said that when the matter came up at Ottawa he had it held up until he had a chance to secure the views of the Council in the matter."

32 On the 1902 strike at Buhl Malleable Iron, see Windsor *Evening Record* "Windsor 'Scabs' Were Maltreated" February 14, 1902; on the Canadian Bridge Strike, see *Evening Record*, "Trouble Last Night" April 9, 1903; "Riot Ended in Bloodshed" April 10, 1903; and "Strike Settled" April 19, 1903—the union had also demanded a clause that "none but union men be employed." But in this they were unsuccessful.

33 Hansard, House of Commons debates, January 12, 1905, 3.

34 On Wigle Park, see Windsor Municipal Archives, By-law 1261, "A By-law Respecting a Public Park" passed February 3, 1908; and see *Evening Record* editorial "The Park Scheme" February 8, 1908—"The latest park scheme, promoted by Mayor Wigle, is more promising than anything that has been attempted for many years;" on Wigle, see *Commemorative Biographical Record of the County of Essex* (Toronto: J.H. Beers, 1905) 56, and Hamilton Wigle ed., *The History of the Wigle Family and their Descendants* (Kingsville: 1931) 80-1.

35 David Roberts, *In the Shadow of Detroit: Gordon M. McGregor, Ford of Canada, and Motoropolis* (Detroit: Wayne State University Press, 2006) 15; much of the comment on the early life of Gordon McGregor is drawn from this book; on McGregor's singing career in Winnipeg, see Windsor *Evening Record* "City Siftings" April 14, 1896.

36 On the origins of the wagon works, see Windsor *Evening Record* "Another Industry" October 21, 1897—that they had come to Walkerville from Chatham to take advantage of the "greater shipping facilities" and supply of lumber. The description of the early phase of the Walkerville Wagon Works is described in detail in *Roberts* (above) at 17 and 20-1; on leaving the area, see "Walkerville Will Lose Wagon Co." January 18, 1904.

37 Much of the account of Gordon McGregor and the founding of Ford of Canada is taken from Roberts, *In the Shadow of Detroit:* p. 21; on Henry Ford in "999" see *Evening Record*, "Automobile on Ice" January 13, 1904.

38 *Evening Record* "By-law Necessary" July 28, 1904.

39 The National Cycle and Automobile Company is shown on the municipal directory of 1900 as occupying the Medbury Block on Ouellette Avenue under the control of Fred Evans, see *Municipal Directory, Windsor, Sandwich & Walkerville* (Ingersoll: Union Publishing, 1900); and see Windsor *Evening Record* "To Make Bicycles" November 20, 1899—"Another gigantic bicycle company has been formed to operate in Toronto."

40 On Bulmer's steam buggy, see *Border Cities Star* "Steam-Driven Buggy Built Only for Fun" December 3, 1938; and Hugh Durnford and Glenn Baechler, *Cars of Canada* (Toronto: McClelland and Stewart, 1973) 43; other comments on the first auto in Windsor come from long-serving constable George Livingstone who in 1931—"recalls the excitement that was caused when the first automobile was driven in Windsor. It was owned by John Kunsky, a man who was determined to become one of Detroit's leading theatrical magnates. Andrew Bowlby was the first Windsor man to own an automobile, George says." *Border Cities Star* March 4, 1931.

41 Bowlby ad, see *Evening Record* March 31, 1904; on the Grosse Pointe tragedy, see *Evening Record* "Killed By Auto" September 10, 1903; and "Tragedy of the Auto" June 18, 1906.

42 Roberts, *In the Shadow of Detroit* 24.

43 Windsor *Evening Record* "Manufacture Autos" July 2, 1905.

44 Roberts, *In the Shadow of Detroit* 33.

45 *Ibid.*, 43.

46 Windsor *Evening Record* "Selling More Autos Than in Other Years" September 28, 1908.

Endnotes to Chapter Two

1 On the Canadian Bridge Company, see Windsor Community Museum, PM 631, *Brief History of the Canadian Bridge Company Limited 1900-1958;* and see Windsor *Evening Record* "Enlarging Their Plant" February 22, 1902—"Page Wire Fence Co. are doing an immense business" and same, "Fence Companies Working Overtime" May 19, 1909.

2 Windsor *Evening Record* "A Model Town" February 22, 1902; on the creation of Garfield Street, see Windsor Community Museum, Walkerville Town Council Minutes, R.G. 5 GI 1.1, p. 375, October 14, 1902; on the "Garden City" see Lewis Mumford, "The Garden City and Modern Planning" in Ebenezer Howard, *Garden Cities of Tomorrow* (London: Faber & Faber, 1946) 31.

3 Thomas Adams, *Rural Planning and Development* (Ottawa: Commission of Conservation, 1917) 17, as quoted in Gerald T. Bloomfield, "Albert Kahn and Canadian Architecture: 1908–1938" *Study of Architecture in Canada Bulletin* vol. 4 December, 1985 p.9; on the plan to tear up the block pavements, see Windsor *Evening Record* "Boulevard Scheme" April 13, 1904.

4 Windsor *Evening Record* "Absolute Victory for the Walkers" December 27, 1909; on the whisky seizure, see *Evening Record* "Walkerville Whisky Seized in Detroit" June 24, 1908; on the whisky war generally, see Francis X. Chauvin, *Hiram Walker His Life and Work...* chapter 32 pp. 4-5, chapter 33 pp. 3-5.

5 On the development of St. Mary's Anglican and the Lincoln Road Methodist Church, see Hoskins, *A Historical Survey of the Town of Walkerville...* 119-30; Catholics had declined to share St. Mary's; on Willistead Manor, see Windsor *Evening Record* "E.C. Walker's Magnificent mansion in Walkerville" October 21, 1905.

6 Windsor *Evening Record* "Ascension Church Crowded to Doors" May 6, 1910; on the enforcement of the *Lord's Day Act* see "Ban on Baseball"—that baseball on Sunday would be prohibited as "Sandwich citizens do not take kindly to the introduction of Sabbath desecration." Windsor *Evening Record* June 9, 1906.

7 On child fights, see Windsor *Evening Record* "Little Locals" March 5, 1902; on dog fights, see Amherstburg *Echo* September 23, 1887—a dog fight "lasting 40 minutes admission 50 cents" was held at a wayside tavern four miles from Windsor.

8 On football, see Windsor *Evening Record* September 16, 1910—Windsor entered a team in the Ontario Rugby League, and October 3, 1910, was trounced in its first game 21-7 by Petrolia; on hockey, see *Evening Record* "Is Hockey Dead?" December 3, 1904.

9 Deneau's nickname of "rube" or country bumpkin was probably attributable to his Amherstburg origins. Deneau played amateur ball for a variety of teams including the Walkerville Crickets. He was also paid to pitch for Michigan teams. Still, he seemed deeply attached to the border area. When not playing sports, he worked part time as a diver. He also coached the indoor baseball teams of the various militia companies. Windsor's team of the early 1900s also owed its success to its catcher George "Stumpy" Loughlin who signed with a professional ball club in Michigan after 1904; see *Evening Record* "We Lose Loughlin" June 24, 1904.

10 Windsor *Evening Record* "Spracklin Yet Undefeated" December 13, 1904; "Went Limit of 25 Rounds" July 6, 1906—describes a brutal 25 round fight with Cleveland star boxer Frank Carney; and "Spracklin Shot" November 9, 1907.

11 On "Patsy" Drouillard, see Windsor *Evening Record* "Lightweight Fights This Evening For Championship" May 5, 1910; the information given on Drouillard in the Windsor-Essex County Sports Hall of Fame is questionable. It lists him as being born in Windsor on October 17, 1893. That would have made him 15 at the time of his first professional bout. Family records record the Drouillards as coming from River Canard and that he was born there on October 23, 1892.

12 On the Canadian Salt Company plant in Sandwich, see *Evening Record* "Work Progressing" September 29, 1910 and "Sandwich" June 9, 1906; "Huge Industry For Sandwich" June 19, 1911; On the ETR branch to Sandwich, see *Evening Record* "Essex Terminal To Sandwich Completed" January 23, 1912.

13 On the Reo Motor Car plant going to St. Catharines see Windsor *Evening Record* "Watch Windsor Win Way To Industrial Renown" February 10, 1909; on the prospect of a steel mill in Sandwich, see *Evening Record* "Sandwich West Sure to Get Steel Plant" May 26, 1909—"Second Gary Will Arise, They Say on River Front in Near Future;".

14 *Detroit News* editorial "The Future of Windsor" as quoted in the Windsor *Evening Record* May 3, 1910.

15 *An Act Respecting the City of Windsor* (1907) *Statutes of Ontario* c. 97; as Mayor Hanna explained to a potential Petrolia investor: "we can offer you splendid inducements in the way of exemption from taxation and free water. The City Council is authorized by special act of Parliament to grant concessions without a vote of the people." Windsor Municipal Archives, City Clerk Letter book, R.G. 2 II/9, Wigle to Littlewood, February 15, 1909.

16 Introducing the industrial by-law in 1910, Mayor Hanna explained that the city's acquisition at a set price protected the land from future speculation. Moreover the

extension of the spur line of the ETR into the property would increase its value, thereby guaranteeing the ratepayers a return on their investment–see Windsor *Evening Record* April 1, 1910.

17 Amherstburg *Echo* "Bridge or Tunnel" April 22, 1904—"This journal has learned that the Michigan Central railroad is weary of the struggle to secure a bridge."… "Under all these circumstances the Michigan Central has begun to think seriously not of a bridge, but of a tunnel." On ice on the Detroit River, see Windsor *Evening Record* "Ferry Boats Battle For Hours With Ice" December 27, 1909.

18 The loss of life and severe injuries incurred in building the MCR tunnel were so appalling that the *Evening Record* ran an article on the issue "Dozen Lives Lost In Digging Tunnel" July 19, 1909; another article "Hardships Endured by Tunnel Workers" described the work done by the muckers, that they worked behind the enormous earth drill, the "shield" and that when the shield got too far in front of them with no supports in place, "accidents usually happen. Owing to the great pressure of earth on top, a large lump of clay will break loose in the intervening distance." On the strike at the tunnel see *Evening Record* "Strike On At Tunnel" March 5, 1907; and "Strike-Breakers Coming to Tunnel" June 9, 1909.

19 Windsor *Evening Record* "He Was Given the Wrong Key" December 17, 1901; on the old electric plant in Windsor and the by-law to replace it, see editorial "The Lighting By-Law" May 3, 1905; on its propensity to break down, see editorial "The City Lighting Plant" October 16, 1906—"To the people on the south side of the city who have been sitting and walking in darkness for the past two months or more… the entire plant is really worn out and serious disablements are liable to occur at any moment."; on the DUR plant, see "New Power Plant" September 9, 1910; and see *Evening Record* "Dark Ways" December 14, 1905.

20 H.V. Nelles, "Sir Adam Beck" vol. XV *Dictionary of Canadian Biography* (Toronto: University of Toronto Press); and see Neil B. Freeman, *The Politics of Power: Ontario Hydro and Its Government, 1906–1995* (Toronto: University of Toronto Press, 1996) 18-21; and Neil B. Freeman, "Turn-of-the-Century State Intervention: Creating the Hydro-Electric Power Commission of Ontario, 1906" 84 *Ontario History* No. 3 (September, 1992) 171—"The potential of water power for generating power inexpensively and relieving dependence on American coal, whose delivery was subject to strikes and price escalations, made it a valuable resource for the province." at 172.

21 Windsor *Evening Record* "Municipal Delegates Welcome Niagara Power" December 12, 1909.

22 *Ibid.*, "Hon. Adam Beck Gives His Stamp of Approval" June 9, 1910—"Electricity for domestic purposes now costs 15 cents per kilowatt hour. When Niagara power comes to the city, Windsorites will pay but 3 cents getting a superior light and a superior service."

23 According to an editorial in the *Evening Record* female property owners tended to be "widows [who] were told that their taxes would be raised... Timid, unthinking women looked at the business standing of some of these canvassers and took their statements for gospel." See "The Morning After" June 21, 1910; on the ambivalence of the mayors, see J.W. Hanna's inauguration address of 1910, Windsor Municipal Archives, City Council Minutes, R.G. 2 AIV 1/9, January 17, 1910; on the passage of the by-law, see *Evening Record* "Power Bylaw Wins By Narrow Margin" June 21, 1910.

Alderman Shepherd inviting Beck to speak—Windsor Municipal Archives, City Clerk Letterbook, R.G. 2 B Box 11, Shepherd to Beck, April 22, 1910; on his opposition to the gas utilities getting any exclusive franchise see *Evening Record* "Ald. Shepherd Is Still On Warpath" February 13, 1909—"Ald. J.H. Shepherd is determined to take no chances of barring Windsor people from the benefit of Niagara power..."

24 Windsor *Evening Record* "Power Bylaw Wins By Narrow Margin" June 21, 1914.

25 On Moise Menard see, *Border Cities Star*, "Pioneer Manufacturer" August 10, 1929; and Durnford and Baechler, *Cars of Canada* 101-2. One of the most unique cars manufactured in Windsor during the early period was the "Tate Cabriolet Roadster," an electric car built by Tate Electric Limited of Walkerville. This company built several cars from 1912 but closed in late 1914. The electrics had their partisans and in the summer of 1914, Windsor's Dr. J.S. Labelle bragged about driving with two of his medical colleagues "each one of the party weighing nearly two hundred pounds" to Pontiac, Michigan; see *Evening Record* "Dr Labelle Establishes Record" June 8, 1914; and *Cars of Canada* 142.

26 Windsor *Evening Record* "Aerial truck..." April 22, 1910; among the other hopefuls was the Canadian Commercial Motor car Co. that produced trucks in an old brewery on Goyeau Street, see *Evening Record* "Turns Out First Car" October 26, 1910.

27 Roberts, *In the Shadow of Detroit* 60.

28 Douglas Brinkley, *Wheels for the World: Henry Ford, His Company, and a Century of Progress 1903–2003* (N.Y: Viking, 2003) 201.

29 Windsor *Evening Record* "Ford Company Will Extend Their Plant" August 16, 1910; and "Mammoth Auto Plant Being Built for Ford Co." September 20, 1912; and see Roberts, *In the Shadow of Detroit* 66.

30 Roberts, *In the Shadow of Detroit* 75.

31 On the death of Alexander Bartlet, see Windsor *Evening Record* December 23, 1910; While Bartlet was the leading establishment figure and a founder of the Presbyterian Church, his empathy was perhaps his most compelling feature. When the train bearing so many dying Norwegians had pulled into Windsor

station in 1857, Bartlet and another man, J.W. Blackadder, were the only non-medical staff who had tried to assist the victims. When Joseph Reaume, a young French-Catholic farmboy, was crippled in an accident, it was Bartlet who helped him get an education. With Bartlet's help and encouragement, Reaume would become a doctor and eventually a member of the provincial legislature and the cabinet.

32 Windsor Public Library, Local History Scrapbook 3d, "Arthur Graham "I Remember When..." and H.R. Wellington, "I Remember When..."

33 Windsor *Evening Record* "New Mammoth Pavilion on Bob-lo Island" June 7, 1913.

34 J. Lewis Robinson, *Windsor, Ontario: A Study in Urban Geography* (Syracuse University, Master of Arts Thesis, may, 1942) 47-8.

35 Windsor *Evening Record* editorial, "Two New Factories" June 6, 1914—"New industries at the rate of one a month or better do not come to any city by accident."

36 Robert Craig Brown and Ramsay Cook, *Canada 1896–1921: A Nation Transformed* (Toronto: McClelland and Stewart, 1974) 179-85; Patrice Dutil and David Mackenzie, *Canada 1911: The Decisive Election that Shaped the Country* (Toronto: Dundurn, 2011); and W.M. Baker, "A Case Study of Anti-Americanism in English-Speaking Canada: The Election Campaign of 1911" LI *Canadian Historical Review* No. 4 (December, 1970) 426.

On Detroit and reciprocity, see the comments of M. McRae the head of Detroit's Board of Trade that "From 70 to 73 percent of Detroit's exports go to Canada...We believe that the broadening of the free exchange list would increase the volume." Detroit *Free Press* September 5, 1911.

37 Windsor *Evening Record* Election Results—September 22, 1911; on Laurier's visit, see *Evening Record* September 9 and 11, 1911; on the Sandwich courthouse meeting—*Evening Record* "Rival Candidates on Same Platform" September 15, 1911; Hiram Walker's placard—*Evening Record* September 16, 1911; on Detroit reaction to the defeat of the Liberals and reciprocity, see Detroit *News* editorial, "No Mistaking Canada's Answer" September 23, 1911.

38 Windsor *Evening Record* "Windsor Will Have Largest Auto Wheel Works in the Empire" May 24, 1913.

39 For example, Dominion Stamping added more space in 1911 as "Their output is consumed chiefly by the local automobile factories although, considerable... output is constantly in demand by different automobile concerns through eastern Ontario." Windsor *Evening Record* "Building A Large Addition To Plant" October 5, 1911; on bonuses see Windsor Municipal Archives, R.G. 2, By-law 15644 bonus to John Kelsey of Detroit, June 9, 1913.

40 See Appendix "A"—Assessment Commissioner Annual Report, 1920.

41 Windsor *Evening Record* "Davis farm Yielded..."—The 608 residential lots had been purchased for $80,000 and 18 months later had sold for about $200,000.

42 For example, Windsor *Evening Record* "Building Operations in Windsor for the Past Month Exceedingly Brisk" October 4, 1910—building lots were being sold as soon as a foundation was in place.

43 Windsor *Evening Record* "$20,000,000 Steel Plant..." January 2, 1913; E.H. Gary, who had founded U.S. Steel in 1901 with Andrew Carnegie and J.P. Morgan, was obviously motivated by the existing tariffs of between $6 and $7 per ton on steel imported into Canadian and British territories. On O.E. Fleming's role in assembling the land, see *Evening Record* "O.E. Fleming Secured the Site..." January 3, 1913—"There was little or no haggling over prices. The owners were paid big figures, running from $10,000 and upwards in some instances."

44 Ojibway was incorporated as a town in 1913, see *An Act to Incorporate the Town of Ojibway* Statutes of Ontario, 1913, c. 108—The provincial government appointed a group of five men (including William Woollatt, the manager of the ETR. as mayor, W.C. Kennedy of Windsor Gas and Alexander Leslie of the L.E. & D.R. Railway) as town councillors rather than have an election.

The naming of the town was the source of some controversy. Gary of U.S. Steel favoured the name "Pontiac" after the great Indian leader who had almost overrun the British at Detroit. Pontiac, Michigan objected and some Canadians considered this name to be unpatriotic. Many of the residents had been calling the place "Ojibwa" after the local tribe. In the end "Ojibway" was applied to the town. The original name of "Petite Côte" does not appear to have been seriously considered. Windsor *Evening Record* "Propose 'Steel City' to replace 'Pontiac'" March 10, 1913.

On land speculation, see *Evening Record* "Stand Ninety Hours to Purchase Land..." April 21, 1913.

In order to accommodate the coming steel mills, the river road that had served the farm communities for centuries was closed and diverted. The farmers protested to no effect. See, "Will Make Sandwich a Mile Farther Away" *Evening Record* March 1, 1913; and Windsor Municipal Archives, Ojibway Town Council Minutes, R.G. 5 B I 1/1. Meeting of February 2, 1914—petition to the Lieutenant Governor to close "the front or Detroit River road."

45 Toronto *Globe* "From Market Gardens to Big Steel City" May 24, 1913—the glowing tone of the report was undoubtedly attributable to the author Charles L. Barker's position as Windsor's Industrial Commissioner.

46 Essex County by-law no. 306, passed December 3, 1912; my thanks to Mary Brennan, the Director of Council Services for the County of Essex for providing this by-law; on the naming of Ford City, see *Evening Record* "New Municipality Looking For Name" December 3, 1912; on François X. Drouillard, see *Evening Record* "French Pioneer..." February 2, 1905; on *Notre Dame du Lac* see Power and Brock, *Gather up the Fragments* 169-70.

47 Windsor *Evening Record* "Ford City..." March 8, 1913; and see *Evening Record* "Ford Continuing to Make Progress" October 10, 1913.

48 In a letter to a Toronto lawyer, Clerk Stephen Lusted had explained the City's motives: "It is felt to be an absolute necessity to the welfare and growth of Windsor that a street to the River be put through the land in question and that sufficient of said land be acquired upon which to construct a commodious dock for the use of lake-going vessels, while there is also a desire to establish a small park for the remainder of the land above the river level." The lands in question were controlled by the Grand Trunk but were not needed by them; see Windsor Municipal Archives, City Clerk Letterbook, R.G. 2 B Box 11 II/9, Lusted to Shepley June 22, 1910 p. 933-4; and see *Evening Record* "City Deputation Secures River Front Property for Park" October 9, 1912.

On Lanspeary's efforts to create more parkland, see *Evening Record* "Preliminary Steps..."—"Ald. Lanspeary paved the way at the council meeting Monday night for the inauguration of a park system in Windsor." July 16, 1912; and "Establish Parks in Both Ends of City" June 24, 1913.

49 See "Dr. Joseph Octave Reaume M.P.P." in *Commemorative Biographical Record of Essex* (Toronto: J.H. Beers, 1905) 32-3; Reaume was denounced by one of the Orange Lodge organs, the Hamilton *Spectator* – "And now Hon. Mr. Reaume wants to perpetuate the absurdity!" (providing bilingual schools in eastern Ontario) and suggested that if he had the best interests of the children at heart, "he would ask for the abolition of the bi-lingual schools." As quoted in the *Evening Record* editorial "On Dr. Reaume's Trail" March 3, 1906.

50 On Regulation 17, see Charles W. Humphries, *'Honest Enough to be Bold': The Life and Times of Sir James Pliny* Whitney (Toronto: University of Toronto Press, 1985) "This was the regulation upon which the battle was joined during the next decade." at 202.

51 Windsor *Evening Record* "City Council Signs up Hydro-Electric Contract" December 21, 1912.

52 See L.S. Treuge, "Pressing of Switch by Sir Adam Beck Gave Light to City" Windsor *Daily Star* September 12, 1939: the article records the work not only of Perry but also of Edgar Wallace and Fred Hubbell who established Windsor Hydro; for the by-law that established the hydro system see Windsor Municipal Archives, R.G. 2, By-law 1654 ½, passed December 29, 1913.

Endnotes to Chapter Three

1 Windsor *Evening Record* "Military Enthusiasm in Windsor..." August 7, 1914; and "Essex French Regiment" October 2, 1914; on Wigle, see "Lt.-Col. Wigle Accepts Command at London" October 21, 1914; on George Wade, see Amherstburg *Echo* December 4, 1914.

2 Windsor *Evening Record* "View of Readers—the Lady Searcher" March 30, 1915; and see Dimmel, "South Detroit, Canada" 202-3.

3 Roberts, *In the Shadow of Detroit* 117.

4 Windsor *Evening Record* April 21, 1915.

5 Woodford, *This Is Detroit* 86-7; on Wigle's warnings, see *Evening Record*, August 22, 1914- "We know that there are 18,000 Germans in Detroit who sympathize with their mother country…" on the reluctance of Windsor men to join the 21st, see "Recruits Drill" November 24, 1914—once all the volunteers for overseas service were gone, "now they [Windsor men] refuse to volunteer to defend their own city."

6 The bombing itself is described in the *Evening Record* of June 21, 1915, and subsequent police investigation on June 22.

7 Detroit *Free Press* editorial, ""War Across the River" June 22, 1915.

8 Grant W. Grams, "Karl Respa and German Espionage in Canada During World War One" *Journal of Military and Strategic Studies*, 8 (Fall, 2005).

9 Brandon Dimmel "Sabotage, Security, and Border-Crossing Culture: The Detroit River during the First World War, 1914–1918" *Histoire Sociale/Social History* 47 No. 94 (June 2014) 415.

10 Windsor *Evening Record* "A City That Found Itself" October 22, 1915.

11 *Ibid.*, "Soldiers Riot" April 3, 1916; to encourage the men, each recruit to the 99th was promised a cash bonus if they could bring in someone else—*Evening Record* December 13, 1915; on the shaming of able-bodied men to join, see *Evening Record* January 15, 1916.

12 Windsor *Evening Record* "Ford the Universal Car" ad March 4, 1916; on Kelsey Wheel, see *Evening Record* October 15, 1915.

13 Windsor *Evening Record* "Windsor Third City on Building List" March 4, 1916; and see "Windsor Growing Faster than any City in Canada" July 6, 1916; on Ford plans for a tent for its workers, see *Evening Record* "Ford Motor Seeks" May 21, 1913.

14 On the Poles of Marion Avenue, see Windsor *Evening Record* "Council Grants Aid" January 20, 1914—Council resolved to build a sewer on Marion as a means of supplying some work in the neighbourhood; see also, *Evening Record* "Conditions on Marion Avenue Are Unchanged" February 14, 1914.

On the early conditions on Marion Avenue, see *Evening Record* "Marion Avenue District a Flagrant Breach of All Health Laws" May 7, 1913; on Poles excluded from Walkerville, see *Evening Record* "Walkerville to segregate Poles in Own District" September 12, 1917; building Holy Trinity, see Agata Rajski, *One*

Century of the Polish Community in Windsor, 1908–2008 (Windsor: Walkerville, Publishing, 2008) 45.

In 1915, Isadore Cherniak, a former newsboy and soon to be medical student, wrote a newspaper account about the 250 families that made up the Polish colony. Both in language and culture, Marion Street resembled a Polish town more than an Ontario neighbourhood. And now that there was regular work at the Ford plant, the squalor of the previous years was over; see *Evening Record* June 23, 1915.

On the Hungarians, see "Hungarian Colony in Windsor" *Evening Record* June 28, 1912.

15 Windsor *Evening Record* W. A Craik, "He Says Many City Girls Are Yet 'Too Proud to Work" August 18, 1916; on the deluge of socks, see *Evening Record* February 26, 1916; on women at the Peabody plant, see *Evening Record* February 11, 1916.

16 Windsor Municipal Archives, R.G. 2, By-law No. 1732 passed May 27 1914 appointing Martha Dickinson acting clerk; and see Windsor *Daily Star* "Woman Clerk Served in Critical Era" April 3, 1954; and *Daily Star* obituary September 11, 1965; on all three women running for the school board, see Amherstburg *Echo* December 25, 1914; Stephen Lusted was ill and apparently unable to function as City Clerk after 1914—he did not officially retire until July 1, 1920 whereupon Martha Dickinson became City Clerk in her own right—*Border Cities Star,* May 26, 1920.

17 Author interview with Walter Hewlitt's granddaughter Tracey Thomas, August 27, 2013.

18 Windsor *Evening Record* "Farewell to Members of New Negro Battalion" September 14, 1916; and see Calvin Ruck, *Canada's Black Battalion: No. 2 Construction, 1916–1920* (Halifax: Black Cultural Centre for Nova Scotia, 1986); on blacks leaving Windsor to enlist elsewhere, see author interview with Tracey Thomas, August 27, 2013—her grandfather Walter Hewlitt left Windsor to go to London to volunteer for service in France.

On racism in Windsor during this period, see *Evening Record* "Colored Citizens" May 6, 1914—that black citizens had to fund a separate tuberculosis ward; on the hiring of Doran Dixon, a black man in the post office, see *Evening Record* "Color Line"- Oliver Wilcox was forthright in maintaining the rights of black citizens and spoke out in Parliament on their behalf. He was praised for this by Windsor's black political organization, the Good Government Club, see *Evening Record* "Colored People Commend Wilcox" May 20, 1913.

19 Windsor Municipal Archives, City Council Minute book, R.G. 2 A IV 1/12, May 22, 1916, p. 61; and see the *Royal Commission in Racing Inquiry Report of the Rutherford Commission* (Ottawa, 1920).

20 Windsor *Evening Record* Minnie Cage, "Scarcity of Workingmen's Houses…" September 9, 1916; the author's family was one of these cross-border migrants.

The family emigrated from the U.S. south in 1912, attracted by industrial work in Detroit. In order to accommodate a growing family, the only suitable dwelling available was in Walkerville and they crossed the border from Detroit in 1916. All of the family members retained U.S. citizenship.

On Detroiters enlisting in Windsor, see Pte. Clarke from Detroit *Evening Record* October 16, 1916; on half the 99th being American, see comments "Injuring Recruiting" November 17, 1916; Three Detroiters killed at Ypres, see "Three Detroit Boys" March 20, 1915; six out of eight enlisting, see "Six Detroit Youths" October 22, 1915.

21 Windsor *Evening Record* editorial "License Reduction" April 22, 1912; on the plebiscites, see *Evening Record* "The Plebiscite"—"The local conditions here are exceptional and worked strongly against prohibition." January 4, 1894.

22 Windsor *Evening Record* "Grant Ford City License" April 25, 1913—Gordon McGregor argued that the Drouillard application was not for a "roadhouse" for travellers, but for a saloon that would pollute his workers and that "If the Windsor commissioners thought of allowing licensed places in the Windsor factory district there would be a howl, and they wouldn't grant them" and see *Evening Record* editorial "Keep Ford City Dry" April 26, 1913; "Ford City to Have two Licenses" April 29, 1913; and the revocation of the licenses May 9, 1913.

23 Toronto *Globe* editorial "Honor to Hearst and Rowell" September 16, 1916; on the prohibition bill, see Brian Douglas Tennyson, "Sir William Hearst and the Ontario Temperance Act" *Ontario History* vol. LV (December, 1963) 233-245.

On the closing of the roadhouses, see *Evening Record* "Five Road Houses Lose Licenses" July 12, 1915—"Wolf" (Wolfgang Fellers) is the pioneer of the roadhouse proprietors. He located in the spot that he has made famous when that part of Sandwich East was nothing more than a marsh... First he established an unpretentious shack, where he began to build up a reputation on both sides of the river." And "Ontario License Board Cuts Off Three Local Bars" July 14, 1915.

24 On the passing of the 'wet' age in Windsor see *Evening Record* "Police of Detroit..." September 18, 1916.

25 Windsor *Evening Record* "Neighbourhood 'Get-the-Paper-Clubs'" November 14, 1916; on the insult to Americans, see the editorial in *Evening Record* "Injuring Recruiting" November 17, 1916: "After giving all kinds of free publicity and displaying a marked friendship for the Canadian cause the editors and publishers of Detroit Sunday papers are told they can't send their editions over here. No word of appreciation for what they have done."

26 *Ibid.*, editorial, "Border Annoyances" December 5, 1916; and see Dimmel, "South Detroit, Canada" 203-5.

27 Dimmel, "South Detroit, Canada" 207.

28 Marilyn Barber, "The Ontario Bilingual Schools Issue: Sources of Conflict" XLVII, No. 3 *Canadian Historical Review* (September, 1966) 236; and see Robert Choquette, *Language and Religion: A History of English-French Conflict in Ontario* (Ottawa: University of Ottawa Press, 1975); and Chad Gaffield, *Language, Schooling, and Cultural Conflict: The Origins of the French-language Controversy in Ontario* (Kingston: McGill-Queen's University Press, 1987; on the Orange streamer, see *Evening Record* "Orange Banner Taken Down" July 12, 1916.

29 Jack D. Cecillon, *Prayers, Petitions, and Protests: The Catholic Church and the Ontario Schools Crisis in the Windsor Border Region, 1910–1928* (Montreal & Kingston: McGill-Queen's University Press, 2013) 72-3.

30 Michael Power, "The Mitred warrior: A Critical Reassessment of Bishop Michael Francis Fallon, 1867–1931" *Catholic Insight* (April, 2000); an individual as flamboyantly combative as Fallon was bound to generate a stream of scholarly articles; see John Farrell, "Michael Francis Fallon Bishop of London Ontario Canada, 1909–1931: the Man and His Controversies" CCHA *Study Sessions* 35 (1968) 73-90; Adrian Ciani, "An Imperialist Irishman': Bishop Michael Fallon, the Diocese of London and the Great War" *Historical Studies* (January, 2008).

31 Windsor *Evening Record* September 10, 1917; The Ford City riot is thoroughly canvassed in Michael Power, *Bishop Fallon And The Riot At Ford City 8 September 1917* (Windsor: Essex County Historical Society, Occasional Paper No. 3, 1986); as well as Jack Cecillon, "Turbulent Times in the Diocese of London: Bishop Fallon and the French Language Controversy, 1910–18" *Ontario History* 87 (December, 1995) 369-92; while Power is sympathetic to Fallon who was concerned with the "future well-being of his flock" (p. 3) and determined to rid them, particularly the French-Canadians, of backward cultural relicts, Cecillon has a different perspective and notes that Fallon:

> "served as a catalyst for the troubles which erupted in Essex and Kent counties. By vocally opposing the bilingual school system and crushing his clerical adversaries, he infuriated even the most passive members of the community." (p. 388)

32 Barbara M. Wilson, ed., *Ontario and the First World War 1914–1918: A Collection of Documents* (Toronto: Champlain Society, 1977) li; and see Amherstburg *Echo*"99th Boys Wounded" September 29, 1916; on the death of Colley Ambery, see *Evening Record* September 25, 1916.

33 Walter McGregor to Mrs. William McGregor, January 26, 1917, as quoted in Roberts, *In the Shadow of Detroit* 151; on the Council resolution to keep the 241st in Windsor, see Windsor Municipal Archives, Council Minutebook, R.G. 2 A IV-½, October 6, 1916, p. 128.

34 *Detroit News* "Throngs Cheer" April 24, 1917; Windsor *Evening Record* "Farewell to 241st" April 24, 1917.

35 Windsor *Evening Record* Minnie Cage, "Feelings of Windsor Women…" March 3, 1917; on Premier Hearst's comments, see Catherine L. Cleverdon, *The Woman Suffrage Movement in Canada* 2nd ed., (Toronto: University of Toronto Press, 1974) 42; on women in banks see *Evening Record,* Minnie Cage, November 17, 1917; on women in the war, see Joan Sangster, "Mobilizing Women for War" in David Mackenzie ed., *Canada and the First World War* (Toronto: University of Toronto Press, 2005) 157-193.

On the No. 3 Stationary Hospital, see *Star* "Lt. Col. Casgrain Protects Nurses" June 29, 1915—the hospital included local nurses Marie Askin, Nelle Girard and Myrtle Fielder; on May Whittaker's OBE, see *Border Cities Era* November 16, 1918—she had been captured and escaped from German confinement early in the war.

On black troops discriminated against in theatre, see *Evening Record* "Drawing of Color Line" February 6, 1917; and on Somme film *Evening Record* March 8, 1917.

36 Desmond Morton, *Fight or Pay: Soldiers' Families in the Great War* (Vancouver: UBC Press, 2004) 185; on payments in Windsor see *Evening Record* "Soldiers' Wives" September 29, 1916—"Windsor, according to reports from the headquarters in Ottawa, is paying 30 percent more in allowances for soldiers' dependants than any other city in this part of the country." On the increase in taxes to pay dependent benefits, see *Evening Record* "City's Tax Rate" April 27, 1918.

37 Windsor *Evening Record* editorial "The City's Health" ; on closing the Bridge Avenue beach, see *Evening Record* "Would Discourage Bathing" April 6, 1916; and Amherstburg *Echo* August 4, 1916; on the chlorination of Windsor's water, see *Evening Record* "Citizens" August 13, 1912; on the I.J.C., see, Joseph Chacko Chirakaikaran, *The International Joint Commission* (N.Y: A.M.S. Press, 1968) report issued August 12, 1911—pp. 269-71.

38 Michael B. Moir, "Samuel Morley Wickett" vol. XIV *Dictionary of Canadian Biography* (Toronto: University of Toronto Press, 1998) 1064; on the early petitions for a border utilities commission, see C.L. Barker, "The Essex Border Utilities Commission" Windsor *Evening Record* March 23, 1917.

39 Morris Knowles' ideas were put forward at a public meeting in January, 1917—*Evening Record* "Border Utilities" January 11, 1917; on the EBUC as a war measure, see *Evening Record* editorial "Border Utilities Commission" February 24, 1916; Ford City was increasingly dissatisfied with the EBUC—"Ford City in its dealings with the Essex border utilities commission, has about reached the parting of the ways, declared Mayor Charles Montreuil" January 5, 1917.

On what to call this greater municipal area, see editorial in *Evening Record* "New Name For Border Cities" November 14, 1917- "Another fusion appellation that has come into general use is "Border Cities."

40 Windsor *Evening Record* "Passport Order" June 9, 1917; and see, Dimmel, "Sabotage, Security and Border Culture…" 416-7.

41 Windsor *Evening Record* "Kennedy Is Easy Victor" December 18, 1917; and see Michael Power, "William Costello Kennedy" vol. XV *Dictionary of Canadian Biography* (Toronto, University of Toronto Press).

42 Windsor *Evening Record* "Foreigners Back Down" June 17, 1918.

43 On war gardens see *Evening Record* April 26, 1918—"The well-to-do classes are doing their bit the same as the working men. A.D. Bowlby has two lots that he intends to work himself." On the 500 acre manufacturer lands, see *Evening Record* March 26, 1918 "Inspection Made" May 4, 1918; on the push for agriculture, see Adam Crerar, "Ontario and the Great War" in Mackenzie ed., *Canada and the First World War* "Few Ontarians traded full-time jobs—even with promises of equal pay on the farm—for summers of trudging behind teams and mucking out barns." at 234.

44 On the Polish recruits, see *Evening Record* "Polish Army Recruits get big Send-off" September 18, 1918; on losses after the battle of Amiens, see *Border Cities Era*, October 19, 1918—reports the death of six local men in France.

On the Jewish recruits, A. Weingarden, Harry and Mike Meretsky for the Jewish battalion, see "For Palestine" *Evening Record* May 15, 1918.

45 Eileen Pettigrew, *The Silent Enemy: Canada and the Deadly Flu of 1918* (Saskatoon: Western Producer, 1983); and *Thirty-Eighth Annual Report of the Provincial Board of Health for the year 1919* (Legislative Assembly of the Province of Ontario, 1920) notes that, "the outbreak spread from east to west across the province and caused great loss of life."

46 *Border Cities Star* editorial "A Joint Board of Health" November 15, 1918; on the virulence of the epidemic in December, see "Will Convert Veterans' Clubhouse" December 16, 1918; on the number of victims, see "Heavy Toll" January 15, 1919.

47 Toronto *Globe* "Armistice Celebrations in Ontario" November 12, 1918.

Endnotes to Chapter Four

1 On the Prince of Wales tour, see *Border Cities Star* October 23 and 24, 1919; on women being denied office work at banks see "Bankers Bar Girls" October 28, 1921.

2 Gregory S. Kealey, "State Repression of Labour and the Left in Canada, 1914–1920: The Impact of the First World War" in Franca Iacovetta, Paula Draper and Robert Ventresca, *A Nation of Immigrants...* (Toronto: University of Toronto Press, 1998) 399; and *Border Cities Star* "Russian Agitator" July 5, 1918, and "Case Against Slavs" October 24, 1918; Language was a decided problem and one Pole found himself charged with writing seditious documents in Russian. The Windsor prosecution staff did not seem to know the difference between Polish and Russian, see *Border Cities Star* "Judge Smith" July 25, 1919.

3 Pearson Wells comments as reported in *Border Cities Star* "Ford Will Assist" February 8, 1919; Carrick's comments to the Chamber of Commerce—"Labor Aims Endorsed" February 13, 1919; The Windsor G.W.V.A. branch passed a resolution in February 1919 to—"have all unfriendly aliens removed… and returned men given their places." They also objected to Windsor restaurants refusing to serve black soldiers in uniform as an "insult to soldiers" February 7, 1919.

4 Craig Heron and Myer Siemiatycki, "The Great War, the State, and Working-Class Canada" in Craig Heron, *The Workers' Revolt in Canada, 1917–1925* (Toronto: University of Toronto Press, 1998) 27; on Archie Hooper and the rise of unionism in Windsor, see *Border Cities Star* "Trouble May Come" March 20, 1919 and on the organization of 3,000 men, see "Great Strides" July 19, 1919.

5 *Border Cities Star* "Organized Labor" May 14, 1919; the arrival of troops in Windsor is described in the previous edition of May 13.

6 David Jay Bercuson, *Confrontation at Winnipeg: Labour, Industrial Relations, and the General Strike* (Montreal: McGill-Queen's University Press, 1974) 116; D.C. Masters, *The Winnipeg General Strike* (Toronto: University of Toronto Press, 1973) on the reaction to the general strike, see Reinhold Kramer and Tom Mitchell, *When the State Trembled…* (Toronto: University of Toronto Press, 2010).

7 Roberts, *The Shadow of Detroit* 174; on General Motors, see *Border Cities Star* April 4, 1919; Dominion Forge, May 30, 1917.

8 *Border Cities Star* "Canadian Ford" May 10, 1919; Studebaker, July 30 and 31, 1919.

9 Byron Lew and Marvin McInnis, "Guns and Butter: World War I and the Canadian Economy" (Trent University) 46; on Algoma Steel, see Dawson McDowall, *Steel at the Sault: Francis H. Clergue, Sir James Dunn and the Algoma Steel Corporation* (Toronto: University of Toronto Press, 1984) 65.

10 Roberts, *The Shadow of Detroit* 164 and 181; on Windsor's growth during the war, see *Border Cities Star* "Industrial Growth is not Hindered by War Conditions" November 1, 1918.

11 *Border Cities Star* "Windsor Leads Over Twelve Cities" February 1, 1919; Windsor Municipal Archives, Assessment Commission Annual report, 1920; and Cancian et al. *Windsor: A Statistical Package* (1983).

12 *Border Cities Star* "Border Building Record" August 1, 1919 and "Walkerville in need of 500 New Houses He Says" August 14, 1918; on Gundy's urging government loans for housing, see "Housing Plan" January 21, 1919.

13 Oxford, *The Ferry Steamers* 77; and see *Star* editorial, "The Ferry Question" September 23, 1919—"His Worship (Mayor Winter) believes that a renewal of the franchise cannot be justified in view of the poor quality of service now furnished

the Border Cities." On the final resolution of the ferry question, see *Star* "Pact Is Made" April 18, 1923.

14 *Border Cities Star* "Beck's Plan" October 27, 1919—Beck had almost single-handedly prolonged the streetcar strike of the previous summer by declaring that if a fare increase was approved that this would increase the value of the SW&A and make it difficult to purchase. Once the fare increase was defeated and the strike renewed, the *Border Cities Star* reminded its readers that Sir Adam was the "disturbing element" and that his machinations had better end up with a publicly owned streetcar system, see editorial "Sir Adam's Move" July 7, 1919.

15 Author interview with Bill Willson, December 5, 2013; The Lincoln Road bus was operated by the Windsor Bus Company, see Windsor municipal Archives, Walkerville council Minutes, March 15 and April 13, 1922.

16 On Adjutant Martin's struggle to fund the construction, see *Border Cities Star* "New Grace Hospital Wing" December 13, 1922; and Windsor *Daily Star* February 22, 1936; on the respect for the Salvation Army after the war, see the *Star* article, June 7, 1924—"Popular favor, guided by the boys who knew the Army in war time swung strongly toward the band banging, Blood and Fire flag waving pacifists…"

17 See Windsor *Daily Star* "Border Chapter Tea To Observe Jubilee" June 5, 1959.

18 Canada, Royal Commission in Racing Inquiry, Report of J.G. Rutherford (Ottawa: 1920); on all-night cafes, see *Border Cities Star* "Protests" October 12, 1918, and on "spooning booths" October 16, 1920.

19 Dorothy Ours, *Man O' War: A Legend Like Lightning* (N.Y: St. Martin's Press, 2006).

20 *Border Cities Star* "Charged With Violation" January 2 and 8, 1919; see editorial "The Prohibition Farce" January 4, 1919—"Men who like a little liquor now and then feel the easiest way to get a prescription is to ask the family doctor to make one out."

21 Gerald Hallowell, *Prohibition in Ontario* (Toronto: Ontario Historical Society Research Publication, No.2, 1972) Chapter III 'Ontario Will Go Dry Forever'; on the Windsor Collegiate Institute debate, see *Border Cities Star* October 17, 1919' on Bishop Fallon's views, see editorial "The Bishop's Comment" June 28, 1920.

22 On Michigan prohibition, see Larry D. Engelmann, "A Separate Peace: The Politics of Prohibition Enforcement in Detroit, 1920-1930" *Detroit in Perspective: A Journal of Regional History* 1 (Autumn, 1972) 51.

23 *Detroit News* "Officers Seize Boats and Rum" September 5, 1920; on Windsor smugglers, *Star* January 14, 1920.

24 *Border Cities Star* "Liquor Deals Give Border Bad Name" February 14, 1920; and see "Ice Swallows Rum Runners" February 10, 1920.

25 Hallowell, *Prohibition in Ontario* 117; on William Raney, see Charles M. Johnson, *E.C. Drury: Agrarian Idealist* (Toronto: University of Toronto Press, 1986) 154-5; and especially Peter Oliver, *Public and Private Persons: The Ontario Political Culture1914–1934* (Toronto: Clarke, Irwin, 1975) 71-2.

26 On J.O.L. Spracklin, see "To Admit Windsor Man to Ministry" *Evening Record* June 2, 1916, and "Rev. Spracklin" *Border Cities Star* March 20, 1920; on the controversies in the Methodist Church, see "Carman-Jackson" controversy, *Evening Record* March 4, 1909; and "Methodists Oppose New Dancing Modes" July 24, 1919.

27 Detroit *News* "Spracklin and Trumble" November 8, 1920; on Ham Trumble arrested for fire alarm prank—*Evening Record* October 3, 1910; on Mrs. Francis Chappell selling liquor without a license—"Fined $300" June 22, 1916.

28 Ontario Archives, R.G. 49-102, *Record of the Special Committee re: Ontario Temperance Act*—In the first session, on September 28, 1920, J.D. Flavelle, chairman of the Board of License Commissioners noted that, "...there has been a great deal of rum running on the Border Towns. In Windsor we have had men fined as high as $2,000, and they went away smiling, saying that they had made five or six thousand dollars out of the transaction." p. 1; on the Toronto *Globe* editorial "The Scandal of the Border" September 28, 1920; and *Border Cities Star* editorial "Enforce the Law" May 29, 1920; on the Toronto *Star* accounts of high adventure along the border, see "Night on the Detroit with Bootleggers" November 3, 1920.

29 *Ibid.* Special Committee Sessions, November 2 and 3, 1920.

30 *Border Cities Star* "Pussyfoot denied Hearing In City" April 12, 1921.

31 *Border Cities Star* "Essex County Goes Wet" April 19, 1921.

32 *Toronto Telegram* April 9, 1921; and see Hallowell, *Prohibition in Ontario* 121.

33 *Detroit Free Press* May 20, 1921—"The reign of terror began, according to the police, shortly after the Province of Quebec closed its border to the export of liquor. The shortage of liquor is being acutely felt by members of "The Bootleggers Union."

34 On Cecil Smith, see *Border Cities Star* "Arrest Taxi Driver" April 5, 1919; February 19 and October 13 and 18, 1921; generally, see Detroit *News* "Rum King Held in Alien plot" May 3, 1929.

Cecil Smith would make legal history when he challenged the right of the government to tax his income from illegal liquor sales. On his legal challenges to the income tax case, see *Smith* v *A.G. of Canada* (1924) Ex.C.R. 193 and (1925) C.T.C. 244; remarkably enough Smith won in the Supreme Court of Canada which ruled that the money obtained from criminal activity was tax-free. A persistent government took the case all the way to Canada's highest court—the Judicial Committee of the Privy Council where the decision was reversed and Smith, now penniless, was ordered to pay $28,630. *Star* July 27, 1926.

35 Toronto *Globe* "Tentacles of Rum-runner" March 25, 1921; *Globe* on Cecil Smith, October 14, 1921; on Smith's career see *Star* "Says he Paid" October 13, 1921 and October 18, 1921.

36 *Border Cities Star* "Idle men" January 19, 1921; and "Provincial Highway" January 18, 1921.

37 Engelmann, "A Separate Peace" 53.

Endnotes to Chapter Five

1 David Roberts, "McGregor, Gordon Morton" *Dictionary of Canadian Biography* vol. 15 (University of Toronto Press) 2003; and see accounts of the McGregor funeral in *Border Cities Star* March 14 and 15, 1922.

2 *Border Cities Star* December 31, 1921.

3 Dimitry Anastakis, "From Independence to Integration: The Corporate Evolution of the Ford Motor Company of Canada, 1904-2004" *Business History Review* 78 (Summer, 2004) 226; and comments by Wallace Campbell that Ford of Canada was autonomous 213.

4 John Herd Thompson and Allen Seager, *Canada 1922–1939: Decades of Discord* (Toronto: McClelland and Stewart1985) 85.

5 Joe Sherman "Like the factories he designed, Albert Kahn lived to work" *The Smithsonian* (September, 1994) 55; on the construction see *Border Cities Star*—"The immensity of the steel erecting job may be gleaned from the fact that the Canadian Bridge Company now have four separate lines of railway running through the factory site to be used for hauling the big steel columns to their location over the twelve acres of land." February 24, 1923.

6 Hugh Durnford and Glenn Baechler, *Cars of Canada* (Toronto: McClelland and Stewart, 1973) 240; on the opening of the new plant, see *Border Cities Star* December 5, 1923; on the impact of the Ford payroll on the Border Cities, see "Ford Plant Keeps Thousands in Food" *Star* February 12, 1924.

7 *Border Cities Star* "From Shack to 9 Million Dollars" September 5, 1925; and see Rolland Jerry, "Hands Across the Border: Canadian Liked Gotfredsons as Well as Yanks" Gotfredson *Truck* (1977); and see *Star* March 30, 1926—"So strong is the demand for the Gotfredson bus that in some parts of Ontario entire passenger lines are being operated by firms using the company's product.."

8 *Border Cities Star* "Steel Is Progress" February 21, 1925.

9 Power, "William Costello Kennedy".

10 *Border Cities Star* "A New Industry" January 20, 1920; and May 26, 1928.

11 On Chrysler of Canada's origins, see Durnford and Baechler, *Cars of Canada* 268-9; and *Border Cities Star* December 31, 1925, December 10, 1926 and November 24, 1927; on the 1928 plant to be built on Tecumseh Road, see "High Spot Chrysler" *Star* December 31, 1928.

12 Desmond Morton, *Working People* (Montreal & Kingston: McGill-Queen's University Press, 2007) Fifth ed., 125; on the early failed auto unions, see James A. Pendergast, "The Attempt at Unionization in the Automobile Industry in Canada, 1928" *Ontario History* 70 (December, 1978) 245- 62; on the firing of Archie Hooper, see *Border Cities Star* January 5, 1921—to add further insult, Hooper was shortly thereafter charged with running a betting house out of his cigar stand; see *Star* January 21, 1921.

13 Author interview with Bill Willson, December 5, 2013; on the growth of the Anglican Church, see *Star* January 5, 1925; on Anglican controversies, see "Rector Flays" February 5, 1924; on the legal profession, see Patrick Brode, *Lawyers of the Southwest: A History of the Essex Law Association, 1884–2009* (Windsor: E.L.A., 2009) 10-1.

14 Dominion of Canada Census, 1921 (pages 458-9) and 1931 (pages 402-3) (Ottawa: King's Printer); on the encouragement of British immigration, see Valerie Knowles, *Strangers at our Gates: Canadian Immigration and Immigration Policy, 1540–2006* (Toronto: Dundurn Press, 2007) 137-8.

15 *Border Cities Star* "Union Church is Dedicated" June 11, 1925—it was later to be called Emmanuel United Church.

16 Cecillon, *Prayers Petitions and Protests* 240; on Eugene Mailloux and the "M. & P. Stores," see *Star* December 28, 1935.

17 Author interview with James Watson, and see *Star* "Barbers Draw Color Line" November 22, 1919—As the head of the barber's union noted, "We have union shops for the colored trade and we have union shops for the white trade;" on train waiters protest, see "Colored Waiters Discuss New Move" August 21, 1926.

18 See the *Archives and Records of the Charles H. Wright Museum of African American History*, Cornelius L. Henderson Collection; on the Askin incident, see *Star* "Council Impotent" June 15, 1925—"Recently residents of Askin Avenue met to protest against the sale of a residence to a colored man who claims to be a lawyer in Detroit."

19 On the Scislowski family, see "Memories of a Long Ago War" essay by Stanley Scislowski; on William Englander, see *Star* "City's Court Interpreter" January 10, 1925; on organized labour's opposition to immigration, see David Goutor, *Guarding the Gates: The Canadian Labour Movement and Immigration, 1872–1934* (Vancouver: UBC Press, 2007) 202-3.

20 *Border Cities Star* "Church for Hungarians" November 26, 1928.

21 *Border Cities Star* "New Canadians" May 24, 1924.

22 *Border Cities Star* "Border Cities Gets Missionary" May 23, 1925: "Protestantism is not making the slightest move to forge ahead, and yet we have a group of people here as large as the City of St. Thomas…"

23 *Border Cities Star* "Use Theatre for Services" January 14, 1924; on the Albert Residence for men, see *Star* December 4, 1923.

24 *Border Cities Star* "Dante Aligheri Society Formed" December 18, 1920.

25 The origins of the Border Cities Italian Club, later the Caboto Club, are detailed in its 1985, 60th anniversary commemorative history; on the early Italians in Windsor, see Windsor *Weekly Record* "The Dago Banana Peddlers" December 16, 1892—"They often accost ladies with 'Here, you buy de banah, five, ten cents a doze'."

26 Starting from a much larger base in population and buildings, Toronto construction values from April 1923 to April 1924 rose from $2.23 million to $2.46 million; Hamilton's from $611,000 to 840,000; Windsor alone in the same period rose from $395,000 to 557,000; the addition of the border cities would have augmented this by at least 50%; *Border Cities Star* "How Windsor Compares" May 24, 1924; in absolute terms, new construction in the Border Cities stood fifth in Canada for the first half of 1926, see *Star* August 28, 1926.

For example, Riverside alone, still a very rural area, had $307,250 in building permits issued in the first 10 months of 1923; *Star* November 2, 1923.

27 *Border Cities Star* September 1, 1923.

28 *Border Cities Star* March 30, 1926; on the development of Ottawa Street, see *Star* "Modern Buildings" April 18, 1925; by 1928, so little land remained to be developed, that the only subdivision in the city was Eastlawn Gardens, see *Star* December 29, 1928.

29 Author interview with Bill Willson December 5, 2013; male nude bathing in the Detroit River was a local tradition and persisted despite the attempts of City Council to impose higher standards of modesty. See *Evening Record,* July 21, 1905—"Persistent complaints have been made to the Windsor police regarding people bathing at the Canadian Pacific railway dock without wearing bathing suits."

30 Evelyn G. McLean, "St. Clare of Assisi Church" *Acorn: The Journal of the Architectural Conservancy of Ontario* vol. XXV (Spring, 2000) 15; on Lothian and St. Clare's construction, see *Star* April 4 & December 31, 1931.

On David Cameron, see obituary "Prominent Architect" July 14, 1959; on James Pennington, see Windsor *Star* February 7, 1987—Pennington had an extended career from 1909 almost to his death in 1963. One of his last works designed in the later 1950s was a modernist structure, the University of Windsor library.

On George Y. Masson selected to design the cenotaph, see "Shaft Design Is Chosen" *Star* May 31, 1924; The work of Masson and Sheppard on the John Campbell School in 1926 has been described in *Canada's Historic Places* as "perhaps the finest and best-preserved example of Neo-Gothic Collegiate architecture in the City of Windsor." In their early years, David Nichols, an architect who favoured the *beaux arts* style made up the firm with Hugh Sheppard. George Masson joined them in 1926 to make it Nichols, Sheppard and Masson. Nichols may well have influenced the design of the federal building on Ouellette Avenue in 1933. In later years, Sheppard and Masson also had a fling with modernism in their design of the 1957 City Hall.

On the Prince Edward Hotel, see *Star* "Flag Marks" September 13, 1921; and on General Byng school in Sandwich, November 16 & 17, 1923.

31 Report of the Minister of Education, Province of Ontario, 1919, see Appendix B, letter from F.W. Merchant the Director of Technical education to the Minister of education, February 18, 1920: that Walkerville was a leading example of the need for technical education that "was heartily supported by the management of the industries in Walkerville and Ford" 9-10; and the opening of the Windsor-Walkerville Technical School, *Border Cities Star* August 29-30, 1923; on Walkerville Collegiate Institute, see *Star* January 29, 1924.

On W.D. Lowe, see obituary in *Star* June 27, 1945 and comments to the Chamber of Commerce, January 14, 1920.

On Walkerville's reluctance to join the project, see "Both Sides of Dispute" Star December 9, 1919; and Tolmie's speech to the mass audience, "Compromise Possible" December 11, 1919.

32 See report of Jim Baxter, secretary of the E.B.U.C. "Utilities Commission a Child of Necessity" *Border Cities Star* December 6, 1919; and Roberts, *The Shadow of Detroit* 212.

33 *Border Cities Star* "Joint Sewers" December 28, 1920; and March 16 and September 18, 1925; on the plebiscite for the filtration plant, see *Star* editorial "Future of the Border Cities" December 1, 1922; and "Wilson's Majority" December 5, 1922—"The biggest surprise of the election was the endorsation of the joint filtration project..."

34 F. Adams, "The Epidemic of Virulent Smallpox in Windsor and Vicinity" *The Canadian Medical Association Journal* (1924) 692- 6; and see *Border Cities Star*—as the community had no isolation unit, the Grand Central Hotel in Windsor was taken over for smallpox cases which could not be isolated in a home—February 25, 1924.

35 Larry Kulisek and Trevor Price, "Ontario Municipal Policy Affecting Local Autonomy: A Case Study Involving Windsor and Toronto" *Urban History Review* 16:3 (1988: Feb) 255 at 258; on comments against Morris Knowles, see University of Windsor Archives, J. Clark Keith Papers (hereinafter "Keith Papers"), Box 1,

newspaper clippings. A comment from the Walkerville *Citizen* July 13, 1917 that Knowles was paid $9,400 to superintend work that the EBUC had not even approved; The Walkerville *Herald* of January 12, 1917 noted a council meeting where Mayor Montreuil stated, "in my opinion the Commission up to date has not fulfilled with any measure of credit the purpose for which it was organized." Councillor Riberdy robustly added, "It is a situation that makes me feel like taking off my coat and fighting."

36 Keith Papers, No. 95-007, R.B. Braid Secretary of EBUC to H.E. Beckett, March 12, 1934.

37 Keith Papers, Box 3, File 18, Knowles to Gordon McGregor, November 5, 1920.

38 *Border Cities Star* September 5, 1925; M.E. Brian was often called a "be-jobbed" man for the number of positions he held in the City's administration. In addition to being the Chief Engineer, Brian was also the Weed Inspector, Pound Keeper, Smoke Inspector, Supervisor of Public Works and the Asphalt Plant, overseer of city streets, and, lastly, superintendant of the golf course. See *Star* "Sees No Need Of Extra Aid" June 25, 1926.

39 Frank Mitchell, in his inaugural address of 1925, promised that his policy would be "one of retrenchment" *Star* January 12, 1925; on closing the Howard Avenue shelter, *Star* January 3, 1925; on the City Hall, see inaugural address of 1926 where Mitchell conceded that the City Hall (the Central School of 1871) was a dilapidated antique, but as there was no money, it would remain "for still another year or so." A new City Hall would not be dedicated until almost thirty years later.

On Cecil Jackson's ideas, see *Star* editorial "The Mayor's Program" Jan. 11, 1927.

On the burning of the Church of the Ascension, see *Star* December 22, 1926—I am grateful to Doug Diet for his suggestions on this point; Fire Chief Clarence DeFields served a remarkable 47 years on the Windsor Fire Department, 30 of them as Chief. Despite a 1907 incident in which he was trapped in a burning basement, barely survived, and was left blind in one eye, DeFields would serve until 1946. He is described in Wilfred List's article "Fire Chief Clarence DeFields" Windsor Public Library, Local scrapbook 16a, p. 4.

40 Windsor Municipal Archives, R.G.2 A City Council Minutes, Book 14: October 18, 1926—Hugh Graybiel addressed City Council on the amalgamation plebiscite. He was supported by a prominent figure, and President of the Chamber of Commerce, Colonel Walter McGregor; on the outcome of the plebiscite, see *Star* December 7, 1926—Windsor voted for 7,232 to 954 against; and see editorial "Yesterday's Vote on Amalgamation" by Walter McGregor in which he notes that 82 percent of Walkerville's voters were opposed as were 66 percent of Sandwich's.

On the 1922 proposal to join Walkerville and Ford City, see *Star* December 7, 1922.

41 Ontario Archives, R.G. 8-35, Walkerville Border Municipalities, B 224 033, J.H. Coburn to J.A. Ellis, October 18, 1928; on the Ellis Report, see Windsor Community Museum, P.M. 47, J.A. Ellis, Director, Bureau of Municipal Affairs September 25, 1928—the five municipalities in Ellis's report were Windsor, Ford City, Sandwich, Walkerville and Riverside. After a thorough review of the five municipalities, he concluded that "The only complete solution in the interests of all the municipalities is for them to enter into a partnership on fair and reasonable terms whereby they will become one municipality" p. 12. With regard to financial problems, he noted that, despite its pretensions, Walkerville was running the highest debenture debt per capita for schools.

42 On the annexation to Walkerville of 540 acres of land from lots 92 and 93 of Sandwich East Township, see *Ontario Gazette*, 53 (November 6, 1920) 2209, and Hoskins, pp. 146-7; on Walkerville as a racially exclusive area, see author interview with Bill Willson December 5, 2013.

43 *Border Cities Star* May 1925; on the construction of the Remington Arms plant, see Amherstburg *Echo* February 14, 1913—"one of the biggest cartridge companies in the world, has let contracts for the construction of a big plant on a 100 acre site in the extreme north of Windsor."

44 Cecillon, *Prayers Petitions and Protest* 178; on growing Sandwich, see *Border Cities Star* "Sandwich to Grow Larger" February 21, 1924; and March 30, 1926—"Practically all of the salt used for manufacture by the [Canadian Salt] company is obtained from wells located below the Windsor plant."

45 *Border Cities Star* "Border's Newest Municipality" November 7, 1925; on the development of "Roseland Park" see *Star* July 7, 1928—"it is in very center of South Windsor's amazing activities." And the advertisement from September 7,1926—"Roseland park will be a community in itself. Its people will be set apart;" on the importance of the golf course, see *Star,* "Work on New Golf Course" January 8, 1927.

46 Author interview with Evelyn McLean, October 20, 2010; on the advertisement for Riverside, see *Border Cities Star* June 23, 1923; The town was incorporated by "An Act to Incorporate the Town of River Side" (1921) Statutes of Ontario, Chapter 121; on dissatisfaction with Sandwich East, see *Star* "Seceders Ask" November 19, 1920.

The *Border Cities Star* ran a series of articles on the French Canadian families of Riverside: the St. Louis family on December 3, 1932; the Janisses December 31, 1932; the Reaumes September 16, 1933; and on Paul Le Duc on April 20, 1933

On LaSalle's incorporation, see "An Act to Incorporate the Town of LaSalle" (1924) Statutes of Ontario, Chapter10; and *Star* "Steady Progress" September 5, 1925; but see Peter H.Blum, *Brewed in Detroit* (Detroit: W.S.U.P., 1999) and his comments on Hofer Brewing Company—"the sole reason for this venture was to export beer to the States" 284; on Vital Benoit, see Francis X. Chauvin, *Men of Achievement* vol. 1, (1927 edition) 42-4.

On Tecumseh, see *Star* "Beautiful Homes" September 5, 1925.

47 *Border Cities Star* "Walkerville Theatre" September 18, 1920; on Loew's Theatre, see *Border Cities Star* December 31, 1920; on Simon Meretsky, "Local Film Houses" Windsor *Daily Star* May 15, 1954.

48 *Border Cities Star* September 3, 1925; on Percy LeSueur see official biography in the Hockey Hall of Fame; Cougars v Americans game, *Star* November 27, 1925.

49 Craig Heron, *Lunch-Bucket Lives: Remaking the Workers' City* (Toronto: Between the Lines, 2015) 35; on the opening of the Masonic Temple, see *Star* February 2, 1922.

50 *Border Cities Star* "Beach Revels Are Revealed" August 31, 1924; on the Charleston see, *Star* September 1, 1925; on Mitchell's condemnation of pool rooms and dance halls, see "Neighborly Spirit Urges" January 24, 1924.

51 *Border Cities Star* "New Smith Store" November 11, 1926; on the 1920 expansion, see *Star* September 22, 1920—"Ouellette Avenue will have an entirely new appearance due to the erection of this temple of service." Bartlet's department store also operated on the block south of the Ferry on Ouellette Avenue and offered finer goods than those available in most retail stores.

52 *Border Cities Star* "Walkerville Boat Club Ladies Take Interest In Sports" June 13, 1925; the Club itself had an unusual history. It originated in a debt held by Hiram Walker in a Detroit boat club. When the Detroit club went bankrupt, he realized on their clubhouse and thought that it might be a place of amusement in his town. He had the structure towed across the river and installed near the foot of Devonshire road where it became the "Tecumseh Boat Club." When this was burned down in 1902, it was rebuilt farther upstream on Walker property and christened the "Walkerville Boat Club." The young men who engaged in racing had to use larger vessels or "barges." At one point, "The Tecumseh Club stood forth as the holder of the barge championship of the Detroit River, a title which it held practically all the time barge racing remained in vogue." See *Star* "Walkerville Boat Club..." January 7, 1933.

On Camilla Stodgell Wigle, see Windsor Community Museum, PM 1737 "Camilla Stodgell Wigle, 'The First Lady of East Windsor';" on the Arts and Letters Club, see Windsor Municipal Archives, Ms. 1; on the symphony, see *Star* "Orchestra to Start Season" October 2, 1925.

53 Accusations of J.W. Roiser in *Star* "Denounces conditions" June 13, 1921—"there are no less than five sewers that empty into the river in this vicinity. The bathers are swimming in undiluted sewage."; City council's response that there was nothing to be done, *Star* July 18, 1921.

54 On the excitement of the 1926 racing season see—*Star* July 3, 1926—that the Jockey Club was thronged with "smartly dressed women." And July 28, "Border Cities society will turn out in numbers tomorrow afternoon for the opening of the racing season."

55 *Border Cities Star* "Gundy Names Evils In Act" January 11, 1926; on the case of Mary Ostopovitch, see "Widowed Mother" October 7, 1925; on the dance marathon, see "Dancers Fighting Exhaustion" July 20, 1928; and "Dancing for Money" July 23, 1928.

56 *Border Cities Star* "Facilities Enjoyed" March 30, 1926.

57 Douglas Brinkley, *Wheels for the World: Henry Ford, His Company, and the Century of Progress 1902–2003* (N.Y. Viking, 2003) 282-3; on Detroit's growth, see David Allan Levine, *Internal Combustion: The Races in Detroit 1915–1926* (Westport: Greenwood Press) 12; on Ford's profits, see Allan Nevins, *Ford: The Times, The Man, The Company* (N.Y., Scribners, 1954) 237-8 and 471-76.

58 *Canadian Machinery and Manufacturing News* (Toronto) as quoted in Roberts *D.C.B.* vol. 15 "Gordon McGregor" at 649; on the Dominion Tariff commission hearings of 1920, see Toronto *Globe* December 1, 1920.

59 *Border Cities Star* "Detroit Gives Aid to Border" January 8, 1927.

60 *Border Cities Star*, October 21, 1925; Morand was a fierce critic of Liberal free trade policies, see *Star* October 3, 1925—"Tinkering with the tariff by Mr. King's government has resulted in many of our factories closing their doors..."

61 Tom Traves, *The State and Enterprise: Canadian Manufacturers and the Federal Government, 1917–1931* (Toronto: University of Toronto Press, 1979) 114.

Endnotes to Chapter Six

1 Philip P. Mason's *The Ambassador Bridge: A Monument to Progress* (Detroit: Wayne State University Press, 1987) is the definitive history of the building of the Ambassador Bridge. What follows is largely taken from Dr. Mason's account.

2 On Fleming's 1919 Windsor conference to develop the waterways, see *Star* November 19, 1919. As news of Fleming's enthusiasms spread, the New York *Tribune* of September 21, 1922 covered Fleming's pronouncement that he was assembling the financiers to enable the deepening of the St. Lawrence.

On the Livingstone Channel, see David H. Bennion and Bruce A. Manny, *Construction of Shipping Channels in the Detroit River: History and Environmental Consequences* (U.S. Geological Survey, 2011)—they record that between 1874 and 1968, 96.5 kilometres of shipping channel were dredged and that this work "greatly altered channel morphology and flow dynamics of the river, disrupting ecological function and fishery productivity…" p. 1.

3 On Fred Martin and the tunnel, see Windsor *Daily Star* Neil Morrison, "Tunnel Was Fulfillment of Fred W. Martin's Dream" November 2, 1946; Engholm presenting the plans to Windsor's City Council, *Star* September 19, 1925.

4 On diver Florent and the retrieval of the first tube section, see *Star* December 21, 1928; and see *Star* "Blazing a Trail Beneath the River" December 31, 1928—"At present, very little work has been done on the land at the end of the tunnel here in Windsor. By agreement with the Sisters of the Holy Names, who own St. Mary's Academy, that venerable pile may not be wrecked until after school at the academy is over for the summer..."

5 See "Fifty Homes" *Star* May 26, 1928—"It was in 1919 that the Kinsey-Doyle Company purchased 1,000 acres of what was then farm land, and considered 'far out.' Two years later they began a quiet, steady program of development, which has continued to the present. This firm was the first to interest itself in the South Windsor district. Today in South Windsor there are 15 miles of sewer, 35 miles of watermains and 15 miles of paved streets which have been laid down in the township of Sandwich West in which South Windsor is located."

6 George A. Nader, *Cities of Canada: Vol. I Theoretical, Historical and Planning Perspectives* (Toronto: Macmillan, 1975)—"In terms of land use system the most important characteristic of the car is its door-to-door convenience; since the entire trip may be made without resorting to any additional form of transportation..." 60.

7 *Star* January 3, 1928; on the first planning report, see Thomas Adams, *Final Report Upon the City Plan* 1930—completed July, 1929.

8 On the September 1928 air race and the inception of Walker Airport, see *Star* September 7-8, 1928; the first flight over Windsor on June 28, 1911was flown by St. Croix Johnstone, "the daring Yankee aviator" *Star* June 29, 1911; he would be killed in a crash two months later.

9 University of Windsor Archives, J. Clark Keith Papers, Box 2, File 7, "A History of Metropolitan Hospital" and Box 3, File 17—letter from Dr. F. Adams to EBUC June 10, 1921, that the Border Cities were operating at 50% of the requirement for six beds per thousand inhabitants; on inadequacy of services, see *Star* February 8, 1924 and September 8, 1924 and by-law to support the hospital September 15, 1925.

10 Stephen T. Moore, "Defining the 'Undefended': Canadians, Americans, and the Multiple Meanings of Border During Prohibition" *The American Review of Canadian Studies* (Spring 2004) 12; on Canada as the "enemy" see Greg Marquis, "Brewers and Distillers' Paradise: American Views of Canadian Alcohol Policies, 1919 to 1935" *Canadian Review of American Studies* 34, no. 2, 2004, 137.

11 See Harry Low's obituary, Windsor *Daily Star* August 23, 1955; *Royal Commission On Customs and Excise* Interim Reports (1928)—"The evidence adduced creates a strong impression that some of the liquor declared at Customs as being for export was resold in Canada to be consumed therein. There is also strong evidence that Harry Low attempted to bribe Customs officers and railway employees to facilitate

the export of liquors into the United States." 61; on his 1931 arrest, see Halifax *Herald* July 27, 1931—"Harry Low told C.B. Smith he was a business man in a fairly big way at Walkerville Ont."

On corruption at the export docks, see *Star* May 4, 1927.

12 Jim Cooper's career and death are covered in the *Border Cities Star* February 10, 1931; on his mansion, see *Star* May 24, 1924; on society, June 23, 1926; and on accounts of the evidence given at the Royal Commission on Customs and Excise, and the *Star*'s account of Cooper's testimony that—"I am glad this commission came here… I wanted you to know about the 'rat fund' that was collected here…"

13 Stephen Schneider, *Iced: The Story of Organized Crime in Canada* (Toronto: Wiley, 2009) 187-9; and see *Star* "Walker Not Sold Yet" January 4, 1927.

14 On July 5, it was reported that two rum-runners were being treated for gunshot wounds incurred in a chase with American coast guard craft who opened up on them with machine guns *Star* July 5, 1929; Walter Petty, the acting customs collector at Detroit, described the action during the summer of 1929: "Our officers have had battles with rum running boats during the present offensive. They have taken place, we say, in American waters…" *Star* July 17, 1929- Most Canadian officials thought that the Americans had little regard for the international border.

15 *Maclean's Magazine* Frederick Edwards, "Men Will Kill For Whiskey" 1 and 15 December 1928; and see Patrick Brode, *Unholy City: Vice in Windsor Ontario, 1950* (Windsor: E.C.H.S. 2012) 74-5; on the Riverside Brewery and the "River Gang" see *Star* February 4 1930 and March 4, 1930.

On the 1926 crackdown, see *Star* "Mop-Up Drive" August 23, 1926; and August 24—as a result of the RCMP action: "The river front is a seething mass of excitement and indignation."

16 Author interview with Evelyn McLean, October 20, 2010; Bertha Thomas would present an innovative series of defences to avoid charges of selling liquor. At first, she denied owing the roadhouse, *Star* October 5, 1929; on another occasion, when the police squeezed out alcohol from the carpets where it had been dumped by her staff and found that it exceeded the allowable 2.5%, she suggested that the fresh shellac on the floor had added to the alcohol content, *Star* February 4, 1930.

17 *Border Cities Star* obituary for W.F. Herman, January 17, 1938; and see Windsor Municipal Archives, W.F. Herman Collection, Ms. 6, see comment in the Lethbridge Herald upon Herman's death in January 1928—"a genius in the newspaper business" and the Ottawa *Journal*—that Herman "thought a big paper necessarily was a good paper, but it had to be printed with an uncommon degree of perfection."

18 Windsor Municipal Archives, R.G. 8 C II 7, Annual Report of the Chief Constable 1926—"Our (identification) Bureau has won respect and admiration all over the United States and Canada, not only amongst the Police officials but among the

criminal element as well who pass the word along from one to the other to be very careful when in Windsor." 51.

19 *Border Cities Star* "Wants Drive To Clean City" June 23, 1925; on Thompson see David Rossell, *Windsor Justice Facility* (1999) 10-11, and Francis X. Chauvin, *Men of Achievement* vol. 1 (1927 ed.) 34-5; *Star* editorial praising Thompson "A Great Success" June 10, 1927.

20 Greg Marquis, *Policing Canada's Century: A History of the Canadian Association of Chiefs of Police* (Toronto: University of Toronto Press, 1993) 149; on the *Star*'s praise for Thompson, see editorial "A Great Success" June 10, 1927.

21 On widespread drinking in other Ontario cities, see Oliver, *G. Howard Ferguson*, 168.

22 Windsor Municipal Archives, R.G. 8 C II 7 Annual Reports of the Chief Constable 1925–1930; on other editorials supporting the *Star*, see "Border Cities Stirred" Montreal *Gazette* as reprinted in the *Star* September 17, 1927—The *Gazette* attributed most of Windsor's problems to its proximity to Detroit; and see *Globe* editorial "Worse Than Ever" September 10, 1927.

23 Mason, *The Ambassador Bridge* 125.

24 *Border Cities Star* November 12, 1929.

25 *Popular Mechanics* December, 1930; on the start of the hydraulic drill from the Windsor side, see *Star* "Tube Shield" October 31, 1929; on how the land side of the tunnel was dug, see *Star* "Sand Hogs Fast Workers," November 1, 1930.

26 Essex County Registry Office, Lot 7 and part lot 8 in Registered Plan 333, sold December 26 1926 for $59,700 and then on February 15 1929 to W.F. Herman for $209,000; Lot 1and Part of lot 2 in Block P in Registered Plan 85 sold in March 15 1929 for $305,000—the same property was sold in 1954 for $230,000: I am grateful to Lucinda Morris for title searches of the above.

On the expansion of Canadian Bridge see *Star* November 7, 1929; Realty Development Corporation of Detroit was selling thousands of lots to American speculators. A typical letter (written just before the stock market collapse) states, "We believe you have made a wise investment. The "Detroit of Canada" district today offers many attractive possibilities to the shrewd investor." Author collection—R.D.C. to G. Krewer and P. Pyszka August 1, 1929.

Endnotes to Chapter Seven

1 Farley Mowat, *Born Naked* (Toronto: Key Porter, 1993) 64.

2 *Border Cities Star* May 17, 1930—Mayor Cecil Jackson further stated that henceforth all groceries for the indigent were to be cut off, and that unemployed men

"are being advised in emphatic terms to make every effort, if they have not already done so, to get jobs and restore themselves and their families to a self-supporting basis."; on the impact of the Depression on Canada's auto industry, see John Herd Thompson and Allen Seager, *Canada1922–1939: Decades of Discord* (Toronto: McClelland and Stewart, 1985) 196.

On the population decline, see Windsor Municipal Archives, Annual Report of the Assessment Commissioner, 1929–1935, R.G. 3 EI 1 / 4; and Appendix D.

3 *Ontario Sessional Papers*, vol. LXIII Part III (1931) pp. 42-3; and vol. LXIV part III (1932) p. 41.

4 University of Windsor Archives, Windsor and District Chamber of Commerce papers, Box 7, file 25, memorandum of February 23, 1931—the Prime Minister "instructed Dr. Skelton (of External affairs) to forward an official note to Washington." There is no record of any positive response.

5 *Border Cities Star* editorial "Mr. Hoover Signs" June 18, 1930.

American scholars seem oblivious to the impacts of Smoot-Hawley: in John J. Bukowczyk, Nora Fairies, David R. Smith and Randy William Widdis, *Permeable Border: The Great Lakes Basin as Transnational Region, 1650–1990* (Pittsburgh: University of Pittsburgh Press, 2005) it is held that "The global crisis of the 1930s exacerbated nationalist tendencies in both Canada and the United States as both nations responded by enacting new protective tariff legislation." (p. 146) This fails to appreciate that there was no "nationalistic tendency" in play in Canada and that prior to 1930, the King government had hoped to lower tariffs. Smoot-Hawley in 1930 was an exclusively American assault on free-trade which inevitably invited retaliation.

6 See Judith A.McDonald, Anthony Patrick O'Brien and Colleen Callahan, "Trade Wars: Canada's Reaction to the Smoot-Hawley Tariff" *The Journal of Economic History* 57 No. 4 (Dec. 1997); and Richard N. Kottman, "Herbert Hoover and the Smoot-Hawley Tariff: Canada, A Case Study" *The Journal of American History* 62 No. 3 (Dec. 1975).

In Ojibway, tinplate manufacturing was a success between 1930 and 1932. The "black plate," which was the material used in the process, had been imported from U.S. plants duty-free. However, as a result of Canadian tariffs, the price of this material became prohibitive. As well, with the elimination of the tariff on British tin plate, Ojibway's prices were no longer competitive, see Windsor *Daily Star* July 28, 1937.

7 Tom Traves, *The State and Enterprise: Canadian Manufacturers and the Federal Government, 1917-1931* (Toronto: University of Toronto Press, 1979) 119; and see Detroit *Free Press* "Border Cities Men Jubilant" February 20, 1931; on Chrysler's reaction, see *Star* February 28, 1931—"Commenting the next day after the tariff change, Mr. Mansfield said the new scale meant Chrysler would have to manufacture in Canada as all its products are sold here." On Studebaker, see March 2, 1931.

8 Windsor *Daily Star* "See Car Made At Chrysler Plant" April 2, 1932.

9 Windsor *Daily Star* "27 Added to Payroll" April 19, 1932.

10 On Ford of Canada selling to the Empire, see Wallace Campbell, Henry and Edsel Ford introducing the V8 in January 1935—"In South Africa Ford sales made an all-time high record this year; in Australia and New Zealand sales were nearly double the 1933 figures;" *Border Cities Star* December 28, 1934.

11 Windsor Municipal Archives, R.G. 2 DVI 2 / 1, p. 3, Coughlin Report—Royal Commission of Inquiry re: Border Cities Amalgamation; as Joan Poole observes in her thorough account of the early Depression years in the Border Cities, *The evolution of social services in the Border Cities*... "One of the most devastating effects of the depression in the Border Cities was the precarious state of municipal finances whose main income was property taxes." 48.

12 University of Windsor Archives, Windsor and District Chamber of Commerce papers, Series II Subseries A, Border Citizens' Service Committee, October 7, 1931.

On the construction of the subway under the Pere Marquette tracks, see Canada Transportation Agency Archives, Order No. 48397 issued April 7, 1932: as the subway had little direct benefit to Walkerville, the town had objected to paying for it. But without the subway, East Windsor was unable to complete the Wyandotte Street connection east to the remainder of the Border Cities, see Windsor Municipal Archives, Walkerville town council minutes, June 23, 1930, resolution that "this municipality should not be charged with the extra cost in the construction of the subway."

13 Leon Paroian memoirs, 1997 p. 4; on Herb Brightmore I am grateful for the comments of his daughter Linda Brightmore.

14 *Border Cities Star* "Doctor Tells" December 17, 1930.

15 Lara Campbell, *Respectable Citizens: Gender, Family, and Unemployment in Ontario's Great Depression* (Toronto: University of Toronto Press, 2009) 32-3; on the sliding scale of relief food, see Windsor Municipal archives, Welfare and Transportation Committee, R.G. 2 AI 1932, file 42- scale of relief as of January 17, 1932.

16 Author's collection, Memoirs of Stan Scislowski p. 2.

17 Windsor Municipal Archives, R.G. 5 GI file 1.2 / 6, Minutes of the Walkerville Welfare Board, June 15, 1933; on Walkerville as giving more relief than other places, see D.B. Harkness of the Unemployed Relief Fund of Toronto before the welfare board on January 19, 1933—"the amount of relief given by Walkerville is higher than in any other municipality in Ontario" and Border Cities Star, September 13, 1931—"Walkerville has been more generous in its grocery orders than the other municipalities. Windsor is in second place."

18 *Border Cities Star* October 4, 1933; and Amherstburg *Echo* "Border Cities Relief Board Objects to Immigration of County Families To The City" December 15, 1933.

19 H. Blair Neatby, *The Politics of Chaos: Canada in the Thirties* (Toronto: Macmillan, 1972) 26; the reference to the bean-bag pants from L.M. Grayson and Michael Bliss, *The Wretched of Canada* (Toronto: University of Toronto Press, 1971 128-9, and see—"the single most pressing problem of the poor people who wrote to R.B. Bennett seems to have been clothes... Few relief organizations considered that the destitute needed such luxuries as newspapers, tobacco, haircuts, lipstick, or the odd night out at the movies." p. xiv.

On *L'Union des Cultivateurs d'Essex et Kent* see *Border Cities Star* February 26, 1935.

On Walkerville inspecting the poor for clothes, see Windsor Municipal Archives, RG 5 G1 file 2/6, Minutes of the Welfare Board January 13, 1933.

Police statistics, see Windsor Municipal Archives, R.G. 8- CII, annual reports, 1930–1933: crime went down from 5,339 arrests to 2,073—the average number of suicides per year went from four to nine. No police reports were published for 1934 or 1935.

20 University of Windsor Archives, Chamber of Commerce Papers, Box 3, File 21—Special Meeting to Deal with the Relief Situation, May 10, 1932; much of the role of the Border Citizens' Service Committee is described in detail in Joan Poole, *The Evolution of social services in the Border Cities during the Great Depression (Ontario)* Masters Thesis, University of Windsor, 1990, Chapter 3.

21 *Border Cities Star* "Authority Is Disputed" August 10, 1933.

22 Ontario Archives, R.G. 47-27-1-27, Interview with David Croll, June 1, 1973; on Croll as a "joiner" and his early career, see R. Warren James, *The People's Senator: The Life and Times of David A. Croll* (Toronto: Douglas & McIntryre, 1990) p. 16; on the "Three Davids" see *Star*, June 21, 1929; 1930 municipal campaign, *Star* "Local Labor" November 6; "Results" December 2, 1930; "Two Women Given Posts" January 9, 1931.

Unfortunately, Croll destroyed many of the files covering his period in government during the 1930s, see *Windsor Star* December 23, 1977 "Missing Quint files" p. A-4.

23 Windsor Municipal Archives, R.G. 2 AIV file 1/16 Windsor City Council Minutes, May 4, 1931.

24 *Report on Provincial Policy in Administrative Methods in the Matter of Direct Relief in Ontario, 1932*: W.R. Campbell, chairman.

25 The rally at the Allied War Veterans Hall is described in detail in the *Star* of June 11, 1932—the editorial after the municipal election of 1932 noted that "He [Curry] has done everything possible to hinder and hamper the Mayor. The people said yesterday what they think of that sort of thing."

26 Croll and Gignac's tour of the north was publicized in the *Border Cities Star* May 23, 1933; comments on it in the editorial "Now It can Be Told" Toronto *Globe* July 10, 1933 and Francis X. Chauvin "David Arnold Croll" *Saturday Night* November 10, 1934.

27 Memorandum to A.G. Price from H.L. Cummings, October 31, 1931, as quoted in Kulisek and Price "Ontario Municipal Policy" 260-1.

28 *Ontario Municipal Board Act, 1932* S.O. 1932, c. 27, Part VI; while commonly referred to as a "Board of Control" the actual term used in Part VI was a "committee of supervisors."

On the passage of this statute, see *Star* March 23, 1932; the defaulting municipalities were Riverside, Sandwich, Tecumseh, East Windsor, Sandwich East and Sandwich West. LaSalle petitioned for a Board but was given more time to get its financial house in order—*Star* May 4, 1932.

29 On the debate to submit to a Board of Control, see *Star* November 22, 1932.

30 Speech by Croll to the Ukrainian-Canadian Citizens' Club, in *Star* November 23, 1932; Croll had been a persistent critic of submitting defaulting municipalities to Boards of Control. He had condemned them as "Dictatorship Gone Mad" (May 4, 1932) for disenfranchising residents; a criticism that was ironic in view of his later actions.; on George Bennett's comments, see *Star* December 31, 1932.

31 James A. Pendergast, "The Attempt at Unionization in the Automobile Industry in Canada, 1928": *Ontario History* LXX (December, 1978) No. 4, 254-8; and see *Star* "Session Called To Organize Auto Workers Here" May 19, 1928.

32 John Manley, "Communists and Auto Workers: The Struggle for Industrial unionism in the Canadian Automobile Industry, 1925–36" *Labour/Le travail* 17 (Spring 1986) 122: The paper is largely a paean to the Communist party of Canada and many of its assertions are questionable: e.g., It is alleged (at p. 111) that in 1927–9 Ford vastly increased output and then fired 2,000 workers and sped up the production line. No citation is given for this remarkable and otherwise undocumented assertion.

33 *Border Cities Star*, "Fascists and Reds Collide" August 10, 1932; R.C.M.P. *Weekly Summary* of "Report On Revolutionary Organizations And Agitators in Canada" see No. 734, November 28, 1934; Raycraft was one of the spokesmen for the Hunger Marchers who confronted Premier Henry in Toronto, see *Star* February 16, 1932.

The Communists on the East Windsor council remained in the minority. In January 1933, Raycraft, Morris, Parashak and Davenport voted for a motion to support an unemployment insurance delegation. They were opposed by five other members, Laurendeau, Lajoie. Gordner, Poission and Mayor Theo Fontaine: see Windsor Municipal Archives, R.G. 5 AI file 1/10, "Minutes of East Windsor City Council" January 12, 1933.

34 Communists fired from the Trades and Labor council, see H.A. Logan, *Trades Unions in Canada* (Toronto: Macmillan, 1948) 338.

On Alderman Laurendeau's motion to stop seditious literature from being circulated in the schools, see *Star* "Propaganda Sent to Local Schools" April 19, 1933—"A dramatic moment in the censorship debate came just before the vote when Alderman Laurendeau cried out that those opposing it would be classed as Reds. The council chamber shook with cheers and boos as he sat down."

35 On the Blue Shirts, see *Star* "Ottawa Eyes Blue Shirts" September 14 1933; R.C.M.P. *Weekly Summary* September 22, 1933- "A curious feature is that there is no membership fee, and that the 'marching dress' is supplied free. There is some mystery as to the source of funds..."; Mayor Croll was aware of the group but advised a Jewish news service that there was no indication that they were anti-semitic *Jewish Telegraphic Agency*, "Canada Blue Shirts not Anti-semitic" October 1, 1933.

36 Desmond Morton, *Working People* (4th ed.) (Montreal: McGill-Queen's University Press, 148-9; on Rev. McRae, *Star* November 8, 1933; on the railwaymen's rejection of Communists, see *Star* August 3, 1933.

37 Author interview with Bruce J.S. Macdonald for the Osgoode Society, September 1984. "That would be about 1932 or 33... I (as city Solicitor) got some law students to help me... we handled, oh, I would say several thousand cases and... and if anything, I think we were able to do a very good job in maintaining morale for these people who felt completely helpless, they couldn't get legal assistance any other way." On doctors on relief, see *Star* March 4, 1933.

38 On the "Hard Times Hop" see *Star* January 30, 1932; Harmsworth Races, September 3, 1932; Miss Kornacki, East Windsor, May 26, 1931; Windsor Bulldogs winning the 1929 championship, April 11, 1929; after 1929 the Bulldogs played in the International Hockey League until that league folded in 1936. The playoff system used in 1931 was a round-robin and, strangely enough, Windsor won the championship game that year against the Buffalo Bisons in a scoreless draw, see *Star* April 8, 1931.

Ruth Kerr in the Olympics, August 4, 1932.

39 *Ontario Sessional Papers*, vol. LXVI Part III (1934) p. 9.

40 University of Windsor Archives, Chamber of Commerce Papers, Box 9, file 4, Women's Section—meeting of September 29, 1921.

41 *Border Cities Star* December 3, 1934; the attack on her at Clay park is reported in *Star* June 13, 1934; on Mrs. L.A. Killen being elected to the Board of Education in 1923, see editorial "The Elections" December 4, 1923.

42 For example, at a meeting held at the Wyandotte School on November 30, communist hecklers tried to shout down their opponents. When non-communists silenced them with blows, the police stepped in. *Border Cities Star* "Man Interrupts" December 1, 1934.

43 Toronto *Globe* December 6, 1934; on the situation in East Windsor see *Star* "Communists Hope" November 24, 1934—"Though the Communists represent a very small minority of the city's voting population, the anti-Communists are not discounting the Red determination to gain control of the city council." A *Star* editorial "East Windsor Elections" concluded "Communism is the issue in East Windsor… No one, of course, would think of lending a five cent piece or extending a dime's worth of credit to an Ontario municipality controlled by the disciples of Moscow" December 1, 1934; the report from the *Daily Worker* of December 8th was quoted in the RCMP Report No. 736, of December 12, 1934.

Endnotes to Chapter Eight

1 Croll's response is carried in the *Star* of May 23, 1933; Cummings' address to the Rotary was reported in the previous edition.

2 Zack Taylor, "If Different, then Why?: Explaining the Divergent Political Development of Canadian and American Local Government" *International Journal of Canadian Studies* vol. 49 (2014) 66.

3 *Border Cities Star* "Will Decide On Payment" January 4, 1932—"Last year default was prevented only by Windsor and Walkerville guaranteeing a payment of $25,000."

4 University of Windsor Archives, J. Clark Keith Papers, Box 3, file 32—Report of the Supervisors of the City of Windsor on the S.W. & A., February 1933: "If the Railway, like any other municipal utility, had been required from its inception to retire its debt, either through serial debentures or by sinking fund payments, it would have been evident that the railway was not at any time self-sustaining." (p. 1)

Keith papers, Box 4, file 34- Operation of the S.W. & A.

Passenger Earnings		1933 Revenues and Losses	
1929-	$1.191,768	Revenues	$492,734
1930-	993,463	Expenditures	498,134
1931-	687,471	Bond Interest	286,048
1932-	533,949	Deficit	298,139
1933-	481,026		

As S.E. McGorman, the SW & A's chairman indicated in 1934, "No money has ever been lost in operating the road. The deficits, which have been reported annually since the Depression, being entirely interest charges on the capital." *Star* December 29, 1934.

5 *Border Cities Star* "Loan By-law" December 14, 1933; on the Essex Border Relief Board assuming control of all relief payments outside of Windsor and Walkerville, see *Star* October 18, 1932.

6 See an extended account of Bradshaw and his works on the Board of Control in *Star* "Civic Finance" July 20, 1934.

7 John T. Saywell, *'Just Call me Mitch': The Life of Mitchell F. Hepburn* (Toronto: University of Toronto Press, 1991) 196.

8 On Macdonald, see Windsor *Star* "50 years of service" December 3, 1977: Macdonald came to Windsor in 1927 as a result of his friendship with Gordon Fraser who had earlier settled in the city and had established a formidable practice. Macdonald appreciated that as a result of his appointment to the civic job in 1930 "I was very much envied, I am certain that I was making more than two-thirds of the lawyers that is right through the Depression."—*supra* author interview.

9 Ontario Archives, R.G. 18-108, file: Royal Commission Border Cities Amalgamation Proceedings, March 2, 1935.

10 Ontario Archives, R.G. 18-108, file: *Report of the Royal Commission on Border Cities Amalgamation*, April 1935.

11 *City of Windsor (Amalgamation Act), 1935* Statutes of Ontario, 1935, chapter 74.

12 *Ladore v Bennett* (1938) 3 D.L.R. 212, [1938] O.R. 324 (para. 126) (Ont. Court of Appeal); and [1939] 3 All E.R. 98 (Judicial Committee of the Privy Council).

On Walkerville's opposition to Croll, see Walkerville *News* editorial "Stand By Walkerville!" December 8, 1934. "The scheme of Hepburn and Croll is to rob Walkerville of its heritage."

13 Toronto *Telegram* editorial, "Windsor Amalgamation Sensible Step" April 17, 1935; and see Larry Kulisek and Trevor Price, "Ontario Municipal Policy Affecting Local Autonomy: A Case Study Involving Windsor and Toronto" *Urban History Review* 16:3 (1988: Feb); "David Croll and his supporters wished to annex these fringe municipalities to Toronto, but Toronto resisted and Toronto was not an adversary that Croll and his fellow Liberals wanted to take on at that time." 262.

14 Windsor *Daily Star* March 3, 1937.

15 Chicago *Tribune* May 19, 1931.

16 Message from "United Traders Limited" one of Walker's trading companies to the parent company—that the long-neck Canadian Club bottle "was vulnerable to breakage and the neck protruded from the sacks in which they were packed." January 5, 1931; by October 10, 1931, United Traders was assuring W.W. Hull their agent on St. Pierre and Miquelon that "these goods have been put up in concave amber gate bottles." The "Gate" bottles had a picture of the ornate gates of the Walkerville headquarters, hence the name. They were constructed of thick glass with concave sides and no neck. They proved so popular that they remained in use after Prohibition.

17 Hiram Walkers & Sons Corporate memorandum "Points as to the Position as it now Stands" April 30, 1933; on the opening of the breweries to the Michigan market, see *Star* "Plants Here on Full Time" May 9, 1933.

18 On Wallace Campbell and the new Ford Foundry, see *Star* March 30, 1935; and Ford employment, March 1, 1935; on the V-8 engine, see "The 1932 Ford V-8" *Ford Educational Affairs Department*; on the Chrysler Airflow, see *Star* March 13, 1934; and James Mays, *The Chrysler Canada Story* Chapter 5; on General Motors, see *Star* April 3, 1934.

19 *Border Cities Star* "Will Mean More Sales" April 18, 1934; and see Wallace Campbell's end of the year account of increased sales throughout the British Empire, *Star* December 28, 1935.

20 Tom Traves, ed. *Essays in Canadian Business History* (Toronto: McClelland & Stewart, 1984) Tom Traves, "The Political Economy of the Automobile Tariff, 1926–31" 134-150; see p. 144; and see *Star* "Bendix Firm" December 28, 1935.

21 Author interview with Bruce Macdonald, September 1984 for the Osgoode Society; and Windsor Municipal Archives, Macdonald Papers Ms. 93, IV 2/4, Macdonald to Minister of Municipal Affairs Croll, September 26, 1936: requesting financial experts to assist him in putting Windsor's case forward for the refinancing—"I have been put in the firing line, so to speak, without a rifle."

22 On Reaume, see *Border Cities Star* "New Sandwich Mayor Asks Assistance" January 9, 1933; Reaume was a regular advocate on behalf of the indigent—Windsor Municipal Archives, Minutes of the Sandwich Town Council, RG DI-1.1/25, April 25, 1932—"Mr. Reaume explained that the meeting had been called to discuss the advisability of all the municipalities taking joint action to have relief extended & to have the real conditions here made known to the Government."

On the riverfront park work, Reaume stated that "I will admit that at 8:00 o'clock one cold morning I did go down and stop that job and sent 100 men home. It was a beautifully cold morning… they would not go to work until they were properly clad." *Daily Star* November 19, 1936.

On Reaume's motion to dismiss Macdonald, see *Daily Star* "City Solicitor Ousted" June 28, 1937.

23 Comments of Jules Fortin, secretary of the Bondholders Protective Association as reported in the *Star* September 24, 1936; and see Order of the Ontario Municipal Board, E.W. Cross chairman, issued April 14, 1937.

Endnotes to Chapter Nine

1 Description of Willie Rogin in Windsor *Daily Star* March 12, 1936—Of the 773 points scored by Assumption in a hugely successful 1935–36 season, Rogin

accounted for 233 points; The Windsor-Walkerville Alumni basketball team regularly won the Eastern Canada or national title between 1930–1933.

Women's basketball also did well in Windsor and in 1934 the Windsor-Walkerville Alumnae won the women's senior provincial title, see *Daily Star* April 9, 1934.

2 On the series between the V8s and Assumption College, see *Daily Star* February-March 1936; during the series, Assumption was also playing a full slate of intercollegiate games. The V8s most dominant player, Julius Goldman, was ineligible for the Canadian Olympic team.

On the opening ceremonies, see David Clay Large, *Nazi Games: The Olympics of 1936* (N.Y: W.W. Norton, 2007) that the Canadian salute was actually the "Olympic greeting" developed in 1924 but which certainly appeared to be the Nazi salute. Teams from Britain and France declined to give any stiff-armed salute, see 125-6. Upon arrival back in Windsor, basketball player Tom Pendlebury admitted that "As far as I could see it was the same as the German salute." *Daily Star* August 27, 1936.

On John Loaring, see *Daily Star* August 4 and 15, 1936; Probably the finest sprinter ever to come out of Windsor, in the Empire games of 1938, he would go on to win a gold medal in the 440 yards hurdle event, a gold team medal in the 4 x 110 yard relay and the 4 x 440 yard relay; Windsor swimmer Gordon Kerr also competed in the Olympics for the Canadian team.

3 Tony Atherton, "Berlin Olympics a breakthrough for Canadian basketball," *Global News* August 9, 2011.

4 *Daily Star* "Board Would Extend Duty-Free Parts List" March 23, 1937; on Dr. Morand's warnings, see *Daily Star* April 24, 1935; on Wallace Campbell's pamphlet, see *Some General Aspects of the Canadian Customs Tariff, the National Economy, and the Automobile Industry in Canada* (1938, Ford of Canada) in *Daily Star* January 13, 1938; and Campbell's comments "Adequate Tariff Vital" January 12, 1938.

On labour's reaction against dropping the excise tax, see "Tax Removal Protest Due" February 25, 1939.

5 Windsor *Daily Star* August 8, 1939; McLarty was attempting to justify Liberal tariff reductions, but the statistics he cited clearly showed the downturn in the auto business after 1937.

6 House of Commons Debates, (1939) vol. II, March 23, 1939 pp. 2185-2193: while Conservative critic R.J. Manion declared that "I am chiefly interested in maintaining employment in this country" Paul Martin seemed to accept the inevitable that his party's policies would foster unemployment and therefore the country needed "a system of contributory unemployment insurance" pp. 2190-1; in his memoirs, in which he discusses many topics in voluminous detail, Martin makes little mention of the reduction in auto tariffs. His one comment is a quote from Dr. Morand in which he warned that the Liberal's tariff reduction would close

down factories and put men out of work. Martin's cryptic response is "I took these remarks to heart and began to do all I could for my constituents." Paul Martin, *A Very Public Life: Volume I, Far From Home* (Ottawa: Deneau, 1983) 213.

On Hudson Motor leaving Tilbury, see *Daily Star* July 24, 1939.

7 On the Chamber of Commerce, see Windsor Public Library, Local History pamphlet, Chamber of Commerce "Windsor: Canada's Most Southern City" 1935; Ford expansion, *Daily Star* "Motor Firm Will Spend $3,300,000" December 9, 1936; on the increase in employment, see *Daily Star* "Employment Shows Gain" August 3, 1937; on the increase in building construction, see Windsor Municipal Archives, Assessment for the Year Ending 1938, R.G. 3, EI file 1/19 p. 26; on the growth rate since 1926, see *Star* "Month of March" March 30, 1937.

On increasing trade with the British Empire, see Ian M. Drummond and Norman Hillmer, *Negotiating Freer Trade: The United Kingdom, the United States, Canada and the Trade Agreements of 1938* (Kitchener: Waterloo Laurier University Press, 1989)—in 1936, 42.4 percent of Canada's exports went to the U.S. while 47 percent went to Britain and the Empire, 11.

8 Windsor Public Library, local history scrapbook 3d, "Institution Opened in 1936 Draws Bright Young Men Across Canada".

9 J. Lewis Robinson, *Windsor, Ontario: A Study in Urban Geography* 90; the same thesis is the source for the statistics on the number of American branch plants in Windsor, 56.

10 On other newspapers commenting on the disparity of relief granted to Windsor, see *Daily Star* editorial "Windsor and Relief" March 16, 1936; on Croll's response see *Daily Star* February 28, 1936—"made it definite that the city will actually receive all of the $2,319,000 and no more and no less... If the city can bring its relief costs down by $500,000 by purging its lists together with probable improvement in business conditions which will take others from the rolls, it will be able to live with the money available."

11 Border Cities Star, "112 Strikers back on Job" July 22 and 24, 1935; on the early life of Nell Wark, see Ottawa *Citizen* August 11, 1965 and *Border Cities Star* April 17, 1926.

12 Windsor *Daily Star* "Relief Rolls Down to 9,785" July 18, 1938—this was due in some part to a riverfront beautification scheme in which unemployed former soldiers were all but guaranteed a job; and see *Daily Star* "102 Removed from List" March 3, 1937; on Ford's expansion see *Daily Star* report from Wallace R. Campbell, December 31, 1938.

13 J.S. Napier, *Memories of Building the UAW* (Canadian Party of Labour Publication, 1976)—this pamphlet provides Napier's account of his family background. He also makes it clear that violence and intimidation was an intrinsic tool of early union organization at 12-3.

14 Windsor *Daily Star* "Police Wield Batons" December 21, 1936; on the origins of the Canadian branch of the U.A.W., see Sam Gindin, *The Canadian Auto Workers: The Birth and Transformation of a Union* (Toronto: Lorimer, 1995) 56-62; on the growth of the UAW, see Nelson Lichtenstein, *The Most Dangerous Man in Detroit: Walter Reuther and the Rise of American Labor* (N.Y. Basic, 1995) 56-61.

15 While Windsor's Ford plant was the main auto producer in Canada, the UAW set their sights on GM "because that's where the American breakthrough emerged." Gindin, *The Canadian Auto Workers* 57.

16 As quoted in James, *The People's Senator* 76—the phrase is frequently misquoted, see Kulisek and Price, *A Centennial Celebration* 73; on the Oshawa Strike, see Irving Abella, ed. *On Strike: Six Key Labour Struggles in Canada, 1919–1949* (Toronto: James Lewis, 1974) "Oshawa 1937" 93- 125.

17 Windsor *Daily Star* September 16 1938.

18 Louis Joseph Veres, *History of the United Automobile Workers in Windsor: 1936–1955* Master of Arts Thesis, University of Western Ontario, 1956, 36; on the bomb attack, see Windsor *Daily Star* August 31, 1938—when the bomb was examined, it exploded with enough force to seriously injure a technician; in Napier, *Memories*, he recalls that during the Walker Metal strike in September 1938 that his union squad "looked after the picket line, making sure the scabs had a good reception and send off every morning and afternoon…" 26—he denied that the union had any involvement with planting the bomb.

On the violence in late 1938, by mid-October, there were wildcat (unauthorized) strikes at Chrysler plant 3, Duplate, L.A. Young as well as the authorized strike at Walker Metal, *Daily Star* "Picket Line" October 19, 1938.

19 Brian F. Hogan, "Catechising Culture: Assumption College, the Pius XI Labour School, and the United Automobile Workers, Windsor, 1940–1950" CCHA *Historical Studies*, 55 (1988) 81; on the background of Fr. Edwin Garvey, see P. Wallace Platt, *Dictionary of Basilian Biography: Lives of the Members of he Congregation of St. Basil* (Toronto: University of Toronto Press, 2015) entry for "Garvey, Edwin Charles."

20 *Daily Star* June 3, 1939; on Protestant and Catholic churches coordinating efforts to assist the West, see "Membership Increases" December 31, 1937.

21 Napier, *Memories* 31; the heading of the chapter of his memoirs from pages 30 to 40 leave no doubt of Napier's feelings: "Capitalist Counter-Attack: Catholic Action: Angels of Destruction."

22 See editorial "Windsor's Municipal Elections" Windsor *Daily Star* December 8, 1936:

> Mayor Bennett literally talked himself out of office. His virulent attacks upon all and sundry who failed to fit into his ideas seemed for a time to

> be the recipe for political success. The onebig thing that defeated Mr. Bennett was his remark about Father Blonde being a disgrace to the cloth. That made a large number of Catholics fighting mad and Mr. Bennett's success at thepolls was in doubt from that day.

The Chamber of Commerce remained politically active in the late 1930s in opposing left-wing policies. While George Bennett sought to regain Windsor's sovereignty in controlling its own finances, the Chamber overwhelmingly voted (by a vote of 87.4% versus 12.6%) that the provincial Department of Municipal Affairs, rather than the socialists on City Council or the Board of Control, should continue to supervise the municipality's financial affairs, see University of Windsor Archives, Windsor and District Chamber of Commerce Papers, Series III, Sub-Series 1, Box 10, file 6, Minutes of Directors Meeting, March 13, 1939.

23 Windsor *Daily Star* "Twice Led Windsor As Mayor" April 3, 1954.

24 The plan to beautify the waterfront of all of Essex County in 1929 was to be entrusted to the "Essex County Waterfront Improvement Association." As J. Clark Keith wrote to Mayor David Croll on July 20, 1932, the plan failed as "there was a distinct cleavage at that time between the urban and rural areas, the former having the opinion that the waterfront development was the outstanding need of the district while the rural section held the opinion that highways should have precedence… the entire legislation collapsed." University of Windsor Archives, J. Clark Keith Papers, 95-007, Box 4, file 36.

See *Daily Star* editorial "Giving a Lead"—commenting on the bill prepared by Charles McTague to create the Essex County Waterfront Improvement Association, that a joint board was essential as "The work cannot be left to individual councils, because the improvement scheme is too extensive for that." March 27, 1927.

25 On the opening of CKOK, see *Daily Star* June 1, 1932 and see Canadian Communications Foundation, *Radio Station History* "CKLW-AM (AM 800)"—that WXYZ of Detroit wrote to the CBC in 1938 complaining that "in view of the fact that CKLW is not a Detroit station" it should not be describing itself as a "Windsor-Detroit station."

26 On the end of the Ouellette Avenue streetcars, see *Daily Star* July 2, 1938, and the end of the service, December 30, 1939.

27 *Daily Star* July 19, 1938; and Oxford, *The Ferry Steamers* 95-6; the Walkerville ferry service ended with far less fanfare on May 15, 1942 when the *Halcyon* made the final landing at the Walkerville dock.

28 On improved health in Windsor, see Windsor *Daily Star* August 28, 1937 and "Health Rate Lower Than Average City" December 31, 1937; and see editorial "Maternal Deaths" November 17, 1938—that previously maternal deaths had dropped from 7.3 per thousand to 2.7; improvements to Metropolitan Hospital, see February 19, 1938.

29 Windsor *Daily Star* "Thousands Join Medical Group" August 22, 1939; on Dr. Fred Adams see Windsor Municipal Archives. MS 19, Windsor Local Council of Women, file 1/1. Adams speech of April 26, 1937.

30 See Windsor *Daily Star* "Health Plan Is Detailed" March 3, 1937.

31 Dan Malleck, *Try to Control Yourself: The Regulation of Public Drinking in Post-Prohibition Ontario, 1927–44* (Vancouver: UBC Press, 2012) 67—This work is a thorough study of the management of public drinking spaces of the period and deals extensively with the situation in Essex County and Windsor; see also, Dan Malleck, "An Innovation from Across the Line: The American Drinker and Liquor Regulation in Two Ontario Border Communities, 1927–1944" *Journal of Canadian Studies* vol. 41 (Winter, 2007) 151.

32 Malleck, "An Innovation from Across the Line;" another problem for enforcers was gambling. A crackdown in January 1939 revealed that "tobacco shops" across the city were fronts for bookies. Betting on horse racing was common in Windsor in the 1930s and the extent of the operation indicates that it was tolerated by the police: *Daily Star* "47 Arrested" January 7, 1939.

33 Malleck, *Try to Control yourself*, 207.

34 Windsor *Daily Star* "Michigan Club" March 1, 1937.

35 Tom Macdonnell, *Daylight Upon Magic: The Royal Tour of Canada—1939* (Toronto: Macmillan, 1989) 182.

36 Windsor *Daily Star* editorial "Riverfront Possibilities" June 7, 1939.

37 Eighth Census of Canada, June 1941: Vol. II, Population by Local Subdivisions, (King's Printer, 1944) 410-43.

38 On the early Lebanese community in Windsor, see *Daily Star* February 20, 1936: one of Windsor's few Muslim residents, Ali Abraham also attended the farewell banquet to pay respects to Msgr. Farah; on the Russian church wars, see *Border Cities Star* March 5, 1934—"Furious parishioners threatened violence to their priest, Rev. Fr. Andrew Federochuk" and April 3, 1934 "Church War Still Raging"—beyond personal animosity, the reports do not disclose any reason for the dispute; on the Hungarian conflict, see Zoltan B. Veres, *Hungarians in Windsor* 1912–2012 (no date or publication details).

39 See author interview with Willie Rogin's son Justice Stephen Rogin May 22, 2015.

40 See Keith Rolland, "Where Italian Community Identifies" Windsor *Star* December 13, 1975.

41 Windsor *Daily Star* "Gold to Help Il Duce" January 27, 1936 and "Meconi Vague on Role as Head of City's Fascist Section" May 18, 1938; on the Brant Street Club supplying black clothes, see author interview with Tullio Meconi, January 14, 2015.

42 On Angelo Zamparo, see Windsor *Daily Star* "Prefers Windsor to Italy" April 12, 1939; on Zamparo's defence of the Italian Club, see *Daily Star* "No-Decision Affair" October 5, 1936; after Croll's dismissal from cabinet, it was Zamparo as vice-president of the Windsor-Walkerville Liberal Association who issued the letter of "complete confidence" in him, April 14, 1937.

43 Windsor *Daily Star* "Chinese in Windsor" August 21, 1937; on the American Chinese athlete, see editorial "Official Red Tape" March 13, 1937; the newspaper reported on November 4 1924 that "Jungo Lee [was the] alleged master mind of a dope ring in the Border Cities"; on the Chinese as good citizens, see author interview with B.J.S. Macdonald, September 1984 for the Osgoode Society—"the Chinese were good citizens, and were honest and paid their bills..."; in March 1939, Loh Tsei, a nationalist activist, spoke to a large crowd of both Chinese and local sympathizers at Patterson High School. Popular attitudes were leaning in favour of the Chinese as being victims of Fascist aggression—see *Daily Star* March 24, 1939.

44 Windsor *Daily Star* "Ten Avoid Nazi Talons," January 6, 1939.

45 Sandy Antal and Kevin R. Shackelton, *Duty Nobly Done: The Official History of the Essex and Kent Scottish Regiment* (Windsor: Walkerville Publishing, 2006) see Chapter Ten—"The Second World War—Getting Ready"; there was no doubt that the uniforms were to be the draw, as an editorial in the *Border Cities Star* wrote: "The new Scottish uniforms with which the regiment is being equipped, will aid greatly to its attractiveness. The history of the kilted regiments is practically the same everywhere. There is never a dearth of recruits..." "The Essex Scottish" October 13, 1927; on the officers as a social elite, see *Daily Star* "Essex Scottish Officers" over a quarter of the initial 23 officers were lawyers, others were insurance executives. All were Protestants except for Lawrence Deziel, the sole French-Canadian officer in the pre-war regiment.

As a measure of the lack of urgency in 1939, Windsor's other militia unit, the Essex Regiment (Tank) was not even ordered to go on active status.

46 *Daily Star* September 20, 1939; and December 30, 1939—"To Be Training Centre For Empire Air Force Pilots;" on Mackenzie King and the BCATP, see Creighton, *The Forked Road* 5.

47 Windsor *Daily Star,* editorial "Striking Quickly" June 13, 1940; the "purge of Windsor's Italian population" is described in the *Star* of June 12, 1940; on the reinstatement of some Italians, see "Utilities Reinstate 4" July 13, 1940; on the end of the Windsor Lodge, see Angelo Principe, "The Fascist-Anti-Fascist Struggle in the Order Sons of Italy of Ontario, 1915–1946" *Ontario History* vol. CVI, No. 1 (Spring 2014) 1.

48 Windsor *Daily Star* "Say Good-Bye" May 27, 1940; In comparison, after the first eleven months of the First World War, Windsor men had already been in several battles and many of them were dead.

Endnotes to Chapter Ten

1 Windsor *Daily Star* "One Windsor for Me" August 21, 1940.

2 Creighton, *The Forked Road* 50; on the armaments contracts, see *Star* "New Efforts" June 17, 1940; and September 13, 1940—Ford gets four more contracts for $6,520,000.

3 Robert Bothwell and William Kilbourn, *C.D. Howe* (Toronto: McClelland and Stewart, 1979) 124 and 129.

4 Windsor *Daily Star* "Home Front Industry" October 5, 1940.

5 *Ibid.*, "Army Put On Wheels" May 29, 1941.

6 See, *Star* "2,050 Have Been Built" June 23, 1943; on the federal program for wartime houses, see *Star* May 3 and 5 1941 and "Small Houses Springing Up" September 6, 1941; on Reaume's idea to build a $3,000 house, see *Star* "Council Thumbs Down" February 8, 1941; on the description of Arthur Reaume, see author interview with Jon Adamac, former City Clerk of the City of Windsor, 2000.

7 On the bill to enable Windsor to draw down its debt, see *The City of Windsor Act,* S.O. 1943, c. 52; on the increase in bus revenues and passengers see *Star* editorial "Railway Finances" April 2, 1943 and "Totals Soar" June 23, 1943—"There have been speedy moves to meet the new demands, but rolling stock remains unobtainable." On Reaume's plan to use bus revenue to reduce debt, see speech covered in *Star* August 3, 1943.

8 Author interview with Raymond Colautti, January 3, 2014; on Frank Sasso, see *Star* April 25, 1941; Utilities Commission restoring Italians to work, see *Star* "MacMillan In Dissent" July 13, 1940—MacMillan alone held that "The people of Windsor will take strenuous objection to the actions of their commission in putting these Italians back to work."

9 Reynolds Farley, Sheldon Danziger, Harry J. Holzer, *Detroit Divided* (N.Y: Russell Sage Foundation, 2000) 19-33; Dominic J. Capeci and Martha Wilkerson, "The Detroit Rioters of 1943: A Reinterpretation" *Michigan Historical Review* 16, no. 1 (Spring, 1990) 51-2.

10 Detroit *Free Press*, July 1, 1940.

11 Windsor *Daily Star* November 7, 1941; in his recollections, George Burt of the Canadian UAW also recalls how Harry Bennett of the Ford US immediately halted parts shipments to Canada under union pressure and thereby crippled Canadian production.

On excluding Canadians as aliens, see *Detroit Free Press* editorial "U.S. Border Officers Turn Back Canadians" July 1, 1940: "United States immigration officers for the first time in a century began turning back Canadians..."; on the opening up of the border to truck traffic, see *Free Press* "Ontario Opens Way" October 3, 1942.

12 Windsor *Daily Star* editorial "Plain Loan Talk" June 17, 1941; on the demobilization of the Essex Tank Regiment, see *Star* "Await Call For Service" December 31, 1940; on the decline in recruiting, see *Star* March 10, 1941.

On American enlistments in the Essex Scots, see *Star* July 27, 1940—many of the Americans came from south-eastern Michigan, but one had hitch-hiked from New Mexico to Windsor to enlist.

13 Graham Broad, *A Small Price to Pay: Consumer Culture on the Canadian Home Front, 1939–45* (Vancouver: U.B.C. Press, 2013) 6; on Christmas shopping in Windsor in 1942, see *Star* "Christmas Buying Here Equal to Pre-War Years" December 21, 1942; on Campbell's report to Ford shareholders, see *Star* "13,188 Average Number." April 28, 1942—as Campbell reported, Ford's "average annual earnings of $2,176 (in 1941) compare with $1,963 in 1940 and $1,474 in 1939."

14 Mock invasion, see *Star* "Invasion Is Success" September 30, 1941; on Reaume's seizure of wartime houses, October 1, 1941.

15 Windsor Municipal Archives, MS 19, Windsor Local Council of Women, file ½ Windsor Civilian Defence Committee, March 28, 1941.

16 Windsor *Daily Star* November 8, 1940.

17 *Ibid.*, "Now" column April 22, 1941.

18 *Ibid.*, "Beer-Drinking Jitterbugs" March 25, 1942; on the 1942 plebiscite, see *Star* "Urban Vote Heavily 'Yes'" April 28, 1942; on the 400 draft evaders, see *Star* "Are Not at Addresses" September 19, 1942.

19 Despite his pleas to stay with a combat unit, Croll would be assigned to administrative duties. He received glowing approvals for his work and would be commissioned an officer and write a manual for dispatch riders.

20 Major Rev. Mike Dalton, *Personal War Diary, 1939–1946* (Charette Church Goods, Windsor) July 2, 1942; and see August 21, 1942—"No Essex officer returned (from Dieppe)… remnant of one proud and gallant outfit" 11.

21 Mark Zuehlke, *Tragedy at Dieppe: Operation Jubilee, August 19, 1942* (Vancouver: DRM Publishers, 2012) citing the criticisms of Rear-Admiral Tom Baillie-Grohman, page 129; on the Essex Scots on the beach, see John Mellor, *Forgotten Heroes: the Canadians at Dieppe* (Toronto: Methuen, 1975).

The Dieppe raid continues to be a source of controversy; some of the publications include Terence Robertson, *Dieppe: The Shame and the Glory* (Toronto: Little. Brown, 1962); and Denis and Shelagh Whitaker, *Dieppe: Tragedy to Triumph* (Toronto: McGraw- Hill Ryerson, 1992); Whitaker's book takes the conciliatory approach that there "were lessons learned" and that Dieppe was "a strategic success." p. 299. Such a conclusion is a way of exonerating those whose lack of ability and experience brought on a costly defeat which served no strategic purpose. Even one of Mountbatten's most sympathetic biographers conceded that no competent military leader should have needed "so elementary a reminder" as to the necessity for air and naval support for an amphibious assault on a heavily defended position; see Philip Zeigler, *Mountbatten* (London: Collins, 1985) 191; Brian Loring Villa's *Unauthorized Action: Mountbatten and the Dieppe Raid* (Toronto: Oxford University Press, 1989) is a thoughtful critique which concludes that not only was the raid poorly planned, it was not even authorized.

22 Windsor *Daily Star* "4 Known Dead, 90 Are Missing" August 24, 1942.

23 *Ibid.*, December 11, 1942; on Detroit's reaction to Dieppe, see Detroit *Free Press* editorial "Windsor's... and Ours" August 22, 1942; and Detroit *News* editorial "Windsor's Loss at Dieppe"—"Deep-felt sympathy flows from Detroit to Windsor, her sister city across the river."

24 *Ibid.*, July 14, 1943—Canadian Bridge had already assembled 16 tugs.

25 Stanley Scislowski, "Memories of a Long Ago War" essay written March 24, 2013.

26 Windsor Historical Society, Veteran's Project, Michael Gladstone White interview with Bill O'Neill and Paul Laforet.

27 Desmond Morton, *A Military History of Canada* (Toronto: McClelland and Stewart, 1999) 4th ed. 186.

28 Author interview with Leon Paroian for the Osgoode Society, May 27, 1998.

29 On Yugoslavs, see *Star* "Windsor Colony" March 28, 1941; on the Polish Legion, see *Star* "Dual Celebration for Poles" May 3, 1941 and June 11, 1941; Lebanese tea wagon, June 13, 1941.

30 On James Watson, see author interview for the Osgoode Society, December 1989, pp. 30-1, the interview details Watson's time in the Canadian army and the refusal of his officers to promote him. In frustration, he applied for a transfer to the Air Force; and see Pamela Sugiman, "Privilege and Oppression: The Configuration of Race, Gender, and Class in Southern Ontario Auto Plants, 1939 to1949" *Labour/Le Travail* vol. 47 (Spring, 2001) pp. 83-113; on Adam Clayton Powell, see *Star* August 1, 1943; on Chief DeFields refusal to appoint any black firemen, see *Star* "Talk About Race, Color" August 26, 1942—"Controller W. Ernest Atkinson asked if there were any colored men in the fire department. The fire chief said there weren't and he was not going to appoint any... He said the difficulty was the men had to eat and sleep together."

On black casualties, see *Star* June 5, 1944—George Day a lifelong resident of McDougall Street killed in action in Italy.

31 Author collection Joyce Brode to Pvt. Joseph Brode, October 15, 1942.

32 Windsor *Daily Star* June 17, 1941; and see author interviews with Mrs. Evelyn Hillman April 24, 2006 (rationing) and Ms. Terry Lillis and Patricia Brode, August 8, 2012 ("it was fun!")

33 On the Windsor Police in the war, see David Rossell, Windsor Police pamphlet, 1999 24-6, the plane was destroyed shortly after the dedication. Gordon Hoben would also be killed on operations; on Eleanor Barteaux and the library, see Windsor Municipal Archives, Eleanor Barteaux Haddrow Collection, Ms. 37, scrapbook box 1; on the "Miss Canada Girls" see *Star* February 2, 1943—the group formed a club of over 100 girls, one of the largest such organizations in Canada.

34 On Sgt. Gubb, see *Star* "Flier Buried in Holland" May 27, 1943; on the mock air raid, see *Star* August 9 and 11, 1943; on the HMCS Hunter opening, see "HMCS Hunter Site" *Star* December 28, 1943.

35 Windsor *Daily Star* "Big Increase Is Expected" March 30, 1942.

36 *Ibid.*, "Lights For War Vehicles" December 31, 1942.

37 Letter from "A War Worker" to "Saleslady" February 2, 1943.

38 Windsor *Daily Star* "Army Put on Wheels" May 29, 1941; on the Canadian Women's Auxiliary Air Force, August 27, 1941; on Truscon Steel, see author interview with Bruno Vendrasco; on the first day care centre, see *Star* "Mothers to Enter War Work Here" November 18, 1942.

39 Windsor *Daily Star* "Plant Near Completion" December 31, 1941; on deaf women employed at the machine gun plant, see *Star* April 2 1943—"Deaf women have this job because the company has found it too noisy a one for hearing persons."

Endnotes to Chapter Eleven

1 Author collection, letter of George W. Brode to Pvt. Joseph Brode, November 24, 1942.

2 Laurel Sefton MacDowell, "The Formation of the Canadian Industrial Relations System During World War Two" in Laurel Sefton MacDowell and Ian Radforth, *Canadian Working Class History* (second edition) (Toronto: Canada Scholars' Press, 2000)—see chapter 22; she concludes that the function of the *Industrial Disputes Investigation Act* was to handicap trade union organization. p. 529.

3 Charlotte A.B. Yates, *From Plant to Politics: The Autoworkers Union in Postwar Canada* (Philadelphia: Temple University Press, 1993)—"The unions saw little equality in the sacrifices being made. While their wages were controlled, profits were not." 32.

4 *Ibid.*, at 30; also on Burt see Windsor *Star* "Thirty Years at Helm of UAW" May 17 1980; and Hogan "Catechising Culture" 85 on Burt's relationship with Fr Garvey.

5 On the Chrysler "loitering" see *Star* November 18 and 19, 1940 and case commentary by Bora Laskin in *Canadian Bar Review* vol. 19, (1941) p. 133—Laskin, a national authority on labour issues wondered how Burt and the picketers could

have been convicted for loitering when the Defence of Canada Regulations were designed to prevent spies from canvassing war plants. Were labour picketers to be equated with spies?

6 Windsor *Daily Star* "Seek Pact Like in U.S." September 29, 1941.

7 Windsor *Daily Star* "Early Pact" October 13, 1941; on George Burt's description of the 1941 rally at the Windsor Market, see George Burt, "The UAW and the Ford Windsor Strike 1945" in Gloria Montero, *We Stood Together: First-hand Accounts of Dramatic Events in Canada's Labour past* (Toronto: Lorimer, 1979) 97.

8 The final results of the recognition vote are carried in *Star* November 14, 1941—on the flight of Burt and England to Ottawa, see Montero, *We Stood Together* 96.

9 Windsor *Daily Star* November 28, 1942.

10 Laurel Sefton MacDowell, *Renegade Lawyer: The Life of J.L. Cohen* (Toronto: University of Toronto Press) 105.

11 Windsor *Daily Star* "Women To Be Placed" October 4, 1943; on Ford's proposal for women to work at a lesser rate, see letter in the George Burt Papers in the Reuther Archives, W.H. Clark, Ford Personnel Manager to Regional War Labor Board, June 3, 1943; on the UAW reaction to this proposal, see Montero, *We Stood Together* 98-9.

12 Windsor *Daily Star* "Accord Is Approved" February 20, 1943; on the comments of Nelson Addes see *Star* "Strike Curb" June 10, 1943.

13 Windsor *Daily Star* "Invited to Take Pulpit" February 20, 1943; Incidents such as the Kirkland Lake gold miner's strike of 1941–42 had shown that the existing system was designed to favour the owners and frustrate workers' attempts to gain union recognition, see Laurel Sefton MacDowell, *Remember Kirkland Lake: The Gold Miners' Strike of 1941–42* (Toronto: Canadian Scholars' Press, 2001).

14 Windsor *Daily Star* April 7, 1943.

15 Yates, *From Plant to Politics*—"The disruptions of production resulting from repeated strikes were accompanied by the growing popularity of the CCF." 39.

16 Ian MacPherson, "The 1945 Collapse of the C.C.F. in Windsor" *Ontario History* vol. LXI (Dec. 1969) No. 4, p. 201; election results reported in *Star* August 5, 1943.

17 Desmond Morton, *Working People* (Fifth Ed.) (Kingston: McGill-Queen's University Press, 2007) 183; on McTague's background see Paul Martin, *A Very Public Life* 100, and Patrick Brode, *Lawyers of the Southwest* 9; on his appointment to the National War Labor Board, see *Star* February 4, 1943—McTague was "Regarded by the government as the best man obtainable for the position." And see *House of Commons Debates,* February 1943, p. 106.

18 Morton, *Working People* 184.

19 Windsor Municipal Archives, Bruce J.S. Macdonald Papers, Ms. 43, Box 5 II33-II, file 1/6, Larry Deziel to Bruce Macdonald, September 5, 1944; and see Antal and Shackelton, *Duty Nobly Done* 473.

20 On the Hadassah show, see *Star* "Huge Crowd At Theatre Night" April 17, 1944; on the HMCS Border Cities, see "Redheaded Sea Vet" April 19, 1944; on the City of Windsor Squadron, see "Houle in City Today" May 13, 1944; on the CWAC, see *Star* "Host Open House" September 27, 1943.

21 Windsor Municipal Archives, MS 19, Windsor Local Council of Women, file ½ Committee annual report, January 25, 1937—"a movement which the Local Council of women launched… a municipal Art gallery, and the gradual accumulation of a permanent collection"; on the "Fakir Art Club" see *Star* April 30, 1937 on the eighth annual exhibit at Willistead featuring 104 canvasses from local painters.

22 Windsor *Daily Star* "Picture Is Presented" February 14, 1944; and "500 Attend Opening of Art Gallery" October 2, 1943; on the early days of the Windsor Art Association, see "Work of 38 County Artists" October 21, 1941.

23 Windsor *Daily Star* "Dr. Walter Given Award" January 29, 1945; and see *Star* "Asks Facing of Reality" January 24, 1945; on Fr. Murphy, see obituary *Windsor Star* "Basilian 'Father Stan' May 24, 1983.

24 Windsor *Daily Star* January 20, 1944; editorial comment in the *Star* on loosening morals, see "Morality Drive" January 19, 1944; on the bus terminal see Windsor Municipal Archives, Minutes of the Meetings of the Board of Commissioners of Police, RG 8 BI file 1/5, April 15, 1943.

25 Patrick Brode, *Unholy City: Vice in Windsor Ontario 1950* (Windsor: ECHS, 2012) 17; on arrests for prostitutes found in a bawdy house in 1943 there were 10, in 1944, 41—these figures are minute when compared with reports on how widespread prostitution was in those years. See Windsor Municipal Archives, Chief Constable Annual Reports for 1943 and 1944, RG 8 C II files 21 and 22.

26 On Bull Fielding and the Elmwood, see *Star* May 22, 1944; on the Metropolitan Store, see *Star* "Modern Structure" January 23, 1945; on Bull Fielding and the police, see author interview with William Willson, November 8, 2006: Willson senior operated a drug store on Monmouth Avenue in Walkerville during the 1930s and 40s which featured a Fielding slot machine. Fielding would telephone Willson as to the time of any police raids so that the machine could be moved out of view.

27 Windsor *Daily Star* editorial "Our Waterfront Is An Asset" June 8, 1944.

28 Faludi set out the problems Windsor faced due to the absence of planning during its growth phase during two speeches in January 1945; see *Star* "Dr. Faludi Speaks"

January 23, 1945 and "Betterment of Windsor Is Debated" January 25, 1945; on Mrs. Cameron Montrose, see her election campaign in December 1943, *Star* December 7, 1943; on Faludi's background, see National Archives of Canada, Faludi fonds, Cain No. 263346.

On the lack of playgrounds in Windsor, see *Star* "Children of the Darkest Spot" May 30, 1944—"These youngsters who are learning to play in the alleys and streets and untidy vacant lots are children of adults who state emphatically that they wish there was a decent place for the kids" on Reaume's tour of the slums, see "Mayor Sees For Himself," August 6, 1942.

29 Windsor *Daily Star* "Men on Train" June 23, 1945.

Endnotes to Chapter Twelve

1 Fudge and Tucker, *Labour Before the Law* 283; on Moulton and Abella, see Irving Abella *On Strike: Six Key Labour Struggles in Canada 1919–1949* (Toronto: James Lewis & Samuel, 1974) xiii, and David Moulton "Ford Windsor 1945" 129; and Herb Colling, *Ninety-Nine Days: The Ford Strike in Windsor, 1945* (Toronto: NC Press, 1995).

2 Montero, *We Stood Together* 99; on union concerns that they appeared to be unpatriotic, see the rally of April 23, 1944 where several veterans addressed the members—*Star* "Union Rejects Ford proposal" April 24, 1944.

3 Yates, *From Plants to Politics*, 50-1.

4 Walter P. Reuther library, Archives of Labor and Urban Affairs, Wayne State University, Detroit Michigan (hereinafter "Reuther Archives") UAW International Executive Board minutes Collection, box 3, Meeting in Flint Michigan, September 10-18, 1945.

5 Windsor *Daily Star* election returns in June 3, 1945; thanks to heavy worker turnout in Windsor's Ward One, the former East Windsor, Alex Parent, the president of UAW-CIO Local 195 was elected for Liberal-Labour in the riding of North Essex. That prominent labour leaders such as Burt and Parent were supporting the party of renowned union-buster Mitchell Hepburn led to much controversy and cries of "turncoat."

6 Reuther Archives, George Burt Collection, box 1, Report to District Council #26, June 23-24 1945.

7 Windsor *Daily Star* "Ford Workers Decide" June 25, 1945.

8 Reports on the conciliation board are contained in the *Daily Star* for September 4–11, 1945. During the hearings, Cohen entertained an appreciative audience with references to Campbell's role during the Depression and that by granting the

union's demands he could redeem himself and thereby put aside the "Campbell eye-dropper budget for relief recipients."

William Kaplan is of the view that "The conciliation board's report was an advance over the status quo and presented a possible public relations coup." William Kaplan, *Canadian Maverick: The Life and Times of Ivan C. Rand* (Toronto: Osgoode Society/University of Toronto Press, 2009), 176. How this is tenable it is difficult to understand. The conciliation board's report denied the essential elements of the union's demands and made the strike all but inevitable.

9 Irving Abella, *Nationalism, Communism, and Canadian Labour: The CIO, the Communist Party, and the Canadian Congress of Labour 1935–1956* (Toronto: University of Toronto Press, 1973) 143; while some writers such as William Kaplan have concluded that "Loyal communist such as (Roy) England" and Alex Parent were Communists, (*Canadian Maverick* 172) that is far from apparent, England had supported the Liberal-Labour party in 1945. While Parent had been active in the Labour-Progressive party, he does not appear to have taken out Party membership. While other international UAW executives such as George Addes were accused of being Communists, they clearly were not. (See Martin, *A Very Public Life* 395).

10 Windsor Municipal Archives, Windsor Police Services, RG 8 BI- file 1/5 Minutes of the Board of Commissioners of Police, September 13, 1945; Peaceful labour picketing had been an exclusion from the criminal offence of besetting (that is, watching another's home or place of business) since 1876. This exclusion was omitted from the Criminal Code of 1892. It was not reintroduced until 1939; Statutes of Canada, 1939, chapter 30, s. 11; Caruthers was convicted of besetting in January 1946 and given a suspended sentence.

On Wallace Campbell's petitions to the Provincial A.G. to force the picket line to the offices, see: Archives of Ontario, Office of the Attorney General correspondence, RG 4-2, letter Wallace Campbell to Attorney General, September 17, 1945; and see John Aylesworth (Ford solicitor) to E.C. Awrey (Essex County Crown Attorney) September 15, 1945—that Local 200's picketing was being conducted to stop the company's access to its offices "except at the imminent risk of serious physical injury and except by the exercise of direct physical force. This action by the union constitutes a breach of the law of the most flagrant kind and the company, despite its desire to avoid any provocative action on its part, simply cannot accept a continuance of this situation."

Campbell remained outraged at Attorney General Blackwell's refusal to act and force an opening, and sent him an extended telegram on September 19, decrying this "solid wall of resistance to any peaceful attempt to enter office… in complete defiance of the rights of office employees…"

11 Mary E. Baruth-Walsh and G. Mark Walsh, *On Strike: 99 Days of the Line* (Toronto: Penumbra Press, 1995) 54; on Clarence Gillis, see House of Commons debates, October 9, 1945.

12 Windsor *Daily Star* "Company Shuts Ford Plants" October 20, 1945; on Ford's profits, see House of Commons debates October 10, 1945—comments from Clarence Gillis.

13 Reuther Archives, UAW District #7 papers, box 136, UAW memo of the Special Conference, October 15-17, 1945; on the meeting in the Royal York, see Montero, *We Stood Together* 104-5.

14 Windsor *Daily Star* November 1, 1945; and see Windsor Municipal Archives, Windsor Police Services, RG * BI file 1/5, Minutes of the Special Meeting, November 1, 1945—"The Chairman (Judge Coughlin) impressed upon the (union) speaker the fact that the Board of Comissioners of Police were not using the police as strike breakers; but that the union could not flout the law by keeping the plant protection personnel from the premises in question"; and see comments on Ford taking no efforts to get security men into the plant in Kaplan, *Canadian Maverick*, 183.

15 Windsor *Daily Star* "Statement Issued" November 2, 1945.

16 Archives of Ontario, George Drew papers, RG 3, 8396-776, Press Release of November 2, 1945.

17 Archives of Ontario, George Drew papers, RG 3, 8396-776; transcript of a telephone conversation between Drew and J.L. Ilsley, November 2, 1945—originally cited in Donald M. Wells, "Origins of Canada's Wagner Model of Industrial Relations: The United Auto Workers in Canada and the Suppression of 'Rank and Rile' Unionism, 1936–1953" *The Canadian Journal of Sociology/Cahiers canadiens de sociologie* Vol. 20, No. 2 (Spring, 1995) 210.

18 Windsor lawyer Leon Parioan: taped comments, author collection pages 7-8.

19 Toronto *Star* "Union Clears Ford Area" November 5, 1945.

20 Toronto *Globe and Mail* editorial "Distinctly Separate Issues" November 6, 1945; Windsor *Daily Star* editorial "Mob Rule" November 5, 1945; *Maclean's* January 1, 1946; Hamilton *Spectator* editorial "How Far Can It Go?" November 3, 1943; Toronto *Telegram* editorial "Union Strike Bulletin An Inflammatory Document" November 7, 1945.

21 Kaplan, *Canadian Maverick,* 185.

22 House of Commons debates, November 5, 1941, Martin's speech at 1841–45; on David Croll leaving Windsor, his biographer states simply and inadequately that "the avenues of political advancement there [Windsor] were blocked off and Spadina offered a new challenge." James, *The People's Senator* 103.

23 London *Daily Worker* November 6, 1945—I am grateful to Keri Ferencz for this citation; on the impact of the blockade on other unions, see *Star* November 6, 1945—recounts several unions eager to stage sympathy strikes for Windsor,

November 8, 1945 "Other unions"—"A demand is evident from all the provinces from sympathy work stoppages..."

On the lack of union shops, see Kaplan, *Canadian Maverick*, 168.

On sympathy strikes in Hamilton, see Hamilton *Spectator* "Decides to Call" November 6, 1945; and support in Winnipeg, see The Winnipeg *Tribune* "Labor Protest" November 6, 1945.

24 Royal Canadian Mounted Police, Monthly Security Bulletins, Part II, bulletin for November 1, 1945; quotes in full the editorial from the *Canadian Tribune* of September 22, 1945; on the activity of the some United Church ministers in supporting the strikers, see the bulletin of December 1, 1945.

25 Abella, *On Strike* 152-3; and see R.M. Harrison's description of a Local 195 meeting as related by a returned soldier—"I noticed that this local is run and dominated entirely by a Communist element. Revolution was preached and applauded at this meeting." *Now* column, *Daily Star* January 19, 1946.

26 Archives of Ontario, George Drew Papers, RG 3, 8396-776, Telephone conversation between Premier Drew and Hon J.L. Ilsley, November 5, 1945 at 1:00 p.m.

27 Reuther Archives, UAW District #7 papers, box 136, letter L.B. Freh, treasurer to George Addes and Patrick Conroy, November 12, 1945; an editorial in the *Star* reflected the chagrin many felt who had been taken in by Ford's plea to preserve property:

> It has come as a surprise to most people that the company did not accept the opportunity to go in and put the powerhouse in operation...There was talk of danger from fire, danger from explosion, danger from flood. Yet no haste is being shown to have the powerhouse operating.

Editorial "The Ford Strike" November 21, 1945.

28 Windsor *Daily Star* November 24, 1945.

29 Paul Martin, *A Very Public Life*, 393-7; on Blackwell's radio address see *Star* November 24, 1945.

30 Reuther Archives, UAW District #7 papers, box 136, letter Mitchell and Daley to George Burt and Wallace Campbell, November 27, 1945.

31 Windsor *Daily Star* "Rejected by Members of Union" November 29, 1945.

32 See the note that was being circulated among the strikers prior to the December vote which stated, among other things, "It is important that we go back to work at once in order to save our homes and everything we hold. Our leaders are only interested in their own protection and not our welfare." *Daily Star* December 17, 1945.

33 Kaplan, *Canadian Maverick*, 430.

34 Toronto *Globe and Mail* editorial, "The Rand Formula" January 31, 1946; and see David Croll speech to the University of Toronto Liberal Club, January 31, 1946.

35 Abella, *On Strike* 149; on Burt's reaction to Rand see Reuther Archives, George Burt Collection: Box 1, report to District Council #26, January 19—20, 1946; on a picketer's response to Rand, see *Daily Star* "Victory for Union" January 30, 1946.

36 Montero, *We Stood Together*, 111; on the union commemorative, see Walsh *Strike* 110; on the Paroian recollections, see Leon Parorian taped comments, author collection, p. 8.

37 Wells "Origins of Canada's Wagner Model" 212-4; and see Judy Fudge and Eric Tucker, "Law, Industrial Relations, and the State: Pluralism or Fragmentation? The Twentieth-Century Employment Law Regime in Canada" in Bryan D. Palmer, ed. *Labouring the Canadian Millennium* (St. John's: Canadian Committee on Labour History, 2000) 276.

38 On the return of the regiment, see *Daily Star* "Welcome Home Scottish" November 21, 1945.

Endnotes to Epilogue

1 Kaplan, *Canadian Maverick* 185.

2 On the *Daily Star* editorial warning of a new Depression, see W.L. Clark, "As We See It" January 18, 1946; on Reaume's urging women to leave the factories, see "Are Needed by Veterans, He Says" January 23, 1946.

3 On the planning exhibit, see *Daily Star* "300 Attend" January 15, 1946; and "Audacious and Yet Feasible Is Windsor's Master Plan" January 16, 1946; A reporter from *Time* magazine attended the display and filed a jaundiced account; see *Daily Star* January 30, 1946:

> "Time Magazine's report follows:
>
> 'Windsor [is] a completely disorganized chaos of everything a human being can build… bad streets, slums, blighted areas, factories alongside of houses, no place for your children to play…
>
> An ugly waterfront hems it in on one side. It is sliced through the middle by three railways clustered with factories. It is scarred by dreary wastelands heaped with the skeletons of discarded automobiles…"

Mayor Reaume was outraged by the article and called Faludi to account. The later hastily explained that he had not made the statements attributed to him in *Time* and he completely denied having anything to do with this slur. See *Daily Star* "Dr. Faludi Denies" January 31, 1946.

And editorial "See the Planning Exhibit" January 14, 1946.

Index

Adair, Ken, 224
Adams, Dr. Fred, 114, 134
Adams, Thomas 134
Addes, George, 247
Adelman, Doris, 225
Air Raid Precautions (ARP), 205
Aircraft, 134-5
Aitchison, Gordon, 175
Albert Residence for Men, 109
All Saints' Anglican Church, 11-12, 30, 79, 106, 184
Amalgamation, 164; proposed 116; and Chapter 8
Ambassador Bridge, 253; constructed, 130-1; opened, 144-5
Ambery, Colley, 68
Amherstburg, 18, 152
American Auto Trimming Company, 102
Argyle Road, 28
Armouries, 11, 47-8, 95
Art, 225-6
Arts and Letters Club, 123
Ascension Church, 30, 115
Ashby, Rev. H.B., 115
Assumption College, 112, 121, 175-7, 183-4
Atkinson, Ernest, 206, 226-7
Auto Blockade, 1945, 241-5, 249, 255
Austin, James, 130-1
Austin, Helen, 131
Auto Specialties Plant, 198
Automobiles, 37-9, 134, 172; early development, 23-26; production increases, 177-8
Automobile Industrial Union of the Border Cities, 158

Baptists,11, 14, 109, 184
Barrett, Gordon, 209
Barteaux, Eleanor, 213
Bartlet Law Firm, 39
Baseball, 31, 40, 49, 120, 161-2
Basketball, 175-6
Beach Grove Golf and Country Club, 189
Beaudoin, Fr. Lucien, 61, 63-5, 66-7
Beauty pageants, 161
Beck, Sir Adam, 35-6, 47-8, 126
Begley Public School, 228
Bell, Mitchell, 81-2
Bendix Eclipse, 172
Bennett, George, 157, 163-4, 178-9, 185, 305n. 22
Bennett, Prime Minister R.B., 149, 153, 165
Benoit, Vital, 118
Berger, Sam, 209
Berlin, Irving, 202
Berlin Olympics 1936, 175-7
Bilingual education, 46-7, decline of, 117
Bernstein, Max, 12
Blacks, 13, 107-8; in First World War, 58-9, 70; discrimination against 117;

in Second World War, 211-12, 311n. 30
Blackwell, A.G. Leslie, 239, 246
"blind pigs" 125, 139, 142-3; and 1927 scandal, 141-4
Blue Shirts of Canada, 159
Board of Health, 57; and Spanish Flu, 75-6; unified, 113
Boards of Control (provincial) 156-8, 166-7
Bob-Lo Island Park, 40, 49, 184
Bonusing, 17, 21, 33
Borden, Sir Robert, 73
Border Aero Club, 134
Border Cities, 8, 71-3, 100, 191; war growth, 84-5; peoples, 106-7; 1920s expansion, 109-11, 113, 126-7; failure to co-operate, 116; planning, 133-4; and Depression, Chapter 7
Border Cities, H.M.C.S., 225
Border Cities Industries, 215-6, 221-2
Border Cities Italian Club, 109
Border Cities Relief Board, 152
Border Cities Star, 76, 79, 89, 91; and Thompson campaign, 140-4, 149, 154
Border Cities Symphony, 123
Border Citizens' Service Committee, 153
Bower, Joseph A., 130, 144
Bourg, Walter, 57
Bovington, Rev., 11, 14
Bowlby, A.D., 24; and Mrs. Bowlby, 123
Boxing, 31-2
Bradshaw, Thomas, 167
Brannagan, Thomas, 224
Brightmore, Bert, 151-2
British Commonwealth Air training Plan, 194
British population, 11-2, 106; and Walkerville, 168-9
Browning machine guns, 215-6, 221
Brian, M.E., 115
Bridge Avenue Bathing Beach, 124
Brodie, Magistrate David, 157
Brown, Rev. W.L., 224
Buhl Malleable iron strike, 21-2
Bulat, Peter, 211
Bulmer, William, 24
Burt, George, 222; background, 218-9; and Ford strike, 231-50

Cadillac (ferry), 186
Cage, Minnie, 58, 70
Cameron, David, 111
Campbell, Malcolm, 181
Campbell, Wallace, 130, 171-2, 178; background 100-1; Depression, 151, 153, 155; Second World War, 195, 198-9, 203, 215; and unions, 219-20, 224; and Ford strike, 231-50
Campbell, Walter, 85
Campbell School, 111
Canadian Auto Lamp, 180
Canadian Bridge Company, 20-1, 25, 101, 108, 111, 209; established, 27; 1920s expansion, 146
"Canadian Club," 29, 55; in "Gate" bottles, 170
Canadian Congress of Labour (CCL) 234-5, 246-7
Canadian Deep Waterways and Power Association, 132
Canadian Machinery, 38
Canadian Motor Lamp, 209, 215
Canadian Salt Company, 32, 42, 117
Canadian Steel Company, 44, 149
Canadian Tariff Commission (1920), 100, 127
Canadian Transit Company, 130
Capitol Theatre, 120
Carpenters' Union, 80
Casgrain, Lt. Col. H.R., 70
Central Methodist (after 1925 United) Church, 12, 106, 184
Central School, 17
C.H. Smith Department Store, 70; expansion, 123
Chadwick, Rev. E.A.P., 11-2
Chalmers Motors, 104
Chamber of Commerce, 80, 113, 116, 127-8, 134, 148, 177, 185; and Depression, 153

Champion Spark Plug, 101-2, 125
Chapman, Rev. O.E., 109
Chappell House, 92-5
Chappus, A., 43
Charleston (dance) 122
Chauvin, Mrs. C.C., 154
Cherniak, Isadore, 275-6n. 14
Chinese, 12, 74, 193, 224, 308n. 43
Chlorination, 71
Christian Culture Series, 226, 247
Chrysler of Canada, 135, 149, 177-8, 212, 218; origins of 104-5; and "Airflow," 171-2
City Hall, 17, 115
City of Windsor Squadron, 225
CKLW radio station, 186
CKOK radio station, 186
Clay, Henry, 48
Cleary, Francis, 14
C.M. Bennet Company, 101
Coburn, J.H., 116
Cody, James, 205
Cohen, J.L., 234
Colautti, Antonio, 192, 195, 201
Coldwell, M.J., 235-6
Colthurst, Guy Butler, 111
Columbia (excursion ship) 40, 184
Collective Bargaining Act, 222
Communists, 180-3, 222-3; as "Bolshevik Menace," 79-83; in 1930s, 158-9, 163-4; Ford strike, 232, 235, 240, 244
Congress of Industrial Organizations (CIO) 180-2
Conroy, Pat, 247
Conscription; 1917, 73-4; and Second World War, 205-6
Cooper, James, 137-8
Co-operative Commonwealth Federation (CCF), 161-3, 184, 222-3, 232, 235; formed 159-60
Copland, Jock, 229
Costa, John, 192
Coughlin, Judge J.J., 143, 167-9; and Ford strike, 235, 238-9
Couzens, James, 91
Creighton, Hec, 177
Crime, 89-97, 136-144, 226-7
Croll, David, 12-3, 163, 193, 197, 199-200, 222; runs for mayor, 154-5; directs welfare, 156-8; and amalgamation, 167-9, 179-80, 182; runs again, 185-6; joins army, 194; Ford strike, 243
Cummings, H.L., 156-7, 165, 172
Curry, Clyde, 142-3, 155, 163
Curry, John, 23, 25, 32, 36

Daily Worker, 164
Dalton, Fr. Mike, 206-8, 225
Dante Aligheri Society, 109
Davis, John, 7, 17, 43
Davies, Rev. M.C., 232
Dean, Lee, 193
DeFields, Clarence, 115, 151, 212
De Grandpré, Joseph, 66, 107
Deneau George "Rube" 31-2, 269n. 9
Depression, see Chapter 7
DeSantis, Msgr. Constantino, 191
Desjarlais, Donald, 175
Desoto, 105, 149
Detroit, 7-8, 40-1, 127, 148, 161, 180-1, 189; growth of 20-1, 50-1; Germans in, 52-3; First World War, 60-1, 69, 77; Prohibition, 91-8, 139; Second World War, 201-2, 218-9; see also Transnational Region
Detroit and Windsor Ferry Company, 85
Detroit, Belle Isle and Windsor Ferry Company, 19, 40
Detroit Free Press, 178, 209
Detroit News, 33, 43, 69, 91
Detroit Red Wings, 121
Detroit River, 8, 16, 124, 131-2; as health hazard, 71; and rum-running, 91
Detroit Theatre, 40
Detroit Tigers, 40
Detroit United Railway (DUR) 18-9, 35-6, 81
Detroit-Windsor International Tunnel, 253; built, 132-3, 145-6
Devonshire Race Track, 59

Dewar, P.A., 42
Dezeil, Larry, 160, 225
Dickert, George, 26, 39
Dickinson, Martha, 58
Dieppe Raid (Operation Jubilee), 206-9, 220, 229-30, 310n. 21; as legend, 256
Diphtheria, 71, 186
Dodge trucks, 149
Doe, Fr. Edward, 112
Dominion Fish Hatchery, 44
Dominion Forge, 83, 102
Dominion Motor, 37
Dominion Police, 73
Dominion Trades Congress, 158
Donaldson, Walter, 206-7
Donnelly, Edward, 93
Douglas, Dr. M.S., 187
Drew, Premier George, 240, 242, 245
Drouillard, Arsas, 60-1
Drouillard, Francis X., 45
Drouillard, Patrice "Patsy," 31-2
Drury, Premier Ernest, 91
Dundalk H.M.C.S., 209

East-Europeans, 56-7, 74, 80, 108-9, 158-9, 191
East Windsor; created in 1929, 126; Depression in 151-3; and Communists, 158-9, 163-4
East Windsor Bathing Beach, 161
Edward, Prince of Wales, 79
Edgewater Thomas Inn, 139, 188
18th Battalion, C.E.F., 50
electric cars, 271n. 25
Ellis, H.T.W., 86-7
Ellis, J.A., 116
Elmwood Hotel, 227-8
E-M-F Canada, 103
Emancipation Day, 13, 49, 211
Emery, William, 183
Emms, Alfred "Hap" 161
England, Roy, 219, 223; Ford strike, 231-50
Englander, William, 12, 108-9
Erie Street, 111

Essex Border Utilities Act, 72
Essex Border Utilities Commission (EBUC); created 72-3, 76; in 1920s, 113-5; insolvency, 166
Essex Border Relief Board, 153, 166
Essex County Golf and Country Club, 99, 117
Essex County Medical Association, 187
Essex County War Memorial, 111
Essex Scottish Regiment, 203, 224-5, 250; formed, 193-6; Dieppe Raid, 206-9, 229-30; as legend, 256, 308n. 45
Essex Tank Regiment, 203
Essex Terminal Railway, 20, 32, 33, 44

Fakir Club, 225
Fallon, Bishop Michael, 64-66, 112
Faludi, Dr. E.G., 228, 256, 314n. 28, 319n. 3
Farah, Msgr. Peter, 191
Farrow, Russell, 168
Feller, Wolfgang, 62
Ferland, Fr. Joseph-Napoléon, 15
Ferrari grocery store, 109
Ferries, 19, 34, 85-6, 128; 266n. 26; service ended 186; see individual ferries, *LaSalle, Pleasure and Promise* 85
Fielding, W.F. "Bull," 227-8
Fire department, 115, 170
Firemen's Field Day, 161
First World War, Chapter 3
Fisher Body, 46, 127
Flavelle, J.D., 94
Fleming, Oscar E., 17, 44, 47; and waterways, 132, 135
Florent, Louis, 133
Football, 31
Ford City, 57, 84, 107, 116; creation of, 45-6; battle of, 63-7; becomes East Windsor, 126
Ford, Edsel, 99, 123
Ford Facts (newspaper) 220
Ford, Henry, 23-25, 99, 171
Ford, Henry II, 246

Ford Motor Company (United States) 23-4, 38, 127, 246
Ford Motor Company of Canada, 128, 135, 171, 180; incorporated and growth, 25-6, 38-9, 43; First World War, 51-2, 56, 83; post-war, 100-1; Second World War, 197-9, 203, 212, 218-20; and 1945 Strike, Chapter 12
Ford powerhouse, 100, 237-246
Ford Trade School, 179
Ford V8 (engine) 171
Ford V8s (basketball), 175-7
Forster, J.L., 212
Fowler, Charles, Evan, 129
Frankensteen, Richard, 181-2
French-Canadians, 15-6, 42, 44-5, 105-6, 117, 253; battle of Ford City, 63-7
Frontier Club, 13
Frontier Handicap, 124
Furlong. W.H., 186
Fuller, Gordon, 175-6

"Garden City" 27-9
Gardner, Dr. G.N., 89, 163
Garvey, Fr. Edwin, 183-4, 218
General Byng School, 111
General Motors of Canada, 83, 100, 127, 135, 172, 182, 218
George VI, King, 184, 189-90
Gignac, Harry, 156
Giles Boulevard, 110
Gillis, Clarence, 235
Glasscoe, Edward, 120
Golf, 120
Gotfredson, Benjamin, 102
Gotfredson Truck Corporation, 102, 135, 240
Goldman, Julius, 175
Graham Paige Motors, 150
Gramm Motor Truck, 37
Grand trunk Railway, 33-4
Great War Veterans' Association, 80
Great Western Railway, 8
Green, Alfred, 213
Gubb, John, 213
Gundy, Magistrate W.E., 84, 125, 142-4

Hamilton, 17, 127, 148, 191
Hanna, J.W., 33
"Hard Times Hop" 160-1
Harmsworth race, 161
Harrison, R.M., 125-6, 205
Hatch, Harry, 138, 171
Healy, A.F., 43, 94
Henderson, Cornelius, 108
Hepburn, Mitchell, 164, 168; fires Croll, 182
Herman, W.F., 154; background of 140; anti-vice campaign, 141-4
Hewlitt, Walter, 58-9
Highland Park factory, 38
Hockey, 31, 121-2, 161
Hofer Brewing, 118
Holy Trinity Church, 57, 75
Hooper, Archie, 80-3, 105, 141, 154
Horseracing, 59, 88-9, 124
Hôtel-Dieu hospital, 15, 75, 110-11, 187
Howe, C.D., 197
Howie, Dr. John, 226
Hiram Walker and Sons Distillery, 8, 29, 41-2, 124 137, 170-1
Home Guard, 54
Hong, Joseph and George, 224
Howard Avenue Mission to the Poor, 115
Hungarians, 57, 108, 188, 191
Hunter, H.M.C.S., 213, 240
Hupp Motor Car Company, 37
Hydro-electricity, 35-6, 72-3; expansion of, 126; see also, Essex Border Utilities Commission
Hydro/Electric Commission of the City of Windsor, 48
"Hungry Hollow" 61

Ilsley, J.L., 240, 242, 245
Immaculate Conception Church, 15, 107
Imperial Order of the Daughters of the Empire (IODE) 68, 108; opens sanatorium, 87
Industry; Windsor lack of, 17; growth of, 23-6, 33-4, 43-4; post-First World war, 80, 83, 100-03
Industrial Disputes Investigation Act 217

International Association of Machinists, Local 718, 80
International Joint Commission, 71
Italians, 109, 191-3; interned, 195, 200-1

Jackson, Mayor Cecil, 63, 115, 142, 145, 147, 154
Jackson Park, 121, 161, 185
Jackson's Corners, 117
Jacques, Percy, 75
Janisse, Joseph, 118
Janisse, Stanislas, 66
Jasperson, Lt. Col. F.K., 208
Jeanne d'Arc School, 107
Jews, 12-3, 75, 117, 154, 175, 177, 193
Johnson, William "Pussyfoot," 96-7
Johnstone, Hughson, 90

Kahn, Albert, 28-9; designs Ford Plant 1, 38, 51; post-war designs, 101
Kahn, Julius, 27, 38, 101
Kaltschmidt, Karl, 53-4
Keith, J. Clark, 114-5, 135
Kelsey Wheel Factory, 43, 55, 102, 198; strike, 181-3
Kenilworth Race Track, 59, 89
Kennedy, William Costello, 73-4, 103
Kennedy Collegiate Institute, 111, 176, 212
Kerr Engine Factory, 25, 27
Kerr, Ruth, 161
Ketcheson, Georgina, 163-4
Kew, G.G., 238
Kildare Road, 28
Killen, Mrs. L.A., 162
King, Prime Minister W.L.M., 103, 128, 178, 190, 194, 197, 203, 223
Kirkland Lake Gold Miners' Strike, 221, 223
Knowles, Maurice, 72, 114-5
Kogan, Oscar, 245
Kornacki, Sophie, 160-1
Krug, Peter, 204-5

Labour Progressive Party (communist) 222, 231
"Lady Searcher" 50-1
Laforet, Paul, 210
Lake Erie, Essex and Detroit Railway, 32
Landsdowne ferry, 34
Lanspeary Park, 158-9
LaSalle, 118
Laskin, Bora, 233-4
Laurendeau, Fr. François, 65-7, 164
Laurendeau, Leo, 159
Laurier, Sir Wilfrid, 41
Lawyers, 106
L.A. Young Industries, 102, 172
Lebanese, 191, 211
Leduc, Paul, 118-9
Lefler, William, 53
LeSueur, Percy, 121
Levert, Ben, 159
Licavoli Mob, 139, 227
Ligue des Patriotes, 107
Lincoln Road Methodist Church, 30, 125
Livingstone Channel, 131
Loaring, John, 177, 205
Loew's Theatre, 119
London (Ontario) 13, 17, 127
Lord's Day Act 30, 39-40, 62, 88
Lothian, Arthur, 112
Low, Harry, 136-7
Lowe, W.D., 112-3
Lowe Tech, see Windsor-Walkerville Technical School
Library (Carnegie) 17-8
Lusted, Stephen, 20, 58
Lynch, Emily, 162

Macdonald, Bruce, 167, 172-3, 224-5, 301n. 8; background of, 168
Maclean, Thomas, 241, 247
Maclean's Magazine 242
MacMillan, Angus, 172, 235, 238-9
Magwood, Rev. J.W., 125
Mailloux, Eugene, 107
Maleyko, Martin, 154
Man o'War, 88-9
Mansfield, John, 104, 149, 171-2
Marathon Dancing, 125

Marion Street Colony, 56-7, 74
"Marriage Mills," 20
Martin, Fred; and Grace Hospital, 86-7; develops tunnel, 132-3, 145
Martin, Paul, 223; tariffs, 178; and Ford strike, 245, 247-9
Masonic Temple, 122
Masson, George Y., 111
Master, Alois, 93
Matty, Fr. John, 108
Maxwell Motor Company, 56, 104
McCaw, Henry, 123
McDermott, Tom, 207-8
McDougall Street Factory Site, 33
McEvoy, Bishop Fergus, 13-5
McGee, Fr. W.P., 175-6
McGregor, Gordon, 42, 51, 56, 60-1, 68, 83-4 113, 251-2; early life, 22-3; starts Ford of Canada, 24-6; expansion, 38-9; heads EBUC and Health Board, 72, 76; death of, 99-100
McGregor, Harriett (Hattie) 22
McGregor, Walter, 61, 68
McGregor, William, 22, 42
McHugh, Judge Michael, 14
McLarty, Norman, 178, 219
McLean, Evelyn, 119
McMath, Francis, 27, 44
McNee, Archibald, 14, 19
McNulty Realty, 41
McPherson, Leon, 160
McTague, Charles, 130, 220; background of and national labour code, 223-4
Meconi, Luigi, 192, 195
Meconi, Mariano, 192
Medbury Block, 24, 32
Memorial Park, 185
Menard, Moise, 37-8
Menard Motor Trucks, 38, 83
Mercury 8, 180
Meretsky, Aaron, 12
Meretsky, David, 154
Meretsky, Irving "Toots," 175, 177
Meretsky, Simon, 119-20
Merifield, Rev. Harry, 164
Merlo and Ray Construction, 109
Methodists, 12, 30, 92, 106, 109
Metropolitan General Hospital, 187; built, 134-5
Metropolitan Store, 228
Meunier, Fr. Joseph, 14-5
Michigan, 59-60, 91, 130
Michigan Central Railway Tunnel; built, 34-5, 270n. 18
Michigan Club, 189
Militia, 11-2, 49
Millson, rev. A.E., 221
Milner Walker Wagon Works, 22-3
Milner, William, 23
"Miss Canada Girls," 213
"Miss Western Ontario," 161
Mitchell, Frank, 115, 123, 130
Mitchell, Humphrey, 234, 246-7
Moceri, Joe, 139
Model A, 23-4
Model C, 25
Model T, 38, 42-3, 83, 101, 135
Moisseiff, Leon, 130
Montrose, Mrs. Cameron, 228
Morand, Dr. Raymond, 118, 128, 177-8;
Mousseau, Insp. M.N., 90-1
Mowat, Farley, 147
Moy Hall, 43-4
M & P Stores, 107
Murphy, Mayor Frank, 145
Murphy, Fr. J. Stanley, 226

Nantais, Stanley "Red," 175, 191
Napier, James; origins of UAW Local 195, 181-4
National Cycle and Automobile Company, 24
National Labour Code, 223-4, 233
National Policy, 8, 21, 128
National War Labour Board, 220, 223
Natural gas, 35
Neale, W.H., 239
Newbury, Charles, 180
New Zealand, 146, 150
99th Battalion C.E.F., 54-5, 67-8
Nude bathing, 112, 123, 286n. 29
No. 2 Construction Battalion, 59

No. 3 Stationary Hospital, 70
No. 7 Elementary Flying Training School, 195

O'Connor, Justice G.B., 233-4
Ojibway, 44-5, 146, 149, 273n. 44
O'Neill, William, 210
Ontario; and Prohibition enforcement, 93-7; Boards of Control, 156-8; forced amalgamation, 165-70
Ontario Provincial Police, 240
Ontario Temperance Act, 62, 90-8, 139-40
Orpen, Abe, 89
Oshawa, 182-3
Osterhout, Peter, 110
Ostschwaben Alliance, 188
Ottawa Agreements, 150-1
Ottawa Street, 111
Ottawa United Church, 106
Ouellette Avenue, 96, 115, 146
Ouellette Square, 22, 42, 76
Our Lady of the Rosary Church (*Notre Dame du Lac)* 45, 61; battle of Ford City, 63-7

Pacaud, Gaspard, 15, 107
Packard Motors, 150-1
Page, Leo, 43
Page Wire Fence, 27
Palmieri, Jack, 195
Palms, Lt. James, 207-8
Parent, Alex, 235, 240, 245-6
Parker, Alton, 212
Parker, I.C., 154
Parks, 16, 22, 115, 158-9, 161, 228; on riverfront, 46, 185, 274n. 48
Paroian, Armand, 152, 241, 249
Paroian, Leon, 210-11, 241, 249
Patriot War, 7, 11
Patriotic fund, 70-1
Paulin, Rev. Hugh, 106, 108
Paull, Rev. F.H., 164
Peabody Overall Company; bombing, 52-4; women in, 58
Pearson, Lt. Col. Arthur, 194
Pendelbury, Tom, 176
Pennington, James, 111
Pere Marquette Railway, 33
Perry, Oliver, 48
Petite Côte, 118, 273n. 44
"Picket Line Chicken" 235-6
Planning report (1929), 134; updated, 228
Plymouth, 105, 149
Poisson, Paul, 156-7
Poles, 56-7, 74-5, 108, 211
Police, 91, 93, 96-8, 170, and 1927 scandal, 141-4, Second World war, 213, 226; Ford strike, 235-41, 245
Polish War Veterans Association, 188
Popular Mechanics, 145
Post Office, 151
Powell, Adam Clayton, 211
Presbyterians, 12, 106, 108, 159
Prince, Alan, 50
Prince Edward Hotel, 111, 139, 189
Prince Road Sanatorium, 87
Le Progrès (newspaper) 15
Prohibition, 60-2, 89-98, 136-40, 170-1
Prostitution, 226-7, 314n. 25
Protestants, 11, 13, 14, 232; and Prohibition, 61, 90, 95-6, 106; and unions, 184, 221
Public Health, 57, 71, 113-4, 134-5, 186-7; Spanish Flu, 75-6; Depression, 152

Railways, 7-8, 33-5
Rand, Ivan and "Rand Formula," 248-50, 256
Raney, William, 91-2
Raycraft, Tom, 158-9, 180
Reaume, Arthur, 173, 212, 222; war-time housing, 199-200, 204; Ford strike, 234-6
Reaume, J.O., 46-7, 75, 274n. 49
Reaume, Stanley, 75
Reaume, Insp. U.G., 188
Regal Motors, 37
Reciprocity Treaty, 41-3
Regulation 17, 47, 63-4, 107
Relief, see Welfare
Religion, 11-2, 30, 164, 184; divides city, 13-5, 47; and French-Canadians, 63-7

Remington Park, 117, 179, 182
Renaud, Claude, 238-9
Reo Motor Car, 32
Respa, Karl, 53-4
Reuther, Walter, 181-2
Richards, Ada C., 108
Richards, Justice S.E., 233
Rivait family, 224
River Rouge, 127, 202, 219
Riverfront park, 46, 185, 190-1, 228, 264n. 15 and 16, 306n. 24
Riverside, 116, 153-4, 289n. 46; created, 118-9
Riverside Brewery, 138
Roach, Mickey, 161
Roads, 17, 115, 133-4, 265n. 18
Robeson, Paul, 245
Robinson, Major S.C., 54, 170
Rodd, John H., 30, 81, 88, 95
Rogin, Willie "Moose," 175-6, 191
Roman Catholics, 30, 47, 63-7, 159, 184, 223; and school question, 13-5
Roseland, 118
Royal Canadian Air Force, 195, 205, 210-11
Royal Canadian Navy, 205, 213
Royal Canadian Mounted Police, 138, 159, 163-4, 240-4
Royal Commission on Customs and Excise, 136-7
Rum-running, 89-98, 136-141, 170-1, 253
Russians, 56-7, 74, 191

Saccaro, Caesar, 154
Saginaw Lumber Company, 17, 20
Saint-Pierre, Dr. Damien, 66
Salvation Army, 86-7
Sanborn, Dr. C.S., 226
Sandwich, 7, 8, 14, 17, 44-5, 72, 92-8, 111, 113, 173; growth of, 32, 117
Sandwich Collegiate, 212
Sandwich Methodist Church, 92
Sandwich Windsor and Amherstburg Railway (SW &A) 18, 71, 166, 186, 200, 300n. 4; 1919 strike, 81-3
Sasso, Frank, 200
Saturday Night 156
Scislowski, Stan, 108, 152, 210
Sclanders, F. Maclure, 127-8
Schools, 111-3, 212
Seagrave, W.E., 38
Second World War, 193-6, and see Chapter 10
Severin, Ducharme, 47
Sewers, 113-4
Shaar Hashomayim synagogue, 154, 193
Sharrey Zedek synagogue, 12
Shepherd, James, 36, 47-8
Sheppard, Hugh, 111
Shulman, Rabbi Nahum, 193
Simpson, James, 158-9
Sir Barton, 88-9
"Slacker Hunts" 69
Small Pox, 114
Smith, Cecil, 97-8, 283n. 34
Smoot-Hawley tariffs, 148-50, 295n. 5
Sorrel, Fred, 212
South Africa, 11, 38, 43, 77, 150
Spanish Influenza, 75-6
Sports, 31-2, 59-60, 120-22, 161, 175-9
Spracklin, Rev. J.O.L., 92-5
Springsteen, Stanley, 233
St. Andrew's Presbyterian Church, 12, 30, 106
St. Alphonsus Church, 15, 103
St. Alphonsus School, 13-5
St. Angela Merici, 192
St. Anthony of Padua, 108
St. Bernard School, 112
St. Clare of Assisi, 112
St. Joseph Sisters, 64
St. Lawrence waterway, 132
St. Louis, William, 119
St. Louis, Maurice and Milton, 209
St. Luke Road Barracks, 194, 209-10, 212
St. Mark's Anglican church, 164
St. Mary's Academy, 133
St. Mary's Anglican Church, 29-30
St. Paul's United Church, 221
St. Peter's Maronite Church, 191
St. Rose de Lima Church, 119, 139

Sts. Vladimir and Olga Ukrainian Catholic Church, 108
Stephen's Inn, 143
Streetcars, 18-9, 35, 71-2, 134; removed, 186
Streetcar men union, 81-3
Strikes; Canadian Bridge, 21-2; SW&A (1919) 81-3; Kelsey Hayes, 181-3; war-time, see Chapter 11; Ford 1945, see Chapter 12
Stodgell, Camilla, 123
Stodgell Park, 120
Studebaker, 37, 83, 103, 127
Sutherland, Robert, 19, 21-2

Tariffs, 8, 21, 41-3, 103, 197, 251-2, 254, 148-50, 172; importance of, 127-8; reduced by Liberals, 177-8; see also, Smoot-Hawley Tariffs
Tate Electric, 53
Teahan, John, 52
Tecumseh, 18-9, 118, 230
Temperance, 47, 602; in Border Cities, 96-7; questioned, 143-4; see also, Prohibition
30th Reconnaissance Battalion, 206
Thomas, Bertha, 139-40, 188, 293n. 16
Thompson, Daniel, 96, 141-4
Tilston, Major Frederick, 229
Timms, Robert, 51
"Tin Can City" 179
Tivoli Theatre, 120
Tolmie, Rev. J.C., 12, 14, 47, 113
Toronto, 11, 13, 17, 127, 144, 148, 169-70, 191, 236; and rum-running, 92-5
Toronto Daily Star, 92, 241-2
Toronto Globe (after 1936, "Globe & Mail"), 45, 62, 92, 98, 144, 164, 242, 245, 249
Toronto Telegram, 92, 97, 170, 242
Trades and Labor Council, 81, 154, 159
Transnational Region, 20-1, 41, 43, 50-1, 60-3, emerges in 1920s, 127-8; closed borders, 148-51
Tregenza, William, 103
Trumble, Hamilton "Ham," 92
Trumble, Beverley "Babe," 92-5
Trussed Concrete Steel "Truscon," 27, 101, 215
21st Regiment, Essex Fusiliers, 11-2, 49-50, 52
241st Battalion, C.E.F., "Canadian Scottish Borderers," 68-9
Tully, Deacon John, 106
Tuson, Charles, 75-6, 87-8, 143

Ukrainians, 108-9
Unemployment, 148-9, 151-5; decreases, 178-9
Union of Russian Workers, 79
United Church of Canada, 106, 162, 244
United Farmers of Ontario, 91
Unions, 21-2, 34; early growth, 80-3; 1920s, 105, 158-9; 1930s, 180-3; and see Chapters 11 and 12
United Auto Workers (UAW) 202, 218-21; Local 195 founded, 180; and Ford strike, 232-50
United Automobile, Aircraft and vehicle Workers of America, local 82, 105
Universal, Carriers, 197
U.S. Steel Corporation, 44
Utilities, 71-3, 113-5

Vedas (rum-runner) 136
Victoria, Queen, 7, 9
Victory Loans, 74,84
von Papen, Franz, 53

Wade, George, 50
War Gardens, 74
Walker, Mrs. E.C., 28-9
Walker, E. Chandler, 29, 134
Walker, Hiram, 8, 23, 30
Walker, Hiram H., 134
Walker, J. Harrington, 135
Walker Land and Building Company, 27
Walker Metal, 183
Walker Road, 8, 17, 27, 83
Walkerside Dairy (baseball) 161
Walkerville, 8, 18, 20, 22-3, 52, 57, 64-5, 71-3, 84-5; as garden city, 27-30,

32; expands, 117, 152, 166; opposes amalgamation, 116, 117, 168-9
Walkerville Boat Club, 123, 290n. 52
Walkerville Brewery, 28
Walkerville Chicks (baseball) 120-1
Walkerville Collegiate Institute, 111-2, 212
Walkerville News, 168-9
Walkerville Wagon Works, 23
"War Guests" 195
Wark, Nell, 179-80
Warnica, Lt. Col. D.C., 203
War Orders-in-Council, 79-80
Watson, James, 107, 211
Watson, Tom, 16
Welfare, 109, 151-2, 166-7, 179-80, 185; indignity of, 152-3; northern settlement, 156
Whiteside, Mrs. W.R., 154
Whittaker, Nurse May, 70
Whyte, Olive, 162-3
Wickett, Samuel Morley, 72
Wigle, Ernest, 73-4, 189; as mayor, 22; in First World War, 49-50, 52, 55; runs again, 184-6
Wigle, John, 123
Wigle Park, 22, 55
Wigle, Roy, 209
Wilcox, Oliver, 42
Wild, Ida, 142
Wilgus, William, 34
Wilkinson, Insp. James, 141
Williams, Maj. E.H. "Ted," 229-30
Willistead Art Gallery, 226
Willistead Manor, 29
Wilson, Frank, 139
Windsor; early 1900s, 11-6; electric lighting, 22, 35-6; growth, 109-16; amalgamation with Border Cities, see Chapter 7
Windsor (Walker) Airport, 134
Windsor (Border Cities) Arena, 121, 125
Windsor Bulldogs, 161-2
Windsor Bus Company, 86
Windsor Collegiate Institute, 90, 120
Windsor Conservancy of Music, 40
Windsor *Daily Star*, 228, 242
Windsor Essex and lakeshore Rapid Railway, 18, 134
Windsor *Evening Record*, 12, 14, 24, 36, 54, 62-3, 72
Windsor Gas Company, 36, 74
Windsor Hornets, 122
Windsor Jockey Club, 55, 88, 115
Windsor Local Council of Women, 225
Windsor Medical Services, 187
Windsor Police Commission, 141-4; vice, 226; and Ford strike, 235, 238-9
Windsor and Tecumseh Railroad, 19
Windsor Trades and Labor Council, 79, 81
Windsor Wagon and Carriage Works, 37
Windsor-Walkerville Technical School, 111, 113
Windsor Yacht Club, 189
Winnipeg, 82, 110, 240, 243-4
Winter, E. Blake, 85, 91, 114-5
Wolsek, Frank, 57
Women, 36, 50-1, 122-3, 125; in First World War, 57-8, 70; blind pigs, 139-40, 142; factories, 149; in politics, 162; in Second World War, 214-16; and unions, 219-20
Women's Auxiliary Motor Service, 215
Women's Patriotic League, 57
Wood, Lavinia, 87
Woolatt, William, 44
Workers' Unity League, 180

Yugoslavs, 211
YW-YMCA, 111-2, 153

Zamparo, Angelo, 193
Zimmerman Dance School, 122-3

Acknowledgements

This book owes a debt of gratitude to my friends and colleagues, Michael Power and David Roberts, for their invaluable advice and encouragement. Sharon Hanna and Chris Andrechek of Biblioasis were instrumental in shepherding this project towards publication. But I especially remember my late brother Michael who first inspired in me a love of history and Professor Peter Oliver who guided me along the way. To all of the above, my thanks.

Photo: Deirdre Brode

Patrick Brode was born in Windsor, Ontario. He was called to the Ontario Bar in 1977 and has practiced law ever since. He has written five works on the history of law in Canada including *Sir John Beverley Robinson: Bone and Sinew of the Compact*, which was a finalist for the City of Toronto Book Award in 1985, and *The Odyssey of John Anderson*, a finalist for the Trillium Award in 1990. His book *The Slasher Killings: A Canadian Sex-Crime Panic, 1945-1946* was nominated for the 2009 Arthur Ellis Award. His most recent book is *The River and the Land: A History of Windsor to 1900* (Biblioasis, 2014).